Theory and Practice of Counseling and Psychotherapy

SECOND EDITION

Jerry Corey, Professor of Human Services at California State University, Fullerton, and a licensed counseling psychologist, received his doctorate in counseling psychology from the University of Southern California. He is a Diplomate in Counseling Psychology, American Board of Professional Psychology, and is registered as a National Health Service Provider in Psychology. Recently a visiting adjunct professor at George Peabody College of Vanderbilt University, Jerry taught counseling courses and conducted workshops in England and West Berlin. With his wife, Marianne Schneider Corey, Jerry conducts regular in-service training workshops for counselors, group workers, and personal-growth groups, as well as occasional workshops in Europe and Mexico.

Jerry, currently a member of the editorial board of the *Journal of Specialists in Group Work,* and Marianne are the co-chairpersons of the Professional Standards and Ethics Committee of the *Association for Specialists in Group Work.* He is also a member of the American Group Psychotherapy Association, the Association for Specialists in Group Work, the American Personnel and Guidance Association, the American Psychological Association, the Western Psychological Association, the Inland Psychological Association, and the Association for Humanistic Psychology.

Jerry and Marianne Corey live in the small mountain community of Idyllwild, California, with their children, Heidi and Cindy.

Recent publications by Jerry Corey—all with Brooks/Cole Publishing Company—include:

Manual for Theory and Practice of Counseling and Psychotherapy, Second Edition
Case Approach to Counseling and Psychotherapy
Theory and Practice of Group Counseling
Manual for Theory and Practice of Group Counseling
Groups: Process and Practice (with Marianne Schneider Corey)
I Never Knew I Had a Choice (in collaboration with Marianne Schneider Corey)
Professional and Ethical Issues in Counseling and Psychotherapy (with Marianne Schneider Corey and Patrick Callanan)
Group Techniques (with Marianne Schneider Corey, Patrick Callanan, and J. Michael Russell)

Theory and Practice of Counseling and Psychotherapy

SECOND EDITION

Gerald Corey

California State University, Fullerton

*Diplomate in Counseling Psychology,
American Board of Professional Psychology*

Brooks/Cole Publishing Company

Monterey, California

Brooks/Cole Publishing Company
A Division of Wadsworth, Inc.

Printed in the United States of America

10   9   8   7   6   5   4   3   2   1

Library of Congress Cataloging in Publication Data

Corey, Gerald F.
  Theory and practice of counseling and
psychotherapy.

  Bibliography: p.
  Includes index.
  1. Counseling.   2. Psychotherapy.
I. Title.   [DNLM: 1. Counseling.   2. Psycho-
therapy.   WM 420 C797t]
BF637.C6C574   1981   158'.3   81-6139
ISBN 0-8185-0455-2   AACR2

Subject Editor: *Claire L. Verduin*
Manuscript Editor: *William Waller*
Production Editor: *Jennifer A. Young*
Interior & Cover Design: *Victoria Van Deventer*
Typesetting: *Graphic Typesetting Service, Los Angeles, California*

To my close friends and colleagues,
who are a source of challenge and
inspiration for me—
Marianne Schneider Corey
J. Michael Russell
Patrick Callanan

Preface

This book is intended primarily for counseling courses for both undergraduate and graduate students in psychology, counselor education, and the human-services and mental health professions. I saw a need for a single book, designed for the first course in counseling, that would survey the major concepts and practices of the contemporary therapeutic systems and, in addition, address some basic issues in counseling, including ethics and the issue of the counselor as a person. The broad goal of the book is to help students learn how to select wisely from all the theories those aspects that can be incorporated into their own developing and, I hope, personalized style of counseling.

In general, I have found that students appreciate an overview of the divergent contemporary forms of counseling and therapy. Because they tend to do wide supplementary reading as they study each therapy system, I have included a reading list after each chapter to guide them to sources that treat various aspects of the material with greater depth and detail than is possible in this survey book. Further, my students have strongly suggested that the first course in counseling means more to them when it emphasizes their personal dimensions as counselors. Therefore, I have made every effort to present the material in a personal and practical manner and to encourage reflection and introspection, so that using this book can be a personal as well as academic growth experience.

The first edition of this book enjoyed success among both students and professors. I therefore made every effort to retain in the new edition the major qualities that people have said they like: the organizational format, which gives a succinct overview of the key concepts of each therapy, a description of its therapeutic process, and a brief survey of the therapeutic techniques and procedures of the model; the personal approach; the focus on ethical and professional issues that students will face when they begin to practice; and the emphasis on the role of the counselor as a person in his or her work as a professional.

Every chapter has been revised to some extent, some more than others. The chapters on the psychoanalytic approach, the existential approach, and behavior therapy have been largely rewritten for the purpose of clarity, accuracy, and updating of information and trends. All of the other therapy approaches have been updated and extended as it seemed appropriate. Although I was tempted to add considerable new material, I resisted this temptation in a serious effort to keep the book relatively brief, so that readers can handle the material in a single course (which often requires the use of other books).

I have added only one chapter in this second edition, Chapter 3—"Extensions and Adaptations of Psychoanalytic Theory." This chapter consists of a survey and summary of the following theorists: Carl Jung, Alfred Adler, Karen Horney, Erich Fromm, Harry Stack Sullivan, Erik Erikson, and Wilhelm Reich. In this way, students see the historical bridge that connects Freudian psychoanalysis with some of the later therapeutic approaches that I discuss at greater length. Those professors who are especially interested in devoting more time to Jungian analysis, Adlerian counseling and therapy, or Reichian therapy can build on the brief treatment in this chapter with supplementary lectures and other assigned readings.

As revised, this book presents 15 approaches to counseling and therapy. I believe that they serve as an excellent base on which students can build a personalized theory that will incorporate the *feeling, thinking,* and *behaving* dimensions of human experience. I consistently encourage readers to remain alert to selecting both concepts and techniques that they can make a part of themselves and can draw on as they work with a particular clientele.

I have retained the "Case of Stan" in Chapter 11 because it helps readers see how various therapies can be applied to a single person. I have added a section that gives some flavor of how I would work with Stan. Further, I have mentioned a basis for integrating all the approaches by considering feeling, thinking, and doing dimensions of counseling practice.

In the last three chapters, which deal with basic issues, ethical issues, and the counselor as a person and as a professional, I have retained most of the original material and added material to round out these discussions. More has been added on topics such as evaluating the effectiveness of counseling and psychotherapy, the use of techniques in counseling, the importance of systematic development of skills, dealing with involuntary clients, and the misuse of power and techniques. To the discussion of ethical issues I have added some material on therapist competence, the client/therapist relationship, confidentiality, and guidelines for ethical practice. In the final chapter I take up the topics of burn-out, self-renewal, and retaining one's dignity and power while working within the system.

I should mention that this text can be used in a flexible way. Some instructors may prefer to begin with the final chapter, because it deals with the student's personal characteristics and effectiveness in the counseling process. Other instructors may feel that students are better able to look at their own impact on clients once they have been exposed to the theories. As you will see in Chapter 1, I do recommend that students at least skim Chapters 11-14 early in the course so that they can begin to think about themselves and the issues that are raised in these chapters. After they have studied the theories, they are encouraged to do an in-depth study of these issues and reconsider them.

In this second edition I have made every effort to incorporate those aspects that have worked best in the courses on counseling theory and practice that I regularly teach. To help readers apply theory to practice, I have also revised the student manual, which is designed for experiential work. The *Manual for Theory and Practice of Counseling and Psychotherapy,* as revised, still contains summary charts, open-ended questions and cases, structured exercises, self-inventories, reading suggestions, and a variety of activities that can be done both in class and out of class. Of course, a revised and updated *Instructor's Resource Manual* is available, with suggestions for teaching the course and a variety of test questions.

Also, I have developed a new book, *Case Approach to Counseling and Psychotherapy,* which is designed to be used in conjunction with this textbook and the student manual. This book is composed of many examples of cases that I have developed to show how the various approaches covered in *Theory and Practice of Counseling and Psychother- apy* can actually work with these clients. The purpose of the book is to give students a chance to see a variety of examples of how a therapist of a particular theoretical ori- entation works. For consistency, I have attempted to demonstrate how I would work with a given client using each of the models. Each chapter contains cases for students to work with. Some of these cases are highly structured, which gives students guidance in learning how to apply techniques from each of the approaches. Some are relatively open-ended and demand that students show how they would work with the case pre- sented using the therapy approach under discussion.

Professors who want to focus on the practice of professional counseling may want to devote more attention to ethical and professional issues than are reflected in the last few chapters. For them I recommend *Professional and Ethical Issues in Counseling and Psychotherapy* (by Gerald Corey, Marianne Schneider Corey, and Patrick Callanan, Brooks/Cole 1979). That book, which is an expansion of the topics introduced in Chap- ters 12, 13, and 14 of this book, is particularly useful for practicum/internship/field-work courses and supervision seminars that deal with professional issues students will have to face.

Acknowledgments

I want to express my appreciation and gratitude to the many people who helped me not only in the original development of this edition, but especially in the revision phase. For their thorough review and helpful critique of the first edition I would like to thank the following people: Terry Anderson, Fraser Valley College; Elsie J. Dotson, Western Kentucky University; Richard J. Kaufman, University of New Hampshire; William Lyon, Lyon Psychological Clinic, Newport Beach; and Beverly B. Palmer, California State Uni- versity at Dominguez Hills.

As the second edition began to take shape, a number of people evaluated selected chapters. Special thanks are extended to my chapter reviewers for their instructive and valuable comments, many of which I incorporated into the final revision. These persons include William H. Blau, Metro State Hospital, Norwalk (Chapters 2, 3, and 10); Con- stance T. Fischer, Duquesne University (Chapter 4); William Coulsen, Center for Studies of Person, La Jolla (Chapter 5); Robert Goulding, Western Institute for Group and Family Therapy (Chapter 7); Treva Sudhalter, California State University at Fullerton (Chapter 7); J. Michael Russell, California State University at Fullerton (Chapter 4); David L. Watson, University of Hawaii (Chapter 8); and Alan Kazdin, University of Pittsburgh (Chapter 8).

Those who read and critiqued the complete draft of the present edition are: David E. Botwin, University of Pittsburgh; Abraham Gelfond, Montclair State College; Garry L. Landreth, North Texas State University; Mark E. Meadows, Auburn University; and Beverly B. Palmer, California State University at Dominguez Hills. To all of them I also express my appreciation and gratitude.

Many of my students in the Human Services Program at California State University at Fullerton reviewed the manuscript and provided constructive feedback. These persons include Donna Robbins, Diane Vasquez, Gary Charleston, Debbie King, David Ferguson, and Matthew Hamlin. I want also to thank those students who have participated in my workshops. The challenge of working with them has helped me to integrate theory with practice, thereby directly influencing the content of this book.

Special appreciation is extended to my wife, Marianne, whose generous help has been vital to the revision of this book, and to J. Michael Russell and Patrick Callanan. Many of the ideas for this edition developed from the assistance, criticism, and encouragement I received from these friends and colleagues.

In closing, I want to thank the dedicated staff at Brooks/Cole—especially Bill Waller, manuscript editor; Jennifer Young, production editor; and Claire Verduin, acquisition editor—for their helpful suggestions and guidance. Claire's special interest in this book and expert advice during the writing and revision phases were particularly inspirational.

Gerald Corey

Contents

1

Introduction and Overview

Introduction

Overview

Suggestions for Using the Book

Other Resources

Introduction

This book surveys a variety of approaches to counseling and psychotherapy. Instead of emphasizing the theoretical foundations of these models, it presents the basic concepts of each and discusses topics such as the therapeutic process (including goals), the client/therapist relationship, and specific techniques and procedures applicable to individual and group practice. This book is not, therefore, primarily a text on theories of counseling, nor is it merely a "how to" book that focuses on techniques and methodology. Instead, it aims at developing a balanced view of the major concepts of various therapies and the practical techniques in the therapeutic process.

My hope is that you will remain open and seriously consider the unique contributions as well as the limitations of each therapeutic system presented in this book. In the present stage of theory development, no single theoretical model fully accounts for all the dimensions of the various therapies. Although attempts have been made to integrate and unify many of the diverse approaches, those practitioners who align themselves with a specialized theoretical viewpoint still tend to assume that their approach contains the entire truth. For instance, a psychoanalytic practitioner may view behavior therapy as technique oriented and superficial and as a quick and economical therapy that fails to produce long-term changes in clients. Some behavior therapists are convinced that psychoanalysis is based on unfounded premises and simply does not work. Some existential psychologists criticize both psychoanalytic therapy and behavior therapy on the ground that they are mechanistic, reductionistic, and deterministic approaches that are very limited in dealing with genuine human struggles to create a purposeful existence. It is not uncommon to find advocates of either conventional or newer therapies who refuse to find validity in any approach other than their own.

The viewpoint assumed in this book is that beginning students of counseling, by familiarizing themselves with the current major approaches to therapeutic practice, can acquire a basis for a style of counseling tailored to their own personalities. Thus, I recommend eclecticism as a framework for the professional education of counselors. The danger in presenting one model that all students are expected to advocate to the exclusion of other fruitful approaches is that it can lead the beginning counselor to unduly limit his or her effectiveness with different clients. Valuable dimensions of human behavior can be overlooked if the counselor is restricted to a single theory.

On the other hand, an undisciplined eclectic approach can be an excuse for failing to develop a sound rationale for systematically adhering to certain concepts and to the techniques that are extensions of them. It is easy to pick and choose fragments from the various therapies that merely support one's biases and preconceived ideas. I hope that a study of the various models presented in this book will show that some form of integration among many of the approaches is possible.

I have a strong conviction that the values and personhood of counselors are the groundwork for creating a philosophy and practice of counseling. Thus, it seems essential to me that counselors explore in depth their own values, attitudes, and beliefs and that they work toward increasing their own awareness. Throughout the book, I encourage you to find ways of personally relating to each of the therapies. Unless these therapeutic approaches are studied and applied to ourselves, I fear that a superficial understanding is the best that can be hoped for. I assume that most beginning counselors have an implicit notion of what counseling is and how they might proceed to help others, even though their views may be fuzzy. I believe that if we discover some way of personally relating to each of the therapies and look for specific concepts and methodologies, we can begin to construct a meaningful frame of reference for understanding and working with clients.

My own philosophical orientation is strongly influenced by the existential force in psychology. The existential view addresses itself to significant issues for the population I work with, and it seems most congruent with my own values and personhood. Because techniques and specific procedures are not indicated in this approach, I find that I continue to invent new techniques that grow out of my work with groups. I also borrow techniques from others and then adapt them to my counseling style. Gestalt-therapy techniques, combined with psychodrama and role-playing techniques, have been very useful to me in my practice. Many specific techniques in my approach are derived from behavior therapy: assertive training, behavior rehearsal, modeling, and a variety of coaching and role-playing techniques. My own counseling philosophy and style continue to take new shape through my experience and therapeutic practice.

As I developed the material for this book, I became increasingly aware that there are useful dimensions of each therapy approach and that accepting the validity of one model does not necessarily imply a rejection of seemingly divergent models. For instance, I am firmly convinced that a practitioner might be oriented toward existential psychology and have as a conceptual and philosophical base the existential view of the person. At the same time, the therapist might use many techniques drawn from behavior therapy and from some of the other cognitively oriented therapies that focus on behavior and action. Thus, in my own framework I do not assume that these therapies are incompatible.

In my individual- and group-therapy practices, I respect the psychoanalytic view of the importance of early psychosexual and psychosocial development. I believe that one's past plays an enormous role in shaping one's current personality and behavior. Although I reject the deterministic stance that humans are the products of their early conditioning and thus the victims of their past, I believe that an exploration of the past is essential, particularly to the degree that the past is related to present emotional or behavioral difficulties.

From the cognitive and behavioral therapies, I value the emphasis on specific goals and on encouraging clients to formulate concrete aims for their own therapy sessions. I find that contracts developed by clients are extremely useful, and I frequently either suggest specific "homework assignments" or ask my clients to devise their own. I find that using those techniques expands the effects of an individual or group session to the client's outside life. Although I accept the validity of insight and increasing awareness on the client's part, I consider it essential that clients actually put into practice in their lives what they are learning in therapy.

A major assumption I make is that my clients are able to exercise increasing freedom to choose how they will be in the future. Although I accept that we are surely shaped by our sociocultural environment and that much of our behavior is a product of learning and conditioning, I assume that, with increased awareness of the forces that have molded us, we are able to transcend these deterministic influences. It seems to me that most of the contemporary models of counseling and therapy operate on the basic assumption that clients are able to accept personal responsibility and that their failure to do so has largely resulted in their present emotional and behavioral difficulties.

My philosophy of psychotherapy does not include the assumption that therapy is exclusively for the "sick" and is aimed at "curing" psychological ailments. I find that the medical model severely restricts therapeutic practice. Counseling and therapy are increasingly regarded as a vehicle for self-exploration to assist "normal" people in more fully realizing their human potentials. My clientele is mainly a relatively healthy population composed of people who seek therapy as a personal growth experience or as a means to help them resolve situational crises.

The existential approach and person-centered therapy both emphasize the client/therapist relationship as the major factor that leads to constructive personal change in clients. I have come to believe in the importance of the therapeutic relationship with more certainty as a result of my experience as a psychologist. Thus, I contend that the character or personhood of the therapist is what leads to significant change. Although I think it important that a psychotherapist or counselor have a comprehensive knowledge of personality dynamics and learning theory and a theoretical understanding of therapeutic intervention skills, I do not think that this knowledge is enough. If a practitioner possesses wide knowledge, both theoretical and practical, yet lacks human qualities of compassion, caring, good faith, honesty, realness, and sensitivity, then he or she is merely a technician. In my judgment, those who function exclusively as technicians do not make a significant difference in the lives of their clients.

I see the process of psychotherapy as a dialogue and engagement between two persons. Therapists must be willing to remain open to their own growth and be willing to struggle in their lives, or else they lose their therapeutic potency. Why should clients seek therapists who are "finished products" and who do not do in their own lives what they expect their clients to do in theirs? In short, I think therapists teach clients by their modeling, and perhaps by being willing to share their own humanity they enrich their clients' lives. Although I emphasize that the human qualities of a therapist are of primary importance, I do not think it is sufficient to be merely a good person with good intentions. To be effective, the therapist also requires life experiences, supervised experiences in counseling, and a knowledge of counseling theory and techniques.

Further, it is essential that as students you be well grounded in the various *theories of personality,* and that you learn how they are related to theories of counseling. As a counselor, your conception of the person will affect the interventions you are likely to make. For example, because of the view of human nature taken by psychoanalysts, they focus on techniques designed to tap unconscious material, for therapy is aimed at making that which is unconscious available to the person. These practitioners use inter-pretations as a way of fostering insight, which is seen as an essential part of therapeutic progress. The person-centered therapist, in contrast, holds that people can move forward in a constructive direction without interpretation or any other active intervention from the therapist. Thus, those who subscribe to this view of human nature tend not to rely on directive techniques, for they have faith in their clients' capacities for self-direction. Still another example of how the therapist's conception of the person affects the inter-ventions made is seen in rational-emotive therapy. This approach, grounded in the assumption that people by nature tend to incorporate uncritically a host of irrational ideas about themselves and about life, emphasizes a therapeutic style characterized by forceful persuasion, active and directive teaching techniques designed to help clients attack these stubborn irrational notions, and a high degree of therapist confrontation to undermine the client's tendencies toward self-sabotage.

Depending on your view of personality and the theory of personality from which you are operating, you will select different forms of intervention. Another factor, of course, is the individual characteristics of the client. Some practitioners make the mistake of relying on one type of intervention (supportive, confrontational, information-giving, or some other) for most of the clients with whom they work. It is extremely important to be aware that different clients may respond to various types of intervention. Thus, practitioners must have a broad base of counseling techniques from which to draw what is best for the individual client, rather than forcing the client to fit their specialized form of intervention.

Overview

In this section I will explain why I selected the therapeutic approaches discussed in this book, present an overview of the plan of the book, and make some suggestions for how you can best use it.

Table 1–1 presents an overview of the nine therapeutic approaches that are explored in Chapters 2–10. These nine models of counseling and psychotherapy fit into four general categories.

First is the psychodynamic approach, based largely on insight, unconscious motiva-tion, and reconstruction of the personality; it is the approach of *psychoanalytic therapy.* The reason for including the psychoanalytic model (and placing it first) is its major influence on all of the other formal systems of psychotherapy. Some of the therapeutic models are basically extensions of psychoanalysis, others are modifications of analytic concepts and procedures, and still others are positions that emerged as a reaction against psychoanalysis. Many of the theories of counseling and psychotherapy have borrowed and integrated principles and techniques from the analytic approach. Thus, from a practical as well as a historical vantage point, this model continues to play an important role in contemporary psychotherapy.

Second are seven *social-psychological theorists* and the *ego psychologists,* who have at times been referred to as "neo-Freudians" or "neo-analytic practitioners." In this new edition I have added a chapter that includes the key ideas of Carl Jung, Alfred Adler, Karen Horney, Erich Fromm, Harry Stack Sullivan, Erik Erikson, and Wilhelm Reich. These theorists were originally influenced by Freud yet chose to part company from

TABLE 1–1 Overview of contemporary counseling and therapy models

Psychoanalytic therapy	Key figure: Freud. Historically, the first system of psychotherapy. Psychoanalysis is a personality theory, a philosophical system, and a method of psychotherapy.
Extensions and adaptations of psychoanalytic therapy	Key figures: Jung, Adler, Horney, Fromm, Sullivan, Erikson, Reich. Influenced by Freud, these theorists broke away from orthodox psychoanalysis. They shared the notion that sociocultural factors, conscious factors, and interpersonal aspects are of great significance in the development of the individual. Most of these theorists are still influential, in that their concepts and techniques are found in approaches developed later.
Existential therapy	Key figures: May, Maslow, Frankl, Jourard. The "third force" in psychology. It developed as a reaction against psychoanalysis and behaviorism, which the existential psychologist asserts do not do justice to the study of humans.
Person-centered therapy	Founder: Carl Rogers. Originally a nondirective approach developed during the 1940s as a reaction against the psychoanalytic approach. Based on a subjective view of human experiencing, it places more faith in and gives more responsibility to the client in dealing with problems.
Gestalt therapy	Founder: Fritz Perls. Largely an experiential therapy stressing awareness and integration, which grew as a reaction against analytic therapy. Integrates body and mind functioning.
Transactional analysis (TA)	Founder: Eric Berne. A contemporary model that leans toward cognitive and behavioral aspects. Designed to help people evaluate decisions they have made in light of their appropriateness at present.
Behavior therapy	Key figures: Bandura, Meichenbaum. Mahoney, Beck, Wolpe, Lazarus, Kazdin. Application of the principles of learning to the resolution of specific behavioral disorders. Results are subject to continual experimentation. This technique is continuously in the process of refinement.
Rational-emotive therapy (RET)	Founder: Albert Ellis. A highly didactic, cognitive, action-oriented model of therapy that stresses the role of thinking and belief systems as the root of personal problems.
Reality therapy	Founder: William Glasser. A reaction against conventional therapy. Short-term, with focus on the present. Stresses a person's strengths. Basically, a way clients can learn more realistic behavior and thus achieve success.

orthodox psychoanalysis because of philosophical differences. Most of them made the assumption that the sociocultural factors are of greater importance than the biological determinants of personality. They reacted against the deterministic view of Freud that stressed the role of the unconscious, the power of the first five years of life as the shaper of later development, and the role of sex and aggression. All of their theories represent extensions and adaptations of the psychoanalytic approach, and they all give attention to critical factors during the entire life span of the individual. Further, they are enjoying a revival of interest in current practice. This is especially true of Jungian analysis, Adlerian counseling and therapy, Erikson's ego psychology and the developmental approach, and the body-oriented psychotherapies (largely pioneered by Reich).

Third are the experiential and relationship-oriented therapies based on humanistic psychology, which include the *existential approach,* the *person-centered approach,* and *Gestalt therapy.* The existential approach stresses a concern for what it means to be fully human. It suggests certain themes that are a part of the "human condition," such as freedom and responsibility, anxiety, guilt, awareness of being finite and the implications for living, creating a meaning in the world, and shaping one's future by making active choices. This approach is not a unified school of therapy with a clear theory and a systematic set of techniques. Rather, it is a philosophy of counseling that stresses the divergent methods of understanding the subjective world of the person. The person-centered approach, which is rooted in existential philosophy, places emphasis on the basic attitudes of the therapist. It maintains that the quality of the client/therapist relationship is the prime determinant of the outcomes of the therapeutic process. Philosophically, this model is grounded on the assumption that clients have the capacity for self-direction without active intervention and direction on the therapist's part. It is in the context of a living and authentic relationship with the therapist that this growth force within the client is released. Another branch of the existential approach is Gestalt therapy. It offers a range of techniques that the therapist can draw on in assisting clients to focus on what they are experiencing now and to provide them with an awareness of the diversity of feelings within them at any moment.

Fourth are the cognitively oriented and behaviorally oriented "action therapies," which include *Transactional Analysis, behavior therapy, rational-emotive therapy,* and *reality therapy.* Transactional Analysis is a popular approach that has contributed to the understanding of how people make early decisions in response to parental messages they receive. It stresses the "life script," or life plan, of individuals, and it focuses on their capacity to make new decisions that are more appropriate to their current level of maturity. Behavior therapy, also an action therapy, puts a premium on *doing* and taking steps to make concrete changes. A current trend in behavior therapy is toward the increasing attention given to cognitive factors as an important determinant of behavior. Rational-emotive therapy highlights the necessity of learning how to challenge irrational beliefs that lead to human misery. This system borrows many cognitive, emotive, and behavioral techniques from behavior therapy. These are used to help people undermine those irrational and self-defeating assumptions that result in negative feelings and to help them form a rational philosophy of life. Reality therapy is another form of behavior therapy that is very popular with many mental-health practitioners. It stresses clients' acceptance of personal responsibility for changing themselves and for developing clear plans for changing their *behavior.*

In my view, practitioners need to pay attention to what their clients are *feeling, thinking,* and *doing.* This view also means that a complete therapy system must be addressed to all three of these facets. Taken in combination, I believe, the therapies that I have included provide you with a broad base of concepts and techniques. Although there are many other newer psychotherapies that purport to offer the royal road to an eternal cure, the range of therapies covered in this book provides diverse approaches to counseling. Some of these therapies place emphasis on the *experiential* aspects and of the role of *feelings* in therapy; others highlight the role that *cognitive factors* and *thinking* should play; and others emphasize putting plans into *action* and learning by *doing.* All of these facets combined form the basis of a powerful therapy, and excluding any of these dimensions by overstressing one factor of human experience leads to an incomplete therapy approach.

For the purpose of consistency, these theory chapters (with the exception of Chapter 3, "Extensions and Adaptations of Psychoanalytic Theory," in which seven theorists are briefly summarized) share a common format. This format includes a discussion of key concepts, a look at the therapeutic process, applications of therapeutic techniques and procedures, a summary and my evaluation, questions for reflection and discussion, and suggestions for further reading.

After the nine-chapter survey of the major counseling approaches, Chapter 11 presents a case illustration of the way each theory might deal with the same client. The illustration also demonstrates a basis for integrating the therapies by highlighting their similarities and differences.

In teaching counseling courses and in supervising interns I have found that certain basic issues permeate all the counseling and therapy approaches. Chapter 12 deals with those underlying issues common to all therapies. Chapter 13 emphasizes ethical issues in counseling practice, including the role of the practitioner's value system and the impact of his or her personality on the client. Because I believe that no book on counselor education is complete without a discussion of the personhood of the counselor, Chapter 14, the final chapter, explores how the counselor as a person is perhaps the most important variable in therapeutic effectiveness—surely more important than theoretical orientation or knowledge of techniques.

A list of suggested readings follows each chapter, so that you can pursue a deeper knowledge of areas of special interest. I encourage supplementary reading, for the limitations of this book necessitated focusing on only the highlights of each approach.

SUGGESTIONS FOR USING THE BOOK

I have some specific recommendations on how to get the fullest value as you read. The personal slant of this book invites you to relate what you are reading to your own experiences. For this reason I strongly encourage you to begin by reading Chapter 14, "The Counselor as a Person and as a Professional." You will assimilate much more knowledge of the various therapies if you are willing to remain open as you read them *and* if you make a conscious attempt to relate the key concepts of each model to your own life. You can make this material come alive for you if you apply the techniques you are studying to your personal growth. Chapter 14 can also help you think about how you can use *yourself as a person* as your single most important therapy instrument. To simply memorize the ideas and procedures of the models is to no avail; what *will* make a difference is your ability to incorporate selected concepts and procedures into a personalized style of counseling that is an expression of your uniqueness as a person. This topic is worth considering in depth again after you have studied the therapy models in the earlier chapters.

I have found that students learn a lot by seeing the applications of a theory in action, preferably in a live demonstration or as part of experiential activities in which they function in the alternating roles of client and counselor. Many students find the case history of one client, "Stan" (Chapter 11), helpful to read *before* they study each therapy, because it gives an overview of how various therapists might view Stan and how they might proceed during the course of the sessions. I also present how I would work with Stan, suggesting concepts and techniques that I would draw on from each of the models. This case should also be read carefully again after you have studied the therapies.

Next, and also before you study each therapy in depth in Chapters 2–10, I suggest that you at least skim Chapters 12 and 13. As mentioned above, these two chapters deal with basic ethical and professional issues, which it would be useful to begin considering at the outset of the course. You will be in a position to explore these issues in greater depth after you have been exposed to the models, and thus a second reading of Chapters 12 and 13 will help you to integrate theory with practice.

OTHER RESOURCES

Although this textbook can stand on its own as a teaching tool, I will make continual references throughout it to further reading. Hopefully, this book will entice you to pursue many of its concepts in greater depth. Reading of primary sources will be especially valuable in rounding out your knowledge of those therapies that you find are most meaningful.

In addition to the reading suggestions, I have developed materials that can be used to amplify this book. A *Manual for Theory and Practice of Counseling and Psychotherapy* is designed to help you integrate theory with practice and to make the concepts covered in the book come alive. It consists of self-inventories, experiential activities and exercises, personal-application questions, summary charts, and brief case illustrations. Because of students' interest in actually seeing various therapy approaches demonstrated in action, I have also written a book that shows how I would work with a variety of clients (using each of the separate models and also drawing on models in an eclectic fashion). This book, *Case Approach to Counseling and Psychotherapy,* also contains many cases in which you are asked to become actively involved by showing how you would work with a client, using a particular therapy model under consideration. For those who want to pursue the section dealing with ethical and professional issues in greater depth, my colleagues and I have developed a combination textbook/manual with a wide variety of practical situations you will face—*Professional and Ethical Issues in Counseling and Psychotherapy* (Corey, Corey, & Callanan, 1979). If you are interested in the application of these theories to group counseling, I would recommend *Theory and Practice of Group Counseling* (which also has a *Manual for Theory and Practice of Group Counseling*). These resources would provide a good way to continue learning more about the theory and practice of counseling that you begin with this course. Other books that are relevant to group counseling include: *Groups: Process and Practice* (Corey & Corey, 1977), *Group Techniques* (Corey, Corey, Callanan, & Russell, 1982), and *I Never Knew I Had a Choice.* All of these books are published by Brooks/Cole Publishing Company, Monterey, California 93940.

2

Psychoanalytic Therapy

Introduction

Most of the theories of counseling and psychotherapy discussed later in this book have been influenced by psychoanalytic theory. Some of these therapeutic approaches extend the psychoanalytic model, others modify its concepts and procedures, and others emerged as a reaction against it. Many of the theories of counseling have borrowed and integrated its principles and techniques.

One of the main currents in the history of psychotherapy is Sigmund Freud's psychoanalytic theory. This system is a model of personality development, a philosophy of human nature, and a method of psychotherapy. Freud created a psychodynamic approach, giving psychology a new look and new horizons. For instance, he called attention to factors that motivate behavior, developed a controversial theory of personality development, focused on the role of the unconscious, and developed most of the first therapeutic procedures for understanding and modifying the structure of one's basic character. Freud stimulated a great deal of controversy, exploration, and further development of personality theory and laid the foundation on which many later systems rest.

Key concepts

STRUCTURE OF PERSONALITY

According to the psychoanalytic view, the personality consists of three systems: the id, the ego, and the superego. These are names for psychological processes and should not be thought of as manikins that separately operate the personality; one's personality functions as a whole rather than as three discrete segments. The id is the biological component, the ego is the psychological component, and the superego is the social component.

The id.   The id is the original system of personality; a person is all id at birth. The id is the primary source of psychic energy and the seat of instincts. It lacks organization, and it is blind, demanding, and insistent. A cauldron of seething excitement, the id cannot tolerate tension, and it functions to discharge tension immediately and return to a homeostatic condition. Ruled by the pleasure principle, which is aimed at reducing tension, avoiding pain, and gaining pleasure, the id is illogical, amoral, and driven by one consideration: to satisfy instinctual needs in accordance with the pleasure principle. The id never matures but remains the spoiled brat of personality. It does not think but only wishes or acts. The id is unconscious, but it can also operate out of the preconscious or conscious.

The ego.   The ego has contact with the external world of reality. It is the "executive" that governs, controls, and regulates the personality. As the "traffic cop" for the id, superego, and external world, its principal job is to mediate between the instincts and the surrounding environment. The ego controls consciousness and exercises censorship. Ruled by the reality principle, the ego does realistic and logical thinking and formulates plans of action for satisfying needs. What is the relation of the ego to the id? The ego is the seat of intelligence and rationality that checks and controls the blind impulses of the id. Whereas the id knows only subjective reality, the ego distinguishes between mental images and things in the external world.

The superego.   The superego is the moral, or judicial, branch of personality. It is a person's moral code, the main concern being whether action is good or bad, right or wrong. It represents the ideal, rather than the real, and strives not for pleasure but for perfection. It represents the traditional values and ideals of society as they are handed down from parents to children. It functions to inhibit the id impulses, to persuade the ego to substitute moralistic goals for realistic ones, and to strive for perfection. The superego, then, as the internalization of the standards of parents and society, is related to psychological rewards and punishments. The rewards are feelings of pride and self-love; the punishments are feelings of guilt and inferiority.

VIEW OF HUMAN NATURE

The Freudian view of human nature is deterministic. According to Freud, people are determined by irrational forces, unconscious motivations, biological and instinctual drives, and certain psychosexual events during the first five years of life.

From the orthodox Freudian perspective, humans are viewed as energy systems. The dynamics of personality consist of the ways in which psychic energy is distributed to the id, ego, and superego. Because the amount of energy is limited, one system gains control over the available energy at the expense of the other two systems. Behavior is determined by this psychic energy.

Instincts are central to the Freudian approach. Taken together, the instincts make up the total psychic energy available to the personality. The id is the original system of personality, and it is the reservoir of psychic energy that provides or supplies the power for the operation of the ego and superego. The id is also related to the concept *libido*. Although Freud originally used the term *libido* to refer to sexual energy, he later broadened it to include the energy of all the *life instincts*. These instincts serve the purpose of the survival of the individual and the human race; they are oriented toward growth, development, and creativity. Libido, then, should be understood as a source of motivation that encompasses but goes beyond sexual energy. Freud included all pleasurable acts in his concept of the life instincts; he saw the goal of much of life as gaining pleasure and avoiding pain.

Freud also postulated the concept *death instincts,* which accounted for the *aggressive drive.* At times, he asserted, people manifest through their behavior an unconscious wish to die or to hurt themselves or others. Freud believed that both the sexual and aggressive drives are powerful determinants of why people act as they do.

Although there may be conflicts between the life instincts (known as Eros) and the death instincts (known as Thanatos), human beings are not condemned to be the victims of aggression and self-destruction. In his book *Civilization and Its Discontents* (1930/1962) Freud gave an indication that the major challenge facing the human race was how to manage the aggressive drive. For Freud, the unrest and anxiety of people was related to their knowledge that the human race could be exterminated. How much more true is this today than it was in Freud's time?

CONSCIOUSNESS AND UNCONSCIOUSNESS

Perhaps Freud's greatest contributions are his concepts of the unconscious and of the levels of consciousness, which are the keys to understanding behavior and the problems of personality. The unconscious cannot be studied directly; it is inferred from behavior.

Clinical evidence for postulating the unconscious includes the following: (1) dreams, which are symbolic representations of unconscious needs, wishes, and conflicts; (2) slips of the tongue and forgetting, for example, a familiar name; (3) posthypnotic suggestions; (4) material derived from free-association techniques; and (5) material derived from projective techniques.

For Freud, consciousness is a thin slice of the total mind. Like the greater part of the iceberg that lies below the surface of the water, the larger part of the mind exists below the surface of awareness. The unconscious, which is out of awareness, stores up all experiences, memories, and repressed material. Needs and motivations that are inaccessible—that is, out of awareness—are also outside the sphere of control. Freud believed that most psychological functioning exists in the out-of-awareness realm. The aim of psychoanalytic therapy, therefore, is to make the unconscious motives conscious, for only when one becomes conscious of motivations can one exercise choice. Understanding the role of the unconscious is central to grasping the essence of the psychoanalytic model of behavior. The unconscious, even though out of awareness, does influence behavior. Unconscious processes are the roots of all forms of neurotic symptoms and behaviors. From this perspective, a "cure" is based on uncovering the meaning of symptoms, the causes of behavior, and the repressed materials that interfere with healthy functioning.

ANXIETY

Also essential to understanding the psychoanalytic view of human nature is grasping its concept of anxiety. Anxiety is a state of tension that motivates us to do something. It develops out of a conflict between the id, ego, and superego over control of the available psychic energy. Its function is to warn of impending danger—that is, to signal to the ego that, unless appropriate measures are taken, the danger may increase until the ego is overthrown. When the ego cannot control anxiety by rational and direct methods, it then relies on unrealistic ones—namely, ego-defense behavior (see below).

There are three kinds of anxiety: reality, neurotic, and moral. Reality anxiety is the fear of danger from the external world, and the level of anxiety is proportionate to the degree of real threat. Neurotic anxiety is the fear that the instincts will get out of hand and cause one to do something for which one will be punished. Moral anxiety is the fear of one's own conscience. People with a well-developed conscience tend to feel guilty when they do something contrary to their moral code.

EGO-DEFENSE MECHANISMS

Ego-defense mechanisms help the individual cope with anxiety and defend the wounded ego. They are not necessarily pathological, and they can have adjustive value if they do not become a style of life to avoid facing reality. The defenses one uses depend on one's level of development and the degree of anxiety. Defense mechanisms have two characteristics in common: they either deny or distort reality, and they operate on an unconscious level. Freud's theory is a tension-reduction model, or a homeostatic system. Following are brief descriptions of some common ego defenses:

1. *Repression.* The mechanism of repression is one of the most important Freudian processes, and it is the basis of many other ego defenses and of neurotic disorders. It is a means of defense through which threatening or painful thoughts and feelings are excluded from

awareness. Freud explained repression as an involuntary removal of something from consciousness. It is assumed that most of the painful events of the first five years of life are so excluded, yet these events do influence current behavior.

2. *Denial.* According to Cameron (1963), denial plays a defensive role similar to that of repression, yet it generally operates at preconscious and conscious levels. Denial of reality is perhaps the simplest of all self-defense mechanisms; it is a way of distorting what the individual thinks, feels, or perceives in a traumatic situation. It consists of defending against anxiety by "closing one's eyes" to the existence of threatening reality. In tragic events such as wars and other disasters, people often tend to blind themselves to realities that would be too painful to accept.

3. *Reaction formation.* One defense against a threatening impulse is to actively express the opposite impulse. By developing conscious attitudes and behaviors that are diametrically opposed to disturbing desires, people do not have to face the anxiety that would result if they were to recognize these dimensions of themselves. Individuals may conceal hate with a facade of love, be extremely nice when they harbor negative reactions, or mask cruelty with excessive kindness.

4. *Projection.* Another mechanism of self-deception consists in attributing to others one's own unacceptable desires and impulses. Lustful, aggressive, or other impulses are seen as being possessed by "those people out there, but not by me." Thus, a man who is sexually attracted to his daughter may maintain that it is *she* who is behaving seductively with him. Thus, he does not have to recognize or deal with his own desires.

5. *Displacement.* One way to cope with anxiety is to discharge impulses by shifting from a threatening object to a "safer target." Displacement consists of directing energy toward another object or person when the original object or person is inaccessible. For example, the meek man who feels intimidated by his boss comes home and unloads inappropriate hostility onto his children.

6. *Rationalization.* Some people manufacture "good" reasons to explain away a bruised ego. Rationalization involves explaining away failures or losses. Thus, it helps justify specific behaviors, and it aids in softening the blow connected with disappointments. When people do not get positions they have applied for in their work, they think of logical reasons why they did not succeed, and they sometimes attempt to convince themselves that they really did not want the position anyway.

7. *Sublimation.* From the Freudian perspective, many of the great artistic contributions consisted of a redirection of sexual energy into creative behaviors. Sublimation involves diverting sexual energy into other channels, ones that are usually socially acceptable and sometimes even admirable. For example, aggressive impulses can be channeled into athletic activities, so that the person finds a way of expressing aggressive feelings and, as an added bonus, is often praised.

8. *Regression.* Some people revert to a form of behavior that they have outgrown. In this regression to an earlier phase of development the demands are not so great. In the face of severe stress or extreme challenge, individuals may attempt to cope with the anxiety they feel by clinging to immature and inappropriate behaviors. For example, children who are frightened in school may indulge in infantile behavior such as weeping, excessive dependence, thumb-sucking, hiding, clinging to the teacher. They are seeking to return to a time in their life when there was security.

9. *Introjection.* The mechanism of introjection consists of taking in and "swallowing" the values and standards of others. For example, in concentration camps some of the prisoners deal with overwhelming anxiety by accepting the values of the enemy through an identification with the aggressor. Another example is the abused child, who assumes the abusing parent's way of handling stresses and thus continues the cycle of child beating. It should be noted that there are also positive forms of introjection, such as the incorporation of parental values or the attributes and values of the therapist (assuming that these are not merely uncritically accepted).

10. *Identification.* Although identification is part of the developmental process by which children learn sex-role behaviors, it can also be a defensive reaction. It can enhance self-worth and protect one from a sense of being a failure. Thus, people who feel basically inferior may identify themselves with successful causes, organizations, or people in the hope that they will be perceived as worthwhile.

11. *Compensation.* Compensation consists of masking perceived weaknesses or developing certain positive traits to make up for limitations. Thus, children who do not receive positive attention and recognition may develop behaviors designed to at least get negative attention. People who feel intellectually inferior may direct an inordinate degree of energy to building up their bodies; those who feel socially incompetent may become "loners" and develop their intellectual capacities. This mechanism can have direct adjustive value, and it can also be an attempt by the person to say "Don't see the ways in which I am inferior, but see me in my accomplishments."

12. *Ritual and undoing.* At times people perform elaborate rituals as a way of undoing acts for which they feel guilty. Undoing is designed to negate some disapproved thought or behavior. Anxiety is sometimes lessened when a person uses methods to right a wrong or to take away the guilt he or she feels for some perceived misdeed. For example, a rejecting father may attempt to alleviate his guilt by showering his child with material goods; he also attempts to demonstrate his caring through this act.

DEVELOPMENT OF PERSONALITY

Importance of early development.   A significant contribution of the psychoanalytic model is the delineation of the stages of psychosocial and psychosexual development from birth through adulthood. It provides the counselor with the conceptual tools for understanding trends in development, key developmental tasks characteristic of the various stages, normal and abnormal personal and social functioning, critical needs and their satisfaction or frustration, origins of faulty personality development that lead to later adjustment problems, and healthy and unhealthy uses of ego-defense mechanisms.

In my opinion, an understanding of the psychoanalytic view of development is essential if a counselor is to work in depth with clients. I have found that the most typical problems that people bring to either individual or group counseling are (1) the inability to trust oneself and others, the fear of loving and forming close relationships, and low self-esteem; (2) the inability to recognize and express feelings of hostility, anger, rage, and hate, the denial of one's own power as a person, and the lack of feelings of autonomy; (3) the inability to fully accept one's own sexuality and sexual feelings, difficulty in accepting oneself as a man or woman, and fear of sexuality. According to the Freudian psychoanalytic view, these three areas of personal and social development (love and trust, dealing with negative feelings, and developing a positive acceptance of sexuality) are all grounded in the first five years of life. This period is the foundation on which later personality development is built.

The first year of life: The oral stage.   Freud postulated infantile sexuality. Society's failure, up until then, to recognize the phenomenon can be explained by cultural taboos and every individual's repression of infantile and childhood experiences in this area.

From birth to the end of the first year the infant experiences the oral stage. Sucking the mother's breasts satisfies the need for food and pleasure. As the mouth and lips are sensitive erogenous zones during this period, the infant experiences erotic pleasure from sucking. The infant does not have a developed ego or a superego, but only an id that needs, demands, and pushes for instant gratification.

Two activities during this developmental period are oral-incorporative behavior and oral-aggressive behavior. These early behaviors are considered to be the prototypes of some of the character traits of adulthood.

First to appear is *oral-incorporative* behavior, which involves pleasurable stimulation of the mouth. Libidinal energy is at first focused on the mouth, and then with maturity other areas of the body develop and become the focal points of gratification. However, adults who exhibit excessive oral needs (such as excessive eating, chewing, talking, smoking, and drinking) may have an *oral fixation.* Deprivation of oral gratification during infancy is assumed to lead to problems in adulthood.

As the infant teethes, the *oral-aggressive* period begins. Biting is one activity at this time. Adult characteristics such as sarcasm, hostility, aggression, gossip, and making "biting" comments to others are related to events of this developmental period.

Greediness and acquisitiveness may develop as a result of not getting enough food or love during the early years of life. Material things that children seek become substitutes for what they really want—namely, food and love from the mother. Later personality problems that stem from the oral stage are the development of a view of the world based on mistrust, fear of reaching out to others, rejection of affection, fear of loving and trusting, low self-esteem, isolation and withdrawal, and inability to form or maintain intense relationships.

The major developmental task of the oral stage is acquiring a sense of trust—trust in others, in the world, and in self. Love is the best safeguard against fear, insecurity, and inadequacy; children who are loved by others have little difficulty in accepting themselves. If children feel unwanted, unaccepted, and unloved, then self-acceptance becomes difficult. Rejected children learn to mistrust the world; they view it as a threatening place. The effect of infantile rejection is a tendency in later childhood to be fearful, insecure, attention seeking, jealous, aggressive, hostile, and lonely.

Ages 1–3: The anal stage.

Ages 1–3: The anal stage.   The anal stage marks another step in development. The tasks to be mastered during this stage are learning independence, personal power, and autonomy and learning how to recognize and deal with negative feelings.

Beginning in the second year and extending to the third year, the anal zone comes to be of major significance in the formation of personality. Now children continually face parental demands, experience frustrations when they handle objects and explore their environments, and are expected to master control of their bowels. When toilet training begins during the second year, children have their first experience with discipline. The method of toilet training and the parents' feelings, attitudes, and reactions toward the child can have far-reaching effects on the formation of personality traits. Many of the attitudes children learn about their own bodily functions are the direct results of the attitudes of their parents. Later personality problems such as compulsivity have roots in the ways parents rear their children during this stage.

Children may attempt to control their parents by either withholding their feces or defecating at inappropriate times. If strict toilet-training methods are used, children may express their anger by expelling their feces at inappropriate places and times. This behavior can lay the foundation for later adult characteristics such as cruelty, inappropriate displays of anger, and extreme disorderliness. Freud described this as the *anal-aggressive* personality. Parents might focus too much attention on their children's bowel movements by giving praise whenever they defecate, which can contribute to a child's exaggerated view of the importance of this activity. This focus might be associated with a person's need for being productive. The important point is that later adult characteristics have their roots in the experiences of this period. Thus, certain adults develop fixations revolving around extreme orderliness, hoarding, stubbornness, and stinginess. This is known as the *anal-retentive* personality.

During the anal period of development, the child will surely experience so-called negative feelings such as hostility, destructiveness, anger, rage, hatred, and so on. It is important that children learn that these are acceptable feelings. Many clients in therapy have not yet learned to accept their anger and hatred toward those they love. Because they were either directly or indirectly taught that these feelings were bad and that parental acceptance would be withheld if they expressed them, they repressed them.

It is also important at this stage that children begin to acquire a sense of their own power, independence, and autonomy. If parents do too much for their children, they really teach them that they are incapable of self-functioning. The message transmitted is "Here, let me do thus-and-so for you, because you are too weak or helpless to do these things for yourself." During this time children need to experiment, to make mistakes and feel that they are still acceptable persons, and to recognize some of their own power as separate and distinct individuals. So many clients are in counseling precisely because they have lost touch with their potential for power; they are struggling to define who they are and what they are capable of doing.

Ages 3–5: The phallic stage.   We have seen that between the ages of 1 and 3 the child discards infantile ways and actively carves a distinctive niche in the world. This is the period when capacities for walking, talking, thinking, and controlling the sphincters develop rapidly. As increased motor and perceptual abilities begin to develop, so also do interpersonal skills. The child's progression from a period of passive/receptive mastery to a period of active mastery sets the stage for the next psychosexual developmental period—the phallic stage. During this period sexual activity becomes more intense, and now the focus of attention is on the genitals—the boy's penis and the girl's clitoris.

According to the orthodox Freudian view, the basic conflict of the phallic stage centers on the unconscious incestuous desires that children develop for the parent of the opposite sex. Because these feelings are of such a threatening nature, they are typically repressed; yet they are powerful determinants of later sexual development and adjustment. Along with the wish to possess the parent of the opposite sex comes the unconscious wish of the child to "do away with" the competition—the parent of the same sex.

Hall (1954) described the Freudian notion of what actually occurs in the development of the boy and the girl. In the *male phallic stage* the boy craves the attention of his mother, feels antagonistic toward his father, and develops fears that his father will punish him for his incestuous feelings toward his mother. This is known as the *Oedipus complex.* Thus, the mother becomes the love object for the boy. Both in his fantasy and his behavior, he exhibits sexual longings for her. He soon realizes that his more powerful father is a rival for the exclusive attention he desires from her. However, about the time when the mother becomes the object of love for the boy, repression is already operating, which prevents a conscious awareness of a part of his sexual aims.

At this time the boy typically develops specific fears related to his penis. Freud described the condition of *castration anxiety,* which is said to play a central role in the boy's life at this time. His ultimate fear is that his father will retaliate by cutting off his offending organ. The reality of castration is emphasized when the boy notices the absence of the penis in girls. As a result of this anxiety of losing his prized possession, the boy is said to repress his sexual desire for his mother. If the Oedipal conflict is properly resolved, the boy replaces his sexual longings for his mother with more acceptable forms of affection; he also develops strong identification with his father. In a sense, it is a matter of realizing that, if he cannot beat his father, then he might as well join him. Through this identification with his father, the boy experiences vicarious satisfaction. He becomes more like his father, and he may adopt many of his father's mannerisms.

The *female phallic stage* was not so clearly described by Freud as was the male stage. Also, the orthodox Freudian view of female development has stirred up considerable controversy and is met with negative reactions from many women. The *Electra complex* is the girl's counterpart to the Oedipus complex. The girl's first love object is her mother, but love is transferred to her father during this stage. She is said to develop negative feelings toward her mother when she discovers the absence of a penis, the condition known as *penis envy.* This is the girl's counterpart to the boy's *castration anxiety.* She is said to have a desire to compete with her mother for the father's attention, and when she realizes that she cannot replace her mother, she begins an identification process by taking on some of the characteristics of her mother's behavior.

The development of sexual attitudes assumes critical importance during this period of life. Perhaps one of the most frequently misunderstood terms in Freud's theory is *sexuality.* He uses it much more broadly than it is typically used. Sexuality refers to organ pleasure of any kind. The type of sexuality that becomes evident during the phallic stage does not necessarily refer to the child's desire for sexual intercourse with the opposite-sex parent. Although the boy's feelings toward his mother may be erotically tinged, this kind of sexuality is more undefined than sexual intercourse. It is during this period of psychosexual development that behaviors such as the following become increasingly evident: curiosity about sexual matters, sexual fantasies, masturbation, sex-role identification patterns, and sex play.

Masturbation, accompanied by sexual fantasies, is a normal accompaniment of early childhood. In the phallic period its frequency increases. Children become curious about their bodies; they desire to explore them and to discover differences between the sexes. Childhood experimentation is common, and because many attitudes toward sexuality originate in the phallic period, the acceptance of sexuality and the management of sexual impulses are vital at this time. This is a period of conscience development, a time when children learn moral standards. One critical danger is the parental indoctrination of rigid and unrealistic moral standards, which can lead to the overcontrol of the superego. If parents teach their children that all of their impulses are evil, children soon learn to feel guilty about their natural impulses and may carry these feelings of guilt into their adult lives and be blocked from enjoying intimacy with others. This kind of parental indoctrination results in an infantile conscience—that is, children are afraid to question or to think for themselves but blindly accept the indoctrination without question; they can hardly be considered moral, but merely frightened. Other effects include rigidity, severe conflicts, guilt, remorse, low self-esteem, and self-condemnation.

During this period children need to learn to accept their sexual feelings as natural and to develop a healthy respect for their bodies. They need adequate models for sex-role identification. They are forming attitudes about physical pleasure, about what is "right" and "wrong," what is "masculine," and what is "feminine." They are getting a perspective of the way women and men relate to each other. They are deciding how they feel about themselves in their roles as boys and girls.

The phallic period has significant implications for the therapist who works with adults. Many clients have never fully resolved their feelings about their own sexuality. They may have very confused feelings about sex-role identification, and they may be struggling to accept their sexual feelings and behavior. In my judgment, it is important that therapists give just recognition to early experiences when they are working with adult clients. I am not suggesting that therapists accept a deterministic view that people are condemned to a lack of sexual responsiveness or impotence if they have not successfully mastered the developmental tasks of the phallic period. What I do see as important, however, is that clients become aware of their childhood experiences in this area, perhaps even relive and reexperience them in fantasy. As they relive events and feel again many of their buried feelings, they become increasingly aware that they are capable of inventing new endings to dramas they experienced as children. Thus, they come to realize that, although their present attitudes and behavior are surely shaped by the past, they are not doomed to remain victims of the past.

Ages 5–12: The latency stage. With the passing of the turbulence of the first expression of the Oedipus complex and the combined stresses of the oral, anal, and phallic stages of psychosexual development, the individual can enjoy a period of relative rest. The major structures of personality (id, ego, superego) are largely formed, as are the relationships between these subsystems.

During this latency period new interests replace infantile sexual impulses. Socialization takes place, and children direct their interests to the larger world. The sexual drive is sublimated to some extent to activities in school, hobbies, sports, and friendships with members of the same sex.

The oral, anal, and phallic periods taken together are known as the pregenital period. A major characteristic of this period is a *narcissistic* orientation, or an inward and self-centered preoccupation. During the middle-childhood years there is a turning outward toward relationships with others. Children of this age have an interest in the things of the external world as well as of their internal world. This period prevails until the onset of puberty; it is during adolescence that the individual begins to establish an adult identity, along with a genital orientation.

Ages 12–Adulthood: The genital stage. Young adults move into the genital stage unless they become fixated at an earlier period of psychosexual development. During adolescence many of the old themes of the phallic stage are revived and recapitulated. Adolescents typically develop interest in the opposite sex, engage in some sexual experimentation, and begin to assume adult responsibilities. As they move out of adolescence and into mature adulthood, they develop intimate relationships, become free of parental influence, and develop the capacity to be interested in others. There is a trend away from narcissism and toward altruistic behavior and concern for others. According to Freud, the goals of *lieben und arbeiten* are core characteristics of the mature adult; that is, the freedom "to love and to work" and to derive satisfaction from loving and working are of paramount importance.

Freudian theory of character types.   The psychoanalytic theories of adult personality emphasize common patterns of behavior that are associated with various types of character structures. Individuals might become adults in the chronological sense yet remain immature in the psychosexual sense. Under certain conditions the libido may become fixated at a particular stage. For example, if some of the basic needs of a stage are not met, then the person's behavior is oriented toward meeting those unfulfilled needs. Thus, if a woman has become fixated at the oral stage, she will manifest characteristics throughout her life that are related to this stage (such as attempts to gratify her oral needs). Each psychosexual stage involves anxiety-arousing tasks; if individuals feel unable to deal with this anxiety, their growth may be halted.

In a summary of these various character types, Blum (1953) and Mullahy (1948) described some of the traits of the oral character, the anal character, the phallic character, and the genital character.

The *oral character* tends to exhibit characteristics that contain many elements of the oral fixations established in early childhood. Some of these include passive/dependent behavior, oral preoccupations (eating, drinking, speaking, and smoking), and the expectation that one will be taken care of eternally. It is possible for a person's entire character to be under "oral influence," in the sense that the individual demands to be "fed" and nurtured by others continually. According to Mullahy (1948), generosity, sociability, open-mindedness, restlessness, curiosity, and ambition are all marked in the oral character.

The *anal character* has characteristics marked by fixations at this stage, which include orderliness, parsimony, and obstinacy. Other traits include frugality, an excessive desire to please others, cleanliness, and reliability. Personality traits are assumed to grow out of conflicts centering on toilet training. Adult characteristics might be related to anxiety from early experiences and attitudes formed during the anal stage.

The *phallic character* exhibits behavior that is aimed at allaying castration anxiety, and there is an excessive need to demonstrate and prove oneself. Narcissism is a central characteristic, as in the male who is driven to prove his masculine qualities. People who have a phallic character are extremely oral-dependent, and their high degree of self-centeredness inhibits the development of mature and intimate relationships.

The *genital character* is considered the ideal type. These people have the capacity to achieve complete satisfaction of the sexual drive through genital orgasm, which supposedly puts an end to the damming up of instinctual energy with its negative impact on personality functioning. The final stage of character development is relatively free of self-centeredness. This stage implies that ambivalence is overcome, and that there is an absence of major internal conflicts. People who reach the genital stage of development are able to give and receive affection; they have also resolved the conflicts associated with the earlier stages of development to the degree that they can focus on the tasks facing them as adults.

The therapeutic process

THERAPEUTIC GOALS

The two goals of Freudian psychoanalytic therapy are to reform the individual's character structure by making the unconscious conscious and to strengthen the ego so that behavior is based more on reality and not so much on the whim of instinctual cravings.

The focus is on using therapeutic methods that open mental doors so that unconscious material can be worked through in therapy. The therapeutic process focuses on reliving childhood experiences, which are reconstructed, discussed, interpreted, and analyzed. It is clear that the goal is not limited to solving problems and learning new behaviors. Rather, there is a deeper probing into the past in order to develop the level of self-understanding that is assumed to be necessary for a change in character. Analytic therapy is oriented toward achieving insight, but not just an intellectual understanding; it is essential that the feelings and memories associated with this self-understanding be experienced.

THERAPIST'S FUNCTION AND ROLE

Classical analysts typically assume an anonymous stance, which is sometimes called the "blank-screen" approach. They engage in very little self-disclosure and maintain a sense of neutrality, because they are attempting to foster a *transference relationship,* in which their client will make projections onto them. If therapists say little about themselves and rarely share their personal reactions, they believe, then whatever the client feels toward them is largely the product of feelings associated with other significant figures from the past. These projections that have their origins in unfinished and repressed situations are considered "grist for the mill," and their analysis is the very essence of therapeutic work.

Not all analytically oriented therapists subscribe to the notion of neutrality and anonymity. Many engage in appropriate self-disclosure with their clients. The classic technique of nondisclosure is often misused in nonclassic situations, such as short-term individual therapy and assessment. Therapists in these situations who adopt the blank-screen aloofness that is called for theoretically only in the "pure" context of classical psychoanalysis may actually be keeping themselves hidden as persons in the guise of "being professional."

One of the central functions of analysts is to help the clients acquire the freedom to love and to work. There are other functions. Analysts are concerned with assisting the client in achieving self-awareness, honesty, and more effective personal relationships, in dealing with anxiety in a realistic way, and in gaining control over impulsive and irrational behavior. They must first establish a working relationship with the patient and then do a lot of listening and interpreting. They pay particular attention to the resistances of the patient. While the client does most of the talking, they listen and learn when to make appropriate interpretations, the function of which is to accelerate the process of uncovering unconscious material. They listen for gaps and inconsistencies in the client's story, infer the meaning of reported dreams and free-associating, carefully observe during the therapy session, and remain sensitive to clues concerning the client's feelings toward them.

Organizing these therapeutic processes within the context of understanding personality structure and psychodynamics enables the analyst to formulate the real nature of clients' problems. One of the central functions of the analyst is to teach clients the meaning of these processes so that they are able to achieve insight into their problems, increase their awareness of ways to change, and thus gain more rational control over their lives.

CLIENT'S EXPERIENCE IN THERAPY

Clients must be willing to commit themselves to an intensive and long-term therapy process. Typically, they come to therapy several times weekly for a period of three to five years. The sessions usually last an hour. After some face-to-face sessions with the analyst, clients then lie on a couch for free-association activity; that is, they say whatever comes to mind. This process of free association is known as the "fundamental rule." Clients report their feelings, experiences, associations, memories, and fantasies. Lying on the couch maximizes conditions for their deep reflections and reduces the stimuli that might interfere with their coming into touch with their internal conflicts and productions.

What has just been described is classical psychoanalysis. It should be noted that many analytically oriented therapists do not use the couch and the free-association method. Yet they do direct their clients to focus on concepts such as transference, and these clients work with their dreams and with other unconscious factors.

Clients enter into an agreement with the analyst regarding paying fees, attending sessions at a certain time, and making a commitment to an intensive process. They agree to talk, because their verbal productions are the heart of psychoanalytic therapy. They are typically asked not to make any radical changes in their life-style during the period of analysis.

During therapy clients progress through certain stages: developing a growing relationship with the analyst, experiencing treatment crises, gaining insight into their past and unconscious, developing resistances to learning more about themselves, developing a transference relationship with the analyst, deepening the therapy, "working through" the resistances and uncovered material, and termination of therapy.

RELATIONSHIP BETWEEN THERAPIST AND CLIENT

The client's relationship with the analyst is conceptualized in the transference process, which is the core of the psychoanalytic approach. Transference allows clients to attribute to the therapist "unfinished business" from their past relationships with significant people. The treatment process involves their reconstruction and reliving of the past. As therapy progresses, childhood feelings and conflicts begin to surface from the depths of the unconscious. Clients regress emotionally. Some of their feelings arise from conflicts such as trust versus mistrust, love versus hate, dependence versus independence, and autonomy versus shame and guilt. Transference takes place when clients resurrect from their early past intense conflicts relating to love, sexuality, hostility, anxiety, and resentment, bring them into the present, reexperience them, and attach them to the analyst. Clients might see the analyst as an authority figure who punishes, demands, and controls. For example, they might transfer unresolved feelings toward a stern and unloving father to the analyst, who, in their eyes, becomes stern and unloving. Hostile feelings are the product of negative transference, but clients might also develop a positive transference and, for example, fall in love with the analyst, wish to be adopted, or in many other ways seek the love, acceptance, and approval of an all-powerful therapist. In short, the analyst becomes a current substitute for significant others.

If therapy is to cure, the transference relationship must be worked through. The working-through process involves clients' exploring the parallels between their past and present experience. They have many opportunities to see the variety of ways in which their core conflicts and core defenses are manifested in their daily life. Because a major dimension of the working-through process is the transference relationship, which takes time to build in intensity and additional time to understand and resolve, working-through requires a lengthy period in the total therapeutic process.

The working-through process consists of an exploration of unconscious material and defenses. Most of these defenses were used in early childhood. It is assumed that for clients to become psychologically independent they must not only become aware of this unconscious material but also achieve some level of freedom from behavior motivated by infantile strivings, such as the need for total love and acceptance from parental figures. If this demanding phase of the therapeutic relationship is not properly worked through, clients simply transfer their infantile wishes for universal love and acceptance to other figures they deem as powerful. It is precisely in the client/therapist relationship that the manifestation of these childhood motivations becomes apparent. It must be emphasized, however, that all traces of our childhood needs and traumas will really never be completely erased. In this sense, transference may not be fully resolved, even though it is worked through with one's therapist. We may need to struggle at times throughout our lives with irrational feelings that we project on others as well as with unrealistic demands that we expect others to fulfill. In this sense our past is always a vital part of the person that we are presently becoming.

This notion of never becoming completely free of past experiences has significant implications for therapists who become intimately involved in the unresolved conflicts of their clients. This intensive relationship is bound to ignite some of the unconscious conflicts within therapists. Even if these conflicts have surfaced to awareness, and even if therapists have dealt with these personal issues in their own intensive therapy, this does not imply that they are now free of any distortions that they may project on clients. *Countertransference* is the term that refers to the needs, unresolved conflicts, and irrational reactions that therapists have toward their clients. For example, a client may become excessively dependent upon his therapist. He may look to her to direct him and tell him how to live, and he may look to her for the love and acceptance that he felt he was unable to secure from his mother. The therapist herself may have unresolved needs to nurture, to foster a dependent relationship, and to be told that she is significant, and she may be meeting her own needs by in some way making her client infantile. Unless she is aware of her own needs as well as her own dynamics, it is very likely that her dynamics will interfere with the progress of therapy.

The analyst's own reactions and problems can stand in the way of dealing with the client's problems. Thus, therapists must be aware of how their conflicts can be triggered by certain clients, so that they can guard against disturbing effects. Therapists are expected to develop some level of objectivity and not to react irrationally and subjectively in the face of anger, love, adulation, criticism, and other intense feeling of their clients. Because therapists are human, however, they do have to be aware of their own areas of vulnerability as well as unresolved problems that may intrude from time to time. As a result, countertransference is seen as an inevitable part of the therapeutic relationship. Most psychoanalytic training programs require that trainees undergo their own extensive analysis as a client. If analysts become aware of symptoms (such as strong aversion to certain types of clients, strong attraction to other types of clients, developing psychosomatic reactions at definite times in therapeutic relationships, and the like) then it behooves them to seek professional consultation or enter their own therapy for a time to work out their unresolved personal issues that stand in the way of their being effective therapists.

It is a mistake to assume that all feelings that clients have toward their therapists are mere manifestations of transference. Many of these reactions may have a reality base, and clients' feelings may well be directed to the here-and-now style that the therapist exhibits. On the one hand, every positive response (such as liking of the therapist) should not be labeled "positive transference." On the other hand, a client's anger toward the therapist may be a function of the therapist's behavior; it is a mistake to label all negative reactions as signs of "negative transference." Likewise, therapists have feelings toward their clients, and they do not react uniformly to all their clients. So it is not precise to contend that all positive and negative feelings of therapists toward their clients are merely countertransference. Countertransference is the phenomenon that occurs when there is an inappropriate affect, when therapists respond in irrational ways, or when they lose their objectivity in a relationship because their own conflicts are triggered.

It should be clear that the client/therapist relationship is of central importance in psychoanalytic therapy. As a result of this relationship, particularly in working through the transference situation, clients acquire insight into their own unconscious psychodynamics. Awareness of and insights into repressed material are the bases of the analytic growth process. Clients are able to understand the association between their past experiences and their current behavior as well as the influence of past situations on the formation of their current character structure. The psychoanalytic approach assumes that without this dynamic self-understanding there can be no substantial personality change or resolution of present conflicts.

Application: Therapeutic techniques and procedures

The techniques in psychoanalytic therapy are geared to increasing awareness, gaining intellectual insights into the client's behavior, and understanding the meanings of symptoms. The therapeutic progression is from the client's talk to catharsis to insight to working through unconscious material toward the goals of intellectual and emotional understanding and reeducation, which, it is hoped, lead to personality change. The five basic techniques of psychoanalytic therapy are (1) free association, (2) interpretation, (3) dream analysis, (4) analysis of resistance, and (5) analysis of transference.

FREE ASSOCIATION

The central technique in psychoanalytic therapy is free association. The analyst instructs clients to clear their mind of day-to-day thoughts and preoccupations and, as much as possible, to say whatever comes to mind, regardless of how painful, silly, trivial, illogical, or irrelevant it may be. In essence, clients flow with any feelings or thoughts by reporting them immediately without censorship. They typically lie on the couch while the analyst sits behind them so as not to distract them during the free flow of associations.

Free association is one of the basic tools used to open the doors to unconscious wishes, fantasies, conflicts, and motivations. This technique often leads to some recollection of past experiences and, at times, a releasing of intense feelings that have been blocked off. This release is not seen as crucial of itself, however. During the free-association process, the analyst's task is to identify the repressed material that is locked in the unconscious. The sequence of associations guides the analyst in understanding the connections clients make among events. Blockings or disruptions in associations serve as cues to anxiety-arousing material. The analyst interprets the material to clients, guiding them toward increased insight into the underlying dynamics that they had been unaware of.

INTERPRETATION

Interpretation is a basic procedure used in analyzing free associations, dreams, resistances, and transferences. The procedure consists of the analyst's pointing out, explaining, and even teaching the client the meanings of behavior that is manifested by dreams, free association, resistances, and the therapeutic relationship itself. The functions of interpretations are to allow the ego to assimilate new material and to speed up the process of uncovering further unconscious material.

It is important that interpretations be well timed, because clients will reject ones that are inappropriately timed. A general rule is that interpretation should be presented when the phenomenon to be interpreted is close to clients' conscious awareness. In other words, the analyst should interpret material that clients have not yet seen for themselves but are capable of tolerating and incorporating as their own. Another general rule is that interpretation should always start from the surface and go only as deep as clients are able to go while experiencing the situation emotionally. A third general rule is that it is best to point out a resistance or defense before interpreting the emotion or conflict that lies beneath it.

DREAM ANALYSIS

Dream analysis is an important procedure for uncovering unconscious material and giving the patient an insight into some areas of unresolved problems. During sleep, defenses are lowered, and repressed feelings surface. Freud saw dreams as the "royal road to the unconscious," for in them one's unconscious wishes, needs, and fears are expressed. Some motivations are so unacceptable to the person that they are expressed in disguised or symbolic form rather than being revealed directly.

Dreams have two levels of content: the *latent content* and the *manifest content.* The *latent content* consists of the hidden, symbolic, and unconscious motives. Because they are so painful and threatening, the unconscious sexual and aggressive impulses that make up the latent content are transformed into the more acceptable *manifest content,* which is the dream as it appears to the dreamer. The process by which the latent content of a dream is transformed into the less threatening manifest content is called *dream work.* The analyst's task is to uncover disguised meanings by studying the symbols in the manifest content of the dream. During the analytic hour the analyst might ask the client to free-associate to some aspect of the manifest content of a dream for the purpose of uncovering the latent meanings.

ANALYSIS AND INTERPRETATION OF RESISTANCE

Resistance, a fundamental concept to the practice of psychoanalysis, is anything that works against the progress of therapy and prevents the client from producing unconscious material. During free association or association to dreams, the patient may evidence an unwillingness to relate certain thoughts, feelings, and experiences. Freud viewed resistance as an unconscious dynamic that attempts to defend people against intolerable anxiety, which would arise if they were to become aware of their repressed impulses and feelings.

As a defense against anxiety, resistance operates specifically in psychoanalytic therapy by preventing the patient and analyst from succeeding in their joint efforts to gain insight into the dynamics of the unconscious. Because resistance prevents threatening material from entering awareness, the analyst must point it out, and clients must confront it if they hope to deal with conflicts realistically. The analyst's interpretation of the resistance is aimed at helping clients become aware of reasons for the resistance so that they can deal with them. As a general rule, the analyst points out and interprets the most obvious resistances in order to lessen the possibility of clients' rejecting the interpretation and to increase the chance that they will begin to look at their resistive behavior.

Resistances are not just something to be overcome. Because they are representative of usual defensive approaches in daily life, they must be recognized as devices that defend against anxiety but that interfere with the ability to experience a more gratifying life.

In the Freudian perspective, resistance is an unconscious dynamic; it is the attempt to defend the self against a high degree of anxiety that would result if the material were to be translated from the unconscious to conscious experience. Resistance, along with the development of transference, is a normal part of psychoanalytic therapy. Any aspect of the therapeutic relationship that the client is attempting to avoid, as well as anything that is blocking the process of uncovering unconscious material, is interpreted by the therapist so that the client can begin to work through it.

ANALYSIS AND INTERPRETATION
OF TRANSFERENCE

Transference, as mentioned earlier, manifests itself in the therapeutic process at the point where patients' past "unfinished business" with significant others causes them to distort the present and to react to the analyst as they did to their mother or father or to another early significant person in their life. Now, in relationship with the analyst, clients reexperience the feelings of rejection and hostility once felt toward their parents or someone else. In classical Freudian analysis it is assumed that clients will eventually develop this "transference neurosis," because their problems originated during the first five years of life and are now being inappropriately carried as a framework for living. In classical analysis this transference is encouraged and fostered by the analyst's neutrality, objectivity, anonymity, and relative passivity. Many analytically oriented therapists, although they focus on transference feelings as well as other unconscious material, do not foster a regressive trend in their clients by assuming a passive and aloof stance.

The analysis of transference is a central technique in psychoanalysis, for it allows clients to relive their past in therapy. It enables them to achieve insight into the nature of their fixations and deprivations, and it provides an understanding of the influence of the past as it relates to present functioning. Interpretation of the transference relationship also enables clients to work through old conflicts that keep them presently fixated and that retard their emotional growth. In essence, the psychopathological effects of an undesirable early relationship are counteracted by working through a similar emotional conflict in the therapeutic relationship with the analyst.

Summary and evaluation

The aim of this chapter has been to outline some of the major concepts of psychoanalytic theory and to discuss their implications for therapeutic practice. These key concepts include the existence of instincts as a part of human nature; the structure of personality as described by the systems of the id, the ego, and the superego; the dynamics of the unconscious and its influence on behavior; the role of anxiety and the emergence of a variety of ego defenses as a way of coping with it; and the influences on the development of personality at various life periods, including the oral, anal, phallic, latency, and genital stages. The therapeutic process was described, with emphasis on the goals of treatment and the therapist's function. A distinction was made between classical (orthodox Freudian) analysts and psychoanalytically oriented therapists, who draw on key analytic concepts but integrate this approach with other approaches. The most important analytic techniques typically employed by both groups were described: free association, interpretation, dream analysis, analysis and interpretation of resistance, and analysis and interpretation of transference.

What are the implications of the psychoanalytic approach (as a view of human nature, as a model for understanding behavior, and as a method of therapy) for counselors? How applicable is this approach to school counseling? How useful is it in community counseling clinics and in other kinds of public and private human-services agencies? In general, considering factors such as time, expense, and availability of trained analysts, I think the practical applications of the *method* are very limited. Further, the goals of analytic therapy—that is, probing the unconscious and working toward radical personality transformations—are inappropriate for typical counseling settings. But, although the method might be limited, I believe that therapeutic counselors can deepen their understanding of clients' current struggles by appreciating the many significant contributions of Freud. Psychoanalysis provides the counselor with a conceptual framework for looking at behavior and for understanding the origins and functions of present symptoms. It can also be extremely useful in understanding the functions of the ego defenses as reactions to anxiety. If counselors ignore the early history of the client, they are truly limiting their vision of the causes of the client's present suffering and the nature of the client's present life-style. This does not mean that they must be preoccupied with the past, dig it up, and dwell on it exclusively; but to deemphasize early experiences as determinants of current conflicts is to restrict their capacity to help the client grow. There is no plea here for blaming the past for the fact that a client is now, for example, unable to love. If the client is fearful of forming close relationships with people, however, counselors must understand the roots of this handicap. In addition, counseling will involve working through some of the barriers of the past that are now preventing the client from loving.

Some specific applications of the psychoanalytic point of view include the following: (1) understanding resistances that take the form of cancellation of appointments, fleeing from therapy prematurely, and refusing to look at oneself; (2) understanding the role of early relationships that lead to weak spots and faulty personality development and recognizing that unfinished business can be worked through, so that clients can put a new ending to some of the events that have crippled them emotionally; (3) understanding the value and role of transference; and (4) understanding how overuse of ego defenses can keep people from functioning effectively and recognizing the ways these ego defenses operate both in the counseling relationship itself and in clients' daily lives.

My teaching experience has demonstrated that students sometimes have a difficult time understanding and accepting some of the Freudian notions about the stages of development. The Oedipus complex, penis envy, castration anxiety, incestual feelings, and connections between past situations and current character formation may seem rather obscure on initial presentation. Personally, I recall that I had many doubts about the validity of these concepts when I first studied them in my undergraduate days. However, my experiences with my own children, my observation of other children, and my work in both individual and group therapy have given me a new and wider perspective on the Freudian view of psychosexual development. It is essential to keep in mind that this view must be understood from the vantage point of the time in which Freud wrote—during the Victorian era of the authoritarian father. Much of what Freud described makes sense when it is seen in historical and cultural perspective.

Moreover, it is a mistake to dismiss these concepts in totality or to see them as merely interesting from a historical point of view. Considered more broadly, many of these developmental themes still have relevance for practicing counselors and therapists. Without taking penis envy and castration anxiety literally in the narrow context in which they were originally presented by Freud, practitioners stand to learn a lot about the dynamics of their clients' problem behaviors by appreciating some of Freud's insights into psychosexual development. Especially in my work with intensive therapeutic groups, I have time and again observed what appear to be universal struggles. A few of these are incestual feelings toward parents of the opposite sex, competition with the parent of the same sex and intense feelings of jealousy, guilt over sexual feelings and actions, fears relating to sexual intimacy and loving, fears of abandonment, struggles in the area of defining one's own sexual identity, anger and even rage over not getting what one wanted as a child, and love/hate conflicts. The psychoanalytic approach provides a framework for a dynamic understanding of the role of these early childhood events and the impact of these experiences on the contemporary struggles faced by clients. Without going to the extreme of accepting the orthodox Freudian position, it is still possible to draw on many of these analytic concepts as a framework for understanding the clients we work with and for helping them achieve a deeper understanding of the roots of their conflicts.

Students of counseling can learn a great deal about the therapeutic process by becoming familiar with the concepts and techniques of the analytic approach. Although many counselors will have neither the training for nor the interest in conducting psychoanalytic therapy per se, they can gain much by adding the analytic perspective to their practice. Even if they do not possess the skills to work toward personality reconstruction that analytic therapy involves, the concepts can give depth to their counseling. Knowledge of the dynamics of behavior, ego defenses, the workings of the unconscious, and the development of personality will help them gain this depth.

In my opinion, it is possible to think in psychoanalytic terms and have an analytic framework that gives structure and direction to a counseling practice and at the same time to draw on other therapeutic techniques. I value the psychoanalytic concepts that I have mentioned, and they are in the background as I work with clients either individually or in groups. At the same time, I am critical of the Freudian emphasis on the biological forces as shapers of personality, as well as the emphasis on people's sexual and aggressive aspects. This is where I find value in the contributions of those writers who have built on the basic ideas of Freud and added emphasis on the social forces affecting personality development. It is these approaches that we will consider in the following chapter.

Questions for reflection and discussion

Consider the following questions as you form your own appraisal of the contributions and limitations of the psychoanalytic approach.

1. Freud's model is based on a deterministic view of human nature: the person is determined by psychic energy, unconscious motives, and childhood experiences. Do you agree with this view? What are its implications for counseling practice?
2. The psychoanalytic approach underscores the importance of early psychosexual development. Do you see evidence that one's current problems are rooted in the significant events of one's first five years of life? When you apply this concept specifically to yourself, what connections between your childhood experiences and your present personality are you aware of?
3. Do you think that a system of counseling and psychotherapy is complete if it does not account for such concepts as the unconscious, ego-defense mechanisms, and the critical influences of one's past on one's current personality? Explain your position.
4. In your work as a counselor, many psychoanalytic techniques such as free association, dream interpretation, probing the unconscious, and interpretation and analysis of resistance and transference may not be appropriate, or they may be beyond your level of training. However, what are some concepts of the psychoanalytic approach that can provide you with a useful framework in deepening your understanding of human behavior? How do you see psychoanalytic views as being potentially related to your work as a counselor?
5. As you study the other therapies described in this book, compare them with the psychoanalytic approach. To what degree are other approaches based on psychoanalytic concepts or on a reaction against supposed limitations of psychoanalysis?
6. What were some of your stereotypes or misconceptions of psychoanalysis before you read about this theory? Is it possible that some of your misconceptions might prevent you from seeing some valid concepts that are related to your work as a counselor?
7. How might Freud's concept of the unconscious be important for you to understand, even though in your work as a counselor you might not deal directly with your clients' unconscious motives and conflicts?
8. The psychoanalytic view of anxiety is that it is largely the result of keeping unconscious conflicts buried, and that the ego defenses develop to help the person curb anxiety. What implications does this view have for your work with people? Do you think defenses are necessary? What are the possible values of defense mechanisms? What do you think might happen if you were able to successfully strip away a client's defenses?
9. What is your evaluation of the psychoanalytic view of personality development? Consider the stages of early development, particularly with respect to how fully a person's basic needs were met at each stage. Do you think it is necessary or important to explore with clients areas of conflict and unmet needs of the early years? Do you believe people can resolve their adult problems that stem from childhood experiences without exploring past events? How much emphasis would you place on a person's past?
10. Can you apply any aspects of the psychoanalytic theory to your own personal growth? Does this approach help you in any way to deepen your self-understanding? If so, how and in what ways?

Recommended supplementary readings

If you are interested in expanding your knowledge of the Freudian approach, a good place to begin is *A Primer of Freudian Psychology* (Hall, 1954), a concise overview. The next step would be to consult *An Elementary Textbook of Psychoanalysis* (Brenner, 1974), an excellent orientation text for those who want to acquaint themselves with psychoanalytic theory. Chapter topics include basic hypotheses, drives, the psychic apparatus, dreams, psychopathology, conflict, and psychoanalysis today.

References and suggested readings

Other books highly recommended as supplementary reading are marked with an asterisk.

* Baruch, D. *One little boy.* New York: Dell (Delta), 1964.

Bettelheim, B. *Love is not enough.* New York: P. F. Collier, 1950.

Blum, G. *Psychoanalytic theories of personality.* New York: McGraw-Hill, 1953.

Blum, G. *Psychodynamics: The science of unconscious mental forces.* Monterey, Calif.: Brooks/Cole, 1966.

Brand, M. *Savage sleep.* New York: Bantam, 1968.

Brenner, C. *An elementary textbook of psychoanalysis* (Revised Edition). Garden City, New York: Anchor Press, 1974.

Brown, N. O. *Life against death.* New York: Random House, 1959.

Cameron, N. *Personality development and psychopathology: A dynamic approach.* Boston: Houghton Mifflin, 1963.

Corey, G. *Theory and practice of group counseling.* Monterey, Calif.: Brooks/Cole, 1981.

Corey, G. *Case approach to counseling and psychotherapy.* Monterey, Calif.: Brooks/Cole, 1982.

Freud, S. *An outline of psychoanalysis.* New York: Norton, 1949.

Freud, S. *The interpretation of dreams.* London: Hogarth Press, 1955.

Freud, S. *Civilization and its discontents.* New York: Norton, 1962. (Originally published, 1930.)

Freud, S. *Beyond the pleasure principle.* New York: Bantam, 1967.

Green, H. *I never promised you a rose garden.* New York: New American Library (Signet), 1964.

Haley, J. *Strategies of psychotherapy.* New York: Grune & Stratton, 1963.

Hall, C. *A primer of Freudian psychology.* New York: New American Library (Mentor), 1954.

Hall, C., & Lindzey, G. *Theories of personality* (3rd ed.). New York: Wiley, 1978.

* Mintz, E. *Marathon groups: Reality and symbol.* New York: Appleton-Century-Crofts, 1971.

Mullahy, P. *Oedipus myth and complex: A review of psychoanalytic theory.* New York: Grove Press, 1948.

*Nye, R. *Three psychologies: Perspectives from Freud, Skinner, and Rogers* (2nd ed.). Brooks/Cole, 1981.

* Schultz, D. *Theories of personality* (2nd ed.). Monterey, Calif.: Brooks/Cole, 1981.

Wolf, A., & Schwartz, E. K. *Psychoanalysis in groups.* New York: Grune & Stratton, 1962.

Wolf, A., Schwartz, E. K., McCarty, G. J., & Goldberg, I. A. *Beyond the couch: Dialogues in teaching and learning psychoanalysis in groups.* New York: Science House, 1970.

3

Extensions and Adaptations of Psychoanalytic Theory

Introduction

Carl Jung and analytic theory
INTRODUCTION
VIEW OF HUMAN NATURE
STRUCTURE AND DYNAMICS OF PERSONALITY
The ego
The personal unconscious
The collective unconscious
The persona
The animus *and* anima
The shadow
The self
Two attitudes: Extraversion and introversion
Four psychological functions
COUNSELING IMPLICATIONS

Alfred Adler and individual psychology
INTRODUCTION
VIEW OF HUMAN NATURE
OTHER KEY CONCEPTS
Basic inferiority and compensation
Striving for superiority
Style of life
Childhood experiences
THERAPEUTIC PROCESS: GOALS AND STAGES IN COUNSELING
The relationship
Analysis and assessment
Insight
Reorientation
COUNSELING IMPLICATIONS

Karen Horney
VIEW OF HUMAN NATURE
BASIC THEME
TEN NEUROTIC NEEDS
NEUROTIC TRENDS AND THREE CHARACTER TYPES
TYRANNY OF THE IDEALIZED IMAGE OF SELF
COUNSELING IMPLICATIONS
THERAPEUTIC TECHNIQUES

Introduction

This chapter deals with theorists who were originally influenced by Freud but who had a number of sharp differences with the classical psychoanalytic approach. Some of them were associated with Freud and broke away from him because of these differences. All of them extended and adapted the psychoanalytic approach. At times some of them have been called neo-Freudians, but it should be noted that each has made significant and unique contributions.

In this chapter you will find a highly condensed summary of the key concepts of seven writers—Carl Jung, Alfred Adler, Erich Fromm, Karen Horney, Harry Stack Sullivan, Erik Erikson, and Wilhelm Reich. They bridged the gap between Freud and some of the more contemporary writers to be considered in this book. I will present the highlights of each theory and their implications for counseling and therapy.

The first five theorists to be discussed—Jung, Adler, Horney, Fromm, and Sullivan—shared themes that separated them from Freud's orthodoxy. They agreed that social and cultural factors were of great significance in the shaping of personality. In some senses they developed a social-psychological point of view, pitted largely against what they considered to be Freud's narrow insistence on the biological determinants of personality, especially the role of sex and aggression and the bodily instincts. Further, they gave less emphasis to the role of the unconscious, maintaining that humans also have a capacity for reason and for consciousness. Although most of them accepted the role of early-childhood experiences as important, they rejected the notion that personality is fixed during that period. They gave attention to critical factors during the whole life span.

Horney, Fromm, and Sullivan are frequently identified with the social-psychological theories. Although they borrowed somewhat from Freud, they extended his approach largely by stressing interpersonal factors. Their emphasis on the social and cultural factors has contributed to the modern interactive models of therapy, in which the focus is on one's interaction with one's environment. Community psychology, a relatively recent thrust in therapy, derives its interest in such factors from these theorists.

Erikson, identified as an ego psychologist, has developed an approach to personality that moves considerably beyond Freud's, even though he maintained the core of Freud's thoughts. His contribution is the psychosocial point of view, which gives a conception of the life span and human development that is different from Freud's psychosexual view.

Reich, who can be considered as the precursor of the contemporary body-oriented psychotherapies, was clearly influenced by Freudian psychoanalytic theory. Reich's early contributions were based on the notion of character "armor," which was related to Freud's view that ego defenses are a reaction against anxiety. He stressed loosening and dissolving the body's muscular armoring in addition to dealing in an analytical fashion with psychological matters.

Because each of these theories is summarized only briefly, additional readings will be presented. The main idea of this chapter is not to give you a complete picture but rather to encourage you to read in these areas.

Carl Jung and analytic theory

INTRODUCTION

Carl Jung was originally a colleague of Freud's, but he broke with the master and went on to develop his own highly complex theory of personality, which differed from orthodox Freudian psychoanalysis in many ways. Jung objected primarily to the emphasis Freud gave to the sexual dynamics and determinants of behavior, as well as Freud's basically pessimistic and deterministic view of human nature.

Jungian analytical psychology is experiencing a reawakening of interest in the United States. This approach finds favor with many youths who have interests in existentialism, Eastern religions, mysticism, and the occult. There are three training institutes in the United States (in New York, San Francisco, and Los Angeles) and several in Europe.

VIEW OF HUMAN NATURE

A central feature of Jung's view of the person is his emphasis on the role of purpose and goals. His theory of personality is also a forward-looking one, for it focuses on what people are becoming (Schultz, 1981). According to Jung, people are influenced not only by what they experienced as children, but also by what they aspire to in the future. Hall and Lindzey (1978) wrote that the distinctive feature of Jung's view of humans is the combination of *teleology* with *causality;* that is, the approach combines the concern of humans about the direction they are heading and their concern over past experiences that are important in the present. Human beings are continually growing and evolving, and in doing so they are moving toward a fuller level of development. The goal of human development is found in the ongoing process of striving for self-realization, or the wholeness of personality. Whereas Freud stressed instinctual drives and impulses (such as sexuality, aggression, and the death urges), Jung focused on the optimistic or creative side of humanity, the striving for wholeness, and the role of living for purpose and meaning.

Jung placed even more emphasis on the unconscious than did Freud, and he broadened this concept considerably. He saw that the unconscious could be tapped, developed, and utilized. Not only did he account for the *personal,* or *individual, unconscious,* but he also described the *collective unconscious,* which includes the inherited experiences of humans as a species. This concept brought history, mythology, primitive rituals, religion, and universal symbols into the Jungian view of human nature (Schultz, 1981). Jung described the unconscious forces as both creative and destructive. More than being merely the sum of repressed childhood experiences, the unconscious is the wellspring of creativity and the source for direction in life.

STRUCTURE AND DYNAMICS OF PERSONALITY

Jungian psychology is based on a variety of personality structures, which are unique yet interdependent, in that each is capable of influencing the other. These major systems are the ego, the personal unconscious, the collective unconscious, the persona, the *anima* and the *animus,* the shadow, and the self. The two attitudes of extraversion and introversion and Jung's four psychological functions will also be briefly described.

The ego. The ego is the center of consciousness and is concerned with thinking, feeling, perceiving, and remembering. It represents our awareness as we go about our daily functions. It provides a sense of continuity and identity, as it is the basis for the way we perceive our world and ourselves.

The personal unconscious. The personal unconscious consists of material that comes out of experience. These are the experiences that were once conscious but have been repressed, suppressed, forgotten, or ignored. Painful ideas and thoughts that are not yet ripe for consciousness are suppressed or ignored. As people continue this process of excluding experiences, these experiences begin to cluster around what Jung called *complexes* (emotionally laden ideas and behavioral impulses). Behavior might assume a compulsive quality because of the preoccupation with a theme. Complexes revolve around themes such as power, striving for perfection, achievement, prestige, control, and so forth. As complexes are formed, they lie outside of conscious control and can interfere with effective living.

The collective unconscious. A controversial aspect of Jungian analytic psychology is the notion of the transpersonal unconscious, which is the deepest and most inaccessible level of the person. The collective unconscious is the storehouse of buried memories inherited from the ancestral past. It is the "racial" inheritance of significant memories (archetypes) passed from generation to generation. This represents a catalog of human experiences that grows out of evolution. Archetypes are the ancient experiences, housed in the collective unconscious, that are expressed in the form of images or partially developed memories. They are discovered through the symbolic interpretation of dreams, fantasies, myths, and beliefs. The collective unconscious contains the wisdom of the ages and serves as a guide for human development. Some of its archetypes are the Great Mother, magic, the hero, the divine child, the Wise Old Man, death, power, God, and wholeness. The following archetypes take on particular meaning because of their central role in the development of personality: the persona, the *anima* and *animus,* the shadow, and the self.

The persona. One's persona is the mask worn in response to social situations, the demands of tradition, and one's inner archetypal needs. It is the role that is assigned to people by society. The persona is the public self, the side one displays to the world, or the social facade.

The persona has several counseling implications. Although people must perform certain functions, there is the danger of getting lost in these functions. People can limit themselves by restricting the development of aspects of their personalities that do not fit their roles. There is the danger that they can be defined by their roles, instead of creating identities that fit for them. Clients often seek therapy because their lives have grown stale or because of a need to broaden their lives. Some clients have recognized the problem of deriving most of their satisfaction from one exclusive role; when this role no longer has meaning, people can be lost unless they learn to create new identities.

The **animus** *and* **anima.** Humans have both feminine and masculine characteristics. The feminine side of men is the *anima,* by which men can understand women. The masculine side of women is the *animus,* by which women can understand men. By living with man throughout the ages, woman has become masculinized, and by living with woman, man has become femininized. According to Jung, these archetypes must be expressed if the person is to develop as a full person. Both sexes must express both dimensions of their personhood, or they will lead restricted lives.

One of the implications for counseling of Jung's concept of the *animus* and *anima* is found in the attempt of some men to deny their feminine side. The "macho male" who denies himself feelings, who strives to present an image of toughness, and who squelches any trace of a feminine trait often times pays a steep price. Counseling can be designed to help clients develop both of these dimensions and decide for themselves the type of men or women they will become. In this connection, mention should be made of the unconscious and uncontrolled development of repressed traits that represent the "flip sides" of strongly developed conscious traits. In the Jungian perspective, much psychopathology is related to the eruption of unconsciously developed patterns into awareness or behavior.

The shadow. The shadow is the part of our personality that we would rather not acknowledge, or the part of us that we would rather not be. The shadow has the deepest roots of all the archetypes, and it contains the primitive and animal instincts. It is often considered the "dark side of the person," and is the part that must be tamed if people are to live together constructively. The shadow contains those things in us that we typically do not permit ourselves to recognize; thus, we project these traits or attributes to others.

It should be added that the shadow is something more than our "evil side"; it is also the source of creativity and spontaneity. With its vital and passionate instincts, the shadow helps people become whole and complete. According to Jung, the ego's function is dual: (1) to direct the forces of the shadow and to control the animal instincts to allow for civilized interaction, yet (2) to allow for adequate expression of the shadow, bringing vigor to living. If the shadow side is fully extinguished, then the result is a lifeless and unexciting person. Thus, even though it is difficult to accept and integrate the shadow into our personality, it is critical that we do so for the sake of living a richer existence.

The self. The most important archetype is the self, for it represents unity, wholeness, and integration of personality; it is the central part of personality, around which all of the other systems are clustered. The self provides the personality with unity and stability. The self archetype does not emerge until the other systems of the personality have fully developed. According to Jung, this development of the self occurs during middle age, a crucial time in the life span. Development of the self involves a future orientation including the plans, goals, and sense of purpose that will lead toward self-realization. Realizing the self is a central goal in everyone's life—a goal that people constantly strive for, yet frequently miss. It is the goal and the process by which individuals are able to discover their uniqueness; it is the basis for centeredness and for finding meaning in life. As such, the self functions as a dominant motivating force: it pulls the person from ahead rather than pushing from behind.

Two attitudes: Extraversion and introversion. The extraverted attitude orients the person toward the external and objective world. The extraverted personality tends to be open, socially oriented, and outgoing. The introverted attitude orients the person toward the internal and subjective world. Some characteristics of the introverted personality include shyness, a focus on self, a tendency toward quietness, and a preoccupation with inner experience.

Although people cannot be neatly categorized into either of these dimensions, one of these attitudes tends to become dominant; it is this attitude that influences a person's behavior.

Four psychological functions. Jung found that he could not summarize the differences in people under the categories of extraversion and introversion. He then developed another framework for describing differences in human behavior, based on the psychological functions of thinking, feeling, sensing, and intuition. Although everyone uses all four of these functions in varying degrees, each person epitomizes one function:

1. The *thinking type* is logical and meets situations in a cool, objective, and rational manner.
2. The *feeling type* emphasizes subjective aspects and values and places less emphasis on thinking.
3. The *sensation type* is able to perceive everything given directly by the senses.

4. The *intuitive type* is intensely alive to all possibilities in a situation. Such a person goes beyond facts, feelings, and ideas and is able to get all the essence of reality.

Jung admitted that there is a wide range of variation in any one of these types of person. These represent dominant orientations, and not rigid types. It should be noted that Jung's approach was far more complicated than a simple categorizing of people into two attitudes and four functions. One basis for studying an individual's personality is to learn which are the dominant functions and attitudes. According to Jung, pure types are the exception; instead, there are variations in any one type.

COUNSELING IMPLICATIONS

One of the major aims of Jungian counseling and therapy is helping people become aware of material in their personal and collective unconscious. If people are to live a full existence, they need to be able to deal with the polarities within them. They need to recognize that their strengths can be their weaknesses, and vice versa. Clients must recognize their shadow side, in both its creative and potentially destructive dimensions. Probably most important of all, they need to learn to integrate two central elements in Chinese philosophy—the *yin* (the feminine principle, or *anima*) and the *yang* (the masculine principle, or *animus*). It is crucial to learn in counseling that these forces do not have to oppose each other (and therefore be repressed); rather, they can complement each other.

A central concept in Jungian psychology that has significant implications for counseling is that of the various dimensions of the self and the importance of recognizing and giving expression to these "sides." When we repress a dimension of ourselves and do not allow it to be expressed, it typically manages to "sneak out" in unpredictable and strange ways. When we recognize and develop the various dimensions of our personality, they become functional.

Finally, Jungian psychology provides an interesting approach to understanding the unconscious through the analysis of dreams. Jung focused on the symbols of dreams as a clue to finding meaning. He believed that dreams are more than unconscious wish fulfillment, sexually derived impulses, or aggressive urges being manifested. Instead, he stressed that dreams can help people prepare for their future; they can also function to bring about a balance between opposites in the personality. This approach utilizes dreams as a central part of the therapeutic process. Hall and Nordby (1973) wrote that Jung was the first person to suggest the importance of analyzing a series of dreams recorded over a period of time by an individual. In contrast to the Freudians, Jung attached little importance to interpreting a single dream. He asked his patients to keep a log of their dreams, for he saw dreams as much like the chapters of a book. For him, each chapter contributes to the total story, and taken together as the pieces of a puzzle, they form an interrelated and coherent picture of personality. Jungians also see a series of dreams as revealing recurrent themes that are appropriate for exploration in therapy.

Alfred Adler and individual psychology

INTRODUCTION

Alfred Adler was an early colleague of Freud's, yet he abandoned Freud's basic contentions because he believed he was excessively narrow in his stress on biological and instinctual determination. On many theoretical grounds Adler was in opposition to

Freud. Yet he did credit Freud with creating a dynamic psychology. He acknowledged his debt to Freud for clarifying the purposefulness of symptoms, pointing out the meaning of dreams, and emphasizing the influence of early-childhood experiences in personality development. With Freud, he believed that what an individual becomes in adult life is largely determined by the first five years of life. In the following section we consider some of the ways he parted company with Freud and describe some of the key concepts of the Adlerian approach to counseling and psychotherapy.

VIEW OF HUMAN NATURE

According to Adler, humans are motivated primarily by social urges. Men and women are social beings, and in relationship with others each person develops a unique style of life. Adler stressed the social determinants of personality, not the sexual determinants. He also emphasized that behavior is purposeful and goal-directed. Life goals provide the source of human motivation, especially those goals that are aimed at bringing security and overcoming inferiority feelings. These basic inferiority feelings can motivate us to strive for mastery, superiority, power, and perfection. Feelings of inferiority can thus be the wellspring of creativity.

Consciousness, not the unconscious, is the center of personality, Adler contended. Humans are capable of directing their own actions with an awareness of meaning. Emphasis is on self-determination. People are the masters, not the victims, of their fate. Adler's focus can thus be contrasted to the Freudian historical and causal approach. From the Adlerian perspective humans are viewed in a holistic and unified way. People cannot be subdivided into various components if they are to be understood.

The Adlerian approach is essentially a *growth model,* for its stress is on responsibility, on the process of becoming a person, and on finding meaning in life. Adlerians are not interested in curing sick people, for their emphasis is more on reeducating individuals and reshaping society. Adler was a forerunner of a subjective approach to psychology, which focuses on *internal* determinants of behavior such as values, beliefs, attitudes, goals, interests, subjective perception of reality, and striving toward self-realization.

OTHER KEY CONCEPTS

Basic inferiority and compensation.   Humans are pushed by the need to overcome inherent inferiority and pulled by the striving for superiority. Perfection, not pleasure, is the goal of life. Adler stressed that all of us have inferiority feelings. The child (small and helpless) feels a sense of inferiority. The individual attempts to overcome this helplessness by compensating—that is, by developing a life-style in which success is possible.

Striving for superiority.   A person copes with basic inferiority by seeking power. By striving for superiority a person seeks to change weakness into strength or to excel in one area of concentration to compensate for defects in other areas. In the phrase *striving for superiority* Adler was not implying that we are motivated to "be first" or to dominate others by using power over them. Rather, his view was that superiority is a striving for perfection, or an upward drive to increase our potential and to become what we might become. This striving is characterized by a search for completion, perfection, mastery, and self-actualization. The unique way in which individuals develop a style of striving for power is what constitutes individuality.

Style of life.   All people have a life-style, but no two people develop exactly the same style. In striving for the goal of superiority, some people develop their intellect; others, their artistic talent; others, athletic talents; and so on. These styles of life consist of people's views about themselves and the world and their distinctive behaviors and habits as they pursue their personal goals. Everything that we do is basically influenced by our unique style of life. Our life-style is learned from early interactions in the family, especially during the first five years. Like Freud, Adler saw one's life-style as being largely set by the age of 5.

Childhood experiences.   Adler believed that we create our *selves* as opposed to being passively shaped and determined by childhood experiences. It is not the child-hood experiences in themselves that are crucial; rather, it is our attitude toward these events that is significant. He emphasized the early influences that predispose the child to a faulty style of life. The family constellation can intensify inferiority feelings. The oldest child, who is given much attention until the second one is born, may become so discouraged by the fall from power that he or she develops hostility toward others and insecurity. The second child may walk in the shadow of the older sibling and may shrink from competition with others. The only child tends to be spoiled by parents and may devote attention to retaining or to regaining the favored position within the family and in outside relationships.

THERAPEUTIC PROCESS: GOALS AND STAGES IN COUNSELING

This section on the goals of Adlerian counseling and the phases involved in the process is based on a summary and adaptation of the work of Dinkmeyer, Pew, and Dinkmeyer (1979). According to these authors, there are four central goals in Adlerian counseling, which correspond to the four stages in the therapeutic process:

1. To establish a client/counselor relationship, characterized by empathy, that will allow the client to feel understood and accepted.
2. To help clients understand the beliefs, feelings, motives, and goals that determine their style of life.
3. To help clients develop insight into their style of life and to become aware of their mistaken goals and self-defeating behaviors.
4. To help clients consider options and alternatives to change and make a commitment to an action-oriented program.

The relationship.   Adlerian counselors are initially concerned with developing mutual trust and respect with their clients. To do this they establish a relationship between equals, one in which there are no superiors and no inferiors. Counseling is viewed as a collaborative effort; both partners are active in this relationship, and both are working toward mutually agreed-on goals. Therapeutic progress is possible only when the goals for counseling are clearly defined and when there is an alignment of goals between the therapist and the client. Dinkmeyer, Pew, and Dinkmeyer (1979) supported the idea of initially formulating a therapeutic plan as a contract that spells out what clients want, how they will attain their goals, what is preventing them from being successful, and how they can use their assets to achieve their purposes. Counselors assist clients to become aware of their assets and strengths, rather than focusing continually on their deficits and liabilities. It is assumed that clients can change only when they recognize their personal power and capacity for change. Thus, the Adlerian counselor focuses on positive dimensions and also makes use of encouragement and support.

Analysis and assessment.   In order to gain a sense of the client's life-style, counselors pay close attention to feelings, motives, beliefs, and goals. They explore feelings to understand motives, to develop empathy, and to enhance the quality of the therapeutic relationship. Adlerian therapists go beyond the feelings to explore the beliefs underlying them. Emphasis is placed on confronting faulty beliefs so that clients will not remain unfree. Counselors begin by exploring the current life situation and the manner in which their clients approach work responsibilities, social relationships, feelings about self, and so on.

The analysis and assessment of the individual consists of an exploration of the *family constellation,* which includes conditions that prevailed when the child was forming a life-style. Open-ended questions are often asked that will provide insight into clients' self-perception, sibling relationships, significant forces they have reacted to in life, and key life decisions that they have made.

Adlerian counselors often use another assessment procedure—asking their clients to report their *earliest recollections* along with a collection of events at various points in life as they are remembered and perceived. The Adlerians contend that people tend to remember those events from early childhood that are consistent with their current view of themselves.

From this life-style investigation, which includes an exploration of family background and one's life story, a pattern of "basic mistakes" can be uncovered. During this assessment phase the counselor's main task is to integrate and summarize findings of the investigation and to interpret how the basic mistakes are influencing the client now. This life-style analysis is a continuing process, and it helps the client and counselor develop a therapy plan.

Insight.   Although Adlerian therapists are supportive, they are also confrontive. They challenge their clients to develop insight into mistaken goals and self-defeating behaviors. They work toward the goal of helping their clients understand the purpose of their behavior. Insight into hidden purposes and goals tends to emerge through a process of both encouragement and challenge, as well as through well-timed interpretations by the therapist that are stated as tentative hypotheses. Although insight may be regarded by the Adlerians as a powerful adjunct to behavioral change, it is not seen as a prerequisite. Insight is viewed as a step toward change, but the emphasis is on translating this self-understanding into some type of constructive action. People are able to make abrupt and significant changes in behavior without much insight.

Interpretation is a technique that facilitates the process of gaining insight. It is focused on here-and-now behavior and on the expectations and anticipations that arise from one's intentions. Adlerian interpretation is done in relationship to the life-style. Clients are not forced to accept interpretations, because these are presented tentatively in the form of open-ended sharings that can be explored in sessions. It is hoped that through this process clients will come to understand their own role in creating a problem, how they are maintaining their difficulties now, and what they can do to improve their life situation.

Reorientation. The final stage of the therapeutic process is the action-oriented phase known as reorientation, or putting insight into action. The goal of Adlerian counseling is constructive behavior that makes clients more effective. This phase of counseling focuses on helping people see new and more-functional alternatives. It consists of considering alternative attitudes, beliefs, goals, and behaviors. Clients are both encouraged and challenged to develop the courage that involves risk taking and making changes in life. Encouragement is a basic part of this phase, for through encouragement clients begin to experience their own strength, inner resources, and the power to choose for themselves and direct their own lives.

During the reorientation phase of counseling, clients make decisions and modify their goals. They are encouraged to act *as if* they were the persons they wanted to be, which can serve to challenge self-limiting assumptions. Clients are asked to catch themselves in the process of repeating old patterns that lead to ineffective behavior. Commitment is an essential part of this phase, for if clients hope to change they must be willing to set tasks for themselves and do something specific about their problems. In this way, they translate their new insights into concrete action.

COUNSELING IMPLICATIONS

Adlerian principles and techniques can be used effectively with diverse populations and in different types of counseling situations. Dinkmeyer, Pew, and Dinkmeyer (1979) wrote about Adlerian counseling of children, adolescents, and college students. Adlerian philosophy lends itself well to group counseling; these authors described Adlerian group methods as well as providing an overview of the nature of group process from this orientation. They also discussed its application in working with teachers in groups and in consulting with the individual teacher. Adlerian theory is also used by a variety of parent-education groups. Furthermore, this approach has been applied to family therapy; family-education centers have been established, as have been marriage-education centers. Adlerian concepts have also been applied to marriage counseling, both with couples and with groups of couples.

Karen Horney

VIEW OF HUMAN NATURE

Karen Horney's view of human nature was considerably more optimistic than Freud's. It was her conviction that we are not victims of biological forces. She is identified with the social-psychological theories, which were formed as a reaction against Freud's mechanistic and biological orientation. She believed that psychoanalysis needed to grow beyond the limitations of a psychology based on instincts.

Horney contended that humans have an inborn potentiality for self-realization. But healthy development can be thwarted if our basic security needs are not met in childhood. According to Horney (1939, 1942), character structure develops out of the totality of childhood experiences. Although this developmental process may stop for some during early childhood, it may continue for others into adolescence, middle age, and—with a few people—until old age. It is clear that Horney differed from Freud on the role of the past in one's current character structure.

There were some other significant differences. Horney did not consider penis envy a determining factor in the psychology of women; rather, she saw feminine psychology as based on a lack of confidence and overemphasis on love relationships. She took exception with Freud on his views of the Oedipus complex as manifested in a sexual/aggressive conflict between the child and the parent. She stressed the role of anxiety that grows out of basic disturbances, such as rejection and overprotection, in the parent/child relationship. She theorized that sex and aggression are not dominant motives but, rather, that the need for security is a critical factor in human behavior.

BASIC THEME

Horney's primary concept is *basic anxiety*, which is the child's feeling of being isolated and helpless in a world that is potentially hostile. Anything that disturbs the child's basic security in relation to intimate family relationships produces anxiety. The child develops strategies to cope with feelings of isolation and helplessness. These strategies may include submissiveness, hostility, detachment, an idealized image of self, and so on. A particular strategy may become central in personality and become a drive or a need. According to Horney, basic anxiety underlies all relationships the person has with others. She did stress that it finds expression in some way, and that people find ways of self-protection in the face of it. One way to understand human behavior as a reaction to dealing with basic anxiety is through a consideration of what Horney called the ten neurotic needs.

TEN NEUROTIC NEEDS

As a result of disturbed human relationships, a person who feels unable to get love may seek to obtain power over others, exploit people, compensate for feelings of helplessness, or withdraw into self-pity. Horney believed that any of these needs (which are basically protective devices) could become a relatively stable part of the personality, assuming the characteristics of a drive that would determine much of a person's behavior. She identified these needs as neurotic because she saw them as irrational solutions to problems. The following ten needs are developed as a way of dealing with the basic anxiety that results from a disturbed parent/child relationship:

1. For *affection and approval:* This consists of an insatiable need to win universal approval. By attempting to live up to others' expectations, such people typically end up pleasing nobody, including themselves. They are highly sensitive to rejection and may attempt to purchase affection from others.
2. For *a dominant partner in life:* Such people are fearful of being deserted and left alone. They may become extremely submissive in their quest to avoid being hurt. If others take over their lives, then they hope that they will be taken care of. Such people tend to lose any sense of unique identity and to repress their own desires, and they are watchful of antagonizing others.
3. For *restricting one's life within narrow borders:* Such people are content with a limited existence, for in their eyes, if they ask for little, then there is less chance that they will fail. They choose a life-style of being somewhat invisible. They rarely challenge themselves by opening new doors that will stretch themselves as persons. They choose security over growth.
4. For *power.* The neurotic need for power might be translated into the statement "If I have power, then others can't hurt me." This kind of power is characterized by disregarding others, controlling and manipulating them, and it grows out of one's basic sense of help-

lessness. It is a form of compensation; it is an attempt to gain security by maintaining a sense of superiority over others. Some people consider most of their actions in light of gaining such power, so that their basic inferiority will not be recognized.

5. For *exploitation of others:* This consists of using others to one's own advantage. Those who exploit people tend to restrict their relationships to those people who will in some way enhance their own egos. They give little consideration to what they might do for others, because most of their focus is on what others can do for them.

6. For *prestige:* Like some of the other needs, the need for prestige is not considered neurotic in itself. But for those who orient most of their behavior toward gaining prestige and public recognition, it can be said that there is a neurotic quality to their behavior. It is as though they determine their own worth as a person by the amount of recognition they get from others. Such people are really not free, for they are continually looking outside of themselves for validation.

7. For *personal admiration:* People who feel basically unworthy may develop an inflated self-image as a way of denying their pain. These people are keenly aware of wanting to be admired on the basis of the picture they present to others.

8. For *personal achievement:* Although the need to achieve can be healthy, those who have a compulsive and insatiable drive to achieve are seen as attempting to protect themselves against the anxiety of recognizing their shortcomings. Such people seem never to be satisfied with any of their accomplishments, or they drive themselves to attain unrealistic standards of perfection. Underneath this striving for personal achievement is the wish that they will be loved for what they have done.

9. For *self-sufficiency and independence:* Again, the need for independence is surely not neurotic, yet it can assume neurotic dimensions when people isolate themselves from others out of repeated attempts to find satisfying relationships. Their behavior of moving away from people is an attempt to protect themselves from the pain of rejection.

10. For *protection and unassailability:* Some people are so frightened of making mistakes that they develop an exaggerated need to be perfect. It is as though they were saying "If I am perfect, then nobody can find anything to criticize about me." Such people devote a lot of time to searching for their own imperfections, so that they can find ways to cover them up; in this way they do not feel a sense of vulnerability.

Horney (1942) developed this list of neurotic needs to explain some irrational ways that people orient their lives in attempting to protect themselves from basic anxiety. She did not consider these needs as neurotic in themselves; everyone has some trace of them, and some of them are positive. They are neurotic to the extent that they become a compulsive pattern and an exclusive form of behavior in dealing with basic anxiety. They are also neurotic when a person focuses on one need in a compulsive way to seek satisfaction in most life situations.

NEUROTIC TRENDS AND THREE CHARACTER TYPES

In her later writings, Horney (1945) classified these neurotic needs under three general neurotic trends, each of which results in a certain pattern of behavior. The three character types are people who move toward other people, those who move against people, and those who move away from people.

1. *Moving toward people—the compliant type:* These individuals demonstrate a marked need for affection and approval. They feel weak and helpless, subordinate themselves to others, and behave in highly dependent ways. Their own esteem is determined by what others think of them. They are rarely assertive. Out of their need for acceptance, they become what others want them to become. Their behavior can be seen as an appeal: "Since I am so helpless alone, you must love me and take care of me!"

2. *Moving against people—the aggressive type:* Such individuals are the opposite of the compliant type. Their world is dominated by the view that everyone is basically hostile, and that in order to survive they must be tough. Life becomes a struggle for survival in which the dominant behavior is control of others. These people are constantly on the alert so that they are not outsmarted by others. They may drive themselves hard in a quest to be perfect. Out of their competitiveness they pit themselves against others; life is seen as a game or a battle. These people may outwardly appear to be self-confident, yet they are driven by their need to cover up insecurity and anxiety.

3. *Moving away from people—the detached type:* These people are characterized by a need to maintain emotional distance from others. They might assume the veneer of self-sufficiency, so that they do not have to become involved with others. Their self-sufficient attitude relates to the anxiety that closeness creates for them. They may have an exaggerated need for privacy, for in keeping people out they do not have to deal with the anxiety of intimacy. Although such people devote much energy to erecting barriers to keep others away from them, they do pay a price for this behavior. They value logic and the rational approach to living, and they take measures to keep their emotions in check.

TYRANNY OF THE IDEALIZED IMAGE OF SELF

Horney's theory of the self is important and relevant for eclectic counselors. According to her, everyone creates a self-image, real or idealized. For healthy, or normal, persons, this self-image is based on a realistic evaluation of their assets and liabilities, and it provides a sense of unity and integration of personality. It is a basis from which they are able to form relationships to others. This realistic self-image is open to experience and open to change; far from being rigid, it incorporates new awareness, growth, and emerging goals.

Neurotic persons, because of their greater basic anxiety, are usually not able to integrate the three orientations of moving toward people, moving away from people, and moving against people. Neurotics create a self-view that is unrealistic and rigid, a view they hold to tenaciously. Thus, they deny reality that is too painful to accept. This idealized self-image takes on the quality of rigid adherence to the model a person sees that he or she *should* be. By attempting to live up to this idealized view of self, people are likely to experience a loss of self-respect, extreme dependency on others, feelings of self-contempt, and increased conflicts and anxiety. Because these people are actually living a life based on an illusion, they are under constant stress to protect this self-image, which rests on a shaky foundation.

COUNSELING IMPLICATIONS

Horney's ten neurotic needs, the three character types, and the notion of an idealized self-image have certain implications for counselors. Counselors can challenge clients to look at their motivations for certain styles of behavior. For example, if a client's central problem seems to relate to pleasing others, he or she can learn something about how this need for approval from others dominates most of his or her activities. Although people cannot be categorized by the framework of neurotic needs, it does provide a basis for discussion of the meaning of behavior.

Likewise, counselors can work with clients within the framework of the three neurotic trends. For example, a detached personality can begin to examine the price that is being paid for the safety of detachment from others. This person can question whether or not barriers are needed in all social situations.

Clients can be challenged to look at the picture they have of themselves, in the hope that they will be able to determine whether their self-image is realistic or not. Counseling can help people acquire increased honesty, which will allow them to pierce some of the illusions that prevent them from changing. They can be encouraged to loosen rigid self-perceptions based on "shoulds" and "oughts." In this way, counseling can build a self-image based on a realistic appraisal of one's potentials and goals, one more in line with the real self.

Compliant types can take a closer look at how they are losing a clear sense of themselves by attempting to win universal approval. They can begin to think of behaving in ways that are pleasing to themselves, and they can work toward gaining love and approval from themselves instead of constantly looking outside of themselves for this acceptance. Once they have recognized some of the factors that have contributed to their submissiveness and dependence, they can begin taking steps toward autonomy.

Finally, counselors can challenge those with aggressive orientations to determine whether they need to be as tough and competitive as they have convinced themselves they need to be in order to survive. Such people might explore the aspects of themselves they have inevitably denied as they moved against themselves.

THERAPEUTIC TECHNIQUES

Horney relied mainly on the Freudian techniques of dream analysis and free association as procedures for understanding the functioning of personality. As we have seen, however, Horney stressed the client's current situation rather than the past. Although she did not ignore historical material, she was mainly concerned with exploring with clients the influence of neurotic needs in their present situation. Horney also argued that therapists should be flexible and use whatever techniques are appropriate to each client.

Erich Fromm

VIEW OF HUMAN NATURE

Fromm argues against Freud's deterministic view that humans are driven by biological forces. He also takes exception to the stress that Freud placed on sex as the shaping force of personality. Instead, Fromm contends that humans are influenced by social and cultural forces. But he does not think that we are passively molded by these forces, even though he does place emphasis on them as influencers of personality. He contends that we shape the social forces ourselves and create our own natures.

In some ways Fromm takes an existential view of humans, for he stresses themes such as loneliness, isolation, a sense of belongingness, and the meaning of life. He also stresses the notion of human freedom and the tendency to escape from the anxiety of it. Because their nature is not fixed, humans have many possibilities. Fromm has an optimistic view of human nature, in that he believes that the tendency toward growth and the full realization of one's potentials is a basic part of being human. For Fromm, the central task in life is to become the person that one has the potential to become. Surely, Fromm's thinking contributed to the development of the existential orientation, which will be treated in the next chapter.

KEY CONCEPTS

Basic Orientation. Fromm is identified with the social-psychological theories. He focuses on describing the ways in which the structure and dynamics of a particular society shape its members so that their social character fits the values of that society.

Basic Theme. Because human beings have been separated from nature and from others, they experience isolation and alienation. People can either unite themselves with others by learning how to love, or they can find some security by conforming their will to an authoritarian society.

The Human Condition. Human beings are unique in that they possess self-awareness, reason, imagination, and the capacities to love and to experience loneliness and up-rootedness. People have five needs that arise from the human condition:

1. *The need for relatedness,* or actively and productively loving others. This implies knowledge, understanding, care, respect, and responsibility.
2. *The need for transcendence,* or rising above animal nature by becoming a creative being.
3. *The need for rootedness,* wanting to feel a sense of connectedness with the world, nature, and others.
4. *The need for identity,* or striving for a sense of personal uniqueness in order to make sense out of the world.
5. *The need for a frame of orientation,* or a stable way of making sense out of the world.

Five Character Types. Fromm identified five character types, having the following orientations:

1. *The receptive orientation:* depending on others for support.
2. *The exploitive orientation:* taking things from others and manipulating others.
3. *The hoarding orientation:* finding security by keeping what one has.
4. *The marketing orientation:* regarding people as objects or mere commodities to be bought and sold.
5. *The productive orientation:* implying the full development of human potentialities as expressed by creativity and loving.

COUNSELING IMPLICATIONS

The five needs that are a part of the human condition give counselors and therapists a focus for therapeutic sessions. Some people come to professional counselors because they feel that they are cut off from meaningful ties with others and with nature. Others seek therapy because they have recognized that their lives are empty, and that they have searched in the wrong places to find a sense of meaning. Still others are seeking therapy because of their quest to discover who they are; they see therapy as one way to strive for a personal identity. Fromm has identified some basic conditions of the human experience, and this framework can guide therapists in their understanding of what leads to troubled lives.

The five character types can also serve as a basis for understanding certain patterns of behavior, and they can help the therapist grasp the dynamics of this behavior. Let's look at an example for each of the orientations.

Receptive types lean passively on authority for knowledge and help in directing their lives. They find it difficult to actively love others, because they are so concerned with getting others to love them. As clients they may attempt to manipulate their therapists to make decisions for them. If that happens, therapy is only an extension of the rest of their life.

Exploitive types use others for what they want. They take what they want with little regard for others. Again, in the therapeutic situation therapists must be alert for clients who try to control them by using them, much as they use everyone else. This is especially true of the sociopathic personality, who seems highly resistant to therapy. Even therapy will be perceived as a game, one in which the person will attempt to exploit or deceive the therapist.

In the *hoarding orientation* people derive their security from the amount they can save up. This hoarding relates not only to material things but also to ideas and feelings. It is a challenge for the therapist to encourage such clients to let down some of the walls they have built. Because suspicion and fear of intimacy typically accompany this orientation, part of the task of the therapist is to build a trusting relationship so that clients will not feel such an absolute need to keep all of their thoughts and feelings private.

Some clients mold themselves to fit whatever qualities are apparently in demand by others. These people with a *marketing orientation* tend to sell themselves out for what they deem to be popular. People are reduced to a commodity that is judged to a large extent by the outside wrappings. Counselors who work with these individuals need to encourage them to look at the price they are paying for being "marketable." They are not individuals with unique qualities, but rather have presented themselves as "things." Counselors might help them to recognize that this orientation makes a real sense of security impossible, for they are left without any genuine basis for relating to others. These are the clients who suffer from alienation and who have not discovered any core.

The *productive orientation* is the ultimate goal, for in this approach people are using all of their capacities to actualize themselves. In a sense, a therapeutic goal might be to assist clients of the other four types to develop a productive orientation.

With respect to specific techniques of counseling and therapy, Fromm uses free-association methods, and he considers dream work to be a valuable therapeutic procedure. However, he does not describe in much detail his therapeutic techniques. As such, his theory has its significance for counselors in providing a conceptual framework of basic human needs.

SUMMARY COMMENTS

Fromm's ideas have more implications for society and for the individual's place in it than for personal and individual growth. Also, his theory stresses *relationships* rather than a concern with individual dynamics.

Fromm brings to his work a wide knowledge of sociology, philosophy, anthropology, and history. It is because of this perspective that his writings have a greater depth than the works of many psychoanalysts. According to Schultz (1981), Fromm's contribution is based on a unique interpretation of the interaction between humanity and society. Fromm has called attention to the continuing and interrelated impact of social, economic, and psychological factors on human nature. He has demonstrated that humans are not shaped by a single factor; rather, human development is the result of an interplay of various forces and events. Schultz contended that Fromm's contribution has extended beyond psychoanalysis and psychology to include a broad spectrum of social problems.

Harry Stack Sullivan's interpersonal theory

VIEW OF HUMAN NATURE

Sullivan parted company with Freud's contention that we form our personality by the age of 5. According to Sullivan, we are capable of changing our personality beyond early childhood. Although early experiences are important, they do not exclusively shape and determine later development.

KEY CONCEPTS

Interpersonal Theory. Sullivan's viewpoint is identified with the social-psychological theories. He emphasized the role of personal relations and the study of humans in relationship with significant others. Thus, the unit of study is the interpersonal situation, not the individual alone. Personality manifests itself in the individual's behavior in relation to others.

The Self System. This is the result of threats to one's security. Underlying all other impulses is the power motive, which operates throughout life to overcome a basic sense of helplessness. One's self system develops as a reaction against the anxiety produced by interpersonal relations.

Unique Contribution. Sullivan stressed the role of cognitive processes in personality development. Three modes of experience are involved in ego formation:

1. *Protaxic mode:* characterizes the first year of life. There are no distinctions of time and place. It is a necessary precondition to the other two modes.
2. *Parataxic mode:* characterized by an undifferentiated wholeness of experience that is broken down into parts without any logical connection. It occurs during early childhood. The child accepts without evaluation whatever happens and reacts to others on an unrealistic basis.
3. *Syntaxic mode:* characterized by lack of distortion. In this mode, children learn to use language. As they learn the verbal symbols that are shared by others in their culture, they learn also to perceive logical relationships. They develop the capacity to verify their perceptions with those of others. Self-attitudes are shaped by the reactions of significant others.

Stages of Development. Sullivan contended that personality may change at any time as new interpersonal relations develop; humans are malleable. He stressed that personality is shaped through definite stages of development—infancy, childhood, the juvenile era, preadolescence, early adolescence, late adolescence, and maturity. The social determinants of personality development are crucial.

COUNSELING IMPLICATIONS

Therapeutic techniques. Sullivan (1954) used the interview as the primary therapeutic procedure for gathering data from clients. He saw the therapist as a *participant/observer* and an expert in interpersonal relations. In the dual role of participant and observer, therapists must be alert not only to the client's behavior but also to their own reactions and behavior. Sullivan did not favor the "blank-screen" image of the classical psychoanalyst, and he cautioned against therapists' assuming a strictly objective observational role. He stressed the importance of personal involvement and the impact of the personality of the therapist on the therapeutic process.

His principal instrument of observation is his self—his personality, *him* as a person. The process-es and the changes in processes that make up the data which can be subjected to scientific study occur, not in the subject person nor in the observer, but in the situation which is created between the observer and his subject [1954, pp. 3–4].

Sullivan viewed the therapeutic process as a unique interpersonal relationship, dif-fering from other intimate relationships in its basic purpose. Clients have a right to expect that they will benefit from the interview, that they will learn something about themselves and the way that they live, and that they might apply this knowledge to living more effectively. In short, the ultimate goal of the psychiatric interview is that clients leave with a greater degree of clarity about themselves and how they are living with others.

The four-stage interview.   The therapeutic process involves a series of inter-views, which proceed through the following four stages: *inception, reconnaissance, detailed inquiry,* and *termination.*

1. *The inception stage:* This is a brief period in which the therapist determines the reason the person is seeking professional help and clarifies the nature of the problem. The development of rapport is a basic task at this stage. These early contacts between the therapist and client are crucial in forming a good working relationship needed for later stages of therapy.

    Sullivan advocated an attitude of quiet observation, one in which the therapist does not ask too many questions. Not only is the *verbal content* noticed but also the manner in which the client makes his or her presentation of self. Nonverbal messages are paid attention to, as well as the way the client relates to the therapist. According to Sullivan, clients bring into the therapeutic situation their habitual modes of living, their preconceptions and expectations, and certain distortions of reality ("parataxic distortions"). The skillful therapist gets an ac-curate perception of the client by paying attention to the subtle aspects of the interpersonal relationship that is beginning even during the initial session.

2. *The reconnaissance:* This step in the therapeutic process consists of obtaining a rough outline of the social or personal history of the person coming for help. The interviewer's task is to grasp some notion of the client's identity. The focus is on the questions Who is this person? What happened to bring him or her into the office? What are some significant aspects in this person's past, present, and future? Although Sullivan did not advocate a rigid line of ques-tioning, he did discourage irrelevant discussion. Again at this stage, it takes skill on the therapist's part to raise questions that will lead to a case history. With this information, it is the therapist's task to develop some hypotheses about the nature and origin of the client's problems.

3. *The detailed inquiry:* In this stage the therapist attempts to determine which of these hy-potheses are of most value. This is accomplished by a continuation of sensitive listening and questioning in areas such as attitudes toward one's body, sexual activities, relationships with others, goals and ambitions, eating habits, and other patterns of daily living.

4. *The termination stage:* The main purpose of this stage of therapy is to summarize and consolidate one's learnings in the previous interviews. The therapist generally makes some summary statements from his or her vantage point and suggests a course for the client to follow.

It should be noted that Sullivan placed considerable emphasis on respecting the individuality of the client. He cautioned against making humiliating comments, stressed the value of sensitivity in the interview, and also emphasized the need for therapists to recognize signs of underlying anxiety in the client. Sullivan cautioned against therapists' using therapy to enhance their own prestige. He admonished them to keep in mind their primary task—helping people who bring themselves to therapy take away some-thing that can benefit them in living fuller lives. According to Sullivan, therapists cannot avoid their own involvement in the interview. To the extent that they are unaware of their influence, they limit the effectiveness of therapy. In some key ways Sullivan was a forerunner of a basic humanistic approach that stresses the importance of the therapist as a person and the power of the client/therapist relationship as an agent for change.

Erik Erikson and the developmental theory

INTRODUCTION

, Erik Erikson (1963) built on Freud's ideas and extended his theory by stressing the *psychosocial* aspects of development beyond early childhood. Erikson can be considered both a neo-Freudian and an ego psychologist. He conceives of ego identity as a combination of what "one feels one is and what others take one to be." One who achieves ego identity feels a sense of belonging. Also, as one's past has meaning in terms of the future, there is a continuity in development, reflected by stages of growth; each stage is related to the other stages.

Erikson's theory of development holds that *psychosexual* and *psychosocial* growth take place together, and that at each stage of life we face the task of establishing an equilibrium between ourselves and our social world. He described development in terms of the entire life span, divided by specific crises to be resolved. According to Erikson, a *crisis* is equivalent to a turning point in life, with the potential to move forward or to regress. At these turning points in our development, we can either achieve successful resolution of our conflicts or fail to resolve them. To a large extent, our lives are the result of the choices we make at each of these stages.

STAGES OF DEVELOPMENT

Stage 1—Infancy: Trust versus mistrust.   An infant's basic task is to develop a sense of *trust* in self, others, and the world. Infancy is a time when the individual needs to count on others, to develop a sense of being wanted and secure; it is a time when the foundations of trust are being established. This sense of trust is learned by being caressed and cared for.

From Erikson's viewpoint, if the significant others in an infant's life provide the necessary love, then the infant develops a sense of trust. When love is absent, the result is a general sense of *mistrust* of others. Clearly, infants who feel accepted are in a more favorable position to successfully meet future developmental crises than are those who do not receive adequate nurturing.

Stage 2—Early childhood: Autonomy versus shame and doubt.   According to Erikson, early childhood is a time for developing a sense of *autonomy*. Children who do not master the task of gaining some measure of self-control and ability to cope with the world develop a sense of *shame* and *doubt* about their abilities. Parents who do too much for their children hamper their independence. Children who are encouraged to stay dependent will doubt their capacities for successfully dealing with the world.

Stage 3—The preschool age: Initiative versus guilt.   Erikson contends that the basic task of the preschool years is to establish a sense of *competence* and *initiative*. He places more stress on social development than on concerns relating to sexuality. During this time children are psychologically ready to pursue activities of their own choosing. If they are allowed the freedom to select meaningful activities, they tend to develop a positive outlook characterized by the ability to initiate and follow through. However, if they are not allowed to make some of their own decisions, or if their choices are ridiculed, they develop a sense of *guilt* over taking the initiative. Typically, they withdraw from taking an active stance and permit others to make decisions for them.

Stage 4—The school age: Industry versus inferiority.   Some of the unique psychosocial tasks that must be met if healthy development is to proceed are expanding one's understanding of the physical and social worlds; continuing to develop an appropriate sex-role identity; continuing to develop a sense of values; engaging in social tasks; learning how to accept people who are different; and learning basic skills needed for schooling.

According to Erikson, the central task of middle childhood is to achieve a sense of *industry*. Failure to do this results in feelings of *inadequacy* and *inferiority*. A sense of industry is associated with creating goals that are personally meaningful and achieving them. If this is not done, it will be difficult to experience a sense of adequacy in later years, and future developmental stages will be negatively influenced.

Some of the following problems originate during middle childhood; they are often manifested in later problems that counselors deal with:

- A negative self-concept.
- Feelings of inadequacy relating to learning.
- Feelings of inferiority in establishing social relationships.
- Conflicts over values.
- A confused sex-role identity.
- Unwillingness to face new challenges.
- A lack of initiative and dependency.

Stage 5—Adolescence: Identity versus identity diffusion.   According to Erikson, the major developmental conflicts of the adolescent years are related to the development of a *personal identity*. Adolescents struggle to define who they are, where they are going, and how to get there. If they fail to achieve a sense of identity, then *identity diffusion* is the result. Because they experience diverse pressures—from parents, peers, and society—they often find it difficult to gain a clear sense of identity.

Adolescents have the task of integrating a system of values that will give their lives direction. In the formation of a personal philosophy of life, they must make key decisions relating to religious beliefs, sexual ethics, values, and so forth. In this search for identity, models are especially important for adolescents.

Stage 6—Young adulthood: Intimacy versus isolation.   In Erikson's view we approach adulthood after we master the adolescent conflicts over identity and role confusion. During young adulthood our sense of identity is tested again by the challenge of *intimacy* versus *isolation*.

One of the key characteristics of the psychologically mature person is the ability to form intimate relationships. A prerequisite to establishing this intimacy with others is a confidence in our own identities. Intimacy involves an ability to share with others and to give to others from our own centeredness.

Stage 7—Middle age: Generativity versus self-absorption or stagnation.   This is a time for learning how to live creatively with both ourselves and others.

On the one hand, it can be one of the most productive periods of life. On the other hand, we may painfully experience the discrepancy between our dreams of young adulthood and the reality of what we have accomplished.

Erikson sees the stimulus for continued growth in middle age as the crisis between *generativity* and *stagnation*. He considers generativity in the broad sense to include a sense of creating through a career, family, leisure-time activities, and so on. The main quality of productive adults is the ability to love well, to work well, and to play well. If adults fail to achieve a sense of productivity, they begin to stagnate and to die psychologically.

Stage 8—Later life: Integrity versus despair. According to Erikson, the core crisis of the elderly is *integrity* versus *despair*. Ego integrity is achieved by those who feel few regrets; they have lived productive and worthwhile lives and have coped with their failures as well as their successes. They are not obsessed with what might have been, and they are able to derive satisfaction from what they have done. They are able to view death as a part of the life process, and they can still find meaning in how they are now living.

The failure to achieve ego integrity leads to feelings of despair, hopelessness, guilt, resentment, and self-disgust. Such people think about all of the things they could have done, and they may yearn for "another chance." This realization that they have wasted their lives leads to a sense of despair.

COUNSELING IMPLICATIONS

Erikson's developmental model provides a useful conceptual framework for counselors with diverse orientations. Regardless of a counselor's theoretical preference, relevant questions such as the following can give direction to the therapeutic process:

- What are some major developmental tasks at each stage in life, and how are these tasks related to counseling?
- What are some themes that give continuity to this individual's life?
- What are some universal concerns of people at various points in life? How can people be challenged to make life-giving choices at these points?
- What is the relationship between an individual's current problems and significant events from earlier years?
- What influential factors have shaped one's life?
- What choices were made at these critical periods, and how did the person deal with these various crises?

Counselors who work with a developmental perspective are able to see a continuity in life and to see certain directions their clients have taken. This perspective gives a broader picture of the individual's struggle, and clients are able to discover some significant connections among the various stages of their life.

Wilhelm Reich: Forerunner of body-oriented therapies

INTRODUCTION

Wilhelm Reich pioneered body-oriented psychotherapy; he put the body at the center of psychology. He was a student of Freud's who broke away, and it is clear that much of his work is rooted in psychoanalytic theory. His early contributions were based on the concepts *character* and *character armor,* which grew out of the Freudian notion of the ego's need to defend itself against instinctual forces.

Reich's central idea was that emotions are an expression of the movement of body energy and that chronic muscle tensions block this flow of energy and thus block emotions. Reich associated forms of character resistances with specific patterns of "muscular armoring." He emphasized the importance of loosening and dissolving this muscular armor, along with dealing with psychological issues in an analytic way. Reich demonstrated that by relaxing these patterns of muscular armoring bottled-up emotions could be released.

KEY CONCEPTS

Emphasis on sexuality. According to Reich, psychotherapy is aimed at allowing life energy to flow freely throughout the body by systematically dissolving blocks of muscular armoring. He discovered that these blocks serve to destroy naturalness and spontaneity; they inhibit sexual feeling and the experience of full sexuality. In Reich's view the ability to experience a full orgasm is related to psychological health. Orgastic potency occurs as a total body response of a convulsive nature, with intense pleasure and gratification. Reich discovered that his patients who in the course of their analysis achieved orgastic potency also freed themselves from neurosis. From the Reichian perspective, undischarged sexual energy will be experienced as anxiety; this sexual excitation is the force that supports neurotic defenses. When orgastic potency is established, however, the energy that maintains these defenses stops, and health is possible. One of the main goals of Reichian therapy is the attainment of orgastic potency.

Reich placed central emphasis on assisting patients to develop free expression of their sexual and emotional feelings with a mature relationship. He found that energy was most strongly blocked around the pelvic area of his patients. He viewed the goal of therapy as freedom from all the blocks in the body that prevent the attainment of full capacity for sexual orgasm. His formula for judging psychological health was related to the frequency and intensity of one's orgasms.

Character. In Reich's view, one's character is composed of habitual attitudes and a consistent pattern of responses. Character includes values, one's style of life, and attitudes towards one's body. Reichian therapy involves interpreting the nature and function of a patient's character, not merely focusing on symptoms.

Character armor. According to Reich, character armor includes all repressing defensive forces; many of these defenses are manifested in some form of bodily expression. Reich paid attention to nonverbal behaviors such as the patient's general appearance, facial expressions, tensions in parts of the body, gestures, and other bodily manifestations. He encouraged his patients to become aware of their character traits. To accomplish this, he asked his patients to repeat and exaggerate certain types of habitual behavior that were thought to be a part of character armor.

It was Reich's contention that character traits (or attitudes) have a corresponding physical attitude. Thus, a person's character is expressed in terms of muscular rigidity.

BODY-ORIENTED TECHNIQUES

Loosening of the muscular armor. Reich postulated several layers of muscular armoring, which are related to the repressive forces of certain ego defenses. He assumed that these defensive layers could be loosened best by direct body-contact techniques rather than by psychoanalytic techniques. He asked that his patients lie seminude on a couch so that he could observe patterns of muscular rigidities. To dissolve the character armor, the major therapeutic procedures are (1) working on the patient's body through deep breathing exercises; (2) directly manipulating the chronic muscular tension through pressure and massage; and (3) dealing with whatever resistances and psychological blockages that arise.

Reich's work included emphasis on breathing in a spontaneous and relaxed way. Through his clinical work, he found that resistance to the expression of feeling was accompanied by restricted breathing. Methods that deepened the patient's breathing led to an opening of the feelings. His therapy also focused on working with muscular tensions, such as a tight jaw, neck, or mouth, frowns, and so forth. One of the aims of Reichian therapy came to be a "giving in" to the body and allowing spontaneous expression to occur. Talking by both patient and therapist was minimized, for work was focused on body-related issues.

The body segments that Reich worked on in a separate and systematic way began with the eyes and ended with the pelvis. Some clues from each of these areas gave information about the patient's character structure, and personality was read through the body:

- The *eyes* can express aliveness or emptiness. Emotional expression is encouraged by rolling the eyes and looking from side to side.
- The *mouth* can be tight or too loose. Armor in this region can be loosened by encouraging crying, yelling, biting, and sucking and by direct work with the mouth and the jaw.
- The *neck* may hold back expressions of anger or crying as well as holding on to tensions.
- The *chest* can develop armor that inhibits the free flow of crying, laughing, and breathing.
- The *diaphragm* can restrict the expression of rage and pain.
- The *abdomen* can develop armor that is related to fear of attack.
- The *pelvis* can be rigid and asexual, or it can become a source of experiencing intense pleasure.

Opening up the feelings. Reich's therapeutic work increasingly dealt with freeing intense emotions such as pleasure, rage, fear, grief, pain, and anxiety. These feelings were released through working with the body. Reich discovered that such work resulted in intense experiencing of primal material. He found that, after repressed emotion was expressed, chronic muscular and psychological tension could also be released. To free the emotions bound up by this muscular armor, he gradually began to work directly on areas of bodily tension manually.

IMPACT OF REICH'S WORK ON LATER BODY-ORIENTED THERAPIES

Kelley (1972) wrote that the extent of Reich's influence on many of the body-oriented therapies can hardly be overestimated. Some of the later therapists who were directly influenced by Reichian concepts and procedures are Alexander Lowen (1958, 1967a, 1967b), with his *bioenergetic* approach; Arthur Janov (1970), with his *primal therapy;*

Fritz Perls (1969), with his *Gestalt therapy;* Charles Kelley (1972, 1974), with his *Radix intensives;* and Ida Rolf (1962), with her *structural integration.*

Lowen was Reich's best-known student, and he developed a neo-Reichian program that is rooted in the body. Yet he has considerably broadened the idea that the orgasm is the sole key to psychological health. Lowen mixes character analysis and body work. This body work includes doing stress positions, experiencing kicking, and performing other Lowenian physical exercises. Reichian breathing exercises are a central part of Lowen's approach, which typically leads to a strong discharge of intense and buried feelings.

The primal therapy of Janov is also rooted in Reichian principles. It consists of a series of long, concentrated, daily individual sessions in deep emotional release that are given over a three-week period. This therapy combines breathing exercises derived from Reich with "dialogues with one's parents." Regression to early scenes is induced as a way of discharging pent-up pain that is related to early-childhood experiences. According to Janov, a cure is not possible unless one relives and literally screams out this primal pain that is locked deeply inside each of us.

Perls was one of Reich's patients and was influenced by Reichian principles as he developed his Gestalt therapy. He suggested that therapy should teach the client how to pay attention to body messages, and thus his approach focused on a here-and-now awareness of body states. This approach will be covered in detail in Chapter 6.

Kelley (1972, 1974) is the developer of a neo-Reichian approach known as *Radix.* (Radix means the source, root, or primary cause. Sometimes thought of as *life force* or *life energy,* the Radix flows through the body producing feeling and movement.) This approach consists of emotional releases brought about by a variety of body-oriented techniques, which are generally done in a small group. By using Reichian concepts and techniques, Kelley contends, powerful involuntary discharges of fear, rage, and pain are typically induced. He believes that "repeated intensives" (or experiences of opening up infantile feelings) can change people in profound ways. The release of blocked emotions opens the person to the experience of profound joy. According to Kelley, the release of rage opens one's capacity for love; the release of repressed pain opens up the capacity for pleasure. One's physical appearance can undergo dramatic changes, mainly as a result of changed emotional expression. The Radix intensives consist of a variety of stress positions, breathing exercises, pounding, hitting, and kicking. The goals of this approach are freeing blocks to feeling, gaining increased spontaneity, learning to give and accept love, expressing anger and fear, and attaining a greater degree of emotional freedom (Kelley, 1972, p. 6).

Structural integration—or, as it is more commonly called, *Rolfing*—is a body-oriented approach that involves techniques developed by Ida Rolf (1962). She devised a system of deep body manipulation aimed at restructuring and realigning the body to its normal position. The basic assumption is that the body becomes misaligned through muscle tensions and through even minor physical injuries. Rolfing works to accomplish a muscular balance and better alignment with gravity through a systematic set of techniques that involves deep and painful stretching of the muscle tissues. In a series of ten one-hour sessions these techniques of stretching and manipulating are applied to the muscles of the chest and abdomen, which govern breathing; to the pelvis and rib cage, to allow for more flexible movement; to the neck and head; and also to the entire body, to integrate it.

Although Rolfing is aimed mainly at physical integration, this process often has psychological ramifications. Schutz (1972) wrote that Rolfing is the most detailed treatment of the body and all of its parts and one of the fastest methods of uncovering emotional blocks. Thus, work on the body in this way will often cause memories to surface along with an intense emotional release. There are fruitful combinations of Rolfing techniques with psychological techniques aimed at freeing people from their psychological blocks, thus opening the way for growth.

Body-oriented therapies appear to be increasing in use; the field includes more than the few approaches that have been mentioned. As one studies Reichian concepts, it becomes clear that he had a direct and significant impact on many of the current body-oriented approaches to psychotherapy.

Summary and evaluation

In this brief section I will point out some of the salient features of each of the theories that I have summarized, with emphasis on the concepts from each that I find most valuable in my therapeutic practice.

From Jung I value the emphasis given to the role of purpose and goals in life. I especially like the notion that we are shaped by the future as well as the past, for in this way we can come to a deeper understanding of people by looking at what they aspire to in the future. Jung made a major contribution to understanding the forces and symbols that connect us all.

Adler's work has impressed me, and I draw on many of his concepts in both my individual and group counseling. I am intrigued with the idea that each of us forms a distinctive style of life, which is influenced by our perceived inferiority feelings. The idea of developing a pattern of behavior that is a form of compensation seems to have many interesting implications. I also value the importance given to the family constellation in the shaping of one's personality. The more I read of Adler, the more I am aware of his influence on most of the theorists and therapeutic approaches that came after him. He truly had a visionary concept of psychotherapy, and most of the therapies that are discussed in this book have significant elements of his thinking.

Horney's conception of basic anxiety and of the child's feeling of isolation in a world that is perceived as potentially hostile has significant therapeutic implications for me. Thinking of the needs and basic orientations that she described helps me in my practice. Her concept of the character types (moving toward people, moving against people, and moving away from people) is both interesting and useful in understanding behavior.

Fromm's view of the human condition, with the basic human needs, provides a meaningful framework for counseling. I agree with Fromm that a core problem of people today is the experience of alienation from others, from themselves, and from nature.

The interpersonal theory of Sullivan stressed the role of the therapist as participant/observer. I am especially drawn to his idea that clients have a right to expect that they will benefit from therapy, and that they can expect to apply what they learn from the relationship to everyday living. His emphasis on the therapist as a person is one that I agree is a major determinant of successful therapy.

Horney, Fromm, and Sullivan stressed the social-psychological aspects of personality formation. I find this perspective broadening, for it goes beyond the instinctual and physical orientation of Freud.

Erikson's developmental theory extends Freud's perspective of human development. Although I find Freud's *psychosexual* concepts of great value, I think that Erikson's stress on the *psychosocial* factors gives a more complete picture of the critical turning points at each stage of development. The key needs and developmental tasks, along with the challenges inherent at each stage of life, provide a model to understand some of the core conflicts that clients explore in their therapy sessions. Also, I find the notion of the continuity of the life cycle to be fascinating. This gives some weight to childhood and adolescent factors that are significant in later stages of development. In this sense, we can find themes and threads running through a client's life.

Reich stressed the centrality of the body in psychotherapy. He also focused on block-ages to feelings and stressed ways of opening the feelings. In my own therapeutic practice I have come to pay attention to what my clients express through their bodies. In my opinion there is considerable value to learning to listen to the messages of our bodies, and there is real value in emotional catharsis at times. I think that many of Reich's notions can be integrated into the structure of some of the more traditional therapies.

All of these theorists have been briefly presented as having built on the foundations of Freudian psychoanalysis. But it is a mistake and an oversimplification to place them in a general category of neo-Freudians. Each has gone beyond Freud in certain ways, discarding certain parts of orthodox psychoanalysis, modifying other aspects, extending certain concepts, and developing new concepts and therapeutic procedures. I do not think that this conclusion is self-evident, however. A Freudian might well argue that most of these subsequent theorists actually *narrowed* the scope of theory by acknowledging only the ego aspects of personality (which are most clearly related to social influences) and ignoring other important aspects of the unconscious, particularly the id.

Another reason that these seven theorists cannot simply be lumped together as neo-Freudians is that some of the differences between them are as great as or even greater than their differences with some of the theorists who follow in this textbook. These seven have been selected because they form a historical link between Freud and some of the more contemporary theorists and because their approaches are still alive and influential in the current practice of psychotherapy. Each of these systems has significant implications for counselors. I hope you will choose further reading of those theories that you have found most exciting, so that you can evaluate what aspects to incorporate into your own counseling. As you continue this reading, you may be surprised to find the degree to which these theorists have had an impact on the writers who have followed them.

Questions for reflection and discussion

1. *Jung*. According to Jung, in order to develop as a full person, a man must express his feminine dimension (*anima*), and a woman must express her masculine side (*animus*). What specific traits do you see in yourself from *both* the feminine and masculine di-mensions? How do you think this is related to your ability as a counselor to understand the subjective worlds of the opposite sex?
2. *Adler*. In Adler's view each of us develops a sense of uniqueness expressed by a style of life. We develop this style of life out of our "striving for superiority," or the quest for power. In what specific ways do you see yourself as working toward power? What gives you a sense of power?
3. *Horney*. Review Horney's list of ten neurotic needs, and determine the one such need

that you see in the greatest degree in yourself. How does this need either enhance or detract from your ability to relate to others effectively? How do you expect this to affect you as a counselor?

4. *Fromm.* The theme of much of Fromm's writing is the human experience of *isolation* and *alienation* because of our separation from nature and from others. How does this plight apply to you? In what ways do you experience alienation at times? How do you deal with such feelings?

5. *Sullivan.* Sullivan stressed the impact of the therapist's personality on the therapeutic process. Applying this to yourself, what major personal characteristic do you see as your greatest asset as a counselor? What is your greatest personal liability?

6. *Erikson.* As you review the eight stages of human development, what can you learn about critical turning points, or life crises, in your own life? Mention *one* important crisis you faced and how you dealt with it. What impact do you think it will have on your ability to deal with clients with similar struggles?

7. *Reich.* In Reich's view our body armor serves as a defense. Does this theory apply to you, and, if so, how? Are you aware of keeping certain feelings locked within you? Are you aware of any areas in your body that store pent-up feelings?

8. As you review the seven theories in this chapter, select the one major concept from each that you find most valuable, perhaps a concept that you would like to incorporate into your personal counseling theory. Which concept is this, and why did you select it?

9. Give a brief critique of each of these seven theories. What limitations do you see in each? In what way do you see each of these approaches as the same as or different from the Freudian psychoanalytic model? What aspect of the theory do you like best? Like least? Why?

10. As you study the remaining chapters, look for any similarities between these and the seven theories you have just studied. For example, in what ways do you see Adler's concepts expressed in the theories that follow?

Recommended supplementary readings

For those of you who want to do further reading of a general nature on these theories, I highly recommend two textbooks: Schultz, D. *Theories of personality* (2nd ed.). Monterey, Calif.: Brooks/Cole, 1981. This is a concise and basic overview of the major personality theories; it would be a good place to begin. Theories are clearly presented, as well as techniques of inquiry and therapeutic implications.

Hall, C. S., & Lindzey, G. *Theories of personality* (3rd ed.). New York: Wiley, 1978. This is an advanced treatment of the major contemporary theories of personality. It has excellent overviews of the social-psychological theories of Adler, Fromm, Horney, and Sullivan. The chapter on Jung's analytic theory is also excellent. This book is a superb resource.

Other books highly recommended as supplementary reading are marked with an asterisk.

References and suggested readings

CARL JUNG

Hall, C. S., & Lindzey, G. *Theories of personality* (3rd ed.). New York: Wiley, 1978.

* Hall, C. S., & Nordby, V. J. *A primer of Jungian psychology.* New York: New American Library, 1973.

Jung, C. G. *Contributions to analytic psychology.* New York: Harcourt, 1928.

Jung, C. G. *Psychological types.* New York: Harcourt, 1933. (a)

Jung, C. G. *Modern man in search of a soul*. New York: Harcourt, 1933. (b)
* Jung, C. G. *Memories, dreams, reflections* (recorded and edited by Aniela Jaffé). New York: Pantheon, 1963.
Jung, C. G. *Man and his symbols*. Garden City, N.Y.: Doubleday, 1964.
Kaufmann, Y. Analytic psychotherapy. In R. J. Corsini (Ed.), *Current psychotherapies* (2nd ed.). Itasca, Ill.: F. E. Peacock, 1979.
Schultz, D. *Theories of personality* (2nd ed.). Monterey, Calif.: Brooks/Cole, 1981.

ALFRED ADLER

Adler, A. *What life should mean to you*. New York: Capricorn, 1958.
Adler, A. *The practice and theory of individual psychology*. Paterson, N.J.: Littlefield, Adams, 1963.
Adler, A. *Social interest: A challenge to mankind*. New York: Capricorn Books, 1964.
Ansbacher, H. L., & Ansbacher, R. R. (Eds.). *The individual psychology of Alfred Adler: A systematic presentation in selections from his writings*. New York: Basic Books, 1965.
* Dinkmeyer, D. C., Pew, W. L., & Dinkmeyer, D. C., Jr. *Adlerian counseling and psychotherapy*. Monterey, Calif.: Brooks/Cole, 1979.

KAREN HORNEY

Horney, K. *Neurotic personality of our time*. New York: Norton, 1937.
Horney, K. *New ways in psychoanalysis*. New York: Norton, 1939.
Horney, K. *Self analysis*. New York: Norton, 1942.
Horney, K. *Our inner conflicts*. New York: Norton, 1945.
* Horney, K. *Neurosis and human growth*. New York: Norton, 1950.

ERICH FROMM

Evans, R. I. *Dialogue with Erich Fromm*. New York: Harper & Row, 1966.
Fromm, E. *Escape from freedom*. New York: Rinehart, 1941.
Fromme, E. *Man for himself*. New York: Rinehart, 1947.
Fromm, E. *The sane society*. New York: Rinehart, 1955.
* Fromm, E. *The art of loving*. New York: Harper & Row, 1956.
Fromm, E. *The heart of man*. New York: Harper & Row, 1964.
Fromm, E. *The revolution of hope*. New York: Harper & Row, 1968.
Fromm, E. *The anatomy of human destructiveness*. New York: Holt, Rinehart & Winston, 1973.
Fromm, E. *Greatness and limitations of Freud's thought*. New York: Harper & Row, 1980.
Schultz, D. *Theories of personality* (2nd ed.). Monterey, Calif.: Brooks/Cole, 1981.

HARRY STACK SULLIVAN

Sullivan, H. S. *Conceptions of modern psychiatry*. New York: Norton, 1953. (a)
Sullivan, H. S. *Interpersonal theory of psychiatry*. New York: Norton, 1953. (b)
* Sullivan, H. S. *The psychiatric interview*. New York: Norton, 1956.

ERIK ERIKSON

* Erikson, E. H. *Childhood and society* (2nd ed.). New York: Norton, 1963.
Erikson, E. H. *Insight and responsibility: Lectures on the ethical implications of psychoanalytic insight*. New York: Norton, 1964.
Erikson, E. H. *Identity: Youth and crisis*. New York: Norton, 1968.

WILHELM REICH

* Baker, E. *Man in the trap*. New York: Avon, 1967.

* Boadella, D. *Wilhelm Reich: The evolution of his work*. London: Vision, 1973.

Fadiman, J., & Frager, R. *Personality and personal growth*. New York: Harper & Row, 1976.

Janov, A. *The primal scream*. New York: Delta, 1970.

Janov, A. *The primal revolution*. New York: Simon & Schuster (Touchstone Book), 1972.

Kelley, C. R. *The new education*. Santa Monica, Calif.: Interscience Research Institute, 1972.

Kelley, C. R. *Education in feeling and purpose*. Santa Monica, Calif.: Interscience Research Institute, 1974.

Lowen, A. *The language of the body*. New York: Collier-Macmillan, 1958.

Lowen, A. *The betrayal of the body*. New York: Collier-Macmillan, 1967. (a)

Lowen, A. *Love and orgasm*. New York: New American Library, 1967. (b)

Lowen, A. *Depression and the body*. New York: Coward, McCann, & Geoghegan, 1972.

Lowen, A. The body in personality theory: Wilhelm Reich and Alexander Lowen. In A. Burton (Ed.), *Operational theories of personality*. New York: Brunner/Mazel, 1974.

* Lowen, A. *Bioenergetics*. New York: Penguin, 1976.

Perls, F. *Gestalt therapy verbatim*. Lafayette, Calif.: Real People Press, 1969.

Reich, W. *Character analysis*. New York: Noonday Press, 1949.

* Reich, W. *The function of the orgasm*. New York: Bantam, 1967.

Reich, W. *Selected writings*. New York: Noonday Press, 1969.

Rolf, I. *Structural integration: Gravity, an unexplored factor in a more human use of human beings*. Boulder, Colo.: Guild for Structural Integration, 1962.

* Schutz, W. *Here comes everybody: Bodymind and encounter culture*. New York: Harper & Row (Harrow Books), 1972.

4

Existential Therapy

Introduction

Psychology has long been dominated by the empirical approach to the study of individual behavior. Many North American psychologists have considered the commitment to operational definitions, testable hypotheses, and empirical data the only valid approach to securing information about behavior. Within this tradition there has not been much serious interest in philosophical aspects of counseling and psychotherapy that do not readily lend themselves to rigorous empirical investigation.

Now, however, there is a growing interest among counselors and therapists in the "third-force" perspective on therapy, a theoretical alternative to the psychoanalytic and behavioral approaches. Under this heading fall existential therapy, the person-centered approach developed by Carl Rogers (the subject of Chapter 5), and the Gestalt therapy developed by Fritz Perls (the subject of Chapter 6). Both person-centered therapy and Gestalt therapy are experiential and relationship-oriented. They are humanistic approaches that grew out of the philosophical background of the existential tradition.

Existential therapy can best be considered as an *approach* to therapeutic practice, or a *philosophy* on which a therapist operates. As such, it is not a separate school of therapy or a neatly defined, systematic model with specific therapeutic techniques. Thus, in this chapter I will focus on the philosophy underlying the existential approach and on some key themes that have significant implications for the existentially oriented practitioner.

It is important to remember that the existential approach developed from a reaction to two other major models—psychoanalysis and behaviorism. Existential therapy reacts against the psychoanalytic and behavioristic positions' deterministic, reductionistic, and mechanistic view of humans. The existential approach is grounded on the assumption that we are free, whereas the psychoanalytic view sees freedom as restricted by unconscious forces, irrational drives, and past events. Also, the behavioristic position sees freedom as restricted by sociocultural conditioning.

Key concepts

VIEW OF HUMAN NATURE

The existential approach to counseling and psychotherapy focuses on what it means to be human and on the basic dimensions of the human condition. These include (1) the capacity for self-awareness; (2) freedom and responsibility; (3) commitment; (4) choice in the face of uncertainty; (5) finding one's uniqueness and identity and relating to others in a meaningful way; (6) the courage to face one's fundamental aloneness to choose for oneself; (7) the search for meaning, values, purpose, and goals; (8) anxiety; and (9) awareness of death and nonbeing.

The existential movement stands for the respect of the person, for exploring new aspects of human behavior, and for divergent methods of understanding people. Rather than espousing a single way to understand people, it uses numerous approaches to therapy based on its assumptions about human nature.

Rollo May (1953) has been instrumental in translating some concepts drawn from existential philosophy and applying them to psychotherapy. May asserts that all individuals have an inborn urge to become a person; that is, they have the tendency to develop their singularity, discover their personal identity, and strive for the full actualization of their potentials. To the extent that they fulfill these potentials, they experience the deepest joy that is possible in human experience, for nature has intended them to do so.

Becoming a person is not an automatic process, yet everyone has the desire to realize this potential. Whereas acorns grow automatically into oak trees, we human beings become the kind of people we choose to become. It is almost as though nature were urging us to become all that we are able to become. It takes courage to be, and whether we want to be or not is our choice. There is a constant struggle within us. Although we want to grow toward maturity, independence, and actualization, we realize that expansion is often a painful process. Hence, the struggle is between the security of dependence and the delights and pains of growth.

Along with May, two other writers have been instrumental in developing the humanistic trend in psychology, which is partly an offshoot of the existential trend. Abraham Maslow (1968, 1970) focused much of his research on the nature of the self-actualizing person. Maslow wrote of the "psychopathology of the average." So-called "normals" may never extend themselves to become what they are capable of becoming. Maslow argued that healthy people differ from normals in kind as well as in degree. He criticized the Freudian preoccupation with the sick and crippled side of human nature. He contended that, if we base our findings on a sick population, we will have a sick psychology. According to Maslow, too much attention has been given to hostility, aggression, neuroses, and immaturities; likewise, too little attention has been given to love, creativity, joy, and "peak experiences." Maslow's (1968, 1970) research with self-actualizing subjects yielded the following characteristics: the capacity to tolerate and even welcome uncertainty in their lives, acceptance of self and others, spontaneity and creativity, a need for privacy and solitude, autonomy, the capacity for deep and intense interpersonal relationships, a genuine caring for others, a sense of humor, an inner-directedness, and an open and fresh attitude toward life.

Rogers (1961) is another major figure who contributed to creating a humanistic psychotherapy, and who built much of his theory on existential concepts. His approach is an extension and development of the existential tradition and an existential view of humans. He believes in a basic trustworthiness of human nature and contends that each of us has a tendency to become a "fully functioning person," a conception much like Maslow's view of the self-actualizing person.

The person-centered approach to counseling, as developed by Rogers, is treated in the next chapter as a separate form of the humanistic approach to therapy. At this point it suffices to say that there are clear implications for counselors who assume that people strive toward self-actualization. Seeing people in this light means that the therapist focuses on the constructive side of human nature, on what is right with the person, and on the assets people bring with them to therapy. Thus, therapy becomes something more than a process of diagnosis and treatment of ailments. It focuses on how clients act in their world with others, how they can move forward in constructive directions, and how they can successfully encounter obstacles (both from within themselves and outside of themselves) that are blocking their growth. The implication is that therapy is more than "adjustment to norms"; and this approach does not stop with merely solving problems. Instead, practitioners with an existential orientation aim at challenging their clients to make changes that will lead to living fully and authentically, with the realization that this kind of existence demands a continuing struggle. People never arrive at a static state of being self-actualized; rather, at best they are continually involved in the process of actualizing themselves.

In the previous discussion of human nature, humanistic psychology was presented as an offshoot of the existential approach. The following section is intended to clarify more completely the distinction between the humanistic approach and the existential approach, two separate but related trends in psychology.

AN OVERVIEW OF HUMANISTIC PSYCHOLOGY: CENTRAL THEMES

Humanistic psychology grew out of a reaction to the limitations of both the psychoanalytic and the behavioristic traditions' deterministic stance. Composing their theories from many divergent fields and approaches, humanistic psychologists emphasized the complexity of human nature. They reacted against any attempt to reduce human behavior to instincts, drives, or the product of conditioning. Rather than believe that humans could be validly studied and understood in a segmented fashion, they asserted that humans must be studied in complete relation to how they interact with others and with the world. From its earliest days, the humanistic movement has been characterized by certain central themes that focus on the capacities unique to humans, namely: love, choice, creativeness, purpose, relatedness, meanings, and values. According to the humanistic psychologists, people will never be understood or appreciated without exploring these dimensions of human existence. Some of the psychoanalytic and behavioral approaches, however, reject these human dimensions. It is this exclusion, which resulted in a limited and narrow conception of human potentiality, that the humanistic psychologists rebutted.

Humanistic psychologists believe that various problems with contemporary society have led to a human crisis, the resolution of which requires a different approach. Alienation is a key word in this context. Because so many humans are seen as alienated from themselves, from others, and from the world, humanistic psychology originally addressed the problem of alienation: How can humans avoid living fragmented existences? How can humans find ways back to themselves, and how can they find a meaningful basis to fully relate to others?

There are several central emphases or themes within humanistic psychology, five of which, according to Shaffer (1978), are interrelated and interdependent.

1. The starting point for psychology in general is conscious experience. Humanistic psychology in particular emphasizes subjective reality, or the uniqueness of each person's experience.
2. There here and now—the immediate experiencing of the present moment—is an experiential approach that is stressed along with the wholeness and integrity of human behavior.
3. Humanistic psychology grants that humans are limited by both biological and environmental factors; and yet, within the framework of these limitations, human freedom is insisted upon.
4. This approach also contends that humans cannot be reduced to drives, need satisfactions, or unconscious determinants.
5. Humanistic psychology, based on existential philosophy, maintains that humans can never be defined as a product or as an entity: humans are continually in the process of self-definition.

Having been exposed to an overview of human nature and humanistic psychology, we are now ready to pursue our study of existential therapy.

AN OVERVIEW OF EXISTENTIALISM: CENTRAL THEMES

Existentialism is a branch of philosophical thought; the key existential writers did not address themselves to psychotherapeutic concerns directly. These writers included the

19th-century philosophers Friedrich Nietzsche and Sören Kierkegaard. Most existential philosophers share with Kierkegaard a respect for a "subjective" exploration of human experience and for the anxiety, or "dread," involved in making choices, which he called the "leap of faith." Existential thought was further developed in the 20th century by such philosophers as Jean-Paul Sartre, Martin Heidegger, Karl Jaspers, Albert Camus, and Maurice Merleau-Ponty. Heidegger portrays human existence as inherently concerned with questions about the nature of one's own unique being. Most existentially minded therapists are concerned with Heideggerian notions stressing "authenticity," and Sartrian concepts stressing "freedom" and "responsibility."

According to Shaffer (1978) there are four central existential themes:

1. We are confronted with the unavoidable uncertainty of a world without any fixed meaning and with the certainty of our own eventual nonbeing, or death.
2. In the face of a potentially meaningless situation, we become aware of our inherent freedom to choose our attitudes toward situations and to choose our actions.
3. There are constraints, both biological and environmental, on human freedom, yet within these limits there is always choice.
4. We cannot evade responsibility for choosing for ourselves, for we are constantly creating ourselves by the choices we make or fail to make. It is this awareness of personal freedom and responsibility that leads to anxiety, and how we deal with this anxiety is to a large degree related to our identity.

The therapeutic process

THERAPEUTIC GOALS

A basic goal of many therapeutic approaches is enabling individuals to act and to accept the awesome freedom and responsibility for action. Existential therapy in particular is rooted in the premise that humans cannot escape from freedom and that freedom and responsibility are interrelated. Thus, existential therapy seeks to expand self-awareness and increase the potential for choice; that is, clients are helped to become aware of the freedom they possess and to be responsible for the direction of their life. Accepting this responsibility is no easy matter, however. Many fear the weight of being responsible for who they are now and what they are becoming. They must choose, for example, whether to cling to the known and the familiar, or to risk opening themselves to a less certain and more challenging life. That there are no guarantees in life is precisely what generates anxiety. Thus, existential therapy aims also at helping clients face the anxiety of choosing for themselves and accepting the reality that they are more than mere victims of deterministic forces outside themselves.

The following letter was written by one of my former clients and is presented here with her consent. Her words describe vividly her struggles with awareness, freedom, and responsibility and the anxiety she feels in making daily decisions regarding the way she wants to lead her life.

> Often now I find myself struggling deep within me with who I really am as a person and how I really feel. Emotions don't come easily to me even now. Feelings of love and hate are new to me, and often very scary. Many times I find it hard to reconcile myself to the fact that sometimes I can miss someone I care about one moment and then wish that they would go away the next. This inconsistency in myself, this dependency-independency struggle is confusing to me at times. Sometimes I think that I would have been better off if I had remained as emotionally dead as I once was. At least then I didn't hurt so much. But I also know that I wasn't fully alive then either.

Today a man embraced me and I felt very warm and safe for a little while. I like that feeling and yet I fear it, too. It's so alien to me. I want to trust and yet I still find it difficult to do so. Perhaps it's because there's always an element of risk involved in any relationship and I still won't allow myself to accept that risk. I worry about whether I will ever be able to overcome all the old hurts and disappointments and learn to live for today.

Occasionally, when I'm feeling especially alone and lost, I try to imagine what it would be like if I had never entered counseling, if I had never acquired the self-insight that I now have. Or what it would be like if I could magically return in time to an earlier stage of my emotional growth when I felt less threatened, and be able to stay there. I saw no beauty in the world then, and I knew no success, nor did I have much peace of mind, but I felt safer then. The pressures that I live with now didn't exist. It was a simpler, less challenging time for me. And yet if I were magically given the ability to go back I know that I wouldn't. I'm not always sure where I'm going these days, but I do know where I've been, and I would never knowingly choose to return to what I once was again. I've come too far to go back now. And yet sometimes I still wonder if it's all been worth it.

THERAPIST'S FUNCTION AND ROLE

Existential therapists are primarily concerned with understanding the present personal and subjective world of the client, to help that person come to new understandings and options. Typically, these therapists show wide latitude in the methods they employ, varying not only from client to client but also with the same client at different phases of the therapeutic process. Techniques of therapy are secondary to the primary purpose of understanding the client.

Therapists with an existential orientation usually deal with people who have what could be called restricted existences. These clients have a limited degree of awareness of themselves and are often vague about the nature of their problems. They may see few if any options to limited ways of dealing with life situations, and they tend to feel trapped or helpless. A central task of the therapist is to directly confront these clients with the ways they are living restricted existences and to help them become aware of their own part in creating this condition. Therapists might hold up a mirror, so to speak, so that clients can gradually engage in a process of self-confrontation. In this way clients can see how they got the way they are and how they might enlarge the way they live. By becoming aware of factors in their past and of stifling modes of their present existence, they can begin to accept responsibility for changing their future.

May (1961) views the therapist's task as helping clients become aware and conscious of their being-in-the-world: "This is the moment when the patient sees that he is the one who is threatened, that he is the being who stands in this world which threatens, and that he is the subject who *has* a world" (p. 81).

Viktor Frankl (1963) describes the role of the therapist as that of an "eye specialist rather than that of a painter," whose task consists of "widening and broadening the visual field of the patient so that the whole spectrum of meaning and values becomes conscious and visible to him" (p. 174).

For an example of what an existentially oriented therapist might actually do in a therapeutic session, refer again to the letter of my former client. If this client were to express her feelings to a therapist in a session, the therapist might

1. Share his or her own personal reactions to what the client is saying.
2. Engage in some relevant and appropriate personal disclosure of experiences similar to those of the client.
3. Ask the client to express her anguish over the necessity to choose in an uncertain world.

4. Challenge her to look at all the ways in which she avoids making decisions and to make a judgment concerning this avoidance.
5. Encourage her to examine the course of her life in the period since she began therapy by asking: "If you could magically go back to the way you remember yourself *before* therapy, would you really do this now?"
6. Share with her that she is learning that her experience is precisely the unique quality of being human: that she is ultimately alone, that she must decide for herself, that she will experience anxiety over not being sure of her decisions, and that she will have to struggle to define her own meaning in a world that often appears meaningless.

CLIENT'S EXPERIENCE IN THERAPY

In behavioristically oriented therapy, clients might get the impression that their own conscious experiences are not especially significant, and that the therapist is an expert technician who uses specialized procedures to cause their behavior to be different. In existential therapy, however, clients are clearly encouraged to take seriously their own subjective experience of their world. They are challenged to take responsibility for how they *now* choose to be in their world. Effective therapy does not stop with this awareness itself, for the therapist encourages clients to take action on the basis of the insights they develop through the therapeutic process. Clients are expected to go out into the world and decide *how* they will live differently. Further, they must be active in the therapeutic process, for during the sessions they must decide what fears, guilts, and anxieties they will explore. Merely deciding to enter psychotherapy is itself often a scary prospect, as indicated by the notes one of my clients kept for herself during the period of her therapy. Sense the anxiety that she experiences as she chooses to leave security and embark on a search for herself:

> I started private therapy today. I was terrified, but I didn't know of what. Now I do. First of all, I was terrified of Jerry himself. He has the power to change me. I'm giving him that power and I can't go back. That's what's really upsetting me. I can't go back ever. Nothing is the same. . . . I don't know myself yet, only to know that nothing is the same. I'm sad and scared of this. I've sandblasted security right out of my life and I'm really frightened of who I'll become. I'm sad that I can't go back. I've opened the door into myself and I'm terrified of what's there, of coping with a new me, of seeing and relating to people differently. I guess I have free-floating anxiety about everything but most specifically I'm afraid of myself.

In essence, clients in existential therapy are engaged in opening the doors to themselves. The experience is often frightening, or exciting, or joyful, or depressing, or a combination of all of these. As clients wedge open the closed doors, they also begin to loosen the deterministic shackles that have kept them psychologically bound. Gradually they become aware of what they have been and who they now are, and they are better able to decide what kind of future they want. Through the process of their therapy, they can explore alternatives for making their visions become real.

RELATIONSHIP BETWEEN THERAPIST AND CLIENT

For the existential therapist the relationship with the client is given central importance. It is the quality of the person-to-person encounter in the therapeutic situation that is the stimulus for positive change. Therapists with this orientation believe that the basic attitudes they hold toward the client, as well as their own personal characteristics of honesty, integrity, and courage, are what they can offer to the client. The therapeutic relationship is seen as a shared journey. Martin Buber's (1970) conception of the I/Thou relationship has significant implications here. Clients are viewed as persons in the process of change, not as fixed entities. Through a process of empathy therapists share their reactions to clients as one way of deepening the therapeutic relationship.

In writing on the therapeutic relationship Sidney Jourard (1971), who based his therapy on existential concepts, called for therapists who, through their own authentic and self-disclosing behavior, invite the client to authenticity. Jourard asked that therapists work toward a relationship of I and Thou, one in which their spontaneous self-disclosure fosters growth and authenticity in the client. As Jourard put it, "Manipulation begets counter-manipulation. Self-disclosure begets self-disclosure" (p. 142). He also pointed out that the therapeutic relationship can change the therapist as much as it does the client. "This means that those who wish to leave their being and their growth unchanged should not become therapists" (p. 150).

Jourard is a good example of a therapist who developed a self-styled existential and humanistic orientation. He demonstrates that it is possible to be unique and authentic and employ a diversity of techniques within an existential framework. Therapists invite clients to grow by modeling authentic behavior. They are able to be transparent when it is appropriate in the relationship, and their own humanness is a stimulus for the client to tap potentials for realness. Jourard contends that, if therapists keep themselves hidden during the therapeutic session, or if they engage in the same inauthentic behavior that generated symptoms in their clients, then the clients will also remain guarded and persist in their inauthentic ways. Thus, therapists can help clients to become less of a stranger to themselves by selectively disclosing their own reactions at appropriate times. Of course, this does not imply an uncensored sharing of every fleeting reaction. Rather, it implies a willingness to share persistent reactions with clients, especially when this sharing can have a facilitating effect.

Application: Therapeutic techniques and procedures

As I mentioned earlier, the existential approach is unlike most of the other therapies in that it does not have a well-defined set of techniques. Because this approach is basically concerned with matters such as the goals of therapy, human nature, and certain basic assumptions regarding the therapeutic relationship, the existential practitioner can choose procedures from many diverse schools of therapy. This eclecticism might include drawing on some psychoanalytic concepts and techniques, as does Bugental (1965, 1967). It might also incorporate techniques from the cognitive and behavioral therapies. In this approach techniques are viewed as tools to help clients become aware of their choices and to challenge them to accept the responsibility that accompanies the use of this personal freedom.

In the remainder of this chapter I will describe six key existential propositions and their implications for the practice of counseling and psychotherapy. Most of these major premises are found throughout the works of many of the writers that have been listed in the reference section.

PROPOSITION 1: THE CAPACITY FOR SELF-AWARENESS

As human beings we can reflect and make choices, because we are capable of self-awareness. The greater our awareness, the greater our possibilities for freedom; and because we are conscious, we can become aware of the responsibility to choose (see Proposition 2).

Thus, to expand one's awareness is to increase one's capacity to fully experience human living. At the core of human existence, awareness discloses the following to all of us:

1. We are finite, and we do not have forever to actualize our potentials.
2. We have the potential to take action or not to take action.
3. We have some measure of choice in what our actions will be, and therefore we can partially create our own destiny.
4. We are basically alone, yet we have a need to relate ourselves to other beings; we recognize that we are separate from, yet related to, others.
5. Meaning is not automatically bestowed on us but is the product of our searching and of our creating a unique purpose.
6. Existential anxiety, which is basically a consciousness of our own freedom, is an essential part of living; as we increase our awareness of the choices available to us, we also increase our sense of responsibility for the consequences of these choices.
7. This consciousness of our own freedom entails uncertainty about our future.
8. Our capacity for self-awareness enables us to experience conditions of loneliness, meaninglessness, emptiness, guilt, and isolation.

Awareness can be conceptualized in the following way: Picture yourself walking down a long hallway with many doors on each side of the hallway. Let yourself imagine that you can choose to open some of the doors either a crack or fully or to leave them closed. Perhaps if you open one of the doors you will not like what you see—it might be fearsome or ugly. On the other hand, you might discover a room filled with beauty. You might debate with yourself whether to leave a door shut or attempt to pry it open.

I believe we can choose to expand our consciousness or to limit our self-knowledge. I witness the struggle between the opposing desires in almost every counseling situation. Because self-awareness is at the root of most other human capacities, the decision to expand it is fundamental to human growth. What follows is a list of some dawning awarenesses that individuals experience in both individual and group counseling:

1. They become aware that, in desperately seeking to be loved, they really miss the experience of feeling loved.
2. They see how they trade the security of dependence for the anxieties that accompany deciding for themselves.
3. They recognize how they attempt to deny their inconsistencies and how they do not want to accept in themselves what they consider unacceptable.
4. They begin to see that their identity is anchored in someone else's definition of them; that is, they seek approval and confirmation of their being in others instead of looking to themselves for confirmation.
5. They learn that in many ways they keep themselves prisoner by some of their past experiences and decisions.
6. They discover a multitude of facets within them and come to realize that, as they repress one side of their being, they repress another. For example, if they repress tragedy, they seal themselves off from joy; if they deny their hate, they deny their capacity to love; if they cast out their devils, they also cast out their angels.
7. They can learn that they are not condemned to a future similar to the past, for they can learn from their past and thereby reshape the future.
8. They can realize that they are so preoccupied with death and dying that they fail to appreciate living.

9. They are able to accept their limitations yet still feel worthwhile, for they understand that they do not need to be perfect to feel worthy.
10. They can come to realize that they fail to live in the present moment because of either preoccupation with the past, planning the future, or trying to do too many things at once.

Counseling implications.   Increasing self-awareness, which includes awareness of alternatives, motivations, factors influencing the person, and personal goals, is an aim of all counseling. I do not believe, however, that the therapist's job is to seek out unaware people and tell them that they need to expand their awareness. Perhaps those people are content and are not the slightest bit interested in consciousness-raising. When a person does come for therapy, seek a group experience, or ask for counseling, then it is a far different matter.

I also believe that it is a therapist's task to indicate to the client that a price must be paid for increased awareness of self. As one becomes more aware, one finds it more difficult to "go home again." Ignorance of one's condition might bring contentment along with a feeling of partial deadness, but, as one opens the doors in one's world, one can expect more struggle as well as the potential for more fulfillment.

PROPOSITION 2: FREEDOM AND RESPONSIBILITY

Because we are essentially free, we must accept the responsibility for directing our lives. We may, of course, attempt to avoid this reality that we are ultimately the ones who influence our destinies.

The existentialists contend that we are thrust into the world, but that how we live and what we become are the results of our choices. As Sartre (1971) put it, our existence is a given, but we do not have a fixed identity or a settled essence. According to him, we are constantly confronted with the choice of what kind of person we are becoming, and to exist is never to be finished with this kind of choosing. Sartre called for *commitment* to choosing for ourselves, and it might be said that existential guilt is a consciousness of evading commitment, or choosing not to choose. Sartre said "We are our choices." It is clear that self-determination, willingness, and decision are at the core of human existence.

Although there are limits to our freedom, and outside factors restrict our choices, we nevertheless retain an element of freedom. As May (1961) wrote, "No matter how great the forces victimizing the human being, man has the capacity to know that he is being victimized and thus to influence in some way how he will relate to his fate" (pp. 41–42). Frankl (1963) emphasized human freedom and responsibility: "Life ultimately means taking the responsibility to find the right answer to its problems and to fulfill the tasks which it constantly sets for each individual" (p. 122). This underlying freedom cannot be taken away from us, for at a minimum we can choose our attitude in any given set of circumstances.

Counseling implications.   The existentialist sees no basis for counseling and therapy without recognition of the freedom and responsibility each individual possesses. The therapist's tasks are to assist clients in discovering how they avoid full acceptance of their freedom and to encourage them to learn to risk using it. Not to do so is to cripple clients and make them neurotically dependent on the therapist. Therapists need to teach clients that they can explicitly accept the fact that they have choice, even though they may have devoted most of their lives to trying to evade this freedom.

People often come to counselors and therapists because they feel that they have lost control of their own lives. They may look to the counselor to direct them, give them advice, or produce "magical cures." In many ways, they may refuse to grapple with the problem of freedom and their anxiety over choosing for themselves. Two central tasks of the therapist are to challenge clients to recognize how they have failed to choose for themselves and have allowed others to decide for them and to encourage them to take steps toward autonomy.

PROPOSITION 3: NEED FOR CENTER AND NEED FOR OTHERS

Individuals have the need to preserve their uniqueness and centeredness; yet at the same time they have the need to go outside themselves and to relate to other beings and to nature. Failure to relate to others and to nature results in loneliness, alienation, estrangement, and depersonalization.

Each of us has a strong need to discover a self—that is, to find our personal identity. But finding out who we are is not an automatic process; it takes courage. Paradoxically, we also have a strong need to go outside our own existence. We need to discover our relationship to other beings. We must give of ourselves to others and be concerned with them. Many existential writers discuss loneliness, uprootedness, and alienation, which can be seen as the failure to develop ties with others and with nature. This failure becomes an acute problem for the individual in an industralized and urbanized society, where, in a desperate attempt to escape from loneliness, the individual has become the outer-directed person in the lonely crowd that Riesman (1950) wrote of. As a result of inward emptiness and hollowness and the lack of a personal sense of being, the individual attempts to immerse himself or herself in the anonymous crowd.

The courage to be.   It does take courage to discover our core and to learn how to live from the inside. We struggle to discover, to create, and to maintain the core deep within our being. One of the greatest fears of clients is that they will discover that there is no core, no self, and no substance, and that they are merely reflections of everyone's expectations of them. A client might say: "My fear is that I'll discover I'm nobody, that there really is nothing to me, and that I have no self. I'll find out that I'm an empty shell, hollow inside, and nothing will exist if I shed my masks."

Existential therapists might begin by asking their clients to allow themselves to intensify the feeling that they are nothing more than the sum of others' expectations and that they are merely the introjects of parents and parent substitutes. How do they feel now? Are they condemned to stay this way forever? Is there a way out? Can they create a self if they find that they are without one? Where can they begin? Once clients have demonstrated the courage to simply recognize this fear, to put it into words and share it, it does not seem so overwhelming. I find that it is best to begin work by inviting clients to accept the ways in which they have lived outside themselves and to explore ways in which they are out of center with themselves.

The trouble with so many of us is that we have sought directions, answers, values, and beliefs from the important people in our worlds. Rather than trusting ourselves to search within and find our own answers to the conflicts in our lives, we sell out by becoming what others expect of us. Our being becomes rooted in their being, and we become strangers to ourselves.

The need for the self relates to the need to have meaningful relationships with other people. If we live in isolation and have no real connection to others, we experience a sense of abandonment, estrangement, and alienation. Perhaps one of the functions of therapy is to help clients distinguish between a neurotically dependent attachment to another and a therapeutic relationship in which both persons are enhanced. The therapist can challenge clients to examine what they get from their relationships, how they avoid intimate contact, how they prevent themselves from having equal relationships, and how they might create therapeutic, healthy, and mature human relationships.

The experience of aloneness.   The existentialists postulate that part of the human condition is the experience of aloneness. However, we can derive strength from the experience of looking to ourselves and sensing our aloneness and separation. The sense of isolation comes when we recognize that we cannot depend on anyone else for our own confirmation; that is, we alone must give a sense of meaning to our lives, we alone must decide how we will live, we alone must find our own answers, and we alone must decide what we will be or not be. If we are unable to tolerate ourselves when we are alone, then how can we expect anyone else to be enriched by our company? Before we can have any solid relationship with another, we must have a relationship with ourselves. We must learn to listen to ourselves. We have to be able to stand alone before we can truly stand beside another.

There is a paradox in the proposition that humans are existentially both alone and related, but this very paradox describes the human condition. To think that we can cure the condition, or that it should be cured, is a mistake. Ultimately we are alone.

The experience of relatedness.   We humans depend on relationships with others for our humanness. We have a need to be significant in another's world, and we need to feel that another's presence is important in our world. When we allow another person to matter in our world, we experience a sense of meaningful relatedness. When we are able to stand alone and dip within ourselves for our own strength, our relationships with others are based on our fulfillment, not our deprivation. If we feel personally deprived, however, we can expect little but a clinging, parasitic, symbiotic relationship with someone else.

Counseling implications.   People who seek therapy are frequently troubled over a sense of loss of self or of being strangers to themselves. They may say that they have lost any sense of internal direction, for they are caught up in meeting the expectations of others and living a life designed by others. In their attempt to please others and win approval, they often find that they neither win acceptance nor feel self-accepting.

Moustakas (1975) described this condition of alienation from self. He called alienation "the developing of a life outlined and determined by others, rather than a life based on one's own inner experience" (p. 31). In the process of basing our identity on what others say, we actually become strangers to ourselves. This is sometimes called an "inauthentic existence," which consists of leading a life of "selling out" by becoming what others expect us to become. Shaffer (1978) wrote that inauthentic existence is playing status-seeking games to gain applause for a life performance. One important lesson for many clients is that they have indeed paid a steep price for striving to play this performance: not only have they lost contact with themselves, but they have also lost any meaningful basis for developing intense or satisfying relationships with others.

Existential counseling aims at confronting clients with their inauthentic ways and encourages them to commit themselves to living with courage. This entails making the stand necessary to define themselves. Assisting clients to live authentically involves confronting them with the reality that they must make choices and take responsibility for the outcomes. It takes courage to *act,* even though we are not certain that we are making the right choices.

PROPOSITION 4: SEARCH FOR MEANING

A distinctly human characteristic is the struggle for a sense of significance and purpose in life. Human beings by nature search for meaning and personal identity.

In my experience, the underlying conflicts that bring people into counseling and therapy are the dilemmas centered in the existential questions Why am I here? What do I want from life? What gives my life purpose? Where is the source of meaning for me in life?

Existential therapy can provide the conceptual framework for helping the client challenge the meaning in his or her life. Questions that the therapist might ask are Do you like the direction of your life? Are you pleased with what you now are and what you are becoming? Are you actively doing anything to become closer to your self-ideal? Do you even know what you want? If you are confused about who you are and what you want for yourself, what are you doing to get some clarity?

The problem of discarding old values. One of the problems in therapy is discarding traditional values (and imposed values) without finding other, suitable ones to replace them. What does the therapist do when clients no longer cling to values that were never really challenged or internalized and now experience a vacuum? They report that they feel like a boat without a rudder. They seek new guidelines and values that are appropriate for newly discovered facets of themselves, and yet for a time they are without them. Perhaps the task of the therapeutic process is to help clients create a value system based on a way of living that is consistent with their way of being.

The therapist's job might well be to trust the capacity of clients eventually to discover an internally derived value system that does provide a meaningful life. They will no doubt flounder for a time and experience anxiety as a result of the absence of clear-cut values. The therapist's trust in them is an important variable in teaching them to trust in their own capacity to discover from within a new source of values.

Learning to challenge the meaning in life. Founded by Frankl, logotherapy is designed to help the person find a meaning in life. According to Frankl (1963), challenging the meaning in life is a mark of being human. "The will to meaning" is the individual's primary striving. Life is not meaningful in itself; the individual must create and discover meaning.

I think that it is important to realize that the issue of meaning changes at various stages in life. Children attempt to discover the sense of the universe on one level. During adolescence, new quests for meaning emerge. Healthy adolescents question their values, challenge the sources of their values, and look critically at inconsistencies in their world. They struggle to discover their uniqueness. Persons in declining years meet another crisis in life. Now that most of their projects are completed and the vitality of living is on the decline, what significance of living do they find? Do their lives really matter? Do they count in anyone else's life? I remember a man in one of our groups who captured precisely the idea of personal significance when he said "I feel like another page in a book that has been quickly turned, and nobody bothered to read the page."

From the existentialist's view, a central task of counseling is deeply exploring issues pertaining to hopelessness, despair, loss of meaning and significance, and existential emptiness. In fact, some existentialists assert that out of a meaningless and absurd world we find the wellspring of creativity. The absurdity and nothingness of life allow us to create our meaning in the world. The task of the therapeutic process is to confront the issue of meaninglessness and help the client make sense out of a chaotic world.

Frankl (1963) contended that the therapist's function is not to tell clients what their particular meaning in life should be but to point out that they can discover meaning even in suffering. This view does not share the pessimistic flavor of existential philosophy but holds that human suffering (the tragic and negative aspects of life) can be turned into human achievement by the stand an individual takes in the face of suffering. Frankl also contended that people can face pain, guilt, despair, and death and, in the confrontation, challenge the despair and thus triumph. Meaninglessness and the existential vacuum are central problems that the process of therapy must face.

Counseling implications. The existential therapist tends to think more in terms of "restricted existence" as a condition that brings people into therapy, rather than of "sickness" and "psychopathology." People who lead restricted lives have only limited self-awareness; many of their potentials are locked up; they find life dull and meaningless; and they often wonder if this is all there is to life. Meaninglessness in life leads to emptiness and hollowness, or a condition that Frankl calls the existential vacuum. At times people who feel trapped by the emptiness of their lives tend to withdraw from the struggle of creating a life with purpose. This is an area that might well be challenged in counseling.

A related concept is what the existential practitioners call existential guilt. This is a condition that grows out of a sense of incompleteness, or a realization that one is not what one might have become. It is the awareness that one's actions and choices express less than one's full range as a person. When one neglects certain potentialities, there is a sense of this existential guilt. This guilt is *not* viewed as "neurotic," nor is it seen as a symptom that needs to be cured. Instead, the existential therapist explores it to see what clients might learn about the ways in which they are living their life. And it can be used to challenge the meaning and direction of life.

PROPOSITION 5: ANXIETY AS A CONDITION OF LIVING

Anxiety as a source of growth. As a basic human characteristic, anxiety is a reaction to threat. It strikes at the core of existence. It is what is felt when the existence of self is threatened.

Anxiety can be a stimulus for growth, in that we experience it as we become increasingly aware of our freedom and the consequences of accepting or rejecting that freedom. In fact, when we make a decision that involves reconstruction of our lives, the accompanying anxiety can be a signal that we are ready for personal change. The signal is constructive, for it tells us that all is not well. If we learn to listen to the subtle messages of anxiety, we can dare to take steps necessary to change the direction of our lives.

Escape from anxiety. The constructive form of anxiety (existential anxiety) is a function of our acceptance of our aloneness. Existential anxiety results also from the guilt we experience when we fail to actualize our potentials.

Yet so many clients who seek counseling want solutions that will enable them not to suffer from anxiety. Although attempts to avoid anxiety by creating the illusion that there is security in life may help us cope with the unknown, we really know on some level that we are deceiving ourselves when we think we have found fixed security. We can blunt anxiety by constricting our lives and thus reducing choices. Opening up to new life, however, means opening up to anxiety, and we pay a steep price when we short-circuit anxiety.

People who have the courage to face themselves are, nonetheless, frightened. I am convinced that those who are willing to live with their anxiety for a time are the ones who profit from personal therapy. Those who flee too quickly into comfortable patterns might experience a temporary relief but in the long run seem to experience the frustration of being stuck in their old ways.

Counseling implications.   Most people seek professional help because they experience anxiety or depression. Many clients enter a counseling office with the expectation that the counselor will remove their suffering or at least provide some formula for the reduction of their anxiety. The existentially oriented counselor is not, however, devoted to mere removal of symptoms or to anxiety reduction per se. In fact, the existential counselor does not view anxiety as undesirable. He or she might work in such a way that the client experiences increased levels of anxiety for a time. Some questions that might be posed are: How is the client coping with anxiety? Is the anxiety a function of growth, or is it a function of clinging to neurotic behaviors? Is the anxiety in proportion to the threat to the client's well-being? Does the client demonstrate the courage to allow himself or herself to experience the anxiety of the unknown?

Anxiety is the material for productive therapy sessions in either individual counseling or group work. If clients experienced no anxiety, their motivation for change would be low. Anxiety can be transformed into the needed energy for enduring the risks of experimenting with new behavior. Thus, the existentially oriented therapist can help the client recognize that learning how to tolerate ambiguity and uncertainty and how to live without props can be a necessary phase in the journey from living dependently to becoming a more autonomous person. The therapist and client can explore the possibility that, although breaking away from crippling patterns and building new lifestyles will be fraught with anxiety for a while, as the client experiences more satisfaction with newer ways of being, anxiety will diminish. As clients begin to learn a confidence in self, their anxiety that results from an expectation of catastrophe becomes less.

PROPOSITION 6: AWARENESS OF DEATH AND NONBEING

Awareness of death is a basic human condition that gives significance to living.

The existentialist does not view death negatively. A distinguishing characteristic of the human being is to be able to grasp the concept of the future and the inevitability of death. The very realization of eventual nonbeing gives meaning to existence, because it makes every human act count.

The existentialist contends that life has meaning because it has a time limitation. If we had eternity to actualize our potentials, no urgency would exist. Because of our temporal nature, however, death does jar us into taking life seriously. To deny the inevitability of death limits the possibility of the richness of life. This does not mean that it is healthy to live in constant terror of dying, nor does it mean that we must be preoccupied with death. The message is that, because of our finite nature, the present moment becomes important to us. The present is precious, for it is all we really have.

The fear of death and the fear of life are correlated. The fear of death looms over those of us who are afraid to outstretch our arms and fully embrace life. If we affirm life and attempt to live in the present as fully as possible, however, we are not obsessed with the termination of life. Those of us who fear death also fear life, as though we were saying "We fear death because we have never really lived."

Because some of us are afraid of facing the reality of our own deaths, we might attempt to escape the fact of our eventual nonbeing. However, when we do try to flee from the confrontation with nothingness, we must pay a price. As May (1961) put it, "The price for denying death is undefined anxiety, self-alienation. To completely understand himself, man must confront death, become aware of personal death" (p. 65).

Frankl (1963) agreed with May and taught that death gives meaning to human existence. If we were immortal, we could put off acting forever, but, because we are finite, what we do now takes on special significance.

Counseling implications. I have come to appreciate that dying and living are counterpoints. In order to grow we must be willing to let go of some of our past. Parts of us must die if new dimensions of our being are to emerge. We cannot cling to the neurotic aspects of our past and at the same time expect a more creative side of us to flourish.

One group technique that I have found useful is to ask people to fantasize themselves in the same room with the same people in the group ten years hence. I ask them to imagine that they have not followed through with their decisions and that they have failed to accept opportunities to change themselves in ways they said they most wanted to change. They are to imagine that they have not faced the parts of themselves they fear, that they have not carried out their projects, and that they have chosen to remain as they are rather than take risks. Then I ask them to talk about their lives as if they knew they were going to die. This exercise can mobilize clients to take seriously the time they have, and it can jar them into accepting the possibility that they could accept a zombie-like existence in place of a fuller life.

Summary and evaluation

As humans, according to the existentialist view, we are capable of self-awareness, which is the distinctive capacity that allows us to reflect and to decide. With this awareness we become free beings who are responsible for choosing the way we live our lives, and we thus influence our own destinies. This awareness of freedom and responsibility gives rise to existential anxiety, which is another basic human characteristic. Whether we like it or not, we are free, even though we may seek to avoid reflecting on this freedom. The knowledge that we must choose, even though the outcome is not certain, leads to anxiety. This anxiety is heightened when we reflect on the reality that we are mortal beings. Facing the inevitable prospect of eventual death gives the present moment significance, for we become aware that we do not have forever to accomplish our projects. Our task is to create a life that has meaning and purpose. As humans we are unique in that we strive toward fashioning purpose and values that give meaning to living. Whatever meaning our lives have is developed through freedom and commitment to make choices in the face of uncertainty.

CONTRIBUTIONS OF THE EXISTENTIAL APPROACH

The existential approach has brought back the person into central focus. It has given a picture of people at their highest levels of being. It has shown that people are constantly becoming, and that they are continually actualizing and fulfilling their potential. The existential approach has focused sharply on the central facts of human existence—self-consciousness and the consequent freedom. To the existentialist goes the credit for giving a new view of death as a positive thing, not a morbid prospect to fear, for death gives life its meaning. Further, the existentialist has contributed a new dimension to the understanding of anxiety, guilt, frustration, loneliness, and alienation.

In my judgment, one of the major contributions of the existential approach is its emphasis on the human-to-human quality of the therapeutic relationship. This aspect lessens the chances of dehumanizing psychotherapy by making it a mechanical process. Also, I find the philosophy underlying existential therapy very exciting. I particularly like the emphasis on freedom and responsibility and the person's capacity to redesign his or her life by choosing with awareness. From my viewpoint, this model provides a sound philosophical base on which to build a personal and unique style of the practice of therapy, because it addresses itself to the core struggles of the contemporary person.

Further, this approach relates to the basic assumptions underlying the practice of counseling and psychotherapy—although we possess the freedom to make choices, this freedom is accompanied by a degree of anxiety; indeed, the more freedom we have, the more anxiety we are likely to experience.

As I have written elsewhere (1978), the central thrust of the existential approach implies that we are *not* the passive victims of life, for we *do* make choices and *do* have the power to change major aspects of our lives as we struggle toward a more authentic existence. This notion is captured in the following words:

> As we recognize that we are not merely passive victims of our circumstances, we can consciously become the architects of our lives. Even though others may have drawn the blueprints, we can recognize the plan, take a stand, and change the design [Corey, 1978, p. 3].

LIMITATIONS OF THE EXISTENTIAL APPROACH

A major criticism often aimed at this approach is that it lacks a systematic statement of the principles and practices of psychotherapy. It is also frequently criticized for lacking rigor in methodology. Some accuse it of mystical language and concepts, and some object to it as a fad based on a reaction against the scientific approach. Those who prefer a counseling practice based on research would contend that the concepts should be empirically sound, that definitions should be operational, that the hypotheses should be testable, and that therapeutic practice should be based on the results of research on both the process and outcomes of counseling.

Another basic limitation that I see in the existential approach is that many of its concepts are quite abstract and difficult to apply in therapeutic practice. Existential theorists such as Sartre, Kierkegaard, Nietzsche, and Heidegger were not writing for practicing counselors and therapists! Both beginning and advanced practitioners who are not of a philosophical turn of mind tend to find many of the existential concepts lofty and elusive. And those counselors who do find themselves close to this philosophy are often at a loss when they attempt to apply it to practice. As we have seen, this approach stresses understanding clients first and holds that techniques follow. The fact that few techniques are generated by this approach makes it essential for practitioners to develop their own innovative procedures or to borrow from other schools of therapy.

Finally, I think that, although this model has much to offer people who function socially and psychologically at a relatively high level, it has limitations in its applicability to clients who function at low levels, to those in crisis states, and often to the poor. But, even though the existential approach may be inappropriate for working with the seriously disturbed, R. D. Laing (1965, 1967) has used this method to successfully treat schizophrenic patients. Laing's positive results provide one further indication that the existential process could help all patients. Practitioners can treat people in humane ways that are in keeping with this model, while at the same time drawing on some of the more active/directive intervention methods to meet the unique needs of these clients.

Questions for reflection and discussion

Because the existential approach to counseling and psychotherapy is based on a philosophy of the human condition and on the encounter between the client and the therapist, it would be well to ask yourself some of the basic questions that your clients may struggle with in therapy. Most of the issues underlying the questions deal with personal freedom and responsibility and the anxiety that is the result of choosing for oneself. I assume that as counselors and therapists we cannot help clients come to grips with those issues unless we have faced them in our own lives.

1. What does personal freedom mean to you? Do you believe that you are what you are now largely as a result of your choices, or do you believe that you are the product of your circumstances?
2. As you reflect on some critical turning points in your life, what decisions appear to have been crucial to your present development?
3. Are you able to accept and exercise your own freedom and make significant decisions alone? Do you attempt to escape from freedom and responsibility? Are you inclined to give up some of your autonomy for the security of being taken care of by others?
4. Do you agree that basically each person is alone? What are the implications for counseling practice? In what ways have you attempted to avoid your experience of aloneness?
5. What is your experience with anxiety? Does your anxiety result from the consideration that you must choose for yourself, the realization that you are alone, the fact that you will die, and the realization that you must create your own meaning and purpose in life? How have you dealt with anxiety in your own life?
6. Do you believe that, unless you take death seriously, life has little meaning?
7. What are some specific things that you value most? What would your life be like without them? What gives your life meaning and a sense of purpose?
8. Have you experienced an "existential vacuum"? Is your life at times without substance, depth, and meaning? What is this experience of emptiness like for you, and how do you cope with it?
9. Do you believe that anxiety is a motivational force toward growth and that personal growth and change usually entail anxiety? What are the implications for the practice of counseling?
10. What is your concept of a self-actualizing person? In what specific areas of your life do you experience a gap between the way you actually see yourself and the way you would like to experience yourself?

Recommended supplementary readings

In my classes I typically highly recommend *Man's Search for Himself* (May, 1953), *Man's Search for Meaning* (Frankl, 1963), and *The Transparent Self* (Jourard, 1971) as good places to start for those students who want to learn more about the key themes of this therapeutic approach.

Humanistic Psychology (Shaffer, 1978) is a clear and brief description of humanistic concepts and existential themes, with applications to counseling.

I Never Knew I Had a Choice (Corey, 1978) is written from an existential viewpoint, with applications for counseling practice. It deals with such themes as autonomy, love, sex, intimacy, making choices, loneliness and solitude, death and loss, the search for meaning and values, work and the meaning of life, and developing a philosophy to live by. The book contains many exercises and activities for personal reflection on choices you have made; it also has numerous annotated suggestions for further reading in each of these areas.

References and suggested readings

Books highly recommended as supplementary reading are marked with an asterisk.

* Arbuckle, D. *Counseling and psychotherapy: An existential-humanistic view.* Boston: Allyn & Bacon, 1975.

Buber, M. *I and thou* (W. Kaufman, trans.). New York: Scribner's, 1970.

* Bugental, J. F. T. *The search for authenticity: An existential-analytic approach to psychotherapy.* New York: Holt, Rinehart & Winston, 1965.

* Bugental, J. (Ed.). *Challenges of humanistic psychology.* New York: McGraw-Hill, 1967.

* Buhler, C., & Allen, M. *Introduction to humanistic psychology.* Monterey, Calif.: Brooks/Cole, 1972.

Camus, A. *The stranger.* New York: Random House, 1942.

Corey, G. *I never knew I had a choice.* Monterey, Calif.: Brooks/Cole, 1978.

Corey, G. *Theory and practice of group counseling.* Monterey, Calif.: Brooks/Cole, 1981.

Corey, G. *Case approach to counseling and psychotherapy.* Monterey, Calif.: Brooks/Cole, 1982.

Corlis, R., & Rabe, P. *Psychotherapy from the center: A humanistic view of change and of growth.* Scranton, Pa.: International Textbook, 1969.

Fabry, J. *The pursuit of meaning.* Boston: Beacon Press, 1968.

Frankl, V. *Man's search for meaning.* New York: Washington Square Press, 1963.

Frankl, V. *The doctor and the soul.* New York: Bantam, 1965.

* Friedman, M. (Ed.). *The worlds of existentialism: A critical reader.* Chicago: University of Chicago Press, 1973.

Greening, T. (Ed.). *Existential-humanistic psychology.* Monterey, Calif.: Brooks/Cole, 1971.

Heidegger, M. *Being and time.* New York: Harper & Row, 1962.

Hodge, M. *Your fear of love.* New York: Doubleday, 1967.

Jourard, S. *Disclosing man to himself.* New York: Van Nostrand Reinhold, 1968.

Jourard, S. *The transparent self* (Rev. ed.). New York: Van Nostrand Reinhold, 1971.

Keen, E. *Three faces of being: Toward an existential clinical psychology.* New York: Appleton-Century-Crofts, 1970.

Kemp, C. G. Existential counseling. *The Counseling Psychologist,* 1971, *2*(3), 2–30.

Kierkegaard, S. *The concept of dread.* Princeton, N.J.: Princeton University Press, 1944.

Kockelmans, J. J. (Ed.). *Phenomenology: The philosophy of Edmund Husserl and its interpretation.* New York: Doubleday, 1967.

* Kübler-Ross, E. *On death and dying.* New York: Macmillan, 1969.

Kübler-Ross, E. *Death: The final stages of growth.* Englewood Cliffs, N.J.: Prentice-Hall, 1975.

Laing, R. D. *The divided self.* Baltimore, Maryland: Pelican, 1965.

Laing, R. D. *The politics of experience.* New York: Ballantine, 1967.

Mahrer, A. R. *Experiencing: A humanistic theory of psychology and psychiatry.* New York: Brunner/Mazel, 1978.

Maslow, A. *Toward a psychology of being* (Rev. ed.). New York: Van Nostrand Reinhold, 1968.

* Maslow, A. *Motivation and personality* (Rev. ed.). New York: Harper & Row, 1970.

Maslow, A. *The farther reaches of human nature.* New York: Viking, 1971.

May, R. *Man's search for himself.* New York: Dell (Delta), 1953.

* May, R. (Ed.). *Existential psychology.* New York: Random House, 1961.

May, R. *Psychology and the human dilemma.* New York: Van Nostrand Reinhold, 1967.

May, R. *Love and will.* New York: Norton, 1969.

May, R. & Ellenberger, H. F. (Eds.). *Existence: A new dimension in psychiatry and psychology.* New York: Basic Books, 1958.

McWaters, B. (Ed.). *Humanistic perspectives: Current trends in psychology.* Monterey, Calif.: Brooks/Cole, 1977.

* Moustakas, C. *Loneliness and love.* Englewood Cliffs, N.J.: Prentice-Hall, 1972.

Moustakas, C. *The touch of loneliness.* Englewood Cliffs, N.J.: Prentice-Hall, 1975.

Perls, F. *Gestalt therapy verbatim.* Moab, Utah: Real People Press, 1969.

Riesman, D., Reuel, D., & Glazer, N. *The lonely crowd.* New Haven, Conn.: Yale University Press, 1950.

Rogers, C. *On becoming a person.* Boston: Houghton Mifflin, 1961.

Russell, J. M. Sartre, therapy, and expanding the concept of responsibility. *The American Journal of Psychoanalysis,* 1978, *38,* 259–269. (a)

Russell, J. M. Saying, feeling, and self-deception. *Behaviorism,* 1978, *6*(1), 27–43. (b)

Russell, J. M. Sartre's theory of sexuality. *Journal of Humanistic Psychology,* 1979, *19*(2), 35–45.

Sartre, J.-P. *No exit.* New York: Knopf, 1946.

Sartre, J.-P. *Being and nothingness.* New York: Bantam, 1971.

Severin, F. *Discovering man in psychology: A humanistic approach.* New York: McGraw-Hill, 1973.

Shaffer, B. P. *Humanistic psychology.* Englewood Cliffs, N.J.: Prentice-Hall, 1978.

Stevens, J. *Awareness: Exploring, experimenting, and experiencing.* Moab, Utah: Real People Press, 1971.

Sutich, A., & Vich, M. *Readings in humanistic psychology.* New York: Free Press, 1969.

Tillich, P. *The courage to be.* New Haven, Conn.: Yale University Press, 1952.

Valle, R. S., & King, M. (Eds.). *Existential-phenomenological alternatives for psychology.* New York: Oxford University Press, 1978.

Van Kaam, A. Counseling and psychotherapy from the viewpoint of existential psychology. In D. Arbuckle (Ed.), *Counseling and psychotherapy: An overview.* New York: McGraw-Hill, 1967.

5

Person-Centered Therapy

Introduction

The person-centered approach, like Gestalt therapy, which follows it in this text, can be considered a humanistic branch of the existential perspective presented in the last chapter. In the early 1940s Carl Rogers developed what was known as *nondirective counseling* as a reaction against the directive and traditional psychoanalytic approaches to individual therapy. Rogers caused a great furor when he challenged the basic assumption that "the counselor knows best." He also challenged the validity of commonly accepted therapeutic procedures such as advice, suggestion, counselor direction, persuasion, teaching, diagnosis, and interpretation. His basic assumptions were that people are essentially trustworthy, that they have a vast potential for understanding themselves and resolving their own problems without direct intervention on the therapist's part, and that they are capable of growth toward self-direction if they are involved in a therapeutic relationship. From the beginning Rogers emphasized the attitudes and personal characteristics of the therapist and the quality of the client/therapist relationship as the prime determinants of the outcome of the therapeutic process. He consistently relegated to a secondary position matters such as the therapist's knowledge of theory and techniques.

Rogers's early interests (1942) were in the practice of individual counseling and psychotherapy. He later developed a systematic theory of personality and applied this self theory to the practice of counseling individuals, which led him to rename his approach *client-centered therapy* (Rogers, 1951). During the next decade he and his associates continued to test the underlying hypotheses of the client-centered approach by conducting extensive research on both the process and the outcomes of psychotherapy. On the basis of this research the approach was further refined (Rogers, 1961).

Client-centered therapy, which originally implied that people seeking psychological assistance were treated as responsible clients with the power to direct their own lives, gradually extended its sphere of influence into a variety of fields far from its point of origin. Client-centered philosophy was applied to education and was called student-centered teaching/learning (Rogers, 1969). In the 1960s and 1970s Rogers did a great deal to spearhead the development of personal-growth groups, and he applied his ideas to the basic encounter group with many types of populations (Rogers, 1970). His influence spread to working with couples and families (Rogers, 1972); and his ideas were also applied to administration, minority groups, interracial and intercultural groups, and international relationships (Rogers, 1977). Because of his ever-widening scope of influence, and especially his recent interest in the politics of power—how people obtain, possess, share, or surrender *power* and *control* over others and themselves—as it applies to the therapeutic relationship, this approach has become known as the *person-centered approach*. Rogers describes further how his approach to therapy has become person-centered.

> This new construct has had a powerful influence on me. It has caused me to take a fresh look at my professional life work. I've had a role in initiating the person-centered approach. This view developed first in counseling and psychotherapy, where it was known as client-centered, meaning a person seeking help was not treated as a dependent patient but as a responsible client. Extended to education, it was called student-centered teaching. As it has moved into a wide variety of fields, far from its point of origin—intensive groups, marriage, family relationships, administration, minority groups, interracial, intercultural, and even international relationships—it seems best to adopt as broad a term as possible: person-centered [Rogers, 1977, p. 5].

Key concepts

VIEW OF HUMAN NATURE

There is a consistent theme that forms the underpinnings of most of Rogers's writings—a deep faith in the tendency of humans to develop in a positive and constructive manner *if* a climate of respect and trust is established. Rogers has little sympathy for systems based on the assumption that the individual cannot be trusted and instead needs to be directed, motivated, instructed, punished, rewarded, controlled, and managed by others who are in a superior and "expert" position. He has consistently maintained that there are three conditions for releasing a growth-promoting climate in which individuals can move forward and become what they are capable of becoming. These conditions are (1) genuineness, or realness; (2) acceptance, or caring; and (3) deep understanding. If these attitudes are communicated by the helper to the one helped, Rogers postulates, these people will become less defensive and more open to the experience within themselves and in their world—and they will behave in ways that are social and constructive.

This positive view of human nature has significant implications for the practice of therapy. Because of the philosophical view that the individual has an inherent capacity to move away from maladjustment toward psychological health, the therapist places the primary responsibility on the client. The person-centered model rejects the roles of the therapist as the authority who knows best and of the passive client who merely follows the dictates of the therapist. Therapy is thus rooted in the client's capacity for awareness and the ability to make decisions.

CHARACTERISTICS OF THE PERSON-CENTERED APPROACH

Rogers has not presented the person-centered theory as a fixed and completed approach to therapy. He has hoped that others will view his theory as a set of tentative principles relating to how the therapy process develops, not as dogma. Rogers and Wood (1974, pp. 213–214) described the characteristics that distinguish the person-centered approach from other models. An adaptation of this description follows.

The person-centered approach focuses on the client's responsibility and capacity to discover ways to more fully encounter reality. Clients, who know themselves best, are the ones to discover more appropriate behavior for themselves.

The person-centered approach emphasizes the phenomenal world of the client. With accurate empathy and an attempt to apprehend the client's internal frame of reference, therapists concern themselves mainly with the client's perception of self and of the world.

The same principles of psychotherapy apply to all persons—"normals," "neurotics," and "psychotics." Based on the view that the urge to move toward psychological maturity is deeply rooted in human nature, the principles of person-centered therapy apply to those who function at relatively normal levels as well as to those who experience a greater degree of psychological maladjustment.

According to the person-centered approach, psychotherapy is only one example of a constructive personal relationship. Clients experience psychotherapeutic growth in and through the relationship with another person who helps them do what they cannot do alone. It is the relationship with a counselor who is congruent (matching external behavior and expression with internal feelings and thoughts), accepting, and empathic that brings about therapeutic change for the client.

Rogers proposes the hypothesis that certain attitudes on the therapist's part (genuineness, nonpossessive warmth and acceptance, and accurate empathy) constitute the necessary and sufficient conditions for therapeutic effectiveness. Person-centered theory holds that the therapist's function is to be immediately present and accessible to the client and to focus on the here-and-now experience created by their relationship.

Perhaps more than any other single approach to psychotherapy, person-centered theory has developed through research on the process and outcomes of therapy. The theory is not a closed one but one that has grown through years of counseling observations, and that continues to change as new research yields increased understanding of human nature and the therapeutic process.

Thus, person-centered therapy is not a set of techniques or a dogma. Rooted in a set of attitudes and beliefs that the therapist demonstrates, it is perhaps best characterized as a way of being and as a shared journey in which both therapist and client reveal their humanness and participate in a growth experience.

A major characteristic of the person-centered approach is its emphasis on the inner strength of individuals and the revolutionary impact of this strength. According to Rogers (1977), there are significant political implications of this point of view, for person-centered practitioners are involved in revolutionizing traditional behaviors of the members of the helping professions. Power and control are given to the client. Rogers (1977) put this issue into perspective:

> The politics of the client-centered approach is a conscious renunciation and avoidance by the therapist of all control over, or decision-making for, the client. It is the facilitation of self-ownership by the client and the strategies by which this can be achieved; the ... locus of decision-making and the responsibility for the effects of these decisions. ... is politically centered in the client [p. 14].

According to Rogers (1977), there are several implications of this shift in power:

- Regardless of one's orientation, one can be effective by being person-centered.
- The focus on persons renders the question of diagnosis unimportant.
- The medical model of therapy and the person-centered approach are mainly at odds.
- The more the person-centered approach is practiced, the more hierarchical methods of organization—the designation of control and power to individuals at the top of a system's hierarchy—are challenged.
- The effectiveness of the person-centered approach challenges and threatens many professional groups, because of its revolutionary impact.

The therapeutic process

THERAPEUTIC GOALS

The therapeutic aims of the person-centered approach are different from those of traditional approaches. The person-centered approach aims toward a greater degree of independence and integration of the individual. The focus is on the person, not on the person's presenting problem. In Rogers's view (1977) the aim of therapy is not merely to solve problems. Rather, it is to assist clients in their growth process, so that they can better cope with problems they are now facing and with future problems.

Rogers (1961) wrote that people who enter psychotherapy are often asking: How can I discover my real self? How can I become what I deeply wish to become? How can I get behind my facades and become myself?

The underlying aim of therapy is to provide a climate conducive to helping the individual become a fully functioning person. Before clients are able to work toward that goal, they must first get behind the masks they wear, which they develop through the process of socialization. Clients come to recognize that they have lost contact with themselves by using these facades. In a climate of safety in the therapeutic session, they also come to realize that there are other possibilities.

When the facades are worn away during the therapeutic process, what kind of person emerges from behind the pretenses? Rogers (1961) described the characteristics of the person who is becoming increasingly actualized: (1) an openness to experience, (2) a trust in one's organism, (3) an internal locus of evaluation, and (4) the willingness to be a process. These characteristics constitute the basic goals of person-centered therapy.

Openness to experience. Openness to experience entails seeing reality without distorting it to fit a preconceived self-structure. The opposite of defensiveness, openness implies becoming more aware of reality as it exists outside oneself. It also means that one's beliefs are not rigid; one can remain open to further knowledge and growth and can tolerate ambiguity. One has an awareness of oneself in the present moment and the capacity to experience oneself in fresh ways.

Trust in one's organism. One goal of therapy is to help clients establish a sense of trust in themselves. In the initial stages of therapy clients often trust themselves and their own decisions very little. They typically seek advice and answers outside themselves, for they basically do not trust their capacity to direct their own life. As clients become more open to their experiences, their sense of trust in self begins to emerge.

An internal locus of evaluation. Related to self-trust, an internal locus of evaluation means looking more to oneself for the answers to the problems of existence. Instead of looking outside for validation of personhood, one increasingly pays attention to one's own center. One substitutes self-approval for the universal approval of others. One decides one's own standards of behavior and looks to oneself for the decisions and choices to live by.

Willingness to be a process. The conception of self in the *process of becoming,* as opposed to the self as a *product,* is crucial. Although clients might enter therapy seeking some kind of formula for building a successful and happy state (an end product), they come to realize that growth is a continuing process. Rather than being fixed entities, clients are in a fluid process of challenging their perceptions and beliefs and opening themselves to new experiences and revisions.

These characteristics provide a general framework for understanding the direction of therapeutic movement. The therapist does not choose specific goals for the client. The cornerstone of person-centered theory is the view that clients in relationship with a facilitating therapist have the capacity to define and clarify their own goals. Many counselors, however, experience difficulty in allowing clients to decide for themselves their specific goals in therapy. Although it is easy to give lip service to the concept of clients' finding their own way, it takes considerable respect for clients and courage on the therapist's part to encourage clients to listen to themselves and follow their own directions—particularly when they make choices that are not what the therapist hoped for.

THERAPIST'S FUNCTION AND ROLE

The role of person-centered therapists is rooted in their ways of being and attitudes, not in techniques designed to get the client to "do something." Research on person-centered therapy seems to indicate that the attitudes of therapists, rather than their knowledge, theories, or techniques, initiate personality change in the client. Basically, therapists use themselves as an instrument of change. When they encounter the client on a person-to-person level, their "role" is to be without roles. Their function is to establish a therapeutic climate that facilitates the client's growth along a process continuum.

The person-centered therapist thus creates a helping relationship in which clients experience the necessary freedom to explore areas of their life that are now either denied to awareness or distorted. They become less defensive and more open to possibilities within themselves and in the world.

First and foremost, the therapist must be willing to be real in the relationship with a client. Instead of perceiving clients in preconceived diagnostic categories, the therapist meets them on a moment-to-moment experiential basis and helps them by entering their world. Through the therapist's attitudes of genuine caring, respect, acceptance, and understanding, they are able to loosen their defenses and rigid perceptions and move to a higher level of personal functioning.

CLIENT'S EXPERIENCE IN THERAPY

With the person-centered model, therapeutic change depends on the clients' perception both of their own experience in therapy and of the counselor's basic attitudes. If the counselor creates a climate conducive to self-exploration, then clients have the opportunity to experience and explore the full range of their feelings, many of which may be denied to their awareness at the outset of therapy. What follows is a general sketch of the experience of the client in therapy.

Clients come to the counselor in a state of incongruence; that is, a discrepancy exists between their self-perception and their experience in reality. For example, a college student may see himself as a future physician, and yet his below-average grades might exclude him from medical school. The discrepancy between how he sees himself (self-concept) or how he would *like* to view himself (ideal-self-concept) and the reality of his poor academic performance might result in anxiety and personal vulnerability, which can provide the necessary motivation to enter therapy. This client must perceive that a problem exists, or at least that he is uncomfortable enough with his present psychological adjustment to want to explore possibilities for change.

Clients initially may expect the counselor to provide answers and direction or view the counselor as the expert who can provide magical solutions. One of the reasons clients seek therapy is the feeling of basic helplessness, powerlessness, and inability to make decisions or effectively direct their own lives. They may hope to find "the way" through the teachings of the therapist. Within the person-centered framework, however, they soon learn that they are responsible for themselves in the relationship and that they can learn to be freer by using the relationship to gain greater self-understanding.

During the beginning stages of therapy, clients' behavior and feelings might be characterized by extremely rigid beliefs and attitudes, much internal blockage, a lack of centeredness, a sense of being out of touch with their own feelings, an unwillingness to communicate deeper levels of the self, a fear of intimacy, a basic distrust of the self, a sense of fragmentation, and a tendency to externalize feelings and problems, just to mention a few. In the therapeutic climate created by the counselor, clients are able to explore in a safe and trusting environment the hidden aspects of their personal world. The therapist's own realness, unconditional acceptance of their feelings, and ability to assume their internal frame of reference allow them gradually to peel away layers of defenses and come to terms with what is behind the facades.

As therapy progresses, clients are able to explore a wider range of their feelings. Now they can express fears, anxiety, guilt, shame, hatred, anger, and other feelings that they had deemed too negative to accept and incorporate into the self-structure. Now they constrict less, distort less, and move to a greater degree of willingness to accept and integrate some conflicting and confusing feelings related to self. Gradually, they discover aspects, negative and positive, of the self that had been kept hidden. They move in the direction of being more open to all experience, less defensive, more in contact with what they feel at the present moment, less bound by the past, less determined, freer to make decisions, and increasingly trusting in themselves to effectively manage their own life. In short, their experience in therapy is like throwing off the deterministic shackles that had kept them in a psychological prison. With increased freedom they tend to become more mature psychologically and more actualized.

RELATIONSHIP BETWEEN THERAPIST AND CLIENT

Rogers (1961) summarized the basic hypothesis of person-centered therapy in one sentence: "If I can provide a certain type of relationship, the other person will discover within himself the capacity to use that relationship for growth and change, and personal development will occur" (p. 33). Rogers (1967) hypothesized further that "significant positive personality change does not occur except in a relationship" (p. 73).

What are the characteristics of the therapeutic relationship? What are the key attitudes of the person-centered therapist that are conducive to creating a suitable psychological climate in which the client will experience the freedom necessary to initiate personality change? According to Rogers (1967), the following six conditions are necessary and sufficient for personality changes to occur:

1. Two persons are in psychological contact.
2. The first, whom we shall term the client, is in a state of incongruence, being vulnerable or anxious.
3. The second person, whom we shall term the therapist, is congruent or integrated in the relationship.
4. The therapist experiences unconditional positive regard for the client.
5. The therapist experiences an empathic understanding of the client's internal frame of reference and endeavors to communicate this experience to the client.
6. The communication to the client of the therapist's empathic understanding and unconditional positive regard is to a minimal degree achieved [p. 73].

Rogers hypothesized that no other conditions are necessary. If the six conditions exist over some period of time, then constructive personality change will occur. The conditions do not vary according to client type. Further, they are necessary and sufficient for all approaches to therapy and apply to all personal relationships, not just to psychotherapy. The therapist need not have any specialized knowledge. Accurate psychological diagnosis is not necessary and may more often than not interfere with effective psychotherapy. Rogers admits that his theory is striking and radical. His formulation has generated considerable controversy, for Rogers asserts that many conditions that other therapists commonly regard as necessary for effective psychotherapy are nonessential.

It is important to note that through the therapeutic relationship the therapist often grows and changes as much as the client. Thus, the power of the relationship that Rogers describes influences *both* the therapist and the client.

From Rogers's perspective (1977) the client/therapist relationship is characterized by a sense of equality, for therapists do not keep their knowledge a secret or attempt to mystify the therapeutic process. The process of change in the client depends to a large degree on the quality of this equal relationship. As clients experience the therapist listening in an accepting way to them, they gradually learn how to listen acceptingly to themselves. As they find the therapist caring for and valuing them (even the aspects that have been hidden and regarded as negative), they begin to see worth and value in themselves. As they experience the realness of the therapist, they drop many of their pretenses and are real with both themselves and the therapist.

Three personal characteristics, or attitudes, of the therapist form a central part of the therapeutic relationship: (1) congruence, or genuineness, (2) unconditional positive regard, and (3) accurate empathic understanding.

Congruence, or genuineness.

Of the three characteristics, congruence is the most important, according to Rogers's recent writings. Congruence implies that therapists are real; that is, they are genuine, integrated, and authentic during the therapy hour. They are without a false front, their inner experience and outer expression of that experience match, and they can openly express feelings and attitudes that are present in the relationship with the client. Authentic therapists are spontaneous and openly *being* the feelings and attitudes, both negative and positive, that flow in them. By expressing (and accepting) any negative feelings, they can facilitate honest communication with the client.

Through authenticity therapists serve as a model of a human being struggling toward greater realness. Being congruent might necessitate the expression of anger, frustration, liking, attraction, concern, boredom, annoyance, and a range of other feelings in the relationship. This does not mean that therapists should impulsively share all feelings, for self-disclosure must also be appropriate. Nor does it imply that the client is the cause of the therapist's boredom or anger. Therapists must, however, take responsibility for their own feelings and explore with the client persistent feelings that block their ability to be fully present with the client.

The goal of therapy is not, of course, for therapists to continually discuss their own feelings with the client. Person-centered therapy does, however, stress the value of a nonexploitive, authentic, personal relationship and the potential value of open and honest reactions when meaningful communication is blocked. It also stresses that counseling will be inhibited if the counselor feels one way about the client but acts in a different way. Hence, if the counselor either dislikes or disapproves of the client but feigns acceptance, therapy will not work.

Rogers's concept of congruence does not imply that only a fully self-actualized therapist can be effective in counseling. Because therapists are human, they cannot be expected to be fully authentic. The person-centered model assumes that, if therapists are congruent in the relationship with the client, then the process of therapy will get under way. Congruence exists on a continuum rather than on an all-or-none basis.

Unconditional positive regard and acceptance.

The second attitude that therapists need to communicate to the client is a deep and genuine caring for him or her as a person. The caring is unconditional, in that it is not contaminated by evaluation or judgment of the client's feelings, thoughts, and behavior as good or bad. Therapists value and warmly accept the client without placing stipulations on the acceptance. It is not an attitude of "I'll accept you when"; rather, it is one of "I'll accept you as you are." Therapists communicate through their behavior that they value the client as the client is and that he or she is free to have feelings and experiences without risking the loss of the therapist's acceptance. Acceptance is the recognition of the client's right to have feelings; it is not the approval of all behavior. All overt behavior need not be approved of or accepted.

It is important also that therapists' caring be nonpossessive. If the caring stems from their own needs to be liked and appreciated, the change in the client is inhibited.

Unconditional positive regard does not imply an all-or-none characteristic. Like congruence, it is a matter of degree on a continuum.

According to Rogers (1977), research indicates that, the greater the degree of caring, prizing, accepting, and valuing the client in a nonpossessive way, the greater the chance that therapy will be successful. He also made it clear that it is not possible for therapists to genuinely feel acceptance and unconditional caring at all times. Apparently Rogers was not saying that therapists should have *unconditional* positive regard for their clients. Nevertheless, "It is simply a fact that unless this is a reasonably frequent ingredient in the relationship, constructive client change is less likely" (p. 10).

One implication of this emphasis on acceptance of the client is that therapists who have little respect for their clients or an active dislike or disgust can anticipate that their work will not be fruitful. Clients will sense this lack of regard and become increasingly defensive.

Accurate empathic understanding.   One of the main tasks of the therapist is to understand sensitively and accurately clients' experience and feelings as they are revealed during the moment-to-moment interaction during the therapy session. The therapist strives to sense clients' subjective experience, particularly the here-and-now experience. The aim of empathic understanding is to encourage them to get closer to themselves, to experience feelings more deeply and intensely, and to recognize and resolve the incongruity that exists within them.

The concept implies that the therapist will sense clients' feelings as if they were his or her own without becoming lost in those feelings. By moving freely in the world as experienced by clients, the therapist not only can communicate to them an understanding of what is already known to them but can also voice meanings of experience of which they are only dimly aware. It is important to understand that high levels of accurate empathy go beyond recognition of obvious feelings to a sense of the less obvious and less clearly experienced feelings of clients. The therapist helps them expand their awareness of feelings that are only partially recognized.

Empathy is more than a mere reflection of feeling. It entails more than reflecting content to the client, and it is more than an artificial technique that the therapist routinely uses. It is not simply objective knowledge ("I understand what your problem is"), which is an evaluative understanding *about* the client from the outside. Instead, empathy is a deep and subjective understanding *of* the client *with* the client. It is a sense of personal identification with the client. Therapists are able to share the client's subjective world by tuning into their own feelings that might be like the client's feelings. Yet therapists must not lose their own separateness. Rogers believes that, when therapists can grasp the present experiencing of the client's private world, as the client sees and feels it, without losing the separateness of their own identity, then constructive change is likely to occur.

As do the other two characteristics, accurate empathic understanding exists on a continuum; it is not an all-or-nothing matter. The greater the degree of therapist empathy, the greater the chance that the client will move forward in therapy.

Extensions of Rogers's core therapeutic attitudes.   Other writers have built on the foundation laid by Rogers, adding other core therapeutic conditions. These authors focus on specific behaviors of counselors as well as their attitudes. Carkhuff (1969), Egan (1975), and Ivey and Authier (1978) have developed an approach to the training of counselors that is based in part on Rogers's philosophy and also includes an emphasis on systematic skills. These writers add dimensions such as levels of empathy, counselor self-disclosure, immediacy, concreteness, and confrontation. Each of these dimensions of the therapeutic process will now be briefly considered:

Levels of Empathy. As I mentioned earlier, Rogers defines empathy as grasping the subjective world of the client and communicating this deep understanding to the client. Carkhuff (1969) and Egan (1975) contended that this basic level of empathy is essential, yet it is not enough. Thus, Carkhuff wrote of "additive dimensions" and Egan described "advanced accurate empathy"—both of which involve steps beyond basic empathy.

Egan (1975) described stage 1 of the counseling process as a focus on assuming the client's subjective frame of reference (basic empathy and responding). At this level the counselor tries to understand clients' feelings, experiences, and behaviors from their own vantage point. At stage 2, however, there is a shift from a subjective to an *objective* level of understanding. At this stage of *advanced accurate empathy* the counselor not only communicates his or her understanding of the client but also employs various techniques to facilitate a deeper level of self-exploration. The counselor uses focused summaries of what clients have said, helps them to see the larger picture by putting their experiences into perspective, helps them find patterns in their behavior and give meaning to these themes, and suggests alternate frames of reference by which they can consider their behavior in a different light. According to Egan, advanced accurate empathy places demands on clients—that they look at themselves on a deeper level, and that they begin to consider courses of action. These demands are made within the climate of genuine care, concern, and respect for the clients.

Counselor Self-Disclosure. Part of stage 2 of the counseling process as described by Egan (1975) involves the counselor's disclosure of his or her reactions in therapy. In discussing the values of this self-disclosure Egan mentioned modeling for the client, being a positive social influence, reducing role distances, increasing the counselor's ability to *work with* clients, and creating a genuine relationship. This kind of disclosure should serve the needs and interests of clients, and as such it should not burden them or hinder them in exploring and understanding themselves more fully. Thus, the quality and timing of counselor self-disclosure are critical. Further, self-disclosure should help clients focus in a clearer and more concrete way on their areas of ineffective living and the resources they can draw on to enhance their lives.

Immediacy. Immediacy is a form of self-disclosure that relates to what is going on in the here-and-now of the client/counselor relationship. It tends to be the most important and powerful kind of disclosure that a counselor can make to a client. Referring to immediacy as "you-me talk," Egan (1975) pointed out that direct, mutual talk is called for when counselors become aware that they or their clients have *unverbalized* thoughts and feelings about what is occurring during sessions, especially if this material is interfering with progress. This immediate talk is especially called for in relation to trust, dependency, counterdependency, boredom, aimlessness, and strong feelings of attraction or dislike. Carkhuff (1969) suggested that counselors think about what clients are trying, in an indirect way, to express. It takes skill and sensitivity to pick up the verbal and nonverbal behavior of clients and help them find more direct avenues of expression.

Concreteness. Whereas Rogers does not discuss concreteness, Carkhuff (1969), Egan (1975), and Ivey and Authier (1978) stressed the importance of this dimension in the counseling process. Concreteness means being specific in discussing one's concerns, feelings, thoughts, and actions. Without this specificity, clients may ramble on vaguely and generally, and much of the intensity of the session is lost. It becomes the counselor's task to help clients become aware that their communication lacks concreteness and to help them convert vague statements about themselves into concrete expressions.

Confrontation. Person-centered counselors sometimes overemphasize support, almost to the exclusion of being challenging. According to Carkhuff (1969), Egan (1975), and Ivey and Authier (1978), effectiveness includes developing the skill of confronting clients in a therapeutic manner, which is done out of caring and in a supportive climate. This is not an attack on clients; rather, it can be an *invitation* for people to take a closer look at discrepancies between attitudes, thoughts, or behaviors. Confrontation that is done in a tentative (yet direct and honest) manner can be an extension of caring and respect for clients. It can encourage them to examine certain incongruities and to become aware of some of the ways that they might be blocking their personal strengths.

Application: Therapeutic techniques and procedures

As Rogers's view of psychotherapy developed, its focus shifted away from therapeutic techniques toward the therapist's personhood, beliefs, and attitudes and toward the therapeutic relationship. The therapeutic relationship, then, is the critical variable, not what the therapist says or does. In the person-centered framework, the "techniques" are expressing and communicating acceptance, respect, and understanding and sharing with the client the attempt to develop an internal frame of reference by thinking, feeling, and exploring. The therapist's use of techniques as gimmicks would depersonalize the relationship. The techniques must be an honest expression of the therapist; they cannot be used self-consciously, for then the counselor would not be genuine.

PERIODS OF DEVELOPMENT OF PERSON-CENTERED THERAPY

To give you an understanding of the place of techniques in the person-centered approach, the following discussion outlines the evolution of Rogers's theory. Hart (1970) divided the development into three phases:

Period 1 (1940–1950): Nondirective psychotherapy. This approach emphasized the therapist's creation of a permissive and noninterventive climate. Acceptance and clarification were the main techniques. Through nondirective therapy clients would achieve insight into themselves and into their life situation.

Period 2 (1950–1957): Reflective psychotherapy. The therapist mainly reflected the feelings of the client and avoided threat in the relationship. Through reflective therapy the client was able to develop a greater degree of congruence between self-concept and ideal self-concept.

Period 3 (1957–1970): Experiential therapy. The therapist's wide range of behavior to express basic attitudes characterizes this approach. Therapy focuses on the client's experiencing and the expression of the therapist's experiencing. The client grows on a continuum by learning to use immediate experiencing.*

In the earliest period, the nondirective therapist conspicuously avoided interaction with the client. The therapist functioned as a clarifier but submerged his or her own personhood. During this period directive techniques such as questioning, probing, evaluating, and interpreting and directive procedures such as taking a case history, psychological testing, and diagnosis were not a part of the therapeutic process, because they were based on external reference points; therapy relied mainly on the innate growth urge of the client.

Later, therapy shifted away from the cognitive emphasis to clarification, which was to lead to insight. The reflective therapist's emphasis was on responding sensitively to the affective, rather than semantic, meaning of the client's expression (Hart, 1970, p. 8). The therapist's role was reformulated and elaborated to emphasize his or her responsiveness to the client's feelings. Instead of merely clarifying clients' comments, the therapist reflected feelings. To implement clients' reorganization of self-concepts, the therapist's basic job was to remove sources of threat from the therapeutic relationship and function as a mirror so that clients might better understand their own world (Hart, 1970). The therapist as a person was still largely left out of this formulation.

The next period, of experiential therapy, emphasized certain "necessary and sufficient" conditions for personality change to occur. This period introduced the crucial elements of the therapist's attitudes of congruence, positive regard and acceptance, and empathic understanding as prerequisites to effective therapy. The focus of the approach shifted from reflection of the client's feelings to the therapist's expression of his or her own immediate feelings in relationship with the client. The current formulation allows for a wider range and greater flexibility of therapist behavior, including expressions or opinions, feelings, and so forth that in earlier periods were undesirable.

The focus on therapists' immediate experiencing leads them to express their feelings to the client when appropriate, and it allows them, more than in earlier conceptions of the model, to bring in their own personhood. The early formulations of the person-centered view stipulated that therapists were to refrain from intruding their own values and biases into the counseling relationship. They were to forgo commonly used procedures such as setting goals, giving advice, interpreting behavior, and selecting topics for exploration. The modern formulation, however, addresses itself less to prohibitions and allows the therapist greater freedom to participate more actively in the relationship. The aim is to create an atmosphere in which the client feels fully accepted regardless of the techniques or style employed.

Summary and evaluation

Person-centered therapy is based on a philosophy of human nature that holds that we have an innate striving for self-actualization. Further, Rogers's view of human nature is phenomenological; that is, we structure ourselves according to our perceptions of reality. We are motivated to actualize ourselves in the reality that we perceive.

*Adapted from Table 1.1 in *New Directions in Client-Centered Therapy* by J. Hart. Copyright 1970 by Houghton Mifflin Co. Reprinted by permission.

Rogers's theory is based on the postulate that clients possess within themselves the capacity to understand the factors in their life that are causing unhappiness. They also have the capacity for self-direction and constructive personal change. Personal change will occur if a congruent therapist is able to establish with the client a relationship characterized by warmth, acceptance, and accurate empathic understanding. Therapeutic counseling is based on an I/Thou, or person-to-person, relationship in the safety and acceptance of which clients drop their rigid defenses and come to accept and integrate into their self system aspects that they formerly denied or distorted.

Person-centered therapy places the primary responsibility for the direction of therapy on the client. The general goals are becoming more open to experience, trusting in one's organism, developing an internal locus of evaluation and a willingness to become a process, and in other ways moving toward higher levels of self-actualization. The therapist does not impose specific goals and values on clients, they choose their own specific values and life goals.

The person-centered model is not a fixed theory. Rogers intended to develop a set of working principles that could be stated in the form of tentative hypotheses about the conditions facilitating personal growth. This is an open system that is still in evolution. Formulations continue to be revised in light of new research findings.

The person-centered approach emphasizes the personal relationship between client and therapist; the therapist's attitudes are more critical than are techniques, knowledge, or theory. If the therapist demonstrates and communicates to clients that he or she is (1) a congruent person, (2) warmly and unconditionally accepting of their feelings and personhood, and (3) able to sensitively and accurately perceive the internal world as they perceive it, then they will use this relationship to unleash their growth potential and become more of the person they choose to become.

CONTRIBUTIONS OF THE PERSON-CENTERED APPROACH

Perhaps one of the dominant methods used in counselor education is the person-centered approach. One reason is its built-in safety features. It emphasizes active listening, respecting clients, adopting their internal frame of reference, and staying with them as opposed to getting ahead of them with interpretations. Person-centered therapists typically reflect content and feelings, clarify messages, help clients to muster their own resources, and encourage them to find their own solutions. Hence, this approach is far safer than many models of therapy that put the therapist in the directive position of making interpretations, forming diagnoses, probing the unconscious, analyzing dreams, and working toward more radical personality changes. For a person with limited background in counseling psychology, personality dynamics, and psychopathology, the person-centered approach offers assurance that prospective clients will not be psychologically harmed.

The person-centered approach contributes in other ways to both individual and group counseling. It offers a humanistic base from which to understand the subjective world of clients. It provides them the rare opportunity to be really listened to and heard. Further, if they feel that they are heard, they probably will express their feelings in their own ways. They can be themselves, because they know that they will not be evaluated or judged. They can feel free to experiment with new behavior. They are expected to take responsibility for themselves, and it is *they* who set the pace in counseling. They decide what areas they wish to explore, on the basis of their own goals for change. The person-centered approach provides clients with an immediate and specific reaction to what they have just communicated. The counselor acts as a mirror, reflecting their deeper feelings. Thus, they have the possibility of gaining sharper focus and deeper meaning to aspects of their self-structure that were previously only partially known to them. Their attention is focused on many things that they have not attended to before. They are thus able to increasingly own their total experiencing.

Another major contribution to the field of psychotherapy has been Rogers's willingness to state his formulations as testable hypotheses and to submit his hypotheses to research efforts. Even his critics give him credit for having conducted and inspired others to conduct the most extensive research on counseling process and outcome of any school of psychotherapy. His theories of therapy and personality change have had tremendous heuristic effect, and, though much controversy surrounds this approach, his work has challenged practitioners and theoreticians to examine their own therapeutic styles and beliefs.

Person-centered therapy has not been confined to one-to-one psychotherapy. Rogers indicates that his theory has had implications for education, business, industry, and international relations. He devoted considerable effort to the group-counseling movement and is one of the fathers of the basic encounter group (Rogers, 1970). He has long been interested in student-centered teaching and has pioneered humanistic education (Rogers, 1969). His efforts contributed to the establishment of the Association for Humanistic Psychology. Clearly, the person-centered approach has implications for psychotherapy, for training mental-health workers and paraprofessionals, for family living, and for all interpersonal relationships (Rogers, 1961, 1977).

LIMITATIONS OF THE PERSON-CENTERED APPROACH

A vulnerability of the person-centered approach lies in the manner in which some practitioners misinterpret or simplify its central attitudes. Not all counselors can practice person-centered therapy, for some do not really believe in the underlying philosophy. Many of Rogers's followers have attempted to be carbon copies of Rogers himself and have misunderstood some of his basic concepts. They limit their own range of responses and counseling styles to reflections and empathic listening. Surely there is value in listening to and really hearing a client and in reflecting and communicating understanding. But psychotherapy is, one hopes, more than this. Perhaps listening and reflecting are prerequisites for a therapeutic relationship, but they should not be confused with therapy itself.

One limitation of the approach is the way some practitioners become "client centered" and lose a sense of their own personhood and uniqueness. Paradoxically, counselors may focus on the client to such an extent that they diminish the value of their own power as a person and thus lose the impact and influence of their personality on the client. Therapists may highlight the needs and purposes of the client and yet at the same time feel free to bring their own personality into the therapeutic hour.

Thus, one must caution that this approach is something more than merely a listening and reflecting technique. It is based on a set of attitudes that the therapist brings to the relationship, and more than any other quality the therapist's genuineness determines the power of the therapeutic relationship. If therapists submerge their unique identity and style in a passive and nondirective way, they may not be harming many clients; but also they may not be really affecting clients in a positive way. Therapist authenticity and congruence are so vitally related to this approach that therapists who practice within this framework must feel natural in doing so and must find a way to express their own reactions to clients. If not, a real possibility is that person-centered therapy will be reduced to a bland, safe, and ineffectual way of working with clients.

The central limitation of the person-centered model lies in what it omits, rather than what it contains. I see this model as an excellent place to begin a counseling relationship, for unless trust is established and attitudes of respect, care, acceptance, and warmth are communicated, most counseling interventions will fail. But it is not a good place to remain as the counseling process develops. Although I see the core conditions that Rogers describes as being necessary for client change to occur, I also see the need for the knowledge and skills of counselors to be applied in a more directive manner than is called for in the person-centered model. It is here that the extensions of this model by those who advocate a systematic-skills approach are especially appealing.

Questions for reflection and discussion

Person-centered therapy is rooted in assumptions about the capacities of the client and the basic attitudes of the therapist. One real problem with the approach is that therapists sometimes give lip service to its basic concepts, but, because they do not deeply believe in some of these attitudes, their behavior as therapists reflects a conception different from their philosophy of counseling. What follow are some questions designed to help you test and challenge the degree to which you accept a person-centered philosophy and thus would be able genuinely to incorporate it into your own counseling practice.

1. The relationship that the therapist creates with the client is the cornerstone of person-centered therapy. Do you accept Rogers's "necessary and sufficient" conditions for therapeutic change? Is it enough that the therapist has unconditional positive regard for the client, possess an accurate empathic understanding, and be genuine in the relationship? Do you believe that other therapeutic procedures and techniques might be essential for change to occur?
2. Do you think that diagnosis and case history are important prerequisites for therapy? Could you proceed without having information about the client? Do you think that gathering data on the client's past experiences is useful?
3. Would you want to interpret the meaning of your client's behavior, or would you let the client form his or her own meanings?
4. Might you feel compelled to give your own opinions or even to persuade your client to a certain action? Might you strongly suggest certain activities if you really believed they were in your client's best interest? Would you want to give advice?
5. Would you be able to refrain from making value judgments if your client had a life-style that was radically different from yours? What if your client's values and beliefs contradicted your own?
6. Would you be able to accept your client? What would you do if you did not feel accepting of a certain person? Do you see any conflict between genuineness and acceptance?
7. How congruent or real could you be if you withheld your own values, feelings, and attitudes from your client? If you feel like making suggestions but refrain from doing so, are you being inauthentic?
8. What factors might interfere with your being genuine with a client? What about your need for the client's approval? Is there a danger that you might avoid a confrontation because you want to be liked?
9. What within yourself might make accurate empathic understanding difficult for you? Do you have broad life experiences that will help you identify with your client's struggles?

10. Can you empathize with clients and understand their subjective worlds without losing your own separateness and overidentifying with them?

Recommended supplementary readings

One of the best sources for further reading is Rogers's *On Becoming a Person* (1961), a collection of his articles on the process of psychotherapy, its outcomes, the therapeutic relationship, education, family life, communication, and the nature of the healthy person.

For readers who are interested in the application of his ideas to group work and encounter groups, see *Carl Rogers on Encounter Groups* (Rogers, 1970); and those who are interested in the application of his ideas to student-centered teaching should see *Freedom to Learn* (Rogers, 1969).

Carl Rogers on Personal Power (Rogers, 1977) is an extension of his philosophy to areas such as management, administration, minority-group relations, interracial and intercultural groups, workshop groups, community relations, and international relationships. The theme of the book is one's capacity to achieve inner strength and personal power and the implications of this power for daily living.

References and suggested readings

Books highly recommended as supplementary reading are marked with an asterisk.

*American Psychological Association. Carl Rogers on empathy. *The Counseling Psychologist,* 1975, *5*(2), whole issue.
* Axline, V. *Dibs: In search of self.* New York: Ballantine Books, 1964.
Carkhuff, R. R. *Helping and human relations* (2 vols.). New York: Holt, Rinehart & Winston, 1969.
Carkhuff, R., & Berenson, B. *Beyond counseling and therapy* (2nd ed.). New York: Holt, Rinehart & Winston, 1977.
Corey, G. *Theory and practice of group counseling.* Monterey, Calif.: Brooks/Cole, 1981.
Corey, G. *Case approach to counseling and psychotherapy.* Monterey, Calif.: Brooks/Cole, 1982.
* Egan, G. *The skilled helper.* Monterey, Calif.: Brooks/Cole, 1975.
* Evans, R. *Carl Rogers: The man and his ideas.* New York: Dutton, 1975.
Hart, J., & Tomlinson, T. *New directions in client-centered therapy.* New York: Houghton Mifflin, 1970.
Ivey, A., & Authier, J. *Microcounseling: Innovations in interviewing, counseling, psychotherapy, and psychoeducation* (2nd ed.). Springfield, Ill.: Charles C Thomas, 1978.
Jourard, S. *The transparent self* (Rev. ed.). New York: Van Nostrand Reinhold, 1971.
* Martin, D. G. *Learning-based client-centered therapy.* Monterey, Calif.: Brooks/Cole, 1972.
Meador, B., & Rogers, C. Person-centered therapy. In R. Corsini (Ed.), *Current psychotherapies* (2nd ed.). Itasca, Ill.: F. E. Peacock, 1979.
Nye, R. *Three psychologies* (2nd ed.). Monterey, Calif.: Brooks/Cole, 1981.
Rogers, C. *Counseling and psychotherapy.* Boston: Houghton Mifflin, 1942.
Rogers, C. *Client-centered therapy.* Boston: Houghton Mifflin, 1951.
Rogers, C. The necessary and sufficient condition of therapeutic personality change. *Journal of Consulting Psychology,* 1957, *21,* 95–103.
* Rogers, C. *On becoming a person.* Boston: Houghton Mifflin, 1961.
Rogers, C. The conditions of change from a client-centered viewpoint. In B. Berenson & R. Carkhuff (Eds.), *Sources of gain in counseling and psychotherapy.* New York: Holt, Rinehart & Winston, 1967.

* Rogers, C. *Freedom to learn*. Columbus, Ohio: Merrill, 1969.
* Rogers, C. *Carl Rogers on encounter groups*. New York: Harper & Row, 1970.
Rogers, C. *Becoming partners: Marriage and its alternatives*. New York: Delacorte, 1972.
* Rogers, C. *Carl Rogers on personal power: Inner strength and its revolutionary impact*. New York: Delacorte, 1977.
Rogers, C. *A way of being*. Palo Alto, Calif.: Houghton Mifflin, 1980.
Rogers, C., & Wood, J. Client-centered theory: Carl Rogers. In A. Burton (Ed.), *Operational theories of personality*. New York: Brunner/Mazel, 1974.

6

Gestalt Therapy

Introduction

Developed by Frederick Perls, Gestalt therapy is a form of existential therapy based on the premise that individuals must find their own way in life and accept personal responsibility if they hope to achieve maturity. Perls (1973) described the term "Gestalt" as originating from a group of German psychologists, who, working in the field of perception, demonstrated that humans do not perceive things as unrelated isolates, but rather as meaningful wholes. For example, when you enter a room, you do not see it in bits and pieces, you see it as a complete unit. Certain elements in the room may stand out more than others, but the room itself is still seen as a whole. Perls says that there is not an equivalent term in English to capture the meaning of the German word "Gestalt." He describes the term as follows:

> A gestalt is a pattern, a configuration, the particular form of organization of the individual parts that go into its make up. The basic premise of Gestalt psychology is that human nature is organized into patterns or wholes, that it is experienced by the individual in these terms, and that it can only be understood as a function of the patterns or wholes of which it is made [1973, p. 5].

The basic assumption of Gestalt therapy is that individuals can themselves deal effectively with their life problems. The central task of the therapist is to help clients fully experience their being in the here and now by becoming aware of how they prevent themselves from feeling and experiencing in the present. Therefore, the approach is basically noninterpretive, and clients carry out their own therapy as much as possible. They make their own interpretations, create their own direct statements, and find their own meanings. Finally, clients are encouraged to experience directly in the present their struggles with "unfinished business" from their past. By experiencing their conflicts instead of merely talking about them, they gradually expand their own level of awareness and integrate the fragmented and unknown parts of their personality.

Key concepts

VIEW OF HUMAN NATURE

The Gestalt view of human nature is rooted in existential philosophy and phenomenology. It stresses expanding one's awareness, accepting personal responsibility, and unifying the person. In its therapy, the approach focuses on integrating the polarities and dichotomies within the self. Therapy aims not at analysis but at integration, which proceeds step by step until clients become strong enough to facilitate their own personal growth.

The Gestalt view is that the individual has the capacity to assume personal responsibility and live fully as an integrated person. Because of certain problems in development, individuals form various ways of avoiding problems and, therefore, reach an impasse in their personal growth. Therapy provides the necessary intervention and challenge that help them gain knowledge and awareness as they proceed toward integration and growth. As they recognize and experience blocks to maturity, their awareness of the blocks increases, and they can then muster the potential for a more authentic and vital existence.

THE NOW

For Perls, nothing exists except the "now." Because the past is gone and the future has not yet arrived, only the present is significant. One of the main contributions of the Gestalt approach is its emphasis on the here and now and on learning to appreciate and experience fully the present moment. Focusing on the past is viewed as one way of avoiding coming to terms with the full experience of the present.

In speaking of the "now ethos," Polster and Polster (1973) developed the thesis that "power is in the present." They held that "a most difficult truth to teach is that only the present exists now and that to stray from it distracts from the living quality of reality" (p. 7). For so many people the power of the present is lost; instead of being in the present moment, they invest their energies in bemoaning their past mistakes and ruminating about how life could and should have been different, or they engage in endless resolutions and plans for the future. As they direct their energy toward what was or what might have been, their capacity to capitalize on the power of the present diminishes.

Perls (1969a) described anxiety as "the gap between the now and the later." According to him, when individuals stray from the present and become preoccupied with the future, they experience anxiety. In thinking of the future they may experience "stage fright," for they become filled with "catastrophic expectations of the bad things that will happen or anastrophic expectations about the wonderful things that will happen" (p. 30). Rather than living in the now, they attempt to fill the gap between the now and the later with resolutions, plans, and visions.

To help the client make contact with the present moment, the Gestaltist asks "what" and "how" questions but rarely asks "why" questions. In order to promote "now" awareness, the therapist encourages a dialogue in the present tense by asking such questions as: What is happening now? What is going on now? What are you experiencing as you sit there and attempt to talk? What is your awareness at this moment? How are you experiencing your fear? How are you attempting to withdraw at this moment? Perls (1969a) contended that without an intensification of feelings the person would speculate *why* he or she felt this way. According to Perls, "why" questions lead only toward rationalizations and "self-deceptions" and away from the immediacy of experiencing. "Why" questions lead to an endless and heady rumination about the past that only serves to encourage resistance to present experience.

The Gestalt therapist actively points out how easily clients can escape from the now into the past or the future. Most people can stay in the present for only a short while. They are inclined to find ways of interrupting the flow of the present. Instead of experiencing their feelings in the here and now, they often *talk about* their feelings, almost as if their feelings were detached from their present experiencing. Perls's aim was to help people make contact with their experience with vividness and immediacy rather than merely talking about the experience. Thus, if a client begins to talk about sadness, pain, or confusion, the therapist makes every attempt to have the client experience that sadness, pain, or confusion *now*. Talking about problems can become an endless word game that leads to unproductive discussion and exploration of hidden meanings. It is one way of resisting growth and also a way of engaging in self-deception; clients attempt to trick themselves into believing that, because they are facing their problems and talking about them, they are resolving their problems and growing as persons. To lessen the danger of this, attempts are made to intensify and exaggerate certain feelings. In a group setting, for example, the therapist may ask a client who reports how conscious he or she is of pleasing others and meeting others' expectations to strive at that very moment to please each person in the group.

Is the past ignored in the Gestalt approach? It is not accurate to say that Gestaltists have no interest in a person's past; the past is important when it is related in some way to significant themes in the individual's present functioning. When the past seems to have a significant bearing on one's present attitudes or behavior, it is dealt with by bringing it into the present as much as possible. Thus, when clients speak about their past, the therapist asks them to bring it into the now by reenacting it as though they were living it now. The therapist directs clients to "be there" in fantasy and to relive some of the feelings they experienced earlier. For example, rather than talking *about* a past childhood trauma with their father, clients become that hurt child, talk directly to the father in fantasy, and, it is hoped, relive and reexperience that hurt.

Perls contended that individuals tend to hang on to the past and play "blaming games" in order to justify their unwillingness to take responsibility for themselves and their growth. He saw most people as having a difficult time in staying in the now. They get caught up in a whirl by making resolutions and by rationalizing their half-dead state. They would rather do anything than become conscious of how they prevent themselves from being fully alive.

UNFINISHED BUSINESS

Another key concept is unfinished business, which involves unexpressed feelings such as resentment, rage, hatred, pain, anxiety, grief, guilt, abandonment, and so on. Even though the feelings are unexpressed, they are associated with distinct memories and fantasies. Because the feelings are not fully experienced in awareness, they linger in the background and are carried into present life in ways that interfere with effective contact with oneself and others. Unfinished business persists until the individual faces and deals with the unexpressed feelings. In speaking of the effects of unfinished business, Polster and Polster (1973) maintained that "these incomplete directions *do seek* completion and when they get powerful enough, the individual is beset with preoccupation, compulsive behavior, wariness, oppressive energy and much self-defeating behavior" (p. 36).

An example of how unfinished business nags at one and manifests itself in current behavior can be seen in the man who never really felt loved and accepted by his mother. He might have developed resentment for his mother, for, no matter how he sought her approval, he was always left feeling that he was not adequate. In an attempt to deflect the direction of this need for maternal approval, he may look to women for his confirmation of worth as a man. In developing a variety of games to get women to approve of him, he reports that he is still not satisfied. The unfinished business has prevented him from authentic intimacy with women. His behavior thus becomes a compulsive search for the love that he never received from his mother. He needs to experience closure of the unfinished business before he can experience real satisfaction; that is, he needs to return to the old business and express his unacknowledged feelings.

Unacknowledged feelings create unnecessary emotional debris that clutter present-centered awareness. According to Perls (1969a), resentment is the most frequent and worst kind of unfinished business. In his view, when people are resentful they become stuck, for they can neither let go nor engage in authentic communication until they express the resentment. Thus, Perls contended that it is imperative to express resentments. Unexpressed resentment frequently converts to guilt. "Whenever you feel guilty, find out what you are resenting and express it and make your demands explicit" (Perls, 1969a, p. 49).

The therapeutic process

THERAPEUTIC GOALS

Gestalt therapy has several important aims. A basic one is to challenge the client to move from "environmental support" to "self-support." According to Perls (1969a), the aim of therapy is "to make the patient *not* depend upon others, but to make the patient discover from the very first moment that he can do many things, *much* more than he thinks he can do" (p. 29).

In keeping with the humanistic spirit, Perls contended that most of us use only a fraction of our potential. This view is like Maslow's concept of the "psychopathology of the average": our lives are patterned and stereotyped; we play the same roles again and again and find very few ways to really reinvent our existence. Perls contended that, if we find out how we prevent ourselves from realizing the full measure of our human potential, we have ways to make life richer. This potential is based on the attitude of living each moment freshly. A major goal of therapy, therefore, is to help the client live a fuller life.

The goal of Gestalt therapy is *not* adjustment to society. Perls considered the basic personality in our time to be neurotic because we are living in an insane society. He argued that we have a choice of becoming part of the collective sickness or taking the risks of becoming healthy. A goal of therapy, then, is to help each individual find his or her center within. Perls (1969a) wrote "If you are centered in yourself, then you don't adjust any more—then, whatever happens becomes a passing parade and you assimilate, you understand, and you are related to whatever happens" (p. 30).

An underlying aim of Gestalt therapy is the attaining of awareness. Awareness, by and of itself, is seen as curative. Without awareness, clients do not possess the tools for personality change. With awareness, they have the capacity to face and accept denied parts of their beings and to get in touch with subjective experiences and with reality. Clients can become unified and whole. When clients are aware, their most important unfinished business will always emerge so that it can be dealt with in therapy.

THERAPIST'S FUNCTION AND ROLE

Gestalt therapy focuses on the client's feelings, awareness at the moment, body messages, and blocks to awareness. Perls's (1969a) dictum is to "lose your mind and come to your senses."

Gestalt therapy is being in touch with the obvious, according to Perls (1969a), who contended that the neurotic does not see the obvious: "He doesn't see the pimple on his nose" (p. 38). Thus, the therapist's job is to challenge clients. In this way they learn to use their senses fully. They can avoid the obvious and can be open to what is there now. Perls asserted that the total being of a person is before the therapist. Gestalt therapy uses the eyes and ears of the therapist to stay in the now. The therapist avoids abstract intellectualization, diagnosis, interpretation, and excessive verbiage.

Although the Gestalt approach is concerned with the obvious, its simplicity should not be taken to mean that the therapist's job is easy. In my judgment one vulnerability of the approach is the danger of slipping into an impersonal and technical role in which therapists hide their own personhood from clients and become directors of endless exercises and games. If therapists do not use their personhood as an instrument of therapeutic change, then they become little more than responders, catalysts, and technicians who play therapeutic games with clients. Developing a variety of Gestalt gimmicks is easy, but employing the techniques in a mechanical fashion allows the clients to continue inauthentic living. If clients are to become authentic, they need contact with an authentic therapist.

Polster and Polster (1973, pp. 18–22) discussed the concept of the "therapist as his own instrument." Like artists who need to be in touch with what they are painting, the therapist is an "artistic participant in the creation of new life." Polster and Polster implored therapists to use their own experiences as essential ingredients in the therapy process. According to them, therapists are more than mere responders or catalysts who do not change themselves. The data of the therapeutic encounter are grounded in the mutual experiences of the client and the therapist. If therapists are to function effectively, they must be in tune with the persons before them, and they must also be in tune with themselves. Thus, therapy is a two-way engagement on a genuine I/Thou basis. Not only does the client change, but so does the therapist. If the therapist is not sensitively tuned in to his or her own qualities of tenderness, toughness, and compassion and to reactions to the client, then "he becomes a technician, ministering to another person and not living the therapy with the full flavor that is available."

How does Gestalt therapy proceed, and what are the functions of the therapist in the process? What follows are Perls's (1969a) key ideas about the role of the therapist. To begin with, the therapist's aim is the client's maturation and the removal of "blocks that prevent a person from standing on his own feet." The therapist's job is to help the client make the transition from external to internal support, and this is done by locating the impasse. The impasse is the point at which individuals avoid experiencing threatening feelings because they feel uncomfortable. It is a resistance to facing one's self and to changing. People often express resistance by saying: "I feel frustrated—like I'm spinning my wheels and getting nowhere." "I don't know where to go from here." "I can't do thus and so." "I feel stuck." According to Perls, people experience "being stuck" because of their "catastrophic expectations." They imagine that something terrible will happen. Their catastrophic fantasies prevent them from fully living, and because of their unreasonable fears they refuse to take the necessary risks for becoming more mature. Typically, "catastrophic expectations" take the form of statements such as "If I am a certain way or have certain feelings, then I won't be loved, or accepted, or approved of. I'll be stupid. I'll perish. I'll feel like a fool. I'll be abandoned."

At the moment of impasse, clients attempt to maneuver their environment by playing phony roles of weakness, helplessness, stupidity, and foolishness. The therapist's task is to help them get through the impasse so that growth is possible. This is a difficult task, for at the point of impasse clients believe that they have no chance of survival and that they will not find the means for survival within. The therapist assists them in recognizing and working through the impasse by providing situations that encourage them to experience fully their conditions of being stuck. By fully experiencing the blockage, they are able to get into contact with their frustrations. Perls contended that frustration is essential for growth, for without frustration people have no need to muster their own resources and to discover that they can well do on their own what they are manipulating others to do for them. If therapists are not careful, they too will be sucked into clients' manipulations.

Perls (1969a, p. 36) wrote that the way to keep from being manipulated by clients is to let them find their own missing potentials. Clients use the therapist as a "projection screen" and look to the therapist to provide them with what they think is missing in themselves. Perls maintained that all people have "holes" in their personalities. Clients' holes might include their giving up their eyes or ears; instead of doing their own seeing and hearing, they look to others to do their seeing and hearing for them. According to Perls (1969a, p. 37) the holes are apparent. The therapist, then, must provide a situation for growth to occur by confronting clients until they face a decision about whether they will develop their potentials. Frustration results in the discovery that the impasse does not exist in reality but only in fantasy. Clients have persuaded themselves that they do not have the resources to cope, and out of their fears of "catastrophic expectations" they prevent themselves from utilizing their resources. When they face and work through their fears, their neurotic anxiety converts to a sense of positive excitement. As Perls (1969a) put it, "We apply enough skillful frustration so that the patient is forced to find his own way, discover that *what he expects from the therapist, he can do just as well himself*" (p. 37).

An important function of the Gestalt therapist is paying attention to the client's body language. The client's nonverbal cues provide the therapist with rich information, because they often betray feelings of which the client is unaware. Perls (1969a) wrote that a client's posture, movements, gestures, voice, hesitations, and so on tell the real story. He warned that verbal communication is usually a lie, and that if therapists are content-oriented they miss the essence of the person. Real communication is beyond words. "The sounds tell you everything. Everything a person wants to express is all there—not in words. What we say is mostly either lies or bullshit. But the voice is there, the gesture, the posture, the facial expression, the psychosomatic language" (p. 54).

Thus, the therapist needs to be alert for splits in attention and awareness and for incongruities between verbalizations and what clients are doing with their body. Clients demonstrate from moment to moment how they avoid being in full contact with their present-centered actuality. Thus, the therapist might direct clients to speak for and become their gestures or body parts. Gestaltists often ask: What do your eyes say? If your hands could speak at this moment, what would they say? Can you carry on a conversation between your right and left hands? Clients may verbally express anger and at the same time smile. Or they may state that they are in pain and at the same time laugh. The therapist could ask them to recognize that their laughter covers up their pain. Clients might be asked to become aware of how they use their laughter to mask feelings of anger or pain. Attention to the messages that clients send nonverbally are grist for the mill, and the therapist needs to focus on the nonverbal cues.

In addition to calling attention to a client's nonverbal language, the Gestalt counselor places emphasis on the relationship between language patterns and personality. This approach suggests that clients' speech patterns are often an expression of their feelings, thoughts, and attitudes. The Gestalt approach focuses on overt speaking habits as a way to increase clients' awareness of themselves, especially by asking them to notice whether their words are congruent with what they are experiencing or instead distance them from their emotions.

A function of the Gestalt counselor is to gently confront clients by interventions that help them become aware of the effects of their language patterns. By focusing on words clients are thus able to increase their awareness of what they are experiencing in the present moment and of how they are avoiding coming into contact with this here-and-now experience. What are some of the aspects of language that the Gestalt counselor might focus on? The following are some examples:

"It talk": When clients say *it* instead of *I,* they are using depersonalizing language. The counselor may ask them to substitute personal pronouns for impersonal ones so that they will assume an increased sense of responsibility. For example, a client says "It is difficult to make friends." The client could be asked to restate this by making an *I* statement—"I have trouble making friends."

"You talk": The counselor will point out generalized use of *you* and ask the client to substitute *I* when this is what is meant. When clients say "You feel sort of hurt when people don't accept you," they may be asked to look at how they distance themselves from intense feelings by using a generalized *you.* Again, they can be encouraged to change this impersonal *you* into an *I* statement such as, "I feel hurt when I am not accepted." They can be asked to notice the difference between these sentences.

Questions: Questions have a tendency to keep the one asking them hidden, safe, and unknown. Gestalt counselors often ask clients to change their questions into statements. In making personal statements clients begin to assume responsibility for what they say. They may become aware of how they keep themselves mysterious through a barrage of questions and how this serves to prevent them from making declarations that express themselves. For example, without stating their investment behind their question, group members often question one another by probing for information. If a member were to ask another member "Why do you try so hard to get your father's approval when it seems so futile?", I am likely to ask the questioning member "Could you tell her what prompts you to ask her this question? Would you be willing to make a statement about yourself, rather than expect her to answer your question?".

Words that deny power: Some clients have a tendency to deny their personal power by adding qualifiers or disclaimers to their statements. Perls asserted that everything said after a *but* is crazy! Thus, when a client says "I typically feel like a victim, but I am powerless to change this," he or she adds to the powerlessness with the appendage of *but.* Often what follows a *but* is a disclaimer and serves to discount the first part of the statement. The counselor may also point out to clients how certain qualifiers subtract from one's effectiveness. In this way, clients become aware of how qualifiers keep them ambivalent. Experimenting with omitting qualifiers such as *maybe, perhaps, sort of, I guess, possibly,* and *I suppose* can help clients change ambivalent messages into clear and direct statements. Likewise, when clients say *I can't* they are really implying *I won't.* Asking them to substitute *won't* for *can't* assists them in owning and accepting their power by taking responsibility for their decisions. Other words that deny power are the *shoulds* and *oughts* that some people habitually use. Clients can at least become aware of the frequency with which they tell themselves and others that they *should* or *ought* to do this or that. By changing these *I shoulds* to *I choose to* or *I want to* they can begin taking active steps that reduce the feeling of being driven and not in control of their life. The counselor must be careful in intervening so that clients do not feel that everything they say is subject to scrutiny. Rather than fostering a morbid kind of introspection, the counselor hopes to foster awareness of what is really being expressed through words.

CLIENT'S EXPERIENCE IN THERAPY

Perls (1969a) expressed his skepticism about those who seek therapy and contended that not very many people really want to invest themselves in the hard work involved in changing. As he wrote:

> Anybody who goes to a therapist has something up his sleeve. I would say roughly ninety percent don't go to a therapist to be cured, but to be more adequate in their neurosis. If they are power mad, they want to get more power. If they are intellectual, they want to have more elephantshit. If they are ridiculers, they want to have a sharper wit to ridicule, and so on [p. 75].

Although Perls may sound pessimistic, not all clients want only the improvement of their neurosis. Clients in the Gestalt therapeutic experience decide for themselves what they want and how much they want. Perls's warning can be used in confrontation with clients to help them examine how much change they really desire. I believe that, if clients have the courage to honestly face the possibility that all they may want is to improve their manipulative skills, there is a greater chance that they might use therapy productively for something other than supporting the status quo of their defense systems. Thus, one of their first responsibilities is to decide what they want for themselves from therapy. If they say they are confused or attempt to have the therapist decide goals for them, then this is a place to begin. The therapist can explore with clients their avoidance of accepting this responsibility.

The general orientation of Gestalt therapy is toward clients' assumption of more and more responsibility for themselves—for their thoughts, feelings, and behavior. The therapist confronts them with the ways in which they are now avoiding their personal responsibilities and asks them to make decisions about continuing therapy, about what they wish to learn from it, and about how they want to use their therapy time. Other issues that can become the focal point of therapy include the client/therapist relationship and the similarities in the ways clients relate to the therapist and to others in their environment. Clients in Gestalt therapy, then, are active participants who make their own interpretations and meanings. It is they who increase awareness and decide what they will or will not do with their personal learning.

RELATIONSHIP BETWEEN THERAPIST AND CLIENT

As an existential brand of therapy, Gestalt practice involves a person-to-person relationship between the therapist and the client. The therapist's experiences, awareness, and perceptions provide the background of the therapy process, and the client's awareness and reactions constitute the forefront. It is important that therapists actively share their own present perceptions and experiences as they encounter clients in the here and now. Further, the therapist gives feedback, particularly of what clients are doing with their bodies. Feedback gives clients tools to develop an awareness of what they are actually doing. The therapist must encounter clients with honest and immediate reactions and challenge clients' manipulations without rejecting them as persons. The therapist needs to explore with clients their fears, catastrophic expectations, blockages, and resistances.

Perls (1969a), Polster and Polster (1973), and Kempler (1973) all emphasized the importance of the therapist's personhood as the vital ingredient in the therapy process. Perls (1969a, p. 1) objected to using techniques as gimmicks that prevent growth and become a brand of "phony therapy." Polster and Polster (1973, pp. 18–23) cautioned that, if therapists ignore personal qualities as an instrument in therapy, they become mere technicians. Polster and Polster encouraged a wide range of behavior by therapists and warned of the dangers of becoming identified with a limited range of techniques. They called on therapists to tap their spontaneity and draw on the relationship with the client for therapeutic technique. Kempler (1973) considered the actual relationship between the client and the therapist as the core of the therapeutic process, and he cautioned against the "use of tactics which might obscure the real identity of the therapist to his patient" (p. 261). Kempler contended that the use of role playing can be a temptation for therapists to keep their personal responses hidden. Although role playing might be an effective means, it is not the end of therapy. He asserted that techniques are often valuable as adjuncts to the therapeutic process; but he emphasized the process of the client/therapist relationship, for it is the quality of their relationship that determines what happens to both of them.

Application: Therapeutic techniques and procedures

Before discussing the variety of Gestalt techniques that you could include in your repertoire of counseling procedures, I think it is important to take up the preparing of clients for Gestalt exercises, the role of confrontation in therapy, and the rationale underlying Gestalt techniques.

PREPARING CLIENTS FOR GESTALT TECHNIQUES

Sometimes I hear students say that they view Gestalt therapy as "gimmicky" and that they would be afraid to introduce many of these techniques into a counseling session for fear that their clients would perceive them as being slightly odd. I believe that counselors need to be familiar with the techniques they introduce and feel comfortable using them, and that they must develop a relationship with their clients based on trust before they spring certain techniques on them. I fully agree with Passons's (1975) general guidelines for counselors:

- Clients will get more from Gestalt exercises if they are oriented and prepared for them.
- To derive maximum benefit from Gestalt approaches, the counselor must be sensitive to timing when introducing certain techniques.
- Counselors should learn which experiments can be best practiced in the session itself, and which can be best carried out beyond the session.
- The counselor should not suggest techniques or experiments that are too advanced for a client.

All of the Gestalt techniques are designed to enhance the awareness of clients, and thus they can be carried out both in the session itself and outside it. I think that counselors will enlist the cooperation of clients to a far greater extent if they avoid ordering and directing clients in a commanding fashion to carry out a certain exercise. Typically, I ask people if they are willing to try out some experiment to see what they might learn from it, and I take care to emphasize that no specific result is expected. I also tell clients that they can stop when they choose to, and in this way the power is with them. If they resist, then I may well ask them to explore what is stopping them, be it fear, lack of trust, concern over making a fool of themselves, or some other concern. Often what comes out of this exploration of resistance is at least as valuable as the suggested experiment. Basically, I attempt to show clients that I do not have an interpretation that I want to push on them. Rather, I hope that they can discover for themselves a pattern in their behavior through the experiment.

It is critical that counselors who want to use Gestalt approaches have themselves experienced these techniques; their own experimentation and learning can ensure that they will use the techniques with greater care, respect, and understanding. I cannot overstress the value of self-experimentation with each of the techniques that I describe in this chapter *before* asking and expecting clients to take the risk of engaging in them. For those who are interested in sources that contain Gestalt self-experiments, I highly recommend James and Jongeward (1971), Passons (1975), Perls, Hefferline, and Goodman (1951), Rainwater (1979), and Stevens (1971).

ROLE OF CONFRONTATION

I have found that students are sometimes put off by Gestalt therapy because of their perception that a counselor's style is direct, confrontational, and even abrasive. They base this perception on the few quotations I have given from Perls or whatever of his they have read. I tell them that it is a mistake to equate the practice of Gestalt therapy with the personality of Perls. Although he could be highly confrontational and sharp with clients, it is still possible to incorporate Gestalt approaches into one's counseling style in a way that is both challenging and gentle.

It is true that most of the Gestalt techniques that I describe *are* confrontational. Counselors who use these methods must be willing to be active and at times challenging. Clients must also be willing to take risks and challenge themselves, and in that sense self-confrontation becomes crucial. I agree with Passons (1975), who wrote that some people tend to ascribe too much power to Gestalt techniques. He viewed these experiments as designed to enhance awareness, with no power of their own; the power lies in the person who uses the techniques. If they are used in a caring and appropriate manner, they can heighten the experiencing of clients. The skill comes in challenging clients to push beyond their usual level of resistance and avoidance without fostering increased defensiveness.

I think it is fair to state that confrontation is a part of most Gestalt techniques, yet it does not have to be viewed as a harsh attack. Confrontation can be done in such a way that clients cooperate, especially when they are *invited* (not commanded) to examine their behaviors, attitudes, and thoughts. Counselors can encourage clients to look at certain incongruities, especially gaps between their verbal expression and nonverbal expression. If a client is speaking of a painful event yet smiling at the same time, calling attention to the lack of congruence between her smile and her stated feelings can be confrontational to the extent that she may become aware of her attempt to avoid feeling the intensity of her pain. Further, confrontation does not have to be aimed at weaknesses or negative traits; clients can be challenged to recognize the ways that they block their strengths and ways that they are not living as fully as they might. In this sense, confrontation can be a genuine expression of caring that results in positive changes in a client, not a brutal assault on a defenseless person.

Perhaps one of the most essential ingredients in effective confrontation is respect for the client. Counselors who care enough to make demands on their clients are telling them, in effect, that they could be in fuller contact with themselves and others. Ultimately, however, clients must decide for themselves if they want to accept this invitation to learn more about themselves. This caveat needs to be kept in mind with all of the techniques that are to be described.

TECHNIQUES OF GESTALT THERAPY

Earlier I stressed that Gestalt therapy consists of more than a collection of techniques and "games." However, techniques can be useful tools to help the client gain fuller awareness, experience internal conflicts, resolve inconsistencies and dichotomies, and work through an impasse that prevents completion of unfinished business.

Levitsky and Perls (1970, pp. 144–149) provided a brief description of a number of games, including (1) games of dialogue, (2) making the rounds, (3) unfinished business, (4) "I take responsibility," (5) "I have a secret," (6) playing the projection, (7) reversals, (8) the rhythm of contact and withdrawal, (9) "rehearsal," (10) "exaggeration," (11) "May I feed you a sentence?" (12) marriage-counseling games, and (13) "Can you stay with this feeling?" The following discussion is based on the games described by Levitsky and Perls, although I have modified the material and added suggestions for implementing these techniques.

The game of dialogue. As was mentioned earlier, a goal of Gestalt therapy is to bring about integrated functioning and the acceptance of aspects of one's personality that have been disowned and denied. Gestalt therapists pay close attention to splits in personality function. A main division is between the "top dog" and the "underdog." Often therapy focuses on the war between the two.

The top dog is righteous, authoritarian, moralistic, demanding, bossy, and manipulative. This is the "critical parent" that badgers with *shoulds* and *oughts* and manipulates with threats of catastrophe. The underdog manipulates by playing the role of victim, by being defensive, apologetic, helpless, and weak, and by playing powerless. This is the passive side, the one without responsibility, and the one that finds excuses. The top dog and the underdog are engaged in a constant struggle for control. The struggle helps to explain why one's resolutions and promises often go unfulfilled and why one's procrastination persists. The tyrannical top dog demands that one be thus-and-so, whereas the underdog defiantly plays the role of disobedient child. As a result of this struggle for control, the individual becomes fragmented into controller and controlled. The civil war between the two sides is never really complete, for both sides are fighting for their existence.

The conflict between the two opposing poles in the personality is rooted in the mechanism of introjection, which involves incorporating aspects of others, usually parents, into one's ego system. Perls implied that the taking in of values and traits is both inevitable and desirable; the danger is in the uncritical and wholesale acceptance of another's values as one's own, which makes becoming an autonomous person difficult. It is essential that one become aware of one's introjects, especially the toxic introjects that poison the system and prevent personality integration.

The empty-chair technique is one way of getting the client to externalize the introject. In this technique two chairs are placed in the center of the room. The therapist asks the client to sit in one chair and be fully the top dog and then shift to the other chair and become the underdog. The dialogue can continue between both sides of the client. Essentially, this is a role-playing technique in which all the parts are played by the client. In this way the introjects can surface, and the client can experience the conflict more fully. The conflict can be resolved by the client's acceptance and integration of both sides. This technique helps clients get in touch with a feeling or a side of themselves that they might be denying; rather than merely talking about a conflicted feeling, they intensify the feeling and experience it fully. Further, by helping clients realize that the feeling is a very real part of themselves, the technique discourages them from disassociating the feeling. The technique can help clients identify distasteful parental introjects. For example, a client might say "That sounds exactly like my father in me!" Parental introjections can keep a "self-torture" game alive as clients swallow parental injunctions and use them to punish and control themselves.

The dialogues between opposing tendencies have as their aim the promotion of a higher level of integration between the polarities and conflicts that exist in everyone. The aim is not to rid oneself of certain traits but to learn to accept and live with the polarities. Perls argued that other therapeutic approaches place too much emphasis on change. He contended that change cannot be forced, but that through the acceptance of polarities an integration can occur, and the client can stop the badgering self-torture game. There are many common conflicts that lend themselves to the game of dialogue. Some that I find applicable include (1) the parent inside versus the child inside, (2) the responsible one versus the impulsive one, (3) the puritanical side versus the sexual side, (4) the "good boy" versus the "bad boy," (5) the aggressive self versus the passive self, and (6) the autonomous side versus the resentful side.

The dialogue technique can be used in both individual and group counseling. Let me describe one example of a common conflict between the top dog and underdog that I have found to be a powerful agent in helping a client become more intensely aware of the internal split and of which side would become dominant. The client, in this case a woman, plays the weak, helpless, dependent game of "poor me." She complains that she is miserable and that she hates and resents her husband, yet she fears that if he leaves her she will disintegrate. She uses him as the excuse for her impotence. She continually puts herself down, always saying "I can't," "I don't know how," "I am not capable." If she decided that she was miserable enough to want to change her dependent style, I would probably ask her to sit on one chair in the center of the room and become fully the underdog martyr and to exaggerate this side of herself. Eventually, if she got disgusted with this side, I would ask her to be the other side—that is, the top-dog side that puts her down—and talk to the "poor me." Then I might ask her to pretend that she were powerful, strong, and independent and to act as if she were not helpless. I might ask "What would happen if you were strong and independent and if you gave up your clinging dependency?" That technique can often energize clients into really experiencing the roles they continue to play, the result frequently being the reinvention of the autonomous aspects of self.

Making the rounds. Making the rounds is a Gestalt exercise that involves asking a person in a group to go up to others in the group and either speak to or do something with each. The purpose is to confront, to risk, and to disclose the self, to experiment with new behavior, and to grow and change. I have employed the technique when I sensed that a participant needed to face each person in the group with some theme. For example, a group member might say: "I've been sitting here for a long time wanting to participate but holding back because I'm afraid of trusting people in here. And besides, I don't think I'm worth the time of the group anyway." I might counter with "Are you willing to do something right now to get yourself more invested and to begin to work on gaining trust and self-confidence?" If the person answers affirmatively, my suggestion could well be "Go around to each person and finish this sentence: I don't trust you because. . . ." Any number of exercises could be invented to help individuals involve themselves and choose to work on the things that keep them frozen in fear.

Some other related illustrations and examples that I find appropriate for the making-the-rounds technique are reflected in clients' comments such as these: "I would like to reach out to people more often." "I'm bored by what's going on in this group." "Nobody in here seems to care very much." "I'd like to make contact with you, but I'm afraid of being rejected (or accepted)." "It's hard for me to accept good stuff; I always discount good things people say to me." "It's hard for me to say negative things to people; I want to be nice always." "I'd like to feel more comfortable in touching and getting close."

"I take responsibility for . . . ."   In this game, the therapist asks the client to make a statement and then add "and I take responsibility for it." Some examples: "I'm feeling bored, and I take responsibility for my boredom." "I'm feeling excluded and lonely, and I take responsibility for my feelings of exclusion." "I don't know what to say now, and I take responsibility for my not knowing." This technique is an extension of the continuum of awareness, and it is designed to help the individuals recognize and accept their feelings instead of projecting their feelings onto others. Whereas this technique may sound mechanical, it is one that can be very meaningful.

"I have a secret."   This technique permits exploration of feelings of guilt and shame. The therapist asks clients to fantasize about a well-guarded personal secret, not to share the secret but to imagine how they would feel and how others would react to them if they were to reveal it. In group settings I have asked participants to allow themselves to imagine standing before the entire group and revealing aspects of themselves that they invest a lot of energy in hiding from others. Then I ask them to imagine what each person in the group might say to them if they were to share their secrets. This technique can also be used as a method of building trust in order to explore why clients might not reveal their secrets and to explore their fears of revealing material they feel ashamed or guilty about.

Playing the projection.   The dynamics of projection consist of one's seeing clearly in others the very things one does not want to see and accept within oneself. One can invest much energy in denying feelings and imputing motives to others. Often, especially in a group setting, the statements an individual makes toward and about others are in fact projections of attributes he or she possesses.

In the playing-the-projection game, the therapist asks the person who says "I can't trust you" to play the role of the untrustworthy person—that is, to become the other—in order to discover the degree to which the distrust is an inner conflict. In other words, the therapist asks the person to "try on for size" certain statements he or she makes to others in the group.

Reversal technique.   Certain symptoms and behavior often represent reversals of underlying or latent impulses. Thus, the therapist could ask a person who claims to suffer from severe inhibitions and excessive timidity to play the role of an exhibitionist in the group. I remember the woman in one of our groups who had difficulty in being anything but sugary sweet. I asked her to reverse her typical style and be as negative as she could be. The reversal worked well; soon she was playing her part with real gusto and later was able to recognize and accept her "negative side" as well as her "positive side."

The theory underlying the reversal technique is that clients take the plunge into the very thing that is fraught with anxiety and make contact with those parts of themselves that have been submerged and denied. This technique can thus help clients begin to accept certain personal attributes that they have tried to deny.

Another time I asked one of the women in a group to become an evil witch. I asked her to go around to all the others in the group to place her curse on them, to wish evil on them, and to tell them the very thing they feared most. As part of her act she delivered a chilling, evil lecture. This was a woman who, because she had never really been allowed to recognize her demonic side, had repressed her devils. She stored up hostility and resentment as by-products of repression. When she was encouraged to release her personal demons, to become fully the witch she had never been allowed to express, the results were dramatic. She felt intensely her denied side and gradually was able to integrate that side into her personality.

The rehearsal game.   According to Perls, much of our thinking is rehearsing. We rehearse in fantasy for the role we think we are expected to play in society. When it comes to the performance, we experience stage fright, or anxiety, because we fear that we will not play our role well. Internal rehearsal consumes much energy and frequently inhibits our spontaneity and willingness to experiment with new behavior.

The members of the therapy group play the game of sharing their rehearsals with one another in order to become more aware of the many preparatory means they use in bolstering their social roles. They become increasingly aware of how they try to meet the expectations of others, of the degree to which they want to be approved, accepted, and liked, and of the extent to which they go to attain acceptance.

The exaggeration game.   This game involves becoming more aware of the subtle signals and cues one sends through body language. Movements, postures, and gestures may communicate significant meanings, yet the cues may be incomplete. The person is asked to exaggerate the movement or gesture repeatedly, which usually intensifies the feeling attached to the behavior and makes the inner meaning clearer.

Some examples of behavior that lends itself to the exaggeration technique are habitually smiling when expressing painful or negative material, trembling (shaking hands, legs), slouched posture and bent shoulders, clenched fists, tight frowning, facial grimacing, crossed arms, and so forth. If a client reports that his or her legs are shaking, for instance, the therapist might ask the client to stand up and exaggerate the shaking. Then the therapist might ask the client to put words to the shaking limbs.

As a variation from body language, verbal behavior also lends itself to the exaggeration game. The therapist can ask a client to repeat a statement that he or she had glossed over and to repeat it each time louder and louder. The effect frequently is that clients begin to really listen to and hear themselves.

Staying with the feeling.   This technique can be used at key moments when a client refers to a feeling or a mood that is unpleasant and from which he or she has a great urge to flee. The therapist urges the client to stay with, or retain, the feeling.

Most clients desire to escape from fearful stimuli and to avoid unpleasant feelings.

The therapist may ask clients to remain with whatever fear or pain they are experiencing at present and encourage them to go deeper into the feeling and behavior they wish to avoid. Facing, confronting, and experiencing feelings not only take courage but are also a mark of the willingness to endure the pain necessary for unblocking and making way for newer levels of growth.

The Gestalt approach to dream work.   In psychoanalysis dreams are interpreted, intellectual insight is stressed, and free association is used as one method of exploring the unconscious meanings of dreams. The Gestalt approach does not interpret and analyze a dream. Instead, the intent is to bring the dream back to life and relive it as though it were happening now. The dream is not told as a past event but is acted out in the present, and the dreamer becomes a part of his or her dream. The suggested format for working with dreams includes making a list of all the details of the dream, remembering each person, event, and mood in it, and then becoming each of these parts by transforming oneself, acting as fully as possible and inventing dialogue. Because each part of the dream is assumed to be a projection of oneself, one creates scripts for encounters between various characters or parts. All of the different parts of a dream are expressions of one's own contradictory and inconsistent sides. Thus, by engaging in a dialogue between these opposing sides, one gradually becomes more aware of the range of one's own feelings.

Perls's concept of projection is central in his theory of dream formation. According to him, every person and every object in the dream represents a projected aspect of the dreamer. Perls (1969a) suggested that "we start with the impossible assumption that whatever we believe we see in another person or in the world is nothing but a projection" (p. 67). He wrote that the recognition of the senses and the understanding of projections go hand in hand. Thus, he did not interpret dreams, play intellectual guessing games, or tell clients the meaning of their dreams. Clients do not think about or analyze the dream but write a script and act out the dialogue among the various parts of the dream. Because clients can act out a fight between opposing contradictory sides, eventually they can appreciate and accept their inner differences and integrate the opposing forces. Whereas Freud called the dream the royal road to the unconscious, Perls (1969a) believed it was the "royal road to integration" (p. 66).

According to Perls (1969a), the dream is the most spontaneous expression of the existence of the human being. It represents an unfinished situation, but it is more than an uncompleted situation or an unfulfilled wish. Every dream contains an existential message of oneself and one's current struggle. Everything is to be found in dreams if all the parts are understood and assimilated. Each piece of work done on a dream leads to some assimilation. Perls asserted that, if dreams are properly worked with, the existential message becomes clearer. According to him, dreams serve as an excellent way to discover personality voids by revealing missing parts and the client's methods of avoidance. If people do not remember dreams, they are refusing to face what is wrong with their lives. At the very least, the Gestaltist asks clients to talk to their missing dreams. For example, as directed by her therapist, a client reported the following dream in the present tense, as though she were still dreaming.

> I have three monkeys in a cage. One big monkey and two little ones! I feel very attached to these monkeys, although they are creating a lot of chaos in a cage that is divided into three separate spaces. They are fighting with one another—the big monkey is fighting with the little monkey. They are getting out of the cage, and they are clinging on to me. I feel like pushing

them away from me. I feel totally overwhelmed by the chaos that they are creating around me. I turn to my mother and tell her that I need help, that I can no longer handle these monkeys because they are driving me crazy. I feel very sad and very tired, and I feel discouraged. I am walking away from the cage, thinking that I really love these monkeys, yet I have to get rid of them. I am telling myself that I am like everybody else. I get pets, and then when things get rough, I want to get rid of them. I am trying very hard to find a solution to keeping these monkeys and not allowing them to have such a terrible effect on me. Before I wake up from my dream, I am making the decision to put each monkey in a separate cage, and maybe that is the way to keep them.

The therapist then asked his client, Brenda, to "become" different parts of her dream. Thus, she "became" the cage, and she "became" and had a dialogue with each monkey, and then she "became" her mother, and so forth. One of the most powerful aspects of this technique was Brenda's reporting her dream as though it were still happening. She quickly perceived that her dream expressed a struggle that she was having with her husband and her two children. From her dialogue work, Brenda discovered that she both appreciated and resented her family. She learned that she needed to let them know about her feelings, and that together they might work on improving an intensely difficult lifestyle. She did not need an interpretation from her therapist to understand the clear message of her dream.

The preceding brief account of dream work is intended to acquaint the reader with the general manner in which dreams are useful in Gestalt therapy. For the reader who wishes an in-depth treatment of the issue, I suggest Downing and Marmorstein's book (1973) *Dreams and Nightmares,* which is possibly the most detailed work available on Gestalt approaches to dreams.

APPLICATION IN INDIVIDUAL AND GROUP THERAPY

Gestalt therapy can be practiced in a variety of ways, either in an individual or a group setting. In counseling, it can be applied in a strict Gestalt fashion, whereby the client's interaction with the therapist is minimal. Clients translate their immediate experience into a role-playing situation in which they personify all aspects of their awareness. In this puristic form even clients' reactions to the therapist are a part of their fantasy projections.

Individual therapy might also proceed in a less puristic form, characterized by a dialogue between the client and the therapist. The therapist might suggest experiments to help clients gain sharper focus on what they are doing in the present, but the therapist also brings his or her own reactions into the dialogue and thus is more than a director of individual therapy. Polster and Polster (1973) and Kempler (1973), leading figures in the Gestalt approach, called for an active, self-disclosing, involved human approach on the therapist's part.

Kempler (1973, pp. 270–271) urged "full personal expression" of the therapist during the therapeutic hour: "The therapist's responsibility is to live it and not merely preach it by interpreting the other person's behavior." Kempler suggested that the therapist express everything he or she thinks or feels "that he expects to be of value or that would diminish his ability to participate if he withheld it." Kempler allows for a wide range of behavior on the therapist's part during the individual encounter. The therapist might suggest, shout, or cry, talk about himself or herself, explore his or her own embarrassment, or admonish a client. According to Kempler, "No behavior is exclusive property of the patient alone. If the patient-therapist process is to be kept alive, it depends as much on the full participation of the therapist as it does on his demand for his patient's full commitment." Clearly, the success of individual therapy is a function of the joint participation of two humans. The therapist must do more than ask questions, make interpretations, and give suggestions. The therapist's own conflicted process is a vital part of the therapy process.

In a group setting, Gestalt practice can also take a puristic form, or it can encourage members to spontaneously become involved in interactions with one another. Perls worked with a group in the puristic way. His contact was focused on a single client at a time, and he diverted the client's attention away from the group and toward the client's internal reactions. In that manner the therapist and client work together, with the other members as observers. When a particular client is finished working, the therapist usually asks members to give reactions or to relate what occurred to their own experiences. With this model, a member of the group volunteers and accepts the invitation to work. The volunteer takes the "hot seat" and focuses as much as possible on his moment-to-moment, here-and-now awareness. A variety of Gestalt techniques, as I described earlier, encourage intensification of the client's experience. The direct and spontaneous interchanges between the members and the client on the hot seat are absent. At certain times the therapist might call on other members of the group, although usually in a structured way aimed at furthering the therapist's work with the client on the hot seat.

As can individual therapy, group therapy can be practiced within a Gestalt context but less puristically. Group members can have more freedom to interact spontaneously, and the therapist can encourage more member-to-member interaction. The important decision is whether the intervention is helpful or distracting. Some interaction distracts from the quality of work and diffuses the energy of the group.

In short, as Kempler (1973) indicated, "The Gestalt therapist is identified more by who he is than by what he does" (p. 273). The therapist, whether doing individual or group work, has latitude to employ psychotherapeutic techniques with a wider range than those originally developed by Perls in his workshops. Perls's hot seat pattern of working suited his own style and needs. As Kempler (1973) pointed out, this pattern put Perls in the top-dog position. Kempler wrote that Perls was his own person and developed a unique style that cannot be mechanically imitated with effective results. "That Fritz followed himself is the essence of him and hopefully also this will be the core of the Gestalt Movement" (p. 253). Thus, it is hoped, the therapist will develop a style of leadership that is consistent with his or her personhood and not fall into the trap of merely mimicking Perls.

In deciding whether or not to employ Gestalt techniques, we need to consider the population with which we are working. Shepherd (1970) addressed this issue with the following:

> In general, Gestalt therapy is most effective with overly socialized, restrained, constricted individuals—often described as neurotic, phobic, perfectionistic, ineffective, depressed, etc.—whose functioning is limited or inconsistent, primarily due to their internal restrictions, and whose enjoyment of living is minimal. Most efforts of Gestalt therapy are therefore directed toward persons with these characteristics [pp. 234–235].*

*From "Limitations and Cautions in the Gestalt Approach," by I. Shepherd. In J. Fagan and I. Shepherd (Eds.), *Gestalt Therapy Now.* Copyright 1970 by Science and Behavior Books, Inc. This and all other quotations from this source are reprinted by permission of the publisher.

According to Shepherd (1970), Gestalt techniques, particularly confrontational or reenacting techniques, are not for use with a psychotic population. She wrote that more severely disturbed clients need considerable support before they can undertake the in-depth experience of reliving the overwhelming rage, pain, and despair underlying the psychotic processes. Rather than involve the client with role playing that releases intense feelings, "It is helpful to use techniques to facilitate the patient's reclaiming freedom to use eyes, hands, ears, body; in general, to increase sensory, perceptual, and motor capacities toward self-support and mastery of his environment" (p. 235).

Summary and evaluation

Gestalt therapy is an experiential therapy stressing here-and-now awareness. This major focus is on the *what* and *how* of behavior and the role of unfinished business from the past that prevents effective functioning in the present. Some of the key goals of the approach are accepting personal responsibility, living in the immediate moment, and direct experiencing as opposed to abstract talking about experiences. The approach helps clients deal with avoidance, unfinished business, and the impasse.

A central therapeutic aim is to challenge the client to move from environmental support to self-support. Expansion of awareness, which is viewed as curative by and of itself, is a basic goal. With awareness, clients are able to reconcile polarities and dichot-omies within themselves and thus proceed toward the reintegration of all aspects of themselves.

In this approach, the therapist assists clients to experience all feelings more fully, and this enables them to make their own interpretations. The therapist avoids making inter-pretations and instead focuses on how clients are behaving. Clients identify their own unfinished business, and they work through the blockages impeding their growth. They do this largely by reexperiencing past situations as though they were happening in the present. Therapists have many techniques at their disposal, all of which have one thing in common: they are designed to intensify direct experiencing and to integrate conflict-ing feelings.

CONTRIBUTIONS OF GESTALT THERAPY

In my own practice, working with both individuals and groups, I make frequent use of Gestalt techniques. I am impressed with the action approach, which brings conflicts and human struggles to life. Through such techniques, I have found, people actually experience their struggles, as opposed to merely talking about problems endlessly in a detached manner. In doing so, they are able to increase their awareness of what they are experiencing in the present moment. I especially like the range of experiments that a therapist can suggest to help clients discover new facets about themselves. I like it that the approach encourages direct contact and expression of feelings and deemphasizes abstract intellectualizing *about* one's problems.

Another of Gestalt therapy's contributions is the exciting way in which the past is dealt with in a lively manner by bringing relevant aspects into the present. Unfinished business from the past is not ignored; rather, practitioners challenge clients in creative ways to become aware of and work with issues that obstruct current functioning. Further, paying attention to the obvious verbal and nonverbal leads provided by the client is a useful way to approach a counseling session. Through the skillful and sensitive use of Gestalt approaches, practitioners can assist people in heightening their present-centered awareness of what they are feeling and thinking as well as what they are doing. Through this awareness they are enabled to assume an increased share of personal responsibility for what they are experiencing.

I especially value the confrontational aspect of this approach in refusing to accept helplessness as an excuse for not changing. The client is provided with a wide range of tools, in the form of Gestalt experiments, for making decisions about changing the course of living.

LIMITATIONS OF GESTALT THERAPY

A danger of Gestalt therapy lies in the deemphasis of the cognitive factors of personality. Thinking about one's experience tends to be discouraged; I believe that *both* the feeling and thinking functions are of critical importance in the counseling process, and I see this approach as not leaving enough room for people to conceptualize and give meaning to what they are feeling. Another major problem is the tendency of some practitioners to use Gestalt techniques as a way of hiding or as a way of mechanically relating to others. Because of the variety of techniques at their disposal, power-hungry therapists can easily misuse these techniques to either impress or manipulate clients. If this is done, clients are prevented from becoming autonomous, rather than learning to accept responsibility for themselves.

I would like to conclude with a few words of caution. For Gestalt experiments to be effective, clients must be prepared for them. Thus, care must be taken to avoid springing techniques on clients who are left wondering about their purpose. It behooves the counselor to lay the necessary groundwork and to build trust with the client so that the techniques do not appear as mere gimmicks. Finally, Gestalt therapy worked dramatically well for Fritz Perls, because he invented it, and it also fit his personality. Unfortunately, many therapists have become so enthralled with his charismatic manner that they have attempted to mimic his style without really understanding and incorporating the conceptual framework of the Gestalt approach. Some of these practitioners have become carbon copies of Perls, and in doing so they have lost any chance of creating an approach that is effectively their own. Further, merely learning the Gestalt jargon and getting the techniques down pat do not automatically make one an effective therapist.

Questions for reflection and discussion

Following are some questions designed to help you critically evaluate this approach to therapeutic practice.

1. What are the values and limitations of the Gestalt focus on the here and now? Do you think that this approach adequately deals with one's past and one's future? Explain.
2. Gestalt therapy discourages *why* questions and focuses instead on the *what* and *how* of experiencing. What are your reactions to this emphasis? Do you agree or disagree that *why* questions generally lead to heady ruminations?
3. Gestalt therapy tends to focus on what people are *feeling* moment to moment. Do you think that this emphasis on feeling precludes thinking about one's experiencing? Explain.
4. Gestaltists tend to be confrontational in their work. Although this confrontation can be done with care, respect, and sensitivity for clients, there are also some dangers. In your view, what risks are inherent in this approach?

5. A wide variety of techniques and experiments were described in this chapter. How comfortable do you think you would feel in using some of the techniques? Do you think that it is important that *you* experience these techniques first *as a client* before you attempt to use them with others? How might you prepare your clients so that they would be more likely to benefit from Gestalt exercises?
6. What are the major values in using Gestalt approaches? What limitations are there to this approach? With what kinds of client might you be most inclined to use Gestalt techniques?
7. What specific aspects (either techniques or concepts) of Gestalt therapy might you most like to incorporate into your style of counseling? Explain.
8. Compare Gestalt therapy with the psychoanalytic approach. Do you see any basis for integrating Gestalt techniques within a psychoanalytic framework? Discuss.
9. Both Gestalt therapy and person-centered therapy are branches of existential therapy, and they share some philosophical views regarding human nature. At the same time, the former model relies on techniques, whereas the latter deemphasizes techniques and therapist direction. Do you see any basis for integrating Gestalt approaches with some person-centered concepts? Why or why not?
10. What are the implications of Gestalt therapy for your own personal growth? How can you use some of the techniques, experiments, and concepts as a way of furthering self-understanding and promoting personality change in yourself?

Recommended supplementary readings

Gestalt Therapy Verbatim (Perls, 1969a) is one of the best places to get a first-hand account of the style in which Perls worked. If you like that book and want to know more about Perls as a person, I recommend *In and Out of the Garbage Pail* (Perls, 1969b).

Life Techniques in Gestalt Therapy (Fagan & Shepherd, 1970a) is an excellent set of articles dealing with the tasks of the therapist; Gestalt techniques, rules, and games; working with dreams; and the limitations of the approach.

Gestalt Approaches in Counseling (Passons, 1975) is one of the books about Gestalt therapy that I most highly recommend, as it deals with the practical applications of Gestalt concepts in a wide variety of counseling situations. It is an excellent resource for techniques, and it stresses the importance of preparing clients for these techniques.

Gestalt Therapy Integrated: Contours of Theory and Practice (Polster & Polster, 1973) is a superb source for those who want a more advanced and theoretical treatment of this model.

References and suggested readings

Books highly recommended as supplementary reading are marked with an asterisk.

Brown, G. *Human teaching for human learning.* New York: Viking, 1971.
Corey, G. *Theory and practice of group counseling.* Monterey, Calif.: Brooks/Cole, 1981.
Corey, G. *Case approach to counseling and psychotherapy.* Monterey, Calif.: Brooks/Cole, 1982.
Downing, J. (Ed.). *Gestalt awareness.* New York: Harper & Row (Perennial Library), 1976.
Downing, J., & Marmorstein, R. (Eds.). *Dreams and nightmares: A book of Gestalt therapy sessions.* New York: Harper & Row, 1973.
* Fagan, J. The tasks of the therapist. In J. Fagan & I. Shepherd (Eds.), *Gestalt therapy now.* New York: Harper & Row (Colophon), 1970.
* Fagan, J., & Shepherd, I. (Eds.). *Life techniques in Gestalt therapy.* New York: Harper & Row, 1970. (a)

Fagan, J., & Shepherd, I. (Eds.). *What is Gestalt therapy?* New York: Harper & Row, 1970. (b)

Feder, B., & Ronall, R. (Eds.). *Beyond the hot seat: Gestalt approaches to group work.* New York: Brunner/Mazel, 1980.

* James, M., & Jongeward, D. *Born to win: Transactional Analysis with Gestalt experiments.* Reading, Mass.: Addison-Wesley, 1971.

Kempler, W. Gestalt therapy. In R. Corsini (Ed.), *Current psychotherapies.* Itasca, Ill.: F. E. Peacock, 1973.

Latner, J. *The Gestalt therapy book.* New York: Bantam, 1973.

Lederman, J. *Anger and the rocking chair.* New York: McGraw-Hill, 1969.

Levitsky, A., & Perls, F. The rules and games of Gestalt therapy. In J. Fagan & I. Shepherd (Eds.), *Gestalt therapy now.* New York: Harper & Row (Colophon), 1970.

* Passons, W. R. *Gestalt approaches in counseling.* New York: Holt, Rinehart & Winston, 1975.

* Perls, F. *Gestalt therapy verbatim.* Moab, Utah: Real People Press, 1969. (a)

* Perls, F. *In and out of the garbage pail.* Moab, Utah: Real People Press, 1969. (b)

* Perls, F. *The Gestalt approach and eye witness to therapy.* New York: Bantam, 1973.

Perls, F., Hefferline, R., & Goodman, P. *Gestalt therapy: Excitement and growth in the human personality.* New York: Dell, 1951.

* Polster, E., & Polster, M. *Gestalt therapy integrated: Contours of theory and practice.* New York: Brunner/Mazel, 1973.

* Rainwater, J. *You're in charge! A guide to becoming your own therapist.* Los Angeles: Guild of Tutors Press, 1979.

Shepherd, I. Limitations and cautions in the Gestalt approach. In J. Fagan & I. Shepherd (Eds.), *Gestalt therapy now.* New York: Harper & Row (Colophon), 1970.

Smith, E. W. L. (Ed.). *The growing edge of Gestalt therapy.* New York: Brunner/Mazel, 1976.

Stevens, J. O. *Awareness: Exploring, experimenting, experiencing.* Moab, Utah: Real People Press, 1971.

Stevens, J. O. *Gestalt is.* New York: Bantam, 1975.

Van De Riet, V., & Korb, M. *Gestalt therapy: An introduction.* New York: Pergamon Press, 1980.

Zinker, J. *Creative process in Gestalt therapy.* New York: Brunner/Mazel, 1977.

7

Transactional Analysis

Introduction

Key concepts

VIEW OF HUMAN NATURE

EGO STATES

AN INTEGRATED THEORY

Injunctions and early decisions

Strokes

Games

Rackets

Life scripts

Redecisions

The therapeutic process

THERAPEUTIC GOALS

THERAPIST'S FUNCTION AND ROLE

CLIENT'S EXPERIENCE IN THERAPY

RELATIONSHIP BETWEEN THERAPIST AND CLIENT

Application: Therapeutic techniques and procedures

APPLICATION TO GROUPS

THERAPEUTIC PROCEDURES

Structural analysis

Didactic methods

Transactional analysis

Empty chair

Role playing

Family modeling

Analysis of rituals and pastimes

Analysis of games and rackets

Script analysis

Summary and evaluation

Questions for reflection and discussion

Recommended supplementary readings

References and suggested readings

Introduction

Transactional Analysis (TA) is an interactional psychotherapy that can be used in individual therapy but that is particularly appropriate for groups. This approach is set apart from most other therapies in that it is both contractual and decisional. It involves a contract, developed by the client, that clearly states the goals and direction of the therapy process. It also focuses on early decisions that each person makes, and it stresses the capacity to make new decisions. TA emphasizes the cognitive, rational, and behavioral aspects of personality and is oriented toward increasing awareness so that the client will be able to make new decisions and alter the course of his or her life.

Developed by Eric Berne, this approach is based on a personality theory that supplies a framework for the analysis of three separate ego states: Parent, Adult, and Child. Clear-cut operational statements characterize the approach. It utilizes several key words and offers a framework that can be easily understood and learned. The key words are *Parent, Adult, Child, decision, redecision, game, script, racket, strokes, discounting,* and *stamps.* Because of the operational nature of TA, including a contract, a client's degree of change can be established.

The contractual nature of the psychotherapeutic process tends to equalize the power of the therapist and the client. It is the responsibility of clients to decide what they will change. To make the changes a reality, clients change behavior in an active manner. During the course of therapy, they evaluate the direction of their life, come to understand some very early decisions that they made, and realize that they can now redecide and initiate a new direction in life. In essence, then, TA assumes that people can learn to trust themselves, think and decide for themselves, and express their feelings.

Key concepts

VIEW OF HUMAN NATURE

Transactional Analysis is rooted in a philosophy that is antideterministic and asserts that human beings are capable of transcending their conditioning and early programming. Further, this theory rests on the assumptions that people are capable of understanding their past decisions and that they can choose to redecide. It places faith in the person's capacity to rise above habit patterns and to select new goals and behavior. This does not imply that people are free from the influences of social forces, nor does it mean that they arrive at critical life decisions totally by themselves. It acknowledges that they were influenced by the expectations and demands of significant others, especially since their early decisions were made at a time in life when they were highly dependent on others. But decisions can be reviewed and challenged, and, if early decisions are no longer appropriate, new decisions can be made.

Harris (1967) wrote that humans have choices and are not bound by their pasts. "Although the early experiences which culminated in the position cannot be erased, I believe that the early positions can be changed. *What was once decided can be undecided*" (p. 66).* Although Berne (1970) wrote that human beings have the capacity to choose, he contended that few people achieve the degree of awareness necessary for becoming autonomous:

---

*From *I'm OK—You're OK,* by T. Harris. Copyright 1967 by Harper & Row, Publishers, Inc. This and all other quotations from this source are reprinted by permission.

Man is born free, but one of the first things he learns is to do as he is told, and he spends the rest of his life doing that. Thus his first enslavement is to his parents. He follows their instructions forevermore, retaining only in some cases the right to choose his own methods and consoling himself with an illusion of autonomy [p. 194].

This view of human nature has definite implications for the practice of TA therapy. The therapist recognizes that one reason a person is in therapy is because he or she has entered into conspiracies and game playing with others. The therapist does not, however, allow the same conspiratorial relationship to develop in therapy. The therapist will not accept "I tried," "I couldn't help it," and "Don't blame me, because I'm stupid." Because of the basic premise that the person can make choices, can make new decisions, and can act, excuses, or "cop-outs," are not accepted in the therapeutic practice of TA. There-fore, if clients are not allowed to perpetuate their cop-out style in the therapeutic relationship, there is a good chance that they will discover their own internal strengths and capacities to use their freedom in redesigning their life in new and effective ways.

Goulding and Goulding (1978) contended that people make certain decisions for survival motives at some point in life. Yet they are not determined by these early deci-sions, for they can make new ones later and thus change the course of their life. The Gouldings wrote that humans have the power to direct their own life, and that they are not victims of their past:

I [Robert Goulding] believe that the power is in the person, and that the therapist's job is to create an environment in which that person can make new decisions in his life, and get out of his script—to live autonomously, responding to the new environment in a way appropriate for this time and place, not hanging onto old feelings from the past, and looking for reasons to justify them [p. 11].

EGO STATES

As mentioned earlier, Transactional Analysis delineates three distinct patterns of be-havior, or ego states: Parent, Adult, and Child (P–A–C).

The Parent part of the personality is an introject of the parents and parental substitutes. In the Parent ego state we reexperience what we imagined were our own parents' feelings in a situation, or we feel and act toward others as our parents felt and acted toward us. The Parent ego state contains *shoulds* and *oughts*. The Parent in each of us can be the "Nurturing Parent" or the "Critical Parent."

The Adult ego state is the processor of data and information. It is the objective part of the personality, and it is the part that knows what is going on. It is not emotional or judgmental, but works with the facts and with external reality. Based on available infor-mation, it produces the best solution to a particular problem.

The Child ego state consists of feelings, impulses, and spontaneous acts. The Child in each of us might be the "Natural Child," the "Little Professor," or the "Adapted Child." The Natural Child is the impulsive, untrained, spontaneous, expressive infant in each of us. The Little Professor is the unschooled wisdom of a child. It is manipulative and creative. It is that part of the Child ego state that is intuitive and plays on hunches. The Adapted Child exhibits modifications of the Natural Child's inclinations. The modifica-tions are the result of traumatic experiences, demands, training, and decisions about how to get attention.

Clients who experience TA are taught how to recognize what ego state they are functioning in at any given time. In this way they can make conscious decisions about the particular ego state in which they want to function. For example, if Susan becomes aware that she typically responds to her children in the same critical way in which her own mother responded to her, she is then in a position to change this stance.

Goulding and Goulding (1979) asserted that, as clients become more aware of the ego state they are in, they also become more aware of their adaptive behavior (both to their internal Parent and to the outside world). With this awareness, they can knowingly choose to adapt or not to adapt.

AN INTEGRATED THEORY

Robert Goulding and Mary McClure Goulding, directors of the Western Institute for Group and Family Therapy in Watsonville, California, are recognized as being among the current leaders in the field of Transactional Analysis. The Gouldings (1976, 1978, 1979) differ from the classical Bernian approach, and they have developed their own modification of TA by combining its principles and techniques with those of Gestalt therapy and behavior modification.

The following sections, which present further key concepts of TA, are to a large extent a modification of writings of the Gouldings. The theory of TA integrates the following concepts: Children grow up with *injunctions,* and on the basis of these parental messages they make *early decisions.* These early decisions are aimed at receiving parental *strokes* (recognition/attention from parents), as well as at ensuring basic survival. *Games* develop as a way of supporting one's early decisions. "*Rackets,*" which are the chronic bad feelings that flow from these early decisions, are collected and "saved up" by people as a result of playing games. All of these elements fit into the *life script,* which includes our expectations of how our life drama will be played out. A major contribution of the Gouldings to therapeutic practice is the focus on the client's capacity for *redecision,* which implies that early decisions can be understood and changed; new decisions can be made that provide the basis for living life fully.

Injunctions and early decisions. A key concept in TA is that of injunctions, which are the parental messages that children accept uncritically. Goulding and Goulding (1978, 1979) referred to an injunction as a message given to the child by the parents' internal Child out of the circumstances of the parents' own pains—anxiety, anger, frustration, and unhappiness. These messages tell children what they have to do and be in order to get recognition. Although some of these injunctions may be given in a verbal and direct manner by parents to children, more often than not these messages are inferred from parental actions. The Gouldings have drawn up a list of what they consider to be the ten basic injunctions: *Don't. Don't be. Don't be close. Don't be important. Don't be a child. Don't grow. Don't succeed. Don't be you. Don't be sane* and *don't be well. Don't belong.*

In response to the injunctions we hear as children, we eventually make early decisions. These decisions are often motivated by the need to be recognized by our parents, by the need to be stroked by them, and often by the sheer need for psychological or physical survival. Goulding and Goulding (1978, p. 74; 1979, p. 39) made the point that as children *we accept* these parental messages, and that we make early decisions based on them. According to the Gouldings, injunctions are not inserted in the child like an electrode. Further, many injunctions were not even given by the parents; rather, as children we invented them or misinterpreted the messages from our parents, and thus in some cases we gave ourselves our own injunctions. The point is that we make early decisions, many of which may have been appropriate in certain situations as children but which are inappropriate as they are carried into adulthood. Much of the therapeutic process in TA consists of becoming aware of the specific nature of injunctions that we have accepted uncritically and the circumstances surrounding the early decisions that we made in response to these parental messages. As we become increasingly aware of injunctions (and the resulting decisions) we are able to critically examine them to determine if we will continue living by them.

The following list, based on an adaptation of the works of Goulding and Goulding (1978, 1979), includes common injunctions and some possible decisions that could be made in response to them.

1. *Don't*: Given by scared parents, this injunction tells children not to do normal things for fear that they could lead to disaster. Children who accept this injunction will believe that nothing they do is right or safe, and they will look to others to protect them and decide for them.

Possible decisions: "I can't decide for myself, so I look to others to tell me what to do." "I'll never decide for myself again." "I'm scared of making wrong decisions for fear I'll make mistakes, so I won't decide."

2. *Don't be*: As one of the most lethal of all messages, this one is often delivered nonverbally through the way the parent holds (or does not hold) the child. The message might be "I wish you hadn't been born, and then I wouldn't have had to put up with all I have!" This *don't exist* message may be implied by brutality or indifference.

Possible decisions: "I'll get you to love me, even if it kills me." "I'll do what you want and pretend I don't exist in this family." "If things get too bad, I'll kill myself."

3. *Don't be close*: This parental message can be given by parents who are not physically close or who push the child aside. Related to this injunction are the messages *Don't trust* and *don't love*.

Possible decisions: "I won't allow myself to get close, for when I do people leave me." "I won't get close, and that way I won't be hurt." "I'll never trust a woman (man) again."

4. *Don't be important:* In some way children may feel personally discounted when they speak, and thus they may decide not to be important and not to ask for what they want and need.

Possible decisions: "I'll never be or feel important." "If I ever do become important, I can never let anyone know about it."

5. *Don't be a child*: A message that oldest children often get is to be responsible and take care of the rest of the children. As they grow up, they may find it extremely difficult to allow themselves to have fun or to be a child.

Possible decisions: "I'll always be mature and won't do anything childish." "I'll take care of others, and I won't ask for anything for myself."

6. *Don't grow*: A series of parental messages may include these: "Don't grow beyond infancy." "Don't grow up and leave me." "Stay a child and don't become sexual." This injunction may be given by parents who are frightened that they cannot handle the fact that their children are able to grow.

Possible decisions: "I won't be sexual, and in that way my father won't reject me." "I'll stay little and helpless, for then I'll get goodies from my parents."

7. *Don't succeed*: If parents typically criticize children, this message comes across: "You can't make it." "You never do anything right." These children actually get stroked for failing, and thus they may buy the *don't succeed* message.

Possible decisions: "I'm basically stupid and meant to be a loser." "I'll show you that I can make it, even if it kills me." "No matter how good I am, I'll never be good enough."

8. *Don't be you*: This message is given by parents with the implication that "you are the *wrong sex*. You should have been a girl (boy), and then I would have loved you." In the attempt to win parental acceptance, children may decide to try to become whatever their parents want them to be.

Possible decisions: "No matter what I ever do or am, I'll never please them." "I'll pretend I'm a boy (girl)."

9. *Don't be sane* and *don't be well*: Some children receive most of their strokes when they are physically ill or when in some way they act crazy. Crazy behavior may be rewarded and modeled.

Possible decisions: "I'll be crazy (ill), and then I'll get noticed." "I am crazy."

10. *Don't belong*: This message may indicate that a family feels that it does not belong in the community or with any group.

Possible decisions: "Nobody will ever like me because I don't belong anywhere." "I'll never feel at home anywhere."

Strokes.   In this description of basic injunctions and early decisions, I have referred to the strokes that children strive for in their interactions with parents. In TA terminology, strokes are a form of recognition. We use them to communicate with each other. *Positive strokes* say "I like you," and they may be expressed by warm physical touches, accepting words, and friendly gestures. *Negative strokes* say "I don't like you," and they too can be expressed both verbally and nonverbally. *Conditional strokes* say "I will like you *if* and *when* you are a certain way"; they are received for *doing* something. *Unconditional strokes* say "I am willing to accept you for who you are and for being who you are, and we can negotiate our differences."

TA pays attention to how people structure their time to get strokes. It also looks at the life plan of individuals to determine which kind of strokes they both get and give. According to TA, it behooves us to become aware of the strokes we survive on, the strokes that we both ask for and receive, and the strokes that we give others.

Positive stroking is essential for healthy psychological development. It takes the form of expressions of affection or appreciation. If strokes are authentic, then we are nourished.

Negative stroking by parents leads to thwarting a child's growth. Negative strokes rob people of dignity by diminishing, humiliating, or ridiculing them. As bad as they may be, getting negative strokes appears to be preferable to receiving no strokes at all—that is, to being ignored.

Games.   A game is a series of transactions that ends in at least one player feeling badly. By their very nature games are designed to prevent intimacy. They develop for the purpose of supporting original decisions, and they are a part of a person's life script (a plan for life, or a conclusion that was reached about how to behave in order to survive in this world). For example, assume that a person was given the message *don't make it*. Also assume that she made the early decision not to succeed, for if she encountered any success this would bring anxiety. As a child she may have engaged in games that were designed to help her fail. As time passes, she may arrange her life in such a way that she continues to sabotage any chances of enjoying success. Thus, games are a vital part of a person's interactions with others, and they need to be understood if the person wants to decrease game-playing behavior and live authentically.

TA proponents encourage people to identify and understand their ego states. Their contention is that, by recognizing and accepting them, people free themselves from outdated Child decisions and irrational Parent messages that complicate their lives. TA teaches the individual which part he or she is using to make important life decisions. Further, TA proponents say that people can understand their internal dialogues between Parent and Child. They can hear and also understand their relationships with others. They can be aware of when they are straight and when they are crooked with others. Using the principles of TA, people can become aware of the kind of strokes they were reared on, and they can change the strokes they respond to from negative to positive. They are able to ask for the strokes they need, but if they are reluctant to do so they can bet that their Critical Parent is dictating to them that they "shouldn't" be so stuck on themselves. In short, one of the aims of TA is to help people understand the nature of their transactions with others so that they can respond to others with directness, wholeness, and intimacy. Game playing is then reduced.

TA views games as exchanges of strokes that lead to pay-offs of bad feelings and advance the script. Games might give the appearance of intimacy, but people who engage in game-playing transactions create distances between themselves by impersonalizing each other. It takes at least two to play a game, so that one way of aborting game transactions is for one of the players to become aware of the game he or she is in and then to decide not to play anymore. The first step is to gain awareness of the subtle nature of the game. Common games include "Poor Me," "Martyr," "Yes, but," "If It Weren't for You," "Look What You Made Me Do!", "Harried," "Uproar," and "Wooden Leg." Parents often resort to a battery of games to control their children, and children counter with games that are even more highly developed; for example, children are masterful at inventing games to avoid doing chores. The problem with a game is that the ulterior motive for it is buried, and the players end up feeling not OK.

The Karpman Drama Triangle (see Figure 7-1) is a useful device to help people understand games. The triangle has a "Persecutor," a "Rescuer," and a "Victim." For example, a family drama might include the interplay of family members, each operating from a different point on the Drama Triangle. The Victim plays the "Kick Me" game by inviting another person to kick him or her. Often the Victim persecutes another person until he or she kicks the Victim. To complete the triangle, another family member may rush in to save the poor, helpless, kicked Victim from the ruthless Persecutor. It is not uncommon for the Victim to persecute the Rescuer. The Rescuer, in the guise of being

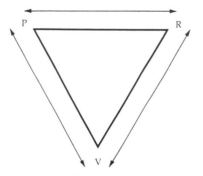

Figure 7-1   The Karpman Drama Triangle *(From "Fairy Tales and Script Drama Analysis," by S. Karpman. In* Transactional Analysis Bulletin, *1968, 7, 39–43. Reprinted by permission.)*

helpful, works to keep others in dependent positions. The feature that distinguishes a game from a straight transaction is the "switch" from one position in the triangle to another, such as the switch from rescuer to persecutor or from victim to persecutor, as illustrated in Figure 7-1.

Rackets.   The unpleasant feelings that we experience following a game are called rackets. These chronic feelings that we hold on to are the ones we often experienced as children with our parents. They are the feelings that we got (from the strokes we received) when we acted in certain ways as children. Like games, rackets support early decisions, and they are a basic part of one's life script. People can develop an anger racket, a guilt racket, or a depression racket, to mention a few. These rackets are maintained by actually choosing situations that will support unpleasant and chronic feelings. For example, if a woman has bought the *don't be close* injunction and made the decision not to trust people and not to get close, she may save up bad feelings of anger to justify her need for distance. If for some reason it appears that she might be getting close to someone, she will probably find certain characteristics or behaviors of the other person that result in her angry feelings, and this way she does not get close. If she collects enough bad feelings, she can eventually prove that she was right all along—that it is dangerous to get close.

Life scripts.   As I mentioned earlier, a life script in many ways resembles a drama with a plot. Our script may have been formed very early in life, when we learned that for psychological or physiological survival we had to be a certain way. Our life scripts include parental messages we have incorporated, the decisions we have made in response to these injunctions, the games we play to maintain our early decisions, the rackets we experience to justify our decisions, and our expectations of the way we think our life drama will be played out and how the story will end. Some TA writers, such as Berne (1964, 1972), Harris (1967), and Steiner (1974), have stressed the script theory. Berne believed that children are "scripted" and that they need direction from a strong Parent figure in the therapist if they hope to change their life scripts. Other well-known TA theorists and practitioners reject the scripting theory. Goulding and Goulding (1978, 1979) asserted that we make decisions in response to real or imagined injunctions and thereby "script" ourselves. In their words: "We believe that the individual writes his own script and can rewrite it with the help of a strong Parent he builds himself, rather than incorporates from a therapist" (1979, p. 42).

Dusay and Dusay (1979) wrote that people's life plan is based on their early existential decisions about themselves and others, and that they assume a basic life position that they are either OK as a person or not OK. Scripts incorporate elements from myths, fairy tales, and dramas in that they include a cast of characters and a range of emotions. One's life script may be a winning or a losing one; it may be tragic or banal. Also, each script includes specific roles to carry out in life. Thus, some people approach life as victims, others as rescuers, and others as persecutors. Once people develop a life script (based on messages they received from their parents and on the patterns of strokes they were reared with), it is characterized by a set of strong beliefs that are resistant to change.

Redecisions.   A major contribution to TA theory and practice has been made by the Gouldings' (1978, 1979) emphasis on the role of *redecisions* by clients in therapy. Throughout their writings, the Gouldings stress that, once early decisions have been made, they are *not* irreversible. In their view we cooperated in making the early decisions that direct our lives, so we can now make new decisions that are appropriate and that will allow us to experience life anew. In working with clients in the redecision process, they have them go back to the early childhood scenes in which they made these decisions. Then, from the Child ego state, they work with them to facilitate a new decision. Simply making an intellectual decision to be different is rarely enough to counteract years of past conditioning. It thus becomes necessary for clients to reexperience the original situation emotionally and to make the new decision emotionally as well as intellectually. For example, if a man were struggling to change an early decision of *not* wanting to live (in response to the *don't be* messages that he accepted as a child), he would be encouraged to go back to an early scene with his parents, work through feelings he had with them at that time, and eventually tell himself (and his parents symbolically) that he *will live,* that he deserves to live even if they wished he had never been born, and that he will make a *new decision* to stop his self-destructive ways and live to the fullest, *for himself*!

With each one of the ten basic injunctions (and some possible decisions that flow from them), there are countless possibilities for new decisions. In each case, the therapist chooses an early scene that fits the client's injunction/decision pattern, so that the scene will help this client make a specific redecision. For example, a client may return to a scene in which she was stroked for not succeeding or was negatively stroked for succeeding and thus made a decision: "I won't make it." After some work on the feelings this early scene stirs up, she can make a new decision: "Whether you like it or not, I *am* succeeding and I like it."

According to the Gouldings (1979), the process of redecision is a beginning rather than an ending. After a redecision, people tend to think, behave, and feel in different ways. They are able to discover an ability to be autonomous, and they can experience a sense of freedom, excitement, and energy.

The therapeutic process

THERAPEUTIC GOALS

The basic goal of Transactional Analysis is to assist clients in making new decisions regarding their present behavior and the direction of their life. It helps individuals gain awareness of how they have restricted their freedom of choice by following early decisions about their life positions, and it provides options to sterile and deterministic ways of living. The essence of therapy is to substitute an autonomous lifestyle characterized by awareness, spontaneity, and intimacy for a lifestyle characterized by manipulative game playing and self-defeating life scripts.

Harris (1967) saw the goal of Transactional Analysis as enabling the individual "to have freedom of choice, the freedom to change at will, to change the responses to recurring and new stimuli" (p. 82). The "restoration of the freedom to change" is based on knowledge of the Parent and the Child and of how these ego states feed into present transactions. The therapeutic process essentially involves freeing the Adult of the contaminating and troublemaking influences of the Parent and Child. As Harris (1967) put it, "The goal of treatment is to *cure* the presenting symptom, and the method of treatment is freeing up of the Adult so that the individual may experience freedom of choice and the creation of new options above and beyond the limiting influences of the past"

(p. 231).   According to Harris, the goal is achieved by teaching the client the basics of P–A–C. Clients in a group setting learn how to recognize, identify, and describe the Parent, Adult, and Child as each appears in transactions in the group.

Berne (1964) implied that the basic objective of Transactional Analysis is the attainment of autonomy, which is manifested by the release and recovery of three characteristics: awareness, spontaneity, and intimacy.

Like Berne, James and Jongeward (1971) viewed achieving autonomy as the ultimate goal of TA, which for them meant "being self-governing, determining one's own destiny, taking responsibility for one's own actions and feelings, and throwing off patterns that are irrelevant and inappropriate to living in the here and now" (p. 263). They made the point that courage is necessary to be a "real winner" at responding to life. It takes courage to accept the freedom that comes with autonomy, courage to choose intimate and direct encounters, courage to accept the responsibility of choosing, and "courage to be the very unique person you really are." They summed up the goal of becoming a healthy person as follows: "The path of an ethical person who is autonomously aware, spontaneous, and able to be intimate is not always easy; but, if such a person recognizes his 'losing streak' and decides against it, he is likely to discover that he was born with what it takes to win" (p. 274).

For Goulding and Goulding (1979), the goal of effective therapy is centered on assisting clients to break through a series of impasses that stem from injunctions and early decisions. Consistent with this goal, the Gouldings have developed redecision therapy, which helps clients work through impasses (or stuck places) on an emotional level. Then, work is done on a cognitive level to understand how archaic patterns of thinking, feeling, and behavior fit together and affect clients' lives in the present.

THERAPIST'S FUNCTION AND ROLE

Transactional Analysis is designed to gain both emotional and intellectual insight, but, as the focus is clearly on rational aspects, the role of the therapist is largely to pay attention to the didactic and cognitive issues. Harris (1967) saw the therapist's role as that of a "teacher, trainer, and resource person with heavy emphasis on involvement" (p. 239). As a teacher, the therapist explains techniques such as structural analysis, transactional analysis, script analysis, and game analysis. The therapist assists clients in discovering the disadvantageous conditions of the past under which they made certain early decisions, adopted life plans, and developed strategies in dealing with people that they might now wish to reconsider. The therapist helps clients gain more realistic awareness and find alternatives for living more autonomously.

Whereas the therapist has an expert knowledge of structural analysis, transactional analysis, and script analysis, he or she does not function in the role of a detached, aloof, superior expert who is there to cure the "sick patient." Most TA theorists—for example, Claude Steiner—stress the importance of an "equal relationship" and point to the contract for therapy as evidence that the therapist and the client are partners in the therapeutic process. Hence, the therapist brings his or her knowledge to bear in the context of a clear, specific contract that the client initiates.

The therapist's job basically is to help clients acquire the tools necessary for change. The therapist encourages and teaches clients to rely on their own Adult rather than on the therapist's Adult. Contemporary TA practice emphasizes that the key job of the leader is to help clients discover their inner power to change by making more appropriate decisions *now,* as opposed to continuing to live by archaic decisions they made in childhood. Goulding and Goulding (1978) stated this point well when they wrote that the therapist's real job is to *allow* clients to find their own power. They stressed that power is in the patient, not in the therapist.

CLIENT'S EXPERIENCE IN THERAPY

One basic prerequisite for being a TA client is the capacity and willingness to understand and accept a therapeutic contract. The treatment contract contains a specific statement of objectives that the client will attain and the criteria to determine how and when these goals are effectively met. Any transactions that are not related to the contract between the client and the therapist are excluded. This means that the therapist will not go on unauthorized "fishing expeditions" in the client's life history. In this way the client knows what he or she is coming to the therapist for, and, when the terms of the contract are completed, the relationship is terminated unless a new contract is established.

The contract implies that clients are active agents in the therapeutic process. From the outset, they state and clarify their own therapeutic goals. To implement these goals the client and therapist may design "assignments" to carry out within a therapy session and in everyday life. For example, Treva Sudhalter, a TA therapist in southern California, designs with her clients "Rehearsals for Change." Clients experiment with new ways of behaving, and thus they can determine whether they prefer the old or the new behavior. They decide whether they want to change and then specify new behavior plans to attain any changes desired. In this way the therapeutic process does not become an interminable one in which clients are dependent on the wisdom of the therapist. Clients demonstrate their willingness to change by actually doing, not by merely "trying" and not by endlessly exploring the past and talking about insights. For therapy to continue, clients act to effect desired changes.

RELATIONSHIP BETWEEN THERAPIST AND CLIENT

Dusay and Dusay (1979) wrote that TA therapy primarily focuses on change as defined by the treatment contract, which is based on an Adult-to-Adult agreement between the therapist and the client on both the goals and the process of the therapy. Therapist and client raise the question that is a basic part of contractual therapy: "How will both of us know when you get what you came for?" The basic attitude is that they are allies and will work together to accomplish a mutually agreed-on goal. During the course of therapy, Dusay and Dusay wrote, the therapist and client define their responsibilities in achieving the goal. The therapist does not assume a passive spectator role, nor does the client sit back passively and wait for the therapist to perform a magical cure.

Goulding and Goulding (1979) agreed that the contract sets the focus for treatment and determines the basis of the therapeutic relationship. They wrote that clients decide the specific beliefs, emotions, and behaviors they plan to change about themselves in order to reach self-designated goals. Clients then work with the therapist to determine the nature of the contract, with the therapist serving as both the witness and facilitator. A therapist will support and work with a contract that is therapeutic for the client.

The emphasis on specific contracts is one of TA's major contributions to counseling and therapy. It is easy in therapy to wander aimlessly without looking at goals or without taking personal responsibility for change. Many clients seek a therapist as the source of a cure-all, and they begin therapy in a passive and dependent stance. One of their difficulties is that they have avoided assuming responsibility, and they attempt to continue their life-styles by shifting responsibility to their therapist. The contractual approach of TA is based on the expectation that clients focus on their goals and make a commitment. It emphasizes the division of responsibility and provides a point of departure for working.

Omnibus contracts, such as "I want to be happy," "I want to understand myself," or "I hope to become better adjusted," are not accepted. The contract must be more specific and must delineate the ways of actually working to fulfill the contract in personal therapy or in a group setting. If a client says "I feel lonely and I'd like to get closer to people," a contract might include a specific exercise or task to actually begin to get close. For example, the client might be asked to experience closeness with other members of the group by spending 15 minutes exploring these feelings with each person in the group.

Some clients complain that they do not know what they want, or that they are too confused to form a clear contract. They can begin by deciding on short-term or easy contracts, perhaps by merely coming for three individual sessions to decide what, if anything, they want from therapy. It is important to keep in mind that a contract is not an end in itself but a means of helping a person accept responsibility for becoming autonomous.

The contract approach clearly implies a joint responsibility. Through sharing responsibility with the therapist the client becomes a colleague in his or her treatment. There are several implications of this relationship. First, there is not an unbridgeable gap of understanding between the client and the therapist. They share the same vocabulary and concepts and have a similar comprehension of the situation. Second, the client has full and equal rights while in therapy. This means that the client is not forced to make any disclosures he or she chooses not to make. Third, the contract reduces the status differential and emphasizes equality between the client and the therapist.

Application: Therapeutic techniques and procedures

APPLICATION TO GROUPS

The concepts and techniques of Transactional Analysis are particularly suited for group situations. In a group people are able to observe other people changing, which gives them more models for increasing their own options. They come to understand the structure and functioning of their individual personalities and learn how they transact with others. They are quickly able to identify the games they play and the scripts they act out. They are able to focus on their early decisions, which may never have been subject to scrutiny. Interaction with other group members gives them ample opportunities to practice assignments and fulfill their contracts. The transactions in the group enable the members to increase their awareness of both self and others and thus focus the changes and redecisions they will make in their lives.

Harris (1967) wrote that "the treatment of individuals in groups is the method of choice by Transactional Analysts" (p. 234). He viewed the beginning phase of a TA group as a teaching and learning process and placed significance on the didactic role of the group therapist. As he put it, "Since the essential characteristic of the group is that of teaching, learning, analyzing, the effectiveness of the Transactional Analyst rests in his enthusiasm and ability as a teacher and his alertness in keeping abreast of every communication or signal in the group, verbal or otherwise" (p. 239). Harris discussed several advantages of a group approach over the traditional one-to-one approach to therapy, some of which are the following: (1) the variety of ways the Parent manifests itself in transactions can be observed; (2) the characteristics of the Child in each individual in the group can be experienced; (3) people can be experienced in a natural milieu, characterized by an involvement with other people; (4) mutual confrontation of games can naturally occur; and (5) patients move faster and get well sooner in group treatment. Harris clarified the last advantage: "By 'get well' I mean achieving the goals stated in the initial hour contract, one of which is the alleviation of the presenting symptom and the other of which is to learn to use P–A–C accurately and effectively" (p. 238).

THERAPEUTIC PROCEDURES

In Transactional practice techniques from a variety of sources, particularly from Gestalt therapy, are used. James and Jongeward (1971) combined concepts and processes from TA with Gestalt experiments and demonstrated a promising avenue toward self-awareness and autonomy.

In their redecision therapy Goulding and Goulding (1979) work within the framework of Transactional Analysis theory, yet their methods are a combination of TA, Gestalt therapy, interactive group therapy, behavior modification, family therapy, psychodrama, and desensitization methods. Realizing the importance of combining the affective and the cognitive levels, the Gouldings draw heavily from TA theory for cognitive structure; and they draw heavily on Gestalt therapy techniques to provide the kind of highly emotional work that breaks through stubborn resistances and impasses. The Gouldings use an intensive residential group format, in which participants stay together anywhere from a weekend to a month.

The remainder of this section is devoted to a brief description of some of the more commonly used processes, procedures, and techniques in TA practice. Most of these therapeutic methods and processes can be applied to individual psychotherapy as well as to group treatment. However, as pointed out earlier, even though TA can effectively work on a one-to-one basis, the group itself is a significant vehicle for educational and therapeutic change.

Structural analysis.   Structural analysis is a tool by which a person becomes aware of the content and functioning of his or her ego states of Parent, Adult, and Child. TA clients learn how to identify their own ego states. Structural analysis helps clients resolve patterns that they feel stuck with. It allows them to find out which ego state their behavior is based on. With that knowledge, they can figure out what their options are.

Two problems related to the structure of personality can be considered by structural analysis: contamination and exclusion. Contamination exists when the contents of one ego state are mixed with those of another. Either the Parent or the Child or both intrude within the boundaries of the Adult ego state and interfere with the clear thinking and functioning of the Adult (see Figure 7-2). Contamination from the Parent is typically manifested through prejudiced ideas and attitudes; contamination from the child involves distorted perceptions of reality. When contamination of the Adult by the Parent or the Child or both exists, "boundary work" is called for so that the demarcation of each ego state is clearly drawn. When the ego-state boundaries are realigned, the person

Both the Parent
and the Child
Contaminating
the Adult

The Parent
Contaminating
the Adult

The Child
Contaminating
the Adult

Figure 7-2 Contamination

understands his or her Child and Parent rather than being contaminated by them. Examples of statements reflecting contamination from the Parent are "Don't mix with people that are not of our kind." "You can't trust those damned minorities." "Always be on the lookout for those mechanics, because they'll cheat you every time." "You can't trust teenagers." Examples of statements reflecting contamination from the Child are "Everyone's always picking on me, and nobody treats me good." "Anything I want I should get right now." "Who could possibly ever want me for a friend?" "The entire universe should revolve around me."

Exclusion exists when, for example, an Excluding-Child ego state can "block out" the Parent or when an Excluding-Parent ego state can "block out" the Child—that is, when rigid ego-state boundaries do not allow for free movement. The person might be relating primarily as Parent, or as Child, or as Adult. The Constant Parent (see Figure 7-3) excludes the Adult and Child and can typically be found in people who are so duty-bound and work-oriented that they cannot play. Such people may be judgmental, moralistic, and demanding of others. They often behave in a domineering and authoritarian manner. The Constant Child excludes the Adult and Parent and, at the extreme, is the sociopath without a conscience. People operating mainly from the Constant Child are perpetually childlike—they refuse to grow up. They do not think or decide for themselves but attempt to remain dependent in order to escape the responsibility for their own behavior. They seek someone who will take care of them. The Constant Adult, who excludes the Parent and the Child, is objective—that is, involved and concerned with

The Constant Parent
Exclusion of Adult
and Child by Parent

The Constant Adult
Exclusion of Parent
and Child by Adult

The Constant Child
Exclusion of Parent
and Adult by Child

Figure 7-3 Exclusion

facts. The Constant Adult is an individual who appears robot-like, with little feeling and little spontaneity.

Didactic methods. Because TA emphasizes the cognitive domain, teaching/ learning procedures are basic to the approach. Members of TA groups are expected to become thoroughly acquainted with structural analysis by mastering the fundamentals of P–A–C. Books are often recommended as an adjunct to therapy. Useful books for the layman include Eric Berne's *Games People Play* and *What Do You Say after You Say Hello?,* Thomas Harris's *I'm OK—You're OK,* Claude Steiner's *Scripts People Live,* Muriel James and Dorothy Jongeward's *Born to Win,* and Mary McClure Goulding and Robert Goulding's *Changing Lives through Redecision Therapy* and *The Power Is in the Patient.* In addition to readings, introductory courses in TA are often recommended as preparation for therapy. Also recommended for members of an ongoing TA group is participation in special workshops, conferences, and educational events related to TA.

Transactional analysis. Transactional Analysis is basically a description of what people do and say to each other. Whatever happens between people involves a transaction between their ego states. When messages are sent, a response is expected. There are three types of transactions: complementary, crossed, and ulterior. Complementary transactions occur when a message sent from a specific ego state gets the predicted response from a specific ego state of the other person. An example is the playful Child/Child transaction illustrated in Figure 7-4. Crossed transactions occur when an unexpected response is made to a message that a person sends out, as shown in Figure 7-5. Ulterior transactions are complex. They involve more than two ego states, and a disguised message is sent, as is illustrated in Figure 7-6.

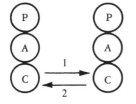

1. "I'd love to go sledding in the snow with you."

2. "Hey, that sounds like fun! Let's go!"

Figure 7-4   Complementary Transactions

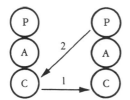

1. "I'd love to go sledding with you in the snow."

2. "Oh, grow up and act your age! I don't have time to waste on foolishness like that!"

Figure 7-5   Crossed Transactions

He to her: "Would you like to go out in the snow and play, or maybe we should finish all this work we should be doing in the house." He is sending a mixed message, which she can hear as (a) Let's go out and play in the snow (Child ⟶ Child) or (b) Let's be responsible and finish our work (Parent ⟶ Child).

Figure 7-6   Ulterior Transactions

Empty chair.   "Empty chair" is a procedure that works well with structural analysis. How does it work? Assume that the client is having difficulty coping with his or her boss (a Parent ego state). The client is asked to imagine that person in the chair before him or her and to carry on a dialogue. This procedure allows the client to express many thoughts, feelings, and attitudes as he or she assumes the roles of the ego states involved. The client sharpens his or her awareness not only of, in this case, the Parent ego state but also of the other two ego states (Child and Adult), which usually have certain characteristics in relation to the imagined state. The empty-chair technique can be useful for people who struggle with strong internal conflicts to get a sharper focus and a concrete grasp on a resolution.

McNeel (1976) described the two-chair technique as an effective tool to assist clients in resolving old conflicts with their parents or others who were in their environment as they were growing up. The goal of two-chair work is to complete unfinished business from the past. McNeel contended "that those therapists who do not make interventions and who sit on the sideline watching the reenactment of an old scene and waiting for the client to make a resolution in this process do not achieve very high results" (p. 62). In order to help clients stop waiting for some unresolved scene in the past to change, it is necessary for therapists to know how to potently intervene in the two-chair work. McNeel provided guidelines for issues to watch for in two-chair work, and he suggested the use of "heighteners" to clarify the issues involved. For example, a client may present himself as a helpless victim when he says "My father never really loved me, so now I don't know how to love anyone else and I don't know what to do about this." An appropriate "heightener" is "So maybe you can stay as you are until you die, unless your father finally decides to love you!"

Role playing.   TA procedures can also be beneficially combined with psychodrama and role-playing techniques. In group therapy, role-playing situations can involve other members. Another group member becomes the ego state that a client is having problems with, and the client talks to that member. Also, group members can rehearse with another member certain kinds of behaviors that they would like to try out in their outside lives. Another possibility is to exaggerate characteristic styles of Constant Parent, Constant Adult, or Constant Child or certain games so that clients can get reactions on their present behavior in the group.

Family modeling.   Family modeling, another approach to working with structural analysis, is particularly useful in working with a Constant Parent, a Constant Adult, or a Constant Child. The client is asked to imagine a scene including as many significant persons in the past as possible, including himself or herself. The client becomes the director, producer, and actor. He or she defines the situation and uses other members of the group as substitutes for family members. The client places them in the way he or she remembers the situation. The subsequent discussion, action, and evaluation can then heighten the awareness of a specific situation and the personal meanings it still holds for the client.

Analysis of rituals and pastimes.   Analysis of transactions includes identification of rituals and pastimes that are used in the structuring of time. Time structuring is important material for discussion and examination, because it reflects the decisions of the script about how to transact with others and how to get strokes. People who fill their time chiefly with rituals and pastimes are probably experiencing stroke deprivation, and thus they lack intimacy in their transactions with others. Because ritual and pastime transactions have low stroke value, such people's social transacting may lead to complaints such as emptiness, boredom, lack of excitement, feeling unloved, and a sense of meaninglessness.

Analysis of games and rackets. The analysis of games and rackets is an important aspect of understanding the nature of transactions with others. Berne (1964) described a game as "an ongoing series of complementary ulterior transactions progressing to a well-defined, predictable outcome" (p. 48). A pay-off for most games is a "bad" feeling that the player experiences. It is important to observe and understand why the games are played, what pay-offs result, what strokes are received, and how these games maintain distance and interfere with intimacy. Learning to understand a person's racket and how the racket relates to the person's games, decisions, and life scripts is an important process in TA therapy.

As I mentioned earlier, a racket consists of the collection of feelings that one uses to justify one's life script and, ultimately, one's decisions. For example, if Jane saves up feelings of depression, the games she plays with others most often have depression as the pay-off. When she has finally gathered enough feelings of depression, she feels justified in suicide, which is the action called for to conclude the life script. This is true of the person who has bought the *don't be* message. A racket is an old, familiar, bad feeling, such as resentment, guilt, fear, hurt, or inadequacy.

Rackets involve the "collection of stamps" that are later traded for a psychological prize. The individual collects archaic feelings by manipulating others to make himself or herself feel rejected, angry, depressed, abandoned, guilty, and so on. The person invites others to play certain roles. For example, Jane, a group member, may invite other members to react to her with anger. She could program this reaction by being extremely closed and hostile and by persuading herself that nobody could ever understand, much less care for, her. Any genuine approach from others would be rebuffed by her refusal to accept anything from anyone. Eventually, Jane would collect enough stamps to prove to the entire group that she was right all along, and then she could say "See, I told you at the beginning that nobody really cares for me and that I'd wind up feeling isolated from and rejected by all of you."

Rackets are as important as games in manipulating others, for they are the primary method of masking a person from the real world. It takes a competent therapist to distinguish between anger, tears, and fears that are used as a racket and the honest expression of emotions. The competent and skillful therapist squarely challenges a client's racket in such a manner that the client becomes aware of his or her behavior without being driven off.

Script analysis. People's lack of autonomy stems from their commitment to their scripting—that is, to a life plan decided on at an early age. An important aspect of the life script is the compelling quality that drives people to play it out.

Scripting initially occurs nonverbally in infancy, from parents' messages. During the early years of development, one learns about one's worth as a person and one's place in life. Later, scripting occurs in direct as well as indirect ways. For example, in a family such messages as the following may be picked up: "In this family, the man is the boss of the house." "Children are to be seen, but not heard." "We always expect the best from you." "The way you are, you'll never amount to a hill of beans." "Never question our authority, and always strive to be respectful and obedient." Because a person's life script forms the core of his or her personal identity and destiny, life experiences may lead a person to conclude, on the one hand: "I'm really dumb, because nothing I do ever turns out right. I suppose I'll always be stupid." On the other hand, the person may conclude: "I can do almost anything that I really decide I want to do. I know I can attain my goals if I channel my efforts in a direction I want to go in."

Script analysis is a part of the therapeutic process by which the life pattern that clients follow is identified. It can demonstrate to clients the process by which they acquired the script and the ways they justify their script actions. When clients become aware of their life script, they are in a position to do something about changing their program- ming. People are not condemned to be a victim of early scripting, for, through awareness, redecision is possible. Script analysis opens up new alternatives from which to choose as people go through life; they need no longer feel compelled to play games to collect pay-offs to justify a certain action that is called for in their life script.

Script analysis can be carried out by means of a script checklist, which contains items related to life positions, rackets, and games—all of which are key functional components of a person's life script.

Summary and evaluation

I find TA's contract method very useful, and I believe that any orientation to counseling can incorporate this aspect. In my judgment, it helps the client assume more personal responsibility for the outcomes of the counseling experience. The analysis of the games that we all play, another contribution of TA, teaches clients to become more aware of game structures and to free themselves from game-playing behavior. They can move from manipulative behavior to more authentic behavior.

Another contribution of TA that I have incorporated into my counseling is challenging clients to become more aware of the early decisions that they made in childhood because of psychological survival motives but that are now not only inappropriate but archaic. A lot of people drag behind them their early decisions about their self-worth and personal power, and they fail to come to terms with their power because they cling to parental messages that they rehearse over and over in their heads. I favor asking people to talk out loud about these inner rehearsals of the messages, many of which keep them in an emotional straitjacket. The TA insistence on examining here-and-now transactions with others to determine what people get from some of their behavior styles is another useful procedure.

Further, the integration of TA concepts and practices with certain concepts from Gestalt therapy is extremely helpful. A good example of how these two approaches can be blended together is found in James and Jongeward's *Born to Win* (1971), which I think is essential reading for any counselor. I frequently use some of the concepts from TA, such as early parental messages or the subtle ways people behave as their parents behaved, as catalysts for role playing or psychodrama. For example, instead of allowing group participants to carry on a lengthy monologue about why they have difficulty expressing affection to those they care about, I will request that they reenact some early scene with their parents that depicts how they learned that "you aren't supposed to get too close." Psychodrama, which can tap the deeper feelings of a current difficulty, tends to be far more meaningful than having people talk about an early decision. The above, then, are a few of the concepts and techniques that I find meaningful and useful in counseling.

What about the limitations of TA? First, because I encourage my students not to subscribe to any approach exclusively, I am somewhat uncomfortable with some proponents of TA, who seem to believe that psychotherapy begins and ends with Eric Berne's model and who follow to the letter Berne's terminology and methodology. The emphasis on many TA terms and on its jargon disturbs me. Although this seems to be characteristic of amateur TA therapists, I do not think that good therapists restrict themselves to structure and terminology.

The emphasis on the structure, to the degree that I find structure in TA, is another disquieting aspect for me. I believe that it is very possible for therapists who are well schooled in TA to become expert in diagnosing game patterns—indicating to the client what type of transaction he or she is now in, labeling every bit of behavior with some cliché phrase, detecting to what degree a person is "OK," and sorting out all kinds of scripting—and yet still practice therapy in such a manner that they leave themselves (their values, feelings, reactions to the client, and so on) out of the transaction with a client. In other words, I do not see in TA a great emphasis on the authenticity of the therapist or on the quality of the person-to-person relationship with the client. As the Rogerian therapist can hide under the blanket of passivity and refrain from directing the client to any degree, the TA therapist can hide under the blanket of categories, structures, labeling, transaction analysis, and the figurative job of directing traffic.

The danger is that TA can be primarily an intellectual experience. TA clients can understand intellectually all sorts of things but perhaps not feel and experience those aspects of themselves. Is the client in TA encouraged to work toward a synthesis of head and gut? Reliance on TA as an exclusive way of growth seems to be limiting in that it stresses understanding on a cognitive level. In my opinion one of the shortcomings of the Gestalt approach is that it deemphasizes intellectual factors. In Gestalt therapy one is frequently called to task if one thinks and is told that one is "bullshitting" or, even worse, "elephantshitting"! In TA, however, one of the shortcomings is its deemphasis of the affective domain. Thus, it is the marriage of many of the concepts and techniques of Gestalt with those of TA that is most useful.

It should be added, however, that contemporary TA stresses the integration of the cognitive and emotional domains. This integration is particularly obvious in the Gouldings' approach, which combines experiential work using Gestalt techniques with the cognitive work of Transactional Analysis. Further, Dusay and Dusay (1979) see the future of TA as shifting from a major reliance on cognitive understanding (which is still considered important) to an approach that is more experiential and deals more with emotions.

Questions for reflection and discussion

Below are questions that are based on the TA framework. I suggest that you apply them to yourself and use them as guidelines for your evaluation of Transactional Analysis and its implications for you.

1. What are some values and standards that you have taken from your parents? What kinds of values do you hold that are in contrast to your parents' values? To what degree have you thought through these values and made them your own or modified them?

2. What are some games and strategies you used as a child with your family and that you are aware of still using in your present relationships with people? What do these games do for you?
3. Can you trace some of the basic early decisions that you made about yourself during your childhood? Are those decisions still operating in your present behavior? Are you aware of changing any of your basic decisions? If so, which ones?
4. What are some parental injunctions that you can identify in your life? Can you identify with any of the following? Don't play. Don't think. Don't touch. Don't talk. Don't stare. Don't be close. Don't succeed. Don't fail. Don't let us down. Don't enjoy. Don't trust. Don't be you. Don't be sexy. Don't be rude. Don't fight. Don't be selfish. Don't be.
5. What are some *dos, oughts,* and *shoulds* in your life? Which of the following fit for you? Be perfect. You should be productive. You ought to work to your potential. You should do what is expected of you. You ought to be responsible. Succeed at everything. Be tough. Do what is right.
6. Can you see how some injunctions that you have internalized might have some effect on you as you counsel others? For example, if you have trouble being spontaneous or being childlike, how might you be affected in working with clients who are impulsive and tend to live for the moment?
7. How do you get your strokes? Are they mainly negative or mainly positive? Do you get strokes from your family? From work? From friends? Are you able to ask for the strokes you want, or are you limited in the amount of positive stroking you can tolerate?
8. Do you really believe that most people are able to change the early decisions that they made about themselves, others, and life? What forces operate against a person in his or her attempt to change and make new decisions? How can a person make and retain new decisions?
9. Are games to some extent necessary for survival? If they are not, why do you suppose that so many of us cling to our manipulative game-playing strategies? What do you suppose would happen if a person gave up all his or her manipulative games and became completely straight and honest in all transactions with others?
10. According to Harris (1967), the essence of a cure in TA therapy is as follows: "If a patient can put into words why he does what he does and how he has stopped doing it, then he is cured, in that he knows what the cure is and can use it again and again" (p. 238). Do you agree? Is this enough? If so, why? If you do not agree, what else do you think is necessary?

Recommended supplementary readings

If you are interested in a popular account of Transactional Analysis, an excellent place to begin is *Born to Win: Transactional Analysis with Gestalt Experiments* (James, M., & Jongeward, 1971). This book not only gives a good overview of TA principles but also includes many Gestalt experiments dealing with topics such as stroking, sexual identity, game playing, adulthood, and autonomy.

Another popularized version, which deals largely with recognizing ego states, transactions, and basic life positions, is *I'm OK—You're OK* (Harris, 1967).

If you are interested in a more advanced treatment of Transactional Analysis as a theory with specific applications to therapeutic practice in groups, I highly recommend *Changing Lives through Redecision Therapy* (Goulding & Goulding, 1979). This is a very readable work that gives a clear and concise overview of Transactional Analysis. It deals in depth with such topics as injunctions and early decisions, contracts, stroking, dealing with emotions, redecisions, and the blending of TA theory with Gestalt therapy techniques. It is an excellent example of integrating the cognitive and the affective dimensions in helping clients to work through early decisions and toward making new decisions.

References and suggested readings

Books highly recommended as supplementary reading are marked with an asterisk.

Barnes, G. (Ed.). *Transactional Analysis after Eric Berne.* New York: Harper College Press, 1977.

Berne, E. *Transactional Analysis in psychotherapy.* New York: Grove Press, 1961.

Berne, E. *Games people play.* New York: Grove Press, 1964.

Berne, E. *Principles of group treatment.* New York: Oxford University Press, 1966.

Berne, E. *Sex in human loving.* New York: Simon & Schuster, 1970.

Berne, E. *What do you say after you say hello?* New York: Grove Press, 1972.

Corey, G. *Theory and practice of group counseling.* Monterey, Calif.: Brooks/Cole, 1981.

Corey, G. *Case approach to counseling and psychotherapy.* Monterey, Calif.: Brooks/Cole, 1982.

Dusay, J., & Dusay, K. M. Transactional Analysis. In R. Corsini (Ed.), *Current psychotherapies* (2nd ed.). Itasca, Ill.: F. E. Peacock, 1979.

* Goulding, M., & Goulding, R. *Changing lives through redecision therapy.* New York: Brunner/Mazel, 1979.

Goulding, R., & Goulding, M. Injunctions, decisions, and redecision. *Transactional Analysis Journal,* 1976, 6(1), 41–48.

* Goulding, R., & Goulding, M. *The power is in the patient: A TA/Gestalt approach to psychotherapy.* San Francisco: TA Press, 1978.

* Harris, T. *I'm OK—You're OK.* New York: Avon, 1967.

James, D., & Scott, D. *Women as winners: Transactional Analysis for personal growth.* Reading, Mass.: Addison-Wesley, 1976.

James, M. *Marriage is for loving.* Reading, Mass.: Addison-Wesley, 1979.

* James, M., & Jongeward, D. *Born to win: Transactional Analysis with Gestalt experiments.* Reading, Mass.: Addison-Wesley, 1971.

Karpman, S. Fairy tales and script drama analysis. *Transactional Analysis Bulletin,* 1968, 7(26), 39–43.

McCormick, P. *Guide for use of a life script questionnaire in Transactional Analysis.* San Francisco: Transactional Publications, 1971.

McNeel, J. The parent interview. *Transactional Analysis Journal,* 1976, 6(1).

Schiff, J. L., with Day, B. *All my children.* New York: Evans, 1970.

Steiner, C. A script checklist. *Transactional Analysis Bulletin,* 1967, 6(22), pp. 38; 39; 56.

Steiner, C. *Games alcoholics play: The analysis of life scripts.* New York: Grove Press, 1971.

Steiner, C. *Scripts people live: Transactional Analysis of life scripts.* New York: Grove Press, 1974.

Weisman, G. *The winner's way: A Transactional Analysis guide for living, working and learning.* Monterey, Calif.: Brooks/Cole, 1980.

Woollams, S., & Brown, M. *Transactional Analysis.* Ann Arbor, Mich.: Huron Valley Institute Press, 1978.

8

Behavior Therapy

Introduction

The theoretical approaches considered so far have emphasized factors such as the individual's psychodynamics, or internal states; the influence of childhood experiences on contemporary functioning; the individual's struggle in making life choices; the quality of the client/therapist relationship; and the experiential aspects of therapy. The behavioral therapies emphasize people's cognitive dimension and various action-oriented methods geared to help them take definite steps to change behaviors. In some respects, Transactional Analysis is a form of behavior therapy, or at least it includes some behavioral features. It emphasizes specific actions and doing; it is based on contracts; it stresses the role of therapist as teacher; and it is a cognitive approach. Likewise, rational-emotive therapy (Chapter 9) is a form of cognitive behavior therapy, and it includes many specific behavioral techniques. Reality therapy (Chapter 10) can be considered a form of behavior modification, and it is essentially a type of nonrigorous operant conditioning.

Behavior therapy is a particular form of behavior modification. While behavior modification relates to the general use of behavioral assumptions, concepts, and techniques to control, change, or modify another's behavior, behavior therapy specifically attempts to eliminate faulty behavior and to help clients acquire new skills. Practiced on a one-to-one or group basis, behavior therapy has undergone important changes and has expanded considerably. It is no longer grounded exclusively in learning theory, nor is it a singular approach or a narrowly defined set of techniques. Kazdin (1978) wrote that behavior modification encompasses a variety of conceptualizations, research methods, and treatment techniques to explain and change behavior. Further, it is quite heterogeneous and eclectic in nature. According to Kazdin, no unifying set of assumptions about behavior can incorporate all the existing techniques in the behavioral field.

The most recent development within behavior therapy is the emergence of a cognitive emphasis. Wilson (1978) described three major forms of cognitive behavior therapy—the rational psychotherapies, the coping-skills therapies, and the problem-solving therapies. According to Wilson, cognitive processes are increasingly a part of behavior therapy. Even with this cognitive emphasis, Wilson asserted, the common core of all behavioral approaches includes a commitment to measurement, methodology, concepts, and procedures derived from experimental psychology.

Key concepts

VIEW OF HUMAN NATURE

The modern behavioral approach is grounded on a scientific view of human behavior that stresses a systematic and structured approach to counseling. Yet it does not exclude the importance of the client/therapist relationship or the potential of clients for making choices. Contemporary behavior therapy does not rest on deterministic assumptions that humans are mere products of their social/cultural conditioning. Rather, the view is emerging that the person is the producer *and* the product of his or her environment (Bandura, 1974, 1977).

Whereas the "radical behaviorists" (Skinner, 1948, 1971) rule out the possibility of self-determination and freedom, the current trend is toward developing procedures that actually give control to clients and thus increase their range of freedom. Kazdin (1978) observed that behavior modification aims to increase individuals' skills so that the number of their response options is increased. Through overcoming debilitating behaviors that restrict choices, individuals are freer to select from possibilities that were not available earlier. Thus, as behavior modification is typically applied, it will increase rather than stifle individual freedom (Kazdin, 1978).

Philosophically, the behavioristic and the humanistic approaches have often been seen as polar opposites. The writings of contemporary behavior therapists suggest that bridges are being built, allowing the possibility of a fruitful synthesis. The strict environmental view of human nature that is based on a stimulus/response model of behavior has been criticized by the pioneer of social-learning theory, Albert Bandura (1974, 1977). He rejected the mechanistic and deterministic model of human behavior because of its exclusive reliance on environmental determinants. Bandura contended that this view, which holds that individuals are passive agents subjected to influences of their surroundings, does indeed fail to take into account the capacity of the individual to actually affect his or her environment.

Other writers have made a case for using behavioristic methods to attain humanistic ends (Mahoney & Thoresen, 1974; Meichenbaum, 1977a; Thoresen & Coates, 1980; Watson & Tharp, 1981). According to Thoresen and Coates (1980), greater attention is being given to the emerging similarities among theories. They identified three interrelated themes that characterize this convergence. First is the focus on therapy as an action-oriented approach. Clients are being asked to act rather than to reflect passively and introspect at length on their problems. They are being helped to take specific actions to change their lives. Therapy is more than merely talking, for it stresses *doing* as a prerequisite for change. Second is the increasing concern of behavior therapists with how stimulus events are mediated by cognitive processes and recognition of the place of private or subjective meanings for the same stimulus events. Third, there is increasing emphasis on the role of responsibility for one's behavior. Given the techniques and skills of self-change, people have the capacity to improve their life by altering one or more of the various factors influencing their behavior. The above three converging themes provide a conceptual framework for a bridge between the behavioral and the humanistic approaches.

Mahoney and Thoresen (1974) stressed self-regulation of behavior, which increases the power of the person. Although they agreed that self-awareness is a factor in change, they stressed that awareness by itself does not result in lasting behavior change. They developed a variety of self-help techniques that can be used to produce behavioral change.

Watson and Tharp (1981) assumed that scientific principles can be used to increase the range of self-directed behavior. They described self-direction as the ability to actualize one's values. For them, self-directed behavior includes the choice of goals, the design of strategies for counseling, the evaluation of outcomes, and the maintenance of valued behavior. Thus, the client is not viewed as a passive agent who is shaped by the therapist; rather, the client is an active and choosing agent and a real partner in the therapeutic process.

Consistent with the notion of how individuals *act on* their environment to produce desired behavioral changes (as opposed to how individuals *react to* their environment) is the self-management approach advocated by Williams and Long (1979). They viewed self-modification as the ultimate application of behavioral concepts. By teaching people how to modify their own behavior, therapists are able to make a permanent impact on the lives of their clients.

In summary, contemporary behavior therapy has become broader in scope to encompass a concern with the cognitive states of individuals, in addition to behavioral dimensions. Behavior therapists are reformulating their techniques in cognitive and social-learning terms instead of the strict conditioning terms of a cause-and-effect model.

THE SCIENTIFIC METHOD

Thoresen and Coates (1980) wrote that behavior therapy is separated from other approaches by its reliance on the principles and procedures of the scientific method. Its concepts and procedures are stated explicitly, tested empirically, and revised continually. Further, treatment and assessment are interrelated, for they occur simultaneously. Research is considered essential to providing effective treatments and advancing beyond current therapeutic practices.

Kazdin (1978) noted that with its emphasis on experimental evaluation of therapy outcomes, contemporary behavior therapy is a scientific approach toward treatment and clinical practice rather than a particular conceptual stance.

BASIC CHARACTERISTICS

Because behavior therapy represents a diversity of procedures, Kazdin (1978) contended that it is difficult to enumerate a set of agreed-on assumptions and features that apply to the entire behavioral field. He did describe the following characteristics that apply most widely, if not universally, to approaches under the term *behavior therapy:*

1. The focus is on current influences on behavior as opposed to the historical determinants.
2. Emphasis is given to observing overt behavior change as the main criterion by which treatment should be evaluated.
3. Treatment goals are specified in concrete and objective terms in order to make replication possible.
4. Reliance is on basic research as a source of hypotheses about treatment and specific therapy techniques.
5. Target problems in therapy are specifically defined, so that treatment and measurement are possible.

According to Kazdin, the above five assumptions represent a basis for unity within the heterogeneity of behavior modification.

The therapeutic process

THERAPEUTIC GOALS

Goals occupy a place of central importance in behavior therapy. The client selects the counseling goals, which are specifically defined at the outset of the therapeutic process. Continual assessment throughout therapy determines the degree to which these goals are being effectively met.

The general goal of behavior therapy is to create new conditions for learning. The rationale is that all behavior is learned, including maladaptive behavior. If neurosis is learned, it can be unlearned, and more effective behaviors can be acquired.

There are several misconceptions regarding the issue of goals in behavior therapy. One common misconception is that the overall goal is simply to remove symptoms of a disturbance and that, once these symptoms are eliminated, new symptoms appear because the underlying causes were not treated. Most behavior therapists would not accept the notion that their approach is merely symptomatic treatment, for they see the therapist's task as eliminating maladaptive behavior and assisting the client to replace it with more adjustive behavior.

Another common misconception is that client goals are determined and imposed by the behavior therapist. There appears to be some truth in this statement, particularly as it pertains to some in situations such as mental hospitals. A clear trend in modern behavior therapy, however, is toward involving the client in the selection of goals. And a good working relationship between the therapist and the client is seen as necessary (though not sufficient) in order to clarify therapeutic goals and cooperatively work toward the means to accomplish them. Whereas the early proponents of this approach seem to have emphasized the expert role of the therapist in deciding goals and behavior, recent practitioners make it clear that therapy cannot be imposed on an unwilling client.

Kazdin (1978) made a case for the use of behavioral technology as a means for accomplishing both societal goals and the individual's goals. He contended that behavioral techniques do not threaten to eliminate or reduce freedom of choice. For example, he cited behavior-modification programs in hospitals and other institutions that have established goals endorsed by society. These aims include returning an individual to the community, fostering self-help, increasing social skills, and alleviating bizarre behaviors. In outpatient therapy, clients come to treatment with a goal—to acquire a skill or to alleviate a problem. In this case Kazdin held that the primary function of the behavior therapist is providing a means to attain the goal of the individual. Freeing individuals from behaviors that interfere with effective living is consistent with the democratic value that individuals should be able to freely pursue their own goals (within the limits of what is consistent with the general social good).

The process of identifying and developing a specific set of goals is a basic part of behavior therapy. These goals provide the framework for determining what treatment procedures will be used as well as what aspects will be given focus. Hence, goals must be refined to the point that they are clear, concrete, and understood and agreed on by both the client and the counselor. This process of determining therapeutic goals entails a negotiation between the client and the counselor, which results in a therapeutic contract that guides the course of therapy.

According to Cormier and Cormier (1979), goals serve three important functions in counseling. Goals that are clearly defined reflect specific areas of client concern, and thus they provide a meaningful direction for counseling. Goals also provide a basis for selecting and using particular counseling strategies and interventions. Most important of all, goals provide a framework for evaluating the outcome of counseling. Both the counselor and the client can monitor progress toward the major goals to compare progress before and after a counseling intervention.

The sequence of selecting and defining goals is described by Cormier and Cormier (1979, p. 165). This process demonstrates the essential nature of a collaborative relationship between the therapist and the client:

1. The counselor explains the nature and purpose of goals.
2. The client decides on the specific changes or goals desired.
3. The client and counselor explore the feasibility of the stated goals.
4. Together they identify any risks associated with the goals, and these risks are explored.
5. Together they discuss the possible advantages of the goals.
6. Based on the information obtained about client-stated goals, the counselor and the client make one of the following decisions: to continue counseling, to reconsider the client's goals, or to seek a referral.

Once the above process of selecting goals is accomplished, a process of defining the goals begins. This process includes a joint effort in which the counselor and client discuss the behaviors associated with the goals, the circumstances of change, the level of behavioral change, the nature of subgoals, and a plan of action to work toward these goals.

After goals have been set and defined, it is the therapist's task to select therapeutic strategies designed to meet them. It is at this point that the client and therapist negotiate a therapeutic contract. Gottman and Leiblum (1974) recommended that a written, signed contract be used that specifies agreement on the goals, methods, and procedural rules of treatment. In their view, there are significant implications of having such a contract (p. 44):

- The therapeutic contract increases the chances of making the counselor/client alliance operational.
- It emphasizes to clients the importance of their active participation in the process, rather than fostering an attitude of being a passive spectator.
- It is the basic link between whatever therapeutic procedures or techniques are used and the concrete goals of the client.

THERAPIST'S FUNCTION AND ROLE

Behavior therapists must assume an active, directive role in treatment, for they apply scientific knowledge to discovering solutions to human problems. The behavior therapist typically functions as a teacher, director, and expert in diagnosing maladaptive behavior and in prescribing curative procedures that, it is hoped, lead to new and improved behavior.

Another important function is the therapist's role modeling for the client. Bandura (1969, 1971a, 1971b, 1977) indicated that most of the learning that occurs through direct experience can also be acquired through observation of others' behavior. He developed the point that one of the fundamental processes by which clients learn new behavior is through imitation, or the social modeling provided by the therapist. The therapist, as a person, becomes a significant role model. Because clients often view the therapist as worthy of emulation, they pattern attitudes, values, beliefs, and behavior after the therapist. Thus, therapists should be aware of the crucial role that they play in the process of identification. For them to be unaware of the power they have in actually influencing and shaping the client's way of thinking and behaving is for them to deny the central importance of their own personhood in the therapeutic process.

CLIENT'S EXPERIENCE IN THERAPY

One of the unique contributions of behavior therapy is that it provides the therapist with a system of well-defined procedures to employ within the context of a well-defined role. It also provides the client with a well-defined role, and it stresses the importance of client awareness and participation in the therapeutic process. Clients must be actively involved in the selection and determination of goals, must possess the motivation to change, and must be willing to cooperate in carrying out therapeutic activities, both during therapy sessions and in real-life situations. If the client is not actively involved in this way, the chances are that therapy will not be successful.

An important aspect of clients' role in behavior therapy is that they are encouraged to experiment with new behavior for the purpose of enlarging their repertoire of adaptive behaviors. They are helped to generalize and transfer the learning acquired within the therapeutic situation to situations outside therapy. Again, this approach underscores the importance of the active involvement and willingness of clients to extend and apply their emerging behaviors to real-life situations.

This therapy is not complete unless actions follow verbalizations. Clients must do far more than merely gather insights; they must be willing to take risks. Successes and failures in the attempts to implement new behavior are a vital part of the therapeutic adventure.

RELATIONSHIP BETWEEN THERAPIST AND CLIENT

There appears to be a tendency on the part of some critics to characterize the relationship between the therapist and the client in behavior therapy as mechanically manipulative and highly impersonal. Most writers in this area, however, assert that establishing a good personal relationship is an essential aspect of the therapeutic process. Behavior therapists do not have to be cast in the cold and impersonal role that reduces them to programmed machines that impose a set of techniques on robot-like clients.

It does appear, however, that most behavior therapies do not assign an all-important role to the relationship variables. Nonetheless, most of them do assert that factors such as warmth, empathy, authenticity, permissiveness, and acceptance are considered necessary, but not sufficient, conditions for behavior change to occur within the therapeutic process.

Application: Therapeutic techniques and procedures

One of the major strengths of the behavioral approach to counseling and psychotherapy is the development of specific therapeutic procedures that lend themselves to refinement through the scientific method. Behavioral techniques must be shown to be effective through objective means, and there is a constant effort to improve them. Although behavior therapists may make mistakes in diagnosis or in applying therapeutic procedures, the results of their mistakes are obvious to them, for they receive continual direct response from their clients. Either their clients improve by attaining their stated goals, or they do not.

In contemporary behavior therapy any technique that can be demonstrated to change behavior may be incorporated into a treatment plan. Lazarus (1971) advocated the use of diverse techniques, regardless of their theoretical origin. He outlined a wide range of techniques that he was using in his clinical practice as supplements to behavioral methods. In his view, the more extensive the range of therapy techniques, the more potentially effective is the therapist. It is clear that behavior therapists do not have to restrict themselves strictly to methods derived from learning theory. Likewise, behavioral techniques can be incorporated into other approaches to therapy.

In the following sections I will describe a range of behavioral approaches and techniques available to the practitioner: relaxation training; systematic desensitization; implosive therapy and "flooding"; aversive-therapy techniques; token economies; modeling methods; a wide range of cognitive techniques, including cognitive-restructuring and thought-stopping; assertion-training programs; and self-management programs. I want to emphasize that these techniques do not encompass the full spectrum of behavioral procedures. Because of the limitations of a survey textbook, I chose to eliminate from discussion operant-conditioning procedures and applied behavioral analysis. In giving such a brief overview of techniques, it is difficult to capture the diversity and full scope of the behavioral field, which is continually developing.

RELAXATION TRAINING AND RELATED METHODS

Relaxation training has become increasingly popular as a method of teaching people to cope with the stresses produced by daily living. It is aimed at achieving muscle and mental relaxation and is easily learned. After clients learn the basics of relaxation procedures, it is essential that they practice these exercises daily in order to obtain maximum results.

Jacobson (1938) is credited with initially developing the progressive relaxation procedure. It has since been refined and modified, and relaxation procedures are frequently used in combination with a number of other behavioral techniques. These include imaginal-desensitization procedures, systematic desensitization, assertion training, self-management programs, tape-recorded instruction, biofeedback-induced relaxation, hypnosis, meditation, and autogenic training—teaching control of bodily and imaginal functions through autosuggestion.

Relaxation training involves several components, which typically involve from four to eight hours of instruction. Clients are given a set of instructions that asks them to relax. They assume a passive and relaxed position in a quiet environment while alternately contracting and relaxing muscles. Deep and regular breathing is also associated with producing relaxation. At the same time, clients learn to mentally "let go"; perhaps by focusing on pleasant thoughts or images. Relaxation becomes a well-learned response, which can become a habitual pattern if practiced daily for about 20 or 25 minutes. During these exercises it helps clients to actually feel and experience the tension building up, to notice their muscles getting tighter and study this tension, and to hold and fully experience the tension. Also, it is useful to experience the difference between a tense and a relaxed state.

Until the last few years relaxation training was primarily used as a part of systematic-desensitization procedures (which will be described later). Recently, relaxation procedures have been applied to a variety of clinical problems, either as a separate technique or in conjunction with related methods. The most common use has been with problems related to stress and anxiety, which often are manifested in psychosomatic symptoms. Other ailments for which relaxation training is helpful include high blood pressure and other cardiovascular problems, migraine headaches, asthma, and insomnia.

Other procedures that are in some ways similar to relaxation methods are hypnosis, biofeedback, autogenic training, and meditation. Relaxation instructions bear many similarities to hypnotic suggestions, including the suggestion to relax and achieve a calm state. Biofeedback employs instruments to provide a person with immediate and continuing feedback about bodily functions, such as the heartbeat, of which people are normally not aware. This procedure can be used as a way of teaching people to become aware of the degree of relaxation. Autogenic training involves a series of instructions to assist clients in gaining control over autonomic functions. Various meditation procedures can be learned as an adjunct to relaxation methods, and meditation can be integrated into daily practice sessions in learning to relax.

SYSTEMATIC DESENSITIZATION

Systematic desensitization is one of the most widely employed and empirically researched behavior-therapy procedures. It is used primarily for anxiety-based maladaptive behaviors or avoidance reactions. It involves, first, a behavioral analysis of stimuli that evoke anxiety and the constructing of a hierarchy of anxiety-producing situations; then, relaxation procedures are taught and are paired with imagined scenes. Situations are presented in a series that moves from the least to the most threatening. Anxiety-producing stimuli are repeatedly paired with relaxation until the connection between those stimuli and the response of anxiety is eliminated (Wolpe, 1958, 1969). The procedure of this counterconditioning model works as follows:

1. Stimuli that elicit anxiety in a particular area, such as rejection, jealousy, criticism, disapproval, or any phobia, are analyzed. The therapist constructs a ranked list of situations that elicit increasing degrees of anxiety or avoidance. The hierarchy is arranged in order from the worst situation that the client can imagine down to the situation that evokes the least anxiety. For example, if it has been determined that the client has anxiety related to fear of rejection, the highest anxiety-producing situation might be rejection by the spouse, next by a close friend, and then by a coworker. The least disturbing situation might be a stranger's indifference toward the client at a party.

2. During the first few sessions the client is given relaxation training, which is based on the technique outlined by Jacobson (1938) and described in detail by Wolpe (1969). Suggesting thoughts and creating imagery of previously relaxing situations, such as sitting by a lake or wandering through a beautiful field, are often employed. It is important that the client reach a state of calm and peacefulness. The client is taught how to relax all the muscles and is taken through the various parts of the body, with emphasis on the facial muscles. The arm muscles are relaxed first, followed by the head, then the neck and shoulders, the back, abdomen and thorax, and then the lower limbs. The client is instructed to practice relaxation outside the session for about 30 minutes each day. When the client has learned to relax quickly, the desensitization procedure begins.

3. The desensitization process involves the client's being completely relaxed with eyes closed. The therapist describes a series of scenes and asks the client to imagine himself or herself in each of the scenes. A neutral scene is presented, and the client is asked to imagine it. If the client remains relaxed, he or she is asked to imagine the least anxiety-arousing scene. The therapist moves progressively up the hierarchy until the client signals that he or she is experiencing anxiety, at which time the scene is terminated. Relaxation is then induced again, and the client continues through all the scenes in the hierarchy. Treatment ends when the client is able to remain in a relaxed state while imagining the scene that was formerly the most disturbing and anxiety producing.

Systematic desensitization is an appropriate technique for treating phobias, but it is a misconception that it can be applied only to the treatment of fears. It can be effectively applied to a large variety of anxiety-producing situations, including interpersonal ones, and to examination fears, generalized fears, neurotic anxieties, and sexual dysfunctions.

In a review of research evidence, Kazdin (1978) commented that systematic desensitization has been extremely effective in alleviating a wide range of maladaptive behaviors such as fears relating to animals, death, injury, and sex. It has also been used effectively in dealing with nightmares, anorexia nervosa, obsessions, compulsions, stuttering, and depression.

IMPLOSIVE THERAPY

One of the earliest alternatives to systematic desensitization was implosive therapy, which is both like and unlike desensitization. Both procedures make use of the imaginal presentation of anxiety-producing material. They differ in that implosive therapy requires that clients (from the very beginning) imagine highly fearful and threatening scenes for a prolonged time without undergoing relaxation exercises, as is the case in desensitization. The purpose of the implosive technique is to produce an anxiety-arousing experience of such magnitude that fears will be lessened in certain situations. Clients are asked not only to visualize strongly arousing stimuli but also, because maximum arousal is desired, to imagine the most terrible and horrible consequences. The therapist provides a running monologue designed to intensify these horrors.

For example, in working with a person with a snake phobia, the therapist might say: "You are in a room that is filled with ugly snakes. See them coming at you, and feel them crawling on you. They are biting you, squeezing you, and their fangs are drawing blood. Feel them tear at your flesh and see the blood!" The rationale of the technique is that, by repeatedly exposing clients to anxiety-ridden situations *without* dire consequences occurring, the anxiety from the stimulus is reduced or eliminated. With repeated exposure in the therapeutic setting, where the expected, feared consequences do not occur, the threatening stimuli lose the effect of producing anxiety, and the neurotic avoidance is supposedly extinguished.

Stampfl (1975) cited several examples of how implosive therapy works. He described a client who complained of obsessive tendencies related to dirt. The client washed his hands up to 100 times a day and had exaggerated fears of germs. The procedures for treating the client included (1) discovering what stimuli trigger what symptoms, (2) assessing how the symptoms are related and how they shape the patient's behavior, (3) asking the client to close his eyes and imagine as vividly as possible what is being described without reflecting on its appropriateness to his situation, (4) moving closer and closer to the client's greatest fears and attempting to have him imagine what he most wants to avoid, and (5) repeating each theme until it no longer arouses anxiety in the client.

Stampfl cited several studies that attest to the efficacy of implosive therapy with hospitalized mental patients, with neurotics, with psychotics, and with people suffering phobic symptoms. He asserted that this approach differs from conventional therapies in its deemphasis of insight as a therapeutic agent. It is a direct method of challenging the patient to "stare down his nightmares."

There are some major limitations of implosive therapy. Because this technique utilizes principles from both learning theory and psychoanalytic theory, therapists using it should be quite knowledgeable in both areas. In contrasting implosive therapy to other behavioral methods, Bellack and Hersen (1977) wrote that it has received relatively little empirical interest, and that most of the research done in this area has been marked by poor experimental design. They also indicated that there is a possibility that fear can be increased rather than decreased with this procedure. It is clear that therapists using this procedure should be familiar with identifying anxiety cues and formulating the scenes and capable of dealing with possible negative experiences in clients. Because implosion is rarely used, there is little evidence about the outcome of this method. Implosion does, however, raise an ethical issue directly related to the possible risks of increasing a client's fears.

 Flooding: An alternative to implosive therapy. Flooding exposes clients to intense anxiety-arousing stimuli—either in real-life situations (*in vivo*) or in imagined ones—for the purpose of heightening anxiety. Kazdin (1978) described flooding as based on the *extinction* of classically conditioned responses to anxiety-provoking cues. When clients are repeatedly exposed to conditioned stimuli at full strength, these stimuli lose their potency to elicit fear responses. The main difference between flooding and implosive therapy lies in the type of scene to which clients are exposed. In implosive therapy, clients are faced with terrible scenes in which dire and aversive consequences occur on an imaginal level. In flooding, scenes are described in which the feared stimuli are presented for a prolonged period of time, but without horrifying consequences.

 In evaluating flooding Bellack and Hersen (1977) concluded that, without clear evidence that it is more effective or quicker than desensitization, there is little justification for using it. They advised therapists to select a less stressful technique of known effectiveness whenever possible. They did point out that many of the subjects in the flooding studies had not responded to other techniques (such as desensitization); thus, the risks involved in flooding were more acceptable in these cases.

AVERSIVE TECHNIQUES

 Aversive techniques are the most controversial of the behavioral methods, although they are widely used for getting people to behave in desired ways. Conditions are created so that people do what is expected of them in order to avoid aversive consequences. Most social institutions use some form of aversive procedure to control the members' behavior and to shape it along expected lines. Churches use excommunication; schools use expulsion, suspension, and failure; industries use layoffs and docking of pay; and governments use fines and prison sentences. Further, parents attempt to regulate their children's behavior through various means of punishment or withholding of rewards.

 Aversion-therapy procedures have been used effectively in treating a wide range of disorders, including alcoholism, cigarette smoking, overeating, and socially unacceptable sexual attraction (Kazdin, 1978). Aversive procedures have been used for the most part to modify behavioral excesses that may involve self-injury, harm, and other violent and aggressive acts. These procedures are typically used in cases of head banging, self-mutilation, hair pulling, self-biting, and hitting, which are common behaviors of some psychotic individuals and mentally retarded patients. Other applications are for sexual deviations such as child molesting, incest, exhibitionism, and cross-dressing.

 There are six common types of aversive method: chemical aversion, electric shock, covert sensitization, "time-out," overcorrection, and response cost.

 1. Chemical aversion. Drugs that induce nausea and vomiting can be used to deter behaviors. This technique has been most prominently used in the treatment of alcoholism. Instead of being forced to refrain from liquor, the alcoholic is asked to drink. Each drink is accompanied by a strong emetic, the effect of which is illness followed by retching and vomiting. The alcoholic will eventually become somewhat ill by simply looking at a drink and will find the odor of alcohol discomforting.

Some clear disadvantages to chemical aversion were listed by Barlow (1978): Because of the unpleasant nature of the treatment, the person may terminate prematurely or refuse to cooperate. Some people develop a tolerance for these chemical agents. Also, there are some possible negative side effects of a physiological nature that make close medical supervision necessary. Barlow contended that patients should be fully informed of the unpleasant effects of such substances. He also maintained that people need a high degree of motivation to complete treatment.

2. Electric shock.   The electric shock used in behavior therapy is of a nonconvulsive nature. It is administered through two electrodes placed on the forearm, calf, or fingertips and held in place by snap fasteners or elastic cloth strips. The intensity levels are adjusted for each patient, and they can vary from one treatment session to the next. Electric shock has been used in treating a variety of behavioral disorders, some of which are chronic vomiting, the self-destructive tendencies of autistic and retarded children, sexual deviations (fetishism, transvestism, pedophilia, exhibitionism, and voyeurism), alcoholism, and aggressive behavior.

Bellack and Hersen (1977) in their summary of research findings concluded that electric shock can be used effectively to decelerate a variety of deviant behaviors. It was found to be more effective in treating sexual deviates than with alcoholics. The long-term effects of electric shock have not been determined. It appears that booster treatments enhance the long-range results. Lasting results also depend on teaching people alternative and positive responses, and not merely eliminating undesirable behaviors.

3. Covert sensitization.   Covert sensitization is a verbal aversion method in which unpleasant scenes are paired imaginally with scenes of deviant behavior. This technique has been used in the treatment of various sexual deviations, alcoholism, obesity, and smoking. Typically, clients imagine themselves engaging in a target behavior. For example, a male exhibitionist would be asked to imagine actual consequences such as the guilt and fear associated with getting caught, the negative reactions from friends and relatives, and being imprisoned for the offense. An alcoholic might be asked to imagine walking into a bar and reaching for a drink, which turns into vomit.

In summarizing the research findings of covert sensitization, Bellack and Hersen (1977) wrote that this method seems to be effective in the treatment of sexual deviation. Again, they pointed out that aversive techniques by themselves do not result in permanent changes unless clients are also taught constructive behaviors to replace those that are eliminated. The results of covert sensitization are far less encouraging with respect to treating obesity, alcoholism, and smoking.

Covert sensitization has some distinct advantages over other aversive procedures that account for its increasing popularity. It can be administered totally on the level of imagination, which results in a wide range of aversive images and facilitates self-administration outside of the therapy session. Further, the scenes can be tape-recorded to save therapist time. Also, covert sensitization is less unpleasant than chemical or electrical methods, does not have the negative side effects, and is less likely to be terminated by the client (Barlow, 1978).

4. Time-out.   Increasing attention has been directed to an aversion procedure known as "time-out from positive reinforcement." This procedure assumes that a target behavior will decrease in frequency if the opportunity to obtain positive reinforcement is denied the individual. For example, in the classroom a disruptive child will be removed for a time from a situation in which reinforcers (other people or some form of entertainment) are present. The child who demonstrates acting-out behavior in the classroom is separated from other children and thus restricted from the opportunity to receive peer reinforcement for attention-getting behavior. Barlow (1978) observed that time-out seems less aversive than other techniques but requires careful attention and consistency from the parent, teacher, or hospital attendant.

5. Overcorrection.   Overcorrection is most often applied to the disruptive behavior of children or institutionalized adults. Classified as a form of punishment, the procedure requires that the individual first restore the environment to its natural condition immediately after the inappropriate behavior (restitution). Then, the individual experiences an appropriate penalty for the disruptive act (overcorrection). For example, children who throw food in a temper tantrum might first be required to clean up the mess they made and then be required to restore the room to a "better-than-normal" state by waxing the floors. Or they might be compelled to clean another room.

6. Response cost.   Response cost is a form of punishment in which a reinforcer is removed after an inappropriate or undesirable behavior. Response cost requires that the relationship between the act and the penalty be clearly explained. This technique entails imposing some penalty, usually in the form of a fine, the loss of points or privileges, or the loss of material goods. Response-cost procedures have been used in combination with hospitalized patients under a token economy, in which constructive behavior earns tokens exchangeable for some tangible reward or privilege. Behavioral infractions often result in the loss of tokens. Combining a reward system with a response-cost procedure often leads to desirable behavior changes.

In discussing the status of response-cost procedures, Bellack and Hersen (1977) noted that the long-term effects had not been fully evaluated. Their summary comment was that, in general, behaviors that are suppressed with response cost tend to remain that way after the contingency has been lifted. Further, with this procedure there is less chance of undesirable side effects, which are often observed when other types of punishment are used.

Ethical issues related to aversion procedures.   The ethical issues involved in aversion-therapy techniques are highlighted when severely painful stimuli are used with nonvoluntary and institutionalized populations. The following guidelines are developed from Barlow (1978), Bellack and Hersen (1977), Kazdin (1978), and Stolz and associates (1978). Therapists who employ aversive therapies must take steps to ensure that they are used appropriately:

• *Informed consent* should be a part of using aversion therapy. Clients should have the right to decide whether they want to participate in a proposed program. Before making the decision, they should be told the type of aversive stimuli and procedures to be used, the possible side effects of the treatment, the chances of success, and the methods used to determine how effective the treatment is. When children are involved, parental consent should be obtained. In cases of institutionalized patients who cannot make an informed decision, the ethical and legal guidelines of the institution should be followed.

- Practitioners who employ aversive techniques must be competent, which implies knowing which technique to select and how to appropriately administer and evaluate the procedure.
- Clear measures of problem behavior should be administered to document effectiveness or the lack of it.
- If aversive methods are used, painless techniques should be attempted before resorting to painful stimuli. Alternative positive measures should be attempted first.

Three excellent points were made by Bellack and Hersen (1977) regarding the use of aversion therapies. *First,* although the short-term effects are known, the long-term effects are not. Ethical practice demands documentation of long-term effects if aversive methods are to be fully legitimized. *Second,* these techniques typically have the goal of suppressing undesirable behavior. Mere suppression is not enough, and complete behavioral treatment requires teaching clients a set of new and adaptive behaviors. *Third,* special ethical issues are involved when aversive techniques are used with homosexuals. Therapists should evaluate whether clients who seek behavioral treatment related to homosexuality actually do want to change their life-style, or whether they are seeking therapy because of societal pressures to conform to basic standards.

TOKEN ECONOMIES

The token economy is a behavioral approach based on the application of the principles of reinforcement and extinction. Instead of using reinforcers directly, however, tokens are awarded that can be exchanged later for a variety of material goods desired by the clients. Instead of being used with individuals, this approach is usually applied to a group environment, such as a classroom, a home for delinquent youths, or a psychiatric ward. The token economy aims at developing adaptive behaviors by reinforcement with the tokens; at times, undesirable behaviors are eliminated by taking away tokens (using the response-cost technique discussed under aversive procedures).

In describing the planning and implementation of a token-economy program, Agras (1978b) contended that it is important to provide a wide range of backup reinforcers as behavior improves. He noted that the main ingredients of a token economy are identifiable target behaviors and a wide range of goods or privileges that can be earned. Target behaviors should not be limited to those that ensure order and discipline, though this may be the first step in the operation of a token system. The choice of reinforcers will depend on the needs and interests of the population, but Agras wrote that the majority of studies suggests that the availability of a wide range of goods and privileges is the main component, not merely setting of goals in themselves.

If a token economy is to work in a psychiatric ward, it is essential that the staff at all levels be educated in its use and also convinced of its value (Agras, 1978b). In cases in which the staff has seen the advantages of a token economy and cooperated with its implementation, research data support the immediate, powerful effects of the contingent application of tokens with a variety of problems. These problems include those of the long-term mental-hospital patient, those related to delinquency, and social and academic problems in the classroom.

A beginning series of controlled-outcome studies suggests that longer-term benefits also occur (Agras, 1978b). Agras emphasized that aspects of the social environment, such as the provision of extra social reinforcement engendered by the use of tokens, are indeed related to the effectiveness of token systems. According to him, success depends largely on the relationship between the various participants and the social atmosphere of the ward or classroom. Thus, such programs are far more than routine, automated procedures of doling out tokens for appropriate behaviors.

It appears that token economies can be applied to shape behavior when approval and other intangible reinforcers do not work. The token system is much like the real-life situation in which workers are paid for their production. Thus, the use of tokens as reinforcers for appropriate behavior has several advantages:

1. Tokens do not lose their incentive value, especially if their earning power and value increase as the specified behavior also improves.
2. Tokens can reduce the delay between an appropriate behavior and its reward.
3. Tokens can be used as concrete motivators to change certain behaviors.
4. Tokens are a form of positive reinforcement.
5. The person has the opportunity to decide how to use earned tokens.
6. Token economies can lead to an increase of staff and client morale.
7. The system allows for social reinforcement measures.
8. Tokens can bridge the gap between an institution and outside life.

MODELING METHODS

The terms *modeling, observational learning, imitation, social learning,* and *vicarious learning* have been used interchangeably. All refer to the process by which the behavior of an individual or a group (the model) acts as a stimulus for similar thoughts, attitudes, and behaviors on the part of observers. Through the process of observational learning, clients can learn to perform desired acts themselves without trial-and-error learning. Bandura (1969, 1971a, 1971b, 1977) has emphasized the role of modeling in the development and the modification of much of human behavior. He has suggested that most fears are developed through social transmission, rather than through direct experience with aversive stimuli.

Effects of modeling. Bandura (1969, 1971a, 1971b) outlined three major effects of modeling, each of which has significant implications for clinical practice. First is the acquisition of new responses or skills and the performance of them. This observational-learning effect refers to integrating new patterns of behavior based on watching a model or models. Examples include learning skills in sports, learning language patterns, training autistic children to speak through the use of models, learning social skills, and teaching hospital patients coping skills necessary for their return to the community.

The second effect of modeling is an inhibition of fear responses, which occurs when the observers' behaviors are inhibited in some way. In this case, the model who performs an inhibited fear response either does not suffer negative consequences or, in fact, meets with positive consequences. Examples include models who handle snakes and are not bitten, models who perform daring feats and do not get hurt, and models who perform prohibited acts. An example of the latter is the worker who walks off the job and strikes. If the person does not lose his or her job, fellow workers may follow suit.

The third effect of modeling is a facilitation of responses, in which a model provides cues for others to emulate. The effect is to increase behaviors that the individual has already learned and for which there are no inhibitions. Examples include models such as attractive teenagers who talk on a television commercial about a brand of jeans. Other youths who see the ad may follow the fad. Another model who channels or influences behavior is the person who is the first one to leave a social gathering. Typically, others soon follow this action.

Types of models. Several types of models can be used in therapeutic situations. A *live model* can teach clients appropriate behavior, influence attitudes and values, and teach social skills. For example, therapists can model the very characteristic to their clients during the therapy session that they hope the clients will acquire. Through their actual behavior during sessions, therapists can best teach self-disclosure, risk taking, openness, honesty, compassion, and the like. They can teach respect, self-acceptance, tolerance, and courage by serving as a model. Therapists are constantly serving as a live model for their clients—for better or for worse! In addition to modeling desired behaviors and attitudes, therapists can also adversely influence their clients by modeling rigidity, lack of regard and respect, fear, rudeness, coldness, and aloofness.

Behavior therapists also use *symbolic models*. A model's behaviors are shown on films, videotapes, and other recording devices. In reviewing the research evidence, Bandura (1969) wrote that symbolic models had been used successfully in a variety of situations. One example is clients who experience a variety of fears. By observing a model or models who successfully encounter certain fearful situations without negative consequences, such clients can decrease or eliminate certain fears.

Multiple models are especially relevant in group therapy. The observer can change attitudes and learn new skills through observation of successful peers in the group (or through observing coleaders). An advantage of multiple models is that observers learn some alternative ways of behaving, for they see a variety of appropriate and successful styles of behavior.

What are the characteristics of effective models? Reviews of research (Bandura, 1969) indicate that a model who is similar to the observer with respect to age, sex, race, and attitudes is more likely to be imitated than a model who is unlike the observer. Models who have a degree of prestige and status are more likely to be imitated than those who have a low level of prestige. However, the status level of the model should not be so high that the observer sees the model's behavior as unrealistic. Further, models who are competent in their performances and who exhibit warmth tend to facilitate modeling effects.

Clinical uses of modeling methods. Perry and Furukawa (1980) presented a comprehensive survey of the uses of modeling with a variety of special populations and problem areas. Clinical applications include treating snake phobias and helping to alleviate fears of children facing surgery. Modeling is used to teach new behaviors to socially disturbed children in the classroom, basic survival skills to retarded individuals, and verbal and motor skills to autistic children. Psychotic adults are taught the social skills they will need on returning to their community, and drug addicts and alcoholics learn new interpersonal skills.

Modeling is also used in teaching counseling skills to staff members in clinical settings. It appears that counselor trainees can learn to increase their empathic level of responding to clients through a combination of modeling with other behavioral methods such as role playing, feedback, and reinforcement.

THE COGNITIVE TREND IN BEHAVIOR THERAPY

As I mentioned earlier, a trend in contemporary behavior therapy is the increased emphasis on the role of thinking and "self-talk" as a factor in behavior. One of the most interesting areas of this approach is cognitive behavior modification, which consists of teaching people to change what they are thinking in order to change how they are acting. The basic assumption of this cognitive approach is that people actually create their own psychological problems, as well as specific symptoms, by the way they interpret events and situations. To a large degree, cognitive behavior therapy is based on the assumption that a reorganization of one's self-statements will result in a corresponding reorganization of one's behavior.

It is clear that the trend is toward considering cognitions as a form of behavior. Meichenbaum (1977a) wrote that within a learning-theory framework the client's cognitions are explicit behaviors that can be modified in their own right, just as are overt behaviors that can be directly observed. Thus, the behavior techniques that have been used to modify overt behaviors, such as operant conditioning, aversive conditioning, modeling, and behavioral rehearsal (practicing a skill in a therapy session in preparation for an anticipated situation) can also be applied to the more covert and subjective processes of thinking and internal dialogue.

In its earlier stages the behavioral approach ruled out subjective and internal states of an individual. Although overt behavior is still the focus of behavior therapy, there is increased recognition that these observable behaviors are not the only factors for which people seek therapy. Contemporary behavior therapy has broadened to make room for thoughts, beliefs, assumptions, feelings, self-verbalizations, and other subjective phenomena. Kazdin (1978) wrote that cognition-based techniques represent a new approach that has grown out of dissatisfaction with stimulus/response explanations of behavior. The new approach arose in response to research that has shown the influence of cognitive processes in controlling behavior.

Mahoney (1977) asserted that there are indications that psychology is undergoing some sort of "revolution." He cited recent efforts to integrate cognitive and behavioristic approaches to psychotherapy. According to Mahoney, the cognitive-learning perspective combines an appreciation for both internal and external environmental factors and addresses the challenge of untangling their relationships. Further, it is a comprehensive approach that recognizes the complex nature of human experience. Thus, this new emphasis is a challenge to those critics of behavior therapy who argue that it focuses only on the mechanistic aspects of behavior and thus loses the person in this reductionist process.

Mahoney suggested that effective therapists who work within the framework of the cognitive-learning perspective will need to master a number of skills. They must be diversified in their teaching skills and their technical knowledge. They must be good listeners, accurate observers, and effective problem solvers. Mahoney argued that such a diversification is long overdue in the field of clinical psychology and may be suited to the awesome complexity of the field of psychotherapy.

Cognitive restructuring.   Although cognitive restructuring is a central part of modern behavior therapy, it has its historical roots in Albert Ellis's rational-emotive therapy, which is the subject of the next chapter. Ellis (1973), Ellis and Grieger (1977), and Ellis and Whiteley (1979) described the theoretical constructs that undergird the practice of rational-emotive therapy, which assumes that human problems are the result of faulty thinking or irrational beliefs. In essence, people create their own emotional and behavioral disorders through their persistence in irrational thinking and self-destructive "self-talk." The assumption is that an individual's cognitive system can be changed directly and that this change will result in an altered and more appropriate set of behaviors. Rational-emotive therapy relies heavily on cognitive-restructuring procedures as well as many of the action-oriented behavioral techniques that are described in this section.

More recently, cognitive restructuring has been developed by Meichenbaum, Beck and his colleagues, and Mahoney. Beck (1967, 1976) contended that specific emotions (such as depression) are typically associated with specific and related interpretations of an experience. His approach consists of an analysis of the stylistic qualities of clients' cognitions, especially those of depressed people. It focuses on directing clients to identify stylistic qualities that involve distortions in their thinking. Through this process, clients become aware of and begin to understand that their emotional experiences (and maladaptive behaviors) are the result of particular thinking processes, which are subject to control and modification.

Beck's cognitive therapy involves assisting clients to critically evaluate their behavior by focusing on negative self-statements. Clients are taught to recognize, observe, and monitor their own thoughts and assumptions, as well as to validate the relationship between cognition and affect. This includes using language or semantic techniques as well as behavioral techniques. It involves doing homework assignments, gathering data on assumptions that are made, using an activity record which allows clients to review their cognitive distortions, and forming alternative interpretations. Beck advocates teaching clients systematic skills of self-observation, so that they can see the relationship between thoughts and emotions. They generate certain hypotheses about their behavior and eventually learn to employ specific problem-solving and coping skills to particular situations.

The following example represents an approach that a client might take in developing alternative interpretations of events and thus changing the feelings surrounding these events (Beck, 1976):

The *situation* is that your professor does not call on you during a particular class session. Your *feelings* may include depression. *Cognitively* you are thinking to yourself and telling yourself: "My professor thinks that I'm stupid, and that I really don't have much of value to offer the class. And furthermore, he's right, because everyone else is brighter and more articulate than I." Some possible *alternative interpretations* are that the professor wants to include others in the discussion, that he is short on time and wants to move ahead, or that he already knows your views.

As can be readily seen from this example, Beck attempts to have clients become aware of the distortions in their thinking patterns. He has them look at their inferences, which may be faulty. They see how they sometimes come to a conclusion (your decision that you are stupid, with little of value to offer) when evidence for such a conclusion is lacking. Clients also learn about the process of magnification of thinking, which involves exaggeration of the meaning of an event (obviously the professor thinks you are stupid because he did not acknowledge you on this one occasion). Beck also stresses such distortions as a disregard for important aspects of a situation, overly simplified and rigid thinking, and generalizing from a single incident of failure.

The role of the therapist is to demonstrate to clients how some of their assumptions about themselves and the world are unrealistic. Clients discover their own cognitive distortions and learn how these assumptions influence their behavior. Finally, in collaboration with the therapist, they learn an alternative set of interpretations.

Meichenbaum's cognitive theory of behavior change.   Cognitive restructuring also plays a central role in Meichenbaum's approach, known as cognitive behavior modification. He described *cognitive structure* as the organizing aspect of thinking, which seems to monitor and direct the strategy, route, and choice of thoughts (1977a). Cognitive structure implies an "executive processor," one that "holds the blueprints of thinking" that determine when to continue, interrupt, or change thinking:

> By cognitive structure I mean to imply that which is *unchanged* by learning a new word but which *is* changed by learning a new word-skill, such as the skill of listening to one's own internal dialogue. The cognitive structure I refer to is, by definition, the source of the scripts from which all such dialogues borrow [p. 213].

Meichenbaum proposed that "behavior change occurs through a sequence of mediating processes involving the interaction of inner speech, cognitive structures, and behaviors and their resultant outcomes" (p. 218). He described a three-phase change process in which those three aspects are interwoven:

Phase 1: Self-Observation. The beginning step in the change process consists of clients' learning how to observe their own behavior. This involves an increased sensitivity to their thoughts, feelings, physiological reactions, and interpersonal behaviors. For example, if depressed clients hope to make constructive changes, they must first realize that they are not a "victim" of negative thoughts and feelings. Rather, they actually contribute to their depression through the kinds of things they tell themselves. Although self-observation is seen as a necessary process if change is to occur, it is not a sufficient condition per se for change.

Phase 2: Starting a New Internal Dialogue. As a result of the early client/therapist contacts, clients learn to attend to their maladaptive behaviors, and they begin to notice opportunities for adaptive behavioral alternatives that will lead to behavioral/cognitive/ affective changes. If clients hope to change, then what they say to themselves must initiate a new behavioral chain, one that is incompatible with their maladaptive behaviors. Clients learn to change the internal dialogue that brought them into therapy. Their new internal dialogue comes to guide new behavior, which results in a form of cognitive restructuring.

Phase 3: Learning New Skills. The third phase of the modification process consists of teaching clients more effective coping skills, which are practiced in real-life situations. (For example, clients who can't cope with failure may avoid appealing activities for fear of not succeeding at them. Cognitive restructuring can help clients change their negative view of failure, thus making them more willing to engage in desired activities.) At the same time, clients continue to focus on telling themselves new sentences and observing and assessing the outcomes. As they behave differently in situations, they typically get different reactions from others. The stability of what they learn is greatly influenced by what they say to themselves about their newly acquired behavior and its consequences.

Meichenbaum (1977a) emphasized the importance of not only speaking to oneself but also listening to oneself. A critical factor determining the behavior-change process is the willingness and ability of clients to *listen* to themselves. Further, Meichenbaum strongly asserted that, if his view of cognitive behavior change is valid and useful from the standpoint of therapeutic practice and research, then therapists must be concerned with all three basic processes: cognitive structures, inner speech, and behaviors and the interpretation of their impact. According to him, focusing on only one will probably prove insufficient.

Thought stopping.   Another form of cognitive behavior therapy is thought stopping, which is used to deal with irrational thoughts that make it difficult for a person to concentrate on anything else. Thought stopping helps a client control unproductive or self-defeating thoughts and images by suppressing or eliminating them. This procedure is appropriate for clients who ruminate about past events that cannot be changed or engage in repetitive and unproductive thinking and anxiety-producing fantasies.

Rudestam (1980) described thought stopping as asking the client to concentrate on the ruminative and anxiety-producing images for a period of time, until the therapist suddenly yells "Stop!" This intervention interrupts the thought sequence, which makes it impossible to continue it. The procedure is repeated until the association between the stop cue and the obsessive thought is strengthened, and until the client takes over the function of intervening with his or her own subvocal "Stop" at any point of becoming aware of the obsessional sequence.

There are six major components of the thought-stopping strategy, which were described as follows by Cormier and Cormier (1979):

1. *Verbal Set.* After clients complain about self-defeating thoughts and images and say that they are willing to work at changing these patterns, the therapist helps them become aware of the nature of these negative thoughts and how they intrude into everyday behavior. The therapist gives some explanation for the rationale of the thought-stopping procedure.

2. *Counselor-Directed Thought Stopping: Overt Interruption.* Initially, the counselor takes the responsibility for interrupting the thoughts with a loud "Stop!"

3. *Client-Directed Thought Stopping: Overt Interruption.* After clients learn to control self-defeating thoughts in response to the counselor's interruption, they then assume the responsibility for the interrupting. They deliberately focus on the troubling thoughts and let all kinds of negative thoughts come to mind. The counselor instructs them to say aloud "Stop!" as soon as they are aware of negative thinking.

4. *Client-Directed Thought Stopping: Covert Interruption.* Because it may be impractical to yell "Stop!" in certain places clients also practice by letting these troubling thoughts and images come to mind and then subvocally saying "Stop."

5. *Shift to Assertive, Positive, and Neutral Thoughts.* Assume that a client continually tells herself that she will falter and fail in giving speeches in her class. In addition to learning to interrupt her self-defeating internal dialogue, she also learns to substitute positive statements, ones that might set up expectancies for success instead of failure. The counselor may help her by modeling or actually giving some constructive sentences to replace the negative self-statements. She is encouraged to practice substituting assertive, positive, or neutral thoughts several times each day—after saying "Stop" to a negative sequence of thoughts and images.

6. *Homework and Follow-Up.* Cormier and Cormier (1979) found that thought stopping works better with clients who are troubled by intermittent, rather than continuous, self-defeating thoughts. They also recommended that, once clients learn the thought-stopping procedure in the interview situation, they need to practice it in everyday situations. Clients are asked to practice thought stopping whenever they notice that they are engaged in negative or self-defeating thinking. They are also told that it takes some time to break a well-learned habit of negative thinking. Clients often keep track of their daily practice with a log sheet, so that they can assess their progress in changing negative thinking to assertive or positive thinking.

ASSERTION TRAINING AND SOCIAL-SKILLS TRAINING

A behavioral approach that has gained popularity is assertion training, also known as social-skills training and personal-effectiveness training. At each developmental stage in life, important social skills must be mastered. For example, children need to learn how to make friends; adolescents need to learn how to interact with the opposite sex; and adults must learn how to effectively relate to mates, peers, and superiors. People who are lacking social skills frequently experience interpersonal difficulties at home, at work, at school, and during leisure time. Behavioral methods have been designed to teach such individuals ways of interacting successfully. Many people have difficulty in feeling that it is appropriate or right to assert themselves. Assertion training can be useful for the following people: (1) those who cannot express anger or irritation; (2) those who have difficulty in saying no; (3) those who are overly polite and who allow others to take advantage of them; (4) those who find it difficult to express affection and other positive responses; and (5) those who feel that they do not have a right to express their thoughts, beliefs, and feelings.

The basic assumption underlying assertion training is that people have the right (but not the obligation) to express their feelings, thoughts, beliefs, and attitudes. One goal of assertion training is to increase people's behavioral repertoire so that they can make the *choice* of whether to behave assertively in certain situations. Another goal is teaching people to express themselves in a way that reflects sensitivity to the feelings and rights of others. Assertion does not mean aggression; thus, truly assertive people do not stand up for their rights at all costs, ignoring the feelings of others.

There are six clinical strategies that therapists typically employ during the course of assertion training: instruction, feedback, modeling, behavior rehearsal, social reinforcement, and homework assignments (Bellack & Hersen, 1977).

1. *Instruction*: The therapist tells the client specific behaviors that are expected. Clear instructions can help clients improve eye contact and speak louder.
2. *Feedback*: This refers to the therapist's comments on the client's behavior after instructions to implement a set of behaviors. Positive and negative feedback have been demonstrated to lead to marked behavioral change.
3. *Modeling*: At times the therapist will actually display the desired behavior for the client to imitate. Both live and videotaped models are used.
4. *Behavior rehearsal*: This involves role playing during the sessions. Both effective and ineffective behaviors in interpersonal situations are critiqued, and performances are practiced in a variety of situations.
5. *Social reinforcement*: This involves praising clients when they acquire the desired responses. A given target response is *shaped* on a gradual basis through the use of praise.
6. *Homework assignments*: An integral part of assertion training is carrying out specific homework assignments of a behavioral nature. Through these assignments, clients bring what they have learned in their sessions into their everyday lives, and they are able to apply this new learning to real-life interpersonal situations. Clients may agree to make and refuse requests, express their feelings and thoughts at appropriate times, and so forth. They may keep a record of their progress in becoming more assertive as well as of the difficulties they are facing in carrying out their assignments.

Assertion training is appropriate in individual counseling situations using the principles mentioned above. Its methods and principles are also well suited to group situations. In assertion-training groups both the therapist and the other members can participate in role-playing activities, offer useful evaluations to the individual, and provide important reinforcement functions.

Shaffer and Galinsky (1974) described how assertive-training, or "expressive-training," groups are structured and how they function. The group is made up of eight to ten members with similar backgrounds, and the sessions last for two hours. The therapist initiates and directs role playing, coaches, reinforces, and acts as a role model. In the group discussions the therapist functions as an expert, lending guidance in the role-playing situations and giving feedback to the members.

As with most behavior-therapy groups, the assertive-training group is characterized by a high degree of leader-provided structure. The sessions are typically structured as follows: The first session, which begins with a didactic presentation on unrealistic social anxiety, focuses on unlearning ineffective internal responses that lead to a lack of assertiveness and on learning a repertoire of new assertive behaviors. The second session may introduce some relaxation training, and each member describes specific behaviors in interpersonal situations that he or she feels are problems. Members then make contracts to carry out previously avoided assertive behavior before the next session. During the third session members describe the assertive behaviors that they tried in real-life situations. Their attempts are evaluated, and, if they have not been fully successful, the group may be directed in role playing. The later sessions consist of additional relaxation training, more contracts for out-of-group assertion experiences, followed by evaluation of new behavior and by more role playing. The later sessions can also be geared to the individual needs of the members. Some groups tend to focus on additional role playing, evaluation, and coaching; others focus on a discussion of attitudes and feelings that make assertive behavior difficult.

Assertive-training group therapy basically consists of behavioral rehearsal applied to groups, and the aim is to help individuals develop more-direct ways of relating in interpersonal situations. The focus is on practicing, through role playing, newly emerging relationship skills so that individuals can overcome their inadequacies and learn how to express their feelings and thoughts more openly, as though they had a right to "own" these reactions.

In many ways assertion-training methods are based on principles of cognitive restructuring, and cognitive procedures are a basic part of most assertion-training programs. As a number of writers have indicated (Beck, 1967, 1976; Beck, Rusch, Shaw, & Emery, 1979; Ellis, 1973; Ellis & Grieger, 1977; Ellis & Whiteley, 1979; Mahoney, 1974; Meichenbaum, 1977a), many of our disturbing emotional reactions are caused by negative self-statements and faulty thinking. Thus, effective programs geared to teaching people how to be assertive must do more than merely give them skills and techniques for dealing with difficult situations. Drawing on the concepts and principles of the above cognitive-behavior therapists, cognitive-restructuring approaches are designed to challenge the beliefs that accompany lack of assertiveness, eliminate irrational beliefs, and change negative thinking to positive thinking that fosters assertive behavior. Cognitive restructuring is a gradual process that occurs in conjunction with behavior rehearsal and homework assignments to be carried out beyond the therapy sessions.

SELF-MANAGEMENT PROGRAMS AND SELF-DIRECTED BEHAVIOR

There is a trend toward "giving psychology away." This trend implies that psychologists will share their knowledge so that the "consumers" can increasingly lead self-managed and self-directed lives and not be dependent on the experts to deal with their problems. Psychologists who share this perspective are primarily concerned with teaching people the skills they will need to manage their own lives effectively.

Self-management is a relatively recent phenomenon in counseling and therapy, and reports of clinical applications have burgeoned since 1970 (Cormier & Cormier, 1979). Self-management strategies include, but are not limited to, self-monitoring, self-reward, self-contracting, and stimulus control.

In self-management programs people make decisions concerning specific behaviors they want to control or change. Some common examples include excessive eating, drinking, or smoking. People frequently discover that a major reason that they do not attain their goals is the lack of certain skills. It is in such areas that a self-directed approach can provide the guidelines for change and a plan that will lead to change.

Steps in self-directed change.   Watson and Tharp (1981) offered a model designed for self-directed change. The following stages of the self-directed model are based on material drawn from several sources, including Watson and Tharp, Cormier and Cormier (1979), Rudestam (1980), Williams and Long (1979), and Mahoney and Thoresen (1974).

1. *Selection of Goals.* The initial stage begins with specifying what specific changes are desired. Goals should be established one at a time, and they should be measurable, attainable, positive, and significant for the person. This last requirement is extremely important, for, if the individual develops a self-change program based on goals determined by someone else, the program has a real possibility of failing.

2. *Translating Goals into Target Behaviors.* Next, questions such as the following are relevant: What specific behaviors do I want to increase or decrease? What chain of actions will produce my goal?

3. *Self-Monitoring.* According to Mahoney and Thoresen (1974), a major first step in self-directed change is the process of self-monitoring, which consists of observing and recording one's own behavior with accuracy. This presumably leads to awareness, focused on concrete and observable behaviors rather than on historical events or feeling experiences. Mahoney and Thoresen suggested the *behavioral diary* as one of the simplest methods for this observation. The occurrence of a particular behavior is recorded, along with comments about the relevant antecedent cues and consequences. For example, if you want to change your eating habits—both in terms of quantity and quality— the behavioral diary will contain entries of what you eat, events and situations before eating or snacking, meal frequency, types of food eaten, and so forth. Total counts can also be transferred at the end of each day or week to a chart, providing a visual illustration of progress (or the lack of it) toward self-selected goals.

Cormier and Cormier (1979) maintained that self-monitoring is indispensable as a measuring device to define problems and to collect evaluative data. They added that, although it is necessary and useful for many clients, it is not sufficient unless it is used in conjunction with other self-management procedures. They suggested that self-monitoring be used in combination with stimulus control, self-reward and self-punishment, and self-contracting.

4. *Working Out a Plan for Change.* An action program that will lead to change might call for gradually replacing an unwanted action with a desirable one or increasing a desirable action. Such a plan of action entails some type of self-reinforcement system and the negotiating of a working contract.

Self-reinforcement is a basic part of this plan. A reinforcer is an event or object that has the effect, when presented or withdrawn, of increasing the probability of the response that precedes it (Rudestam, 1980). The use of reinforcement to change behavior is the cornerstone of modern behavior therapy. It is important to choose appropriate self-rewards, ones that are personally motivating. Watson and Tharp (1981) suggested a question for self-examination: "Do I really think I'll stop performing the undesired behavior (or start the desired behavior) just because I will get X (the reinforcer)?" (p. 176).

Self-contracting is the other facet of a plan for change. It is a self-management strategy that involves determining in advance the external and internal consequences that will follow the execution of the desired or undesired action. This method may help clients keep their commitment to carry out their action plan with some degree of consistency. Six features of good self-contract were described by Cormier and Cormier (1979, p. 507):

1. It must be clear and specific.
2. It should include a balance of rewards and sanctions appropriate to the desired behavior.
3. It should emphasize the positive.
4. It should involve the participation of another person who has a positive role to perform.
5. It should be in writing and be signed by all parties involved.
6. It should include a recording system that illustrates progress toward the goals.

After the plan of action is set forth, it must be readjusted and revised as more is learned about what is necessary to meet the goals and as one finds parts of it that are not working well (Watson & Tharp, 1981).

Summary and evaluation

The contemporary form of behavior therapy (unlike traditional behaviorism and the radical behaviorists) places emphasis on the interplay between the individual and the environment. Cognitive factors and the subjective reactions of people to the environment now have a place in the practice of behavior therapy. Thus, a case was made for using behavioristic technology to attain humanistic ends. It is clear that bridges can connect the humanistic and the behavioristic therapies, especially with the current focus of attention on cognitive behavior modification and the self-directed approaches to helping clients.

The heart of this chapter dealt with a description of commonly used therapeutic techniques and procedures by behavior therapists; these techniques can also be incorporated into other orientations. Even though a dozen or so techniques were described, they represent only a few of the procedures in the behavior therapist's repertoire.

CONTRIBUTIONS OF BEHAVIOR THERAPY

I have found that students sometimes approach behavior therapy with a closed mind, thinking that it is associated with a strictly deterministic and scientific approach to human behavior. Some students make the mistake of perceiving the behavior therapist as a technician and researcher who treats people like laboratory animals. It is clear that, although contemporary behavior therapy rests on a scientific view of human behavior that calls for a structured and systematic approach to counseling and therapy, this does not mean that factors such as the importance of the therapeutic relationship or the potential of clients to choose their own way are diminished.

In my view the behaviorists have contributed to the counseling field with their focus on specifics and their systematic way of applying counseling techniques. They challenge us to reconsider our global approach to counseling. Although we might assume that we know what a client means by the statement "I feel unloved; life has no meaning," the behavior therapist will work with the client in defining what is meant so that therapy can proceed. Whereas a humanist might nod in acceptance to such a statement, the behaviorist might retort with: "Who specifically is not loving you? What is going on in your life to bring about this meaninglessness? What are some specific things that you might be doing that contribute to the state you are in?"

In my opinion there are two major contributions of behavior therapy, both of which can be incorporated into other therapeutic approaches. One is the emphasis on research and assessment of treatment outcomes. This approach places a premium on validation of results, so it is not enough for practitioners to merely have hunches that their techniques are working. It is up to them to demonstrate that therapy is working. If progress is not occurring, then they take a careful look at the original diagnosis and the treatment plan that was formulated. Of all the therapies presented in this book, no other approach and its techniques have been subjected to the degree of empirical research that behavior therapy has. This may account for the fact that this model has changed so dramatically since its origin. Behavior therapy is diverse in terms of its concepts and techniques.

The other major contribution is the wide variety of specific cognitive and behavioral techniques at the disposal of the therapist. Because behavior therapy stresses *doing,* as opposed to merely talking about problems and gathering insights, practitioners have many behavioral strategies that assist clients in formulating a plan of action for changing behavior.

LIMITATIONS AND CRITICISMS OF BEHAVIOR THERAPY

In my view one of the central limitations of this approach is that it deemphasizes the role of feelings and emotions in the therapy process. In the attempt to focus on client behaviors as well as the cognitive patterns that lead to undesirable behavior, the role of feelings tends to be underplayed. This leads to a related concern that I have—namely, the tendency of some behaviorally oriented practitioners to overly stress problem solving and treating a condition. Behavior therapists need to listen very carefully to their clients, and it would be well to allow them to express and explore their feelings *before* implementing a treatment plan. The basic therapeutic conditions that are stressed by the person-centered therapist—such as active listening, empathy, positive regard, respect, mutuality, and immediacy—can be integrated into a behavioral framework. However, too often counselors are so anxious to work toward resolution of client problems that they fail to fully listen to their clients. I am convinced that, before action programs can be effectively implemented and problems resolved, it is necessary for clients to be given full latitude to identify and express their feelings about their problem areas. A mistake some counselors make is only getting at a minor problem as they focus on the presenting issue. They then work with this instead of listening to the client and establishing an atmosphere of trust to get at more pressing and major problems.

Below are some common criticisms and misconceptions that people have about behavior therapy, together with my reactions.

Criticism 1: Behavior therapy may change behaviors, but it does not change feelings. Some critics argue that feelings must change before behavior can change. The behaviorist's point of view is that, if one changes another's behavior, one has effectively been an agent in changing his or her feelings also. Empirical evidence has not borne out the criticism that feelings must be changed first before behavior change takes place.

Criticism 2: Behavior therapy ignores the important relational factors in therapy. The charge is often made that the importance of the relationship between the client and the therapist is discounted in behavior therapy. Although it appears to be true that behavior therapists do not place primary weight on the relationship variable, this does not mean that the approach is condemned to a mechanical and nonhumanistic level of functioning. As was discussed above in the section dealing specifically with the relationship between therapist and client, behavior therapy is most effective when there is cooperation and a working relationship—that is, when both the client and the therapist are working toward the client's goal. It is undoubtedly true that some therapists are attracted to behavior therapy because they can be directive, can play the role of expert, or can avoid the anxieties and ambiguities of establishing a personal relationship. This is not an intrinsic characteristic of the approach, however, and many behavior therapists are more humanistic in practice than some of the therapists are who profess to practice existentially oriented humanistic therapy.

Criticism 3: Behavior therapy does not provide insight. If this assertion is indeed true, the behavior-modification theorist would probably respond that insight isn't necessary. Behavior is changed directly. If the goal of insight is an eventual change of behavior, then behavior modification, which has proven results, has the same effect as insight. If the goals are the same, then the efficacy of the two techniques should be an empirical one. On the other hand, many people want not just to change their behavior but also to gain an understanding of why they behave the way that they do. The answers are often buried deep in past learning and in historical events. Although it is possible for behavior-modification therapists to give explanations in this realm, in fact they usually do not.

Criticism 4: Behavior therapy ignores historical causes of present behavior. This is in opposition to the historical approach or traditional psychoanalytic approach of Freud and others. The Freudian assumption is that early traumatic events are the root of present dysfunction. Discover the original causes, induce insight in the client, and then the present behavior will change. The behavior modifiers may acknowledge that the deviant responses have historical origins, but they would maintain that the responses are still in effect because they are still being maintained by reinforcing stimuli. Relearning of new responses or changing environmental stimuli is what is necessary for behavior change.

Although it is true that there are some limitations to the practice of counseling and therapy with the behavior-therapy approach, I hope that you will come to realize that the approach does offer some unique contributions. The specificity of the approach helps the practitioner to keep clearly in focus the client's goals and to define ways of checking on the therapist's and the client's mutual progress in reaching those goals. I emphasize again that a therapist need not subscribe totally to behavior therapy in order to derive practical benefits from the specific behavioral techniques. Most therapists, often without their awareness, do in fact employ in an unsystematic fashion many behavioral techniques. Their behavior does reinforce and shape client behavior, in much the same way that the behavior therapist systematically and consciously applies reinforcement to shape client behavior. Moreover, therapists can systematically use many behavioral techniques and incorporate them into their own repertoire of therapeutic procedures, even though they do not consider themselves behavior therapists. Therapists, knowingly or unknowingly, shape the responses of their clients by means of a wide range of social reinforcers or by the absence of reinforcement. Many behavioral procedures can be incorporated into a more eclectic framework and even into an existential or humanistic theory. Some of the techniques and methods are tools that a therapist can use with the client and for the client as they both work toward clear goals determined by the client. I hope that the reader can see that it may even be possible to be a humanistically oriented behavior therapist!

Questions for reflection and discussion

1. Compare behavior therapy with the other therapeutic approaches you have studied thus far. In what ways do you think behavior therapy is unique? What are some distinct advantages? What are some disadvantages or limitations of the approach?

2. In what ways might behavior therapy be amalgamated with the humanistic, relationship-oriented approaches? What are the bases on which bridges can be built between the two approaches?

3. How might you as a behavior therapist go about defining and narrowing down therapy goals with clients? What are some ways to translate broad goals into concrete ones?

4. What are your reactions to the focus on behaviors and actions—as opposed to insight and experiencing of feelings—characteristic of behavior therapy?

5. Which behavioral techniques would you be most inclined to use? Why? Explain what types of problem and client would best fit with the techniques you have selected.

6. What ethical issues are involved in the use of certain behavior-therapy techniques? List the techniques, as well as the issues, that you see as being central.

7. Some criticize behavior therapy for working too well; that is, some are concerned that conditioning techniques will be too effective and that they will be used to manipulate the client. What are your reactions to using behavioral strategies for social control?

8. What is your view of the role of empirical research and validation of therapy results stressed by this approach? As a practitioner, how might you attempt to assess the process and the outcomes of therapy?

9. What are the practical applications of behavior modification for parents? For teachers? For society? (How can parents and teachers use behavioral techniques effectively?)

10. What aspects of behavior therapy could you apply to yourself in order to increase your own level of effective functioning in everyday life? Mention some specific problem areas you have or behaviors you want to change, and then discuss the behavioral strategies you could draw on in making the changes you desire.

Recommended supplementary readings

The literature in the field of behavior therapy is vast. One excellent starting place is a comprehensive textbook for counselors interested in a behavioral approach with an emphasis on techniques and procedures, *Interviewing Strategies for Helpers: A Guide to Assessment, Treatment, and Evaluation* (Cormier & Cormier, 1979).

Some of the sources that are most helpful in giving a picture of the cognitive trend in behavior therapy are *Cognitive Therapy and Emotional Disorders* (Beck, 1976), *Cognitive Behavior Modification: An Integrative Approach* (Meichenbaum, 1977a), and *Reflections on the Cognitive-Learning Trend in Psychotherapy* (Mahoney, 1977).

For the area of application of behavioral principles and procedures to assertion training, I think the best resources include the works of Alberti and Emmons: *Your Perfect Right: A Guide to Assertive Behavior* (Alberti & Emmons, 1979) and *Assertiveness: Innovations, Applications, Issues* (Alberti, 1977).

For readings in the area of self-management and using behavioral principles to initiate and direct self-change programs I most recommend *Self-Directed Behavior: Self-Modification for Personal Adjustment* (Watson & Tharp, 1981), *Behavioral Self-Control* (Thoresen & Mahoney, 1974), and *Toward a Self-Managed Life-Style* (Williams & Long, 1979).

In *Clinical Behavior Therapy* (Goldfried & Davison, 1976), the authors do an excellent job of describing their clinical practice of behavior therapy.

References and suggested readings

Agras, W. S. (Ed.). *Behavior modification: Principles and clinical applications* (2nd ed.). Boston: Little, Brown, 1978. (a)

Agras, W. S. The token economy. In W. S. Agras (Ed.), *Behavior modification: Principles and clinical applications* (2nd ed.). Boston: Little, Brown, 1978. (b)

Alberti, R. E. (Ed.). *Assertiveness: Innovations, applications, issues.* San Luis Obispo, Calif.: Impact Publishers, 1977.

Alberti, R. E., & Emmons, M. L. *Your perfect right: A guide to assertive behavior* (3rd ed.). San Luis Obispo, Calif.: Impact Publishers, 1978.

American Psychological Association. The behavior therapies—Circa 1978. *The Counseling Psychologist,* 1978, 7(3).

Bandura, A. *Principles of behavior modification.* New York: Holt, Rinehart & Winston, 1969.

Bandura, A. (Ed.). *Psychological modeling: Conflicting theories.* Chicago: Aldine-Atherton, 1971. (a)

Bandura, A. Psychotherapy based upon modeling principles. In A. E. Bergin & S. L. Garfield (Eds.), *Handbook of psychotherapy and behavior change.* New York: Wiley, 1971. (b)

Bandura, A. Behavior therapy and the models of man. *American Psychologist,* 1974, *(29),* 859–869.

Bandura, A. *Social learning theory.* Englewood Cliffs, N. J.: Prentice-Hall, 1977.

Bandura, A., & Walters, R. Y. *Social learning theory and personality development.* New York: Holt, Rinehart & Winston, 1963.

Barlow, D. H. Aversive procedures. In W. S. Agras (Ed.), *Behavior modification: Principles and clinical applications* (2nd ed.). Boston: Little, Brown, 1978.

Beck, A. T. *Depression: Clinical, experimental, and theoretical aspects.* New York: Harper & Row, 1967.

Beck, A. T. *Cognitive therapy and emotional disorders.* New York: International Universities Press, 1976.

Beck, A. T., Rusch, A. J., Shaw, B. F., & Emery, G. *Cognitive therapy of depression.* New York: Guilford Press, 1979.

Bellack, A. S., & Hersen, M. *Behavior modification: An introductory textbook.* Baltimore: Williams & Wilkins Co., 1977.

Binder, V. Behavior modification: Operant approaches to therapy. In V. Binder, A. Binder, & B. Rimland (Eds.), *Modern therapies.* Englewood Cliffs, N. J.: Prentice-Hall, 1976.

Carkhuff, R., & Berenson, B. *Beyond counseling and therapy.* New York: Holt, Rinehart & Winston, 1967.

Chambless, D. L., & Goldstein, A. J. Behavioral psychotherapy. In R. J. Corsini (Ed.), *Current psychotherapies* (2nd ed.). Itasca, Ill.: F. E. Peacock, 1979.

Coates, T. J., & Thoresen, C. E. *How to sleep better.* Englewood Cliffs, N. J.: Prentice-Hall, 1977.

Corey, G. *Theory and practice of group counseling.* Monterey, Calif.: Brooks/Cole, 1981.

Corey, G. *Case approach to counseling and psychotherapy.* Monterey, Calif.: Brooks/Cole, 1982.

Cormier, W. H., & Cormier, L. S. *Interviewing strategies for helpers: A guide to assessment, treatment, and evaluation.* Monterey, Calif.: Brooks/Cole, 1979.

Cotler, S. B., & Guerra, J. *Assertion training.* Champaign, Ill.: Research Press, 1976.

Craighead, W. E., Kazdin, A. E., & Mahoney, M. J. *Behavior modification: Principles, issues, and applications.* Boston: Houghton Mifflin, 1976.

Ellis, A. *Humanistic psychotherapy.* New York: McGraw-Hill, 1973.

Ellis, A., & Grieger, R. (Eds.). *Handbook of rational-emotive therapy.* New York: Springer, 1977.

Ellis, A., & Whiteley, J. M. (Eds.). *Theoretical and empirical foundations of rational-emotive therapy.* Monterey, Calif.: Brooks/Cole, 1979.

Foreyt, J. P., & Rathjen, D. P. (Eds.). *Cognitive behavior therapy: Research and application.* New York: Plenum, 1978.

Gambrill, E. *Behavior modification: Handbook of assessment, intervention, and evaluation.* San Francisco: Jossey-Bass, 1977.

Goldfried, M. R., & Davison, G. C. *Clinical behavior therapy.* New York: Holt, Rinehart & Winston, 1976.

Goldfried, M. R., & Goldfried, A. P. Cognitive change methods. In F. H. Kanfer & A. P. Goldstein (Eds.), *Helping people change.* New York: Pergamon Press, 1975.

Goldstein, A. P. *Structured learning therapy: Toward a psychotherapy for the poor.* New York: Pergamon Press, 1973.

Gottman, J. M., & Leiblum, S. *How to do psychotherapy and how to evaluate it.* New York: Holt, Rinehart & Winston, 1974.

Jacobson, E. *Progressive relaxation.* Chicago: University of Chicago Press, 1938.

Jeffery, D. B., & Katz, R. C. *Take it off and keep it off! A behavioral program for weight loss and exercise.* Englewood Cliffs, N. J.: Prentice-Hall, 1977.

Kanfer, F. H., & Goldstein, A. P. (Eds.). *Helping people change* (2nd ed.). New York: Pergamon Press, 1980.

Kazdin, A. E. *History of behavior modification: Experimental foundations of contemporary research.* Baltimore: University Park Press, 1978.

Kendall, P. C., & Hollon, S. D. (Eds.). *Cognitive-behavioral interventions: Theory, research, and procedures.* New York: Academic Press, 1979.

Krasner, L. The reinforcement machine. In B. Berenson & R. Carkhuff (Eds.), *Sources of gain in counseling and psychotherapy.* New York: Holt, Rinehart & Winston, 1967.

Krumboltz, J. D., & Thoresen, C. E. *Behavioral counseling: Cases and techniques.* New York: Holt, Rinehart & Winston, 1969.

Krumboltz, J. D., & Thoresen, C. E. (Eds.). *Counseling methods.* New York: Holt, Rinehart & Winston, 1976.

Lange, A., & Jabubowski, P. *Responsible assertive behavior: Cognitive-behavioral procedures for trainers.* Champaign-Urbana, Ill.: Research Press, 1976.

Lange, A. J., Rimm, D. C., & Loxley, J. Jr. Cognitive-behavioral assertion training procedures. In J. M. Whiteley & J. V. Flowers (Eds.), *Approaches to assertion training.* Monterey, Calif.: Brooks/Cole, 1978.

Lazarus, A. A. *Behavior therapy and beyond.* New York: McGraw-Hill, 1971.

Leitenberg, H. (Ed.). *Handbook of behavior modification and behavior therapy.* Englewood Cliffs, N. J.: Prentice-Hall, 1976.

Mahoney, M. J. *Cognition and behavior modification.* Cambridge, Mass.: Ballinger, 1974.

Mahoney, M. J. Reflections on the cognitive-learning trend in psychotherapy. *American Psychologist,* 1977, *32*(1), 5–13.

Mahoney, M. J., & Thoresen, C. E. *Self-control: Power to the person.* Monterey, Calif.: Brooks/Cole, 1974.

Marquis, J. Behavior modification theory: B. F. Skinner and others. In A. Burton (Ed.), *Operational theories of personality.* New York: Brunner/Mazel, 1974.

Meichenbaum, D. *Cognitive behavior modification: An integrative approach.* New York: Plenum, 1977. (a)

Meichenbaum, D. *Cognitive behavior modification newsletter.* University of Waterloo, No. 3, May 1977. (b)

Meichenbaum, D. *Cognitive behavior modification newsletter.* University of Waterloo, No. 4, January 1979.

Mikulas, W. *Behavior modification: An overview.* New York: Harper & Row, 1972.

Murray, E. J., & Jacobson, L. I. Cognition and learning in traditional and behavior therapy. In

S. L. Garfield & A. E. Bergin (Eds.), *Handbook of psychotherapy and behavior change* (2nd ed.). New York: Wiley, 1978.

Nye, R. *Three psychologies* (2nd ed.). Monterey, Calif.: Brooks/Cole, 1981.

Osipow, S. Y., & Walsh, W. B. *Strategies in counseling for behavior change*. New York: Meredith, 1970.

Patterson, C. H. *Theories of counseling and psychotherapy* (2nd ed.). New York: Harper & Row, 1973.

Paul, G. L. *Insight vs. desensitization in psychotherapy*. Stanford, Calif.: Stanford University Press, 1966.

Perry, M. A., & Furukawa, M. J. Modeling methods. In F. H. Kanfer & A. P. Goldstein (Eds.), *Helping people change* (2nd ed.). New York: Pergamon Press, 1980.

Rachman, S. Behavior therapy. In B. Berenson & R. Carkhuff (Eds.), *Sources of gain in counseling and psychotherapy*. New York: Holt, Rinehart & Winston, 1967.

Rimm, D. C., & Masters, J. C. *Behavior therapy: Techniques and empirical findings*. New York: Academic Press, 1974.

Rose, S. D. *Group therapy: A behavior approach*. Englewood Cliffs, N. J.: Prentice-Hall, 1977.

Rudestam, K. E. *Methods of self-change: An ABC primer*. Monterey, Calif.: Brooks/Cole, 1980.

Shaffer, J., & Galinsky, M. D. *Models of group therapy and sensitivity training*. Englewood Cliffs, N. J.: Prentice-Hall, 1974.

Shelton, J., & Ackerman, M. *Homework in counseling and psychotherapy*. Springfield, Ill.: Charles C Thomas, 1974.

Sherman, A. R. *Behavior modification: Theory and practice*. Monterey, Calif.: Brooks/Cole, 1973.

Skinner, B. F. *Walden II*. New York: Macmillan, 1948.

Skinner, B. F. *Beyond freedom and dignity*. New York: Knopf, 1971.

Stampfl, T. Implosive therapy: Staring down your nightmares. *Psychology Today,* February 1975.

Stolz, S. B., & Associates. *Ethical issues in behavior modification*. San Francisco: Jossey-Bass, 1978.

Storms, L. H. Implosive therapy: An alternative to systematic desensitization. In V. Binder, A. Binder, & B. Rimland (Eds.), *Modern therapies*. Englewood Cliffs, N. J.: Prentice-Hall, 1976.

Thoresen, C. E. (Ed.). *The behavior therapist*. Monterey, Calif.: Brooks/Cole, 1980.

Thoresen, C. E., & Coates, T. J. What does it mean to be a behavior therapist? In C. E. Thoresen (Ed.), *The behavior therapist*. Monterey, Calif.: Brooks/Cole, 1980.

Thoresen, C. E., & Mahoney, M. J. *Behavioral self-control*. New York: Holt, Rinehart & Winston, 1974.

Ullman, L., & Krasner, L. (Eds.). *Case studies in behavior modification*. New York: Holt, Rinehart & Winston, 1965.

Walker, C. E. *Learn to relax*. Englewood Cliffs, N. J.: Prentice-Hall, 1975.

Wanderer, Z., & Cabot, T. *Letting go*. New York: Putnam's, 1978.

Watson, D. L., & Tharp, R. G. *Self-directed behavior: Self-modification for personal adjustment* (3rd ed.). Monterey, Calif.: Brooks/Cole, 1981.

Whiteley, J. M., & Flowers, J. V. (Eds.). *Approaches to assertion training*. Monterey, Calif.: Brooks/Cole, 1978.

Williams, R., & Long, J. *Toward a self-managed life-style* (2nd ed.). Boston: Houghton Mifflin, 1979.

Wilson, T. Cognitive behavior therapy: Paradigm shift or passing phase? In J. P. Foreyt & D. P. Rathjen (Eds.), *Cognitive behavior therapy: Research and applications*. New York: Plenum, 1978.

Wolpe, J. *Psychotherapy by reciprocal inhibition*. Stanford, Calif.: Stanford University Press, 1958.

Wolpe, J. *The practice of behavior therapy*. New York: Pergamon Press, 1969.

Wolpe, J., & Lazarus, A. *Behavior therapy techniques*. New York: Pergamon Press, 1966.

Yates, A. J. *Theory and practice in behavior therapy*. New York: Wiley, 1975.

9

Rational-Emotive Therapy

Introduction

I selected Albert Ellis's rational-emotive therapy (RET) for inclusion because I think that it can challenge the student to think through some basic issues underlying counseling and psychotherapy. RET departs radically from several of the other systems presented in this book—namely, the psychoanalytic, existential, person-centered, and Gestalt approaches. RET has more in common with the therapies that are cognitive/behavior/action oriented in that it stresses thinking, judging, deciding, analyzing, and doing. RET is highly didactic, very directive, and concerned more with thinking than with feeling.

More than most other systems of psychotherapy, RET emphasizes the philosophic disputing of clients' self-defeating and irrational beliefs. This system is reeducational as well as disputational. It emphasizes cognitive restructuring, which is done along with a variety of other emotive and behavioral methods. This approach is based on the assumption that cognitions, emotions, and behaviors interact significantly and have a reciprocal cause-and-effect relationship (Ellis, 1979 c).

Ellis developed rational-emotive therapy in 1955, after he found that his training as a psychoanalyst was inadequate in dealing with his clients. Ellis (1979d) believed that the psychoanalytic approach is more than inefficient, in that people sometimes seem to get worse instead of better. He also acknowledged that he had had emotional problems as a youth, including inhibitions and a fear of speaking in public. In working with his own problems, Ellis developed a cognitive/philosophic approach combined with real-life practice situations in which he gave himself homework assignments to speak in public regardless of his discomfort. According to Ellis, RET uses scientific principles and procedures in directly confronting the sources of emotional and behavioral problems and in substituting a rational basis for living.

The concepts of rational-emotive therapy raise several thorny questions that it would be well to keep in mind as you read this chapter: Is psychotherapy essentially a process of reeducation? Should the therapist function mainly as a teacher? Is it appropriate for therapists to use propaganda, persuasion, and highly directive suggestions? How effective is it to attempt to rid clients of their "irrational beliefs" by using logic, advice, information, and interpretations?

Finally, Ellis and Carl Rogers are in sharp contrast in regard to the value and necessity of a personal relationship between the client and the therapist. As you read, try to clarify and define your position on the central issue of whether the client/therapist relationship is the core variable that determines client change or whether other variables, such as the therapist's skill, insightfulness, knowledge, and ability to help the client cut through self-defeating attitudes, are even more important.

Key concepts

VIEW OF HUMAN NATURE

Rational-emotive therapy is based on the assumption that human beings are born with a potential for both rational, straight thinking and irrational, crooked thinking. People have predispositions for self-preservation, happiness, thinking and verbalizing, loving, communion with others, and growth and self-actualization. They also have propensities for self-destruction, avoidance of thought, procrastination, endless repetition of mistakes, superstition, intolerance, perfectionism and self-blame, and avoidance of actualizing growth potentials.

Taking for granted that humans are fallible, RET attempts to help them accept themselves as creatures who will continue to make mistakes yet at the same time learn to live more at peace with themselves. Ellis (1979c) listed some of the key RET assumptions:

1. People condition themselves to feel disturbed, rather than being conditioned by external sources.
2. People have the biological and cultural tendency to think crookedly and to needlessly disturb themselves.
3. Humans are unique in that they invent disturbing beliefs and keep themselves disturbed about their disturbances.
4. People have the capacity to change their cognitive, emotive, and behavioral processes; they

can choose to react differently from their usual patterns, refuse to allow themselves to become upset, and train themselves so that they can eventually remain minimally disturbed for the rest of their lives.

Another basic assumption of RET is that humans think, emote, and behave simultaneously. In some of his earlier writings, Ellis (1962) pointed out that people's thinking significantly affects their feelings and behaviors; that their emotions have a major impact on their thoughts and actions; and that their actions influence their thoughts and feelings. To modify dysfunctional patterns, it is necessary to employ a comprehensive approach that makes use of a variety of cognitive, emotive, and behavioral reeducational methods. Ellis (1979d) maintained that, if people are helped to change in any one of these modalities, they are simultaneously helped to modify the others.

Regarding human nature, Ellis (1967, pp. 79–80) contended that both the Freudian psychoanalytic approach and the existential approach are mistaken and that the methodologies founded on those psychotherapeutic systems are ineffective and inadequate. Ellis charged that the Freudian view of human nature is false because the existential view is partly correct. He asserted that the individual is not completely a biologically determined animal driven by instincts. Rather, people are unique and have the power to understand limitations, to change basic views and values that they uncritically introjected as a child, and to challenge self-defeating tendencies. People have the capacity to confront their value systems and reindoctrinate themselves with different beliefs, ideas, and values. As a result, they will behave quite differently from how they behaved in the past. Thus, because they can think and work until they actually make themselves different, they are not passive victims of past conditioning.

Ellis does not fully accept the existential view of the self-actualizing tendency, because of the fact that humans are biological animals with strong instinctual tendencies to behave in certain ways. Thus, Ellis contends that, once people are conditioned to think or feel in a certain way, they tend to continue behaving in that manner even though they might realize that their behavior is self-defeating. Ellis thinks it is incorrect to assume that an existential encounter with an accepting, permissive, authentic therapist will usually root out an individual's deeply ingrained patterns of self-defeating behavior.

VIEW OF EMOTIONAL DISTURBANCE

Neurosis, defined as "irrational thinking and behaving," is a natural human state that afflicts all of us to some degree. This state is deeply rooted merely because we are human beings and live with other human beings in society.

Psychopathology is originally learned and aggravated by the inculcation of irrational beliefs from significant others during childhood. However, we actively reinstill false beliefs by the processes of autosuggestion and self-repetition. Hence, it is largely our own repetition of early-indoctrinated irrational thoughts, rather than a parent's repetition, that keeps dysfunctional attitudes alive and operative within us.

Emotions are the products of human thinking. When we *think* something is bad, then we *feel* bad about that thing. Ellis (1967) maintained that "emotional disturbance, therefore, essentially consists of mistaken, illogical, unvalidatable sentences or meanings which the disturbed individual dogmatically and unchallengingly *believes,* and upon which he therefore emotes or acts to his own defeat" (p. 82).

RET insists that blame is the core of most emotional disturbances. Therefore, if we are to cure a neurosis or psychosis, we had better stop blaming ourselves and others. We had better learn to accept ourselves in spite of our imperfections. Anxiety stems from internal repetition of the sentence "I don't like my behavior and would like to change" and the self-blaming sentence "Because of my wrong behavior and my mistakes, I am a rotten person and I am to blame, and I deserve to suffer." According to RET, this anxiety is unnecessary. A person can be helped to see that precise, irrational sentences are false, self-blaming traps that he or she has acquired.

RET contends that people do not need to be accepted and loved, even though it might be desirable. The therapist teaches clients how to feel unhurt even when they are unaccepted and unloved by significant others. Although RET allows people to experience sadness over being unaccepted, it attempts to help them find ways of overcoming all deep-seated manifestations of depression, hurt, loss of self-worth, and hatred.

RET hypothesizes that, because we are raised in society, we tend to be victims of fallacious ideas, that we tend to keep reindoctrinating ourselves over and over with those ideas in an unthinking and autosuggestive manner, and that consequently we keep the ideas operant in our overt behavior. Some of the main irrational ideas that we continually internalize and that inevitably lead to self-defeat are, according to Ellis (1967), the following:

1. The idea that it is a dire necessity for an adult human being to be loved or approved by virtually every significant other person in his community.
2. The idea that one should be thoroughly competent, adequate, and achieving in all possible respects if one is to consider oneself worthwhile.
3. The idea that certain people are bad, wicked, or villainous and they should be severely blamed and punished for their villainy.
4. The idea that it is easier to avoid than to face certain life difficulties and self-responsibilities.
5. The idea that it is awful and catastrophic when things are not the way one would very much like them to be.
6. The idea that human unhappiness is externally caused and that people have little or no ability to control their sorrows and disturbances.
7. The idea that one's past history is an all-important determiner of one's present behavior and that, because something once strongly affected one's life, it should indefinitely have a similar effect [p. 84].

In Ellis's view, it is absolutistic and *must*urbatory thinking that is the foundation of human problems. The basic irrational beliefs of individuals can be summarized by three major *musts*:

1. "I *must* perform well and be approved of by significant others. If I don't, then it is *awful,* I *cannot stand* it, and I am a *rotten person.*"
2. "You *must* treat me fairly. When you don't, it is *horrible,* and I *cannot bear* it."
3. "Conditions *must* be the way I want them to be. It is *terrible* when they are not, and I *cannot stand* living in such an *awful* world."

Ellis (1979a) contended that, if people subscribe to these three basic *musts* (and their derivatives), disturbances will follow.

A-B-C THEORY OF PERSONALITY

The following diagram will clarify the interaction of the various components being discussed:

A (Activating Event) ◄— B (Belief) —► C (Emotional Consequence)

↑

D (Disputing Intervention)

The A-B-C theory of personality is central to RET theory and practice. A is the existence of a fact, an event, or the behavior or attitude of an individual. C is the emotional consequence or reaction of the individual; the reaction can be either appropriate or inappropriate. A (the activating event) does not cause C (the emotional consequence). Instead, B, which is the person's belief about A, causes C, the emotional reaction. For example, if a person experiences depression after a divorce, it may not be the divorce itself that causes the depressive reaction but the person's *beliefs* about being a failure, being rejected, or losing a mate. Ellis would maintain that the beliefs about the rejection and failure (at point B) are what causes the depression (at point C), not the actual event of the divorce (at point A). Thus, human beings are largely responsible for creating their own emotional reactions and disturbances. Showing people how they can change the irrational beliefs that directly cause their disturbed emotional consequences is the heart of RET (Ellis, 1979e).

After the A-B-C comes D, disputing. Essentially, D is the application of the scientific method to help clients challenge their irrational beliefs. Because the principles of logic can be taught, these principles can be used to destroy any unrealistic, unverifiable hypothesis. This logicoempirical method can help clients give up self-destructive ideologies.

How is an emotional disturbance fostered? It is fed by the illogical sentences that the person continually repeats to himself or herself such as "I am totally to blame for the divorce," "I am a miserable failure, and everything I did was wrong," "I am a worthless person," "I feel lonely and rejected, and that is a terrible catastrophe." Ellis (1974) made the point that "you feel the way you think" (p. 312). Disturbed emotional reactions such as depression and anxiety are initiated and perpetuated by the self-defeating belief system, which is based on irrational ideas that one has incorporated. Although Ellis (1974) contended that emotional disturbances can be eliminated or modified by directly working with the feelings (depression, anxiety, hostility, fear, and so on), he added that

> the quickest, most deep-seated, most elegant, and longest-lasting technique of helping people to change their dysfunctional emotional responses is probably through enabling them to see clearly what they are strongly telling themselves—at B, their Belief System—about the stimuli that are impinging on them at A (their Activating Experiences) and teaching them how to actively and vigorously Dispute (at D) their irrational Beliefs [pp. 312–313].

Theory of personality change. Ellis (1979d) agreed that people get pay-offs or neurotic gains from originating and maintaining their disturbed behavior. RET does not look for deep-seated or dramatic pay-offs, as do many of the psychodynamically oriented therapies. Instead, RET is grounded on the assumption that people seek the easy way out in order to avoid pain. Thus, RET theory holds that most people have a natural tendency to resist basic personality change. Even though they may want to behave differently, they still have to *force* themselves to change ineffectual acts before they can comfortably behave in new ways. It takes *sustained* and *hard work* over a considerable period of time to change self-defeating ways of behaving.

Other dimensions of personality change were described as follows by Ellis (1979e):

1. Because people largely create their own disturbances by inventing irrational and illogical ideas, they also have the capacity to understand and change these irrational beliefs, along with the self-sabotaging behaviors that flow from these beliefs.
2. The most effective way to bring about personality change is by a combination of cognitive awareness and philosophic restructuring.
3. People tend to behave dysfunctionally and to return to self-defeating behaviors after they

have taught themselves to function more effectively. Thus, if change is to be long lasting, it is necessary to continue to interrupt disturbed behaviors with strong counterbeliefs, along with consistently practiced behavioral changes.

4. It is best to use a variety of cognitive, emotive, and behavioral methods in an experimental way to determine which methods work best for a given individual's change.

The therapeutic process

THERAPEUTIC GOALS

Ellis (1979b) indicated that the many roads taken in RET are aimed at one major goal: "minimizing the client's central self-defeating outlook and acquiring a more realistic, tolerant philosophy of life" (p. 205).

RET strives for a thorough philosophical reevaluation based on the assumption that human problems are philosophically rooted. Thus, RET is not aimed primarily at symptom removal. It is mainly designed to induce people to examine and change some of their most basic values, especially those values that keep them disturbed (Ellis, 1979b). If a client's presenting problem is a fear of failing in his or her marriage, the aim is not merely to reduce that specific fear; instead, the therapist attempts to work with the client's exaggerated fears of failing in general.

Ellis (1979d) listed the following goals toward which RET therapists work with their clients:

1. *Self-Interest.* Without becoming completely absorbed in themselves, emotionally healthy people have the capacity to be interested in themselves.
2. *Social Interest.* Humans rarely choose a lonely existence, and they have an interest in living effectively with others in a social group.
3. *Self-Direction.* Although emotionally healthy people may prefer the cooperation and support of others, they do not demand this support. They are able to assume responsibility for their own life, and they can work at solving independently most of their own problems.
4. *Tolerance.* Mature people are able to allow others to make mistakes or to be wrong; and they do not condemn them for such behavior.
5. *Flexibility.* Healthy people remain flexible in their ideas, are open to change, and have an unbigoted view of others.
6. *Acceptance of Uncertainty.* Mature individuals realize that they live in an uncertain world. Although they might enjoy a good degree of order, they do not whiningly demand this order and a false sense of certainty.
7. *Commitment.* Healthy individuals have the capacity to become vitally absorbed in something outside of themselves.
8. *Scientific Thinking.* Mature people can feel deeply and act concertedly. However, they can also regulate their emotions and actions by reflecting on them and their consequences.
9. *Self-Acceptance.* Healthy people accept themselves *because* they are alive, and they avoid measuring their basic worth by their external achievements or the evaluations of others.
10. *Risk Taking.* Emotionally healthy people tend to be adventurous, though not foolhardy.
11. *Nonutopianism.* Mature and emotionally healthy people accept the fact that they will never achieve a utopian existence. They realize that they will never get everything they want, nor will they completely avoid everything they do not want.

THERAPIST'S FUNCTION AND ROLE

The main therapeutic activities of RET are carried out with one central purpose: to help the client get free of illogical ideas and learn to substitute logical ideas in their place. The aim is to get the client to internalize a rational philosophy of life, just as he or she internalized a set of dogmatic, irrational, and superstitious beliefs from both parents and culture.

To achieve this aim, the therapist has specific tasks. The first step is to show clients that they have incorporated many irrational "shoulds," "oughts," and "musts." Clients must learn to separate their rational beliefs from their irrational ones. To foster this client awareness, the therapist serves the function of a counterpropagandist who challenges the self-defeating propaganda that the client originally accepted without question as truth. The therapist encourages, persuades, and at times even commands the client to engage in activities that will act as counterpropaganda agents.

A second step in the therapeutic process takes clients beyond the stage of awareness by demonstrating that they keep their emotional disturbances active by continuing to think illogically and by repeating self-defeating sentences that keep the influence of earlier years functional. In other words, because clients keep reindoctrinating themselves, they are responsible for their own problems. That the therapist merely shows clients that they have illogical processes is not enough, for a client is apt to say: "Now I understand that I have fears of failing and that these fears are exaggerated and unrealistic. Nevertheless, I *still feel* fearful of failing!"

To get beyond clients' mere recognition of irrational thoughts and feelings, the therapist takes a third step: attempting to get clients to modify their thinking and abandon their irrational ideas. Rational-emotive psychology assumes that their illogical beliefs are so deeply ingrained that clients will not normally change them by themselves. The therapist must assist clients to come to the understanding of the relationship between their self-defeating ideas and their unrealistic philosophies that leads to the vicious cycle of the self-blaming process.

Thus, the final step in the therapeutic process is to challenge clients to develop rational philosophies of life so that they can avoid becoming the victims of other irrational beliefs. Tackling only specific problems or symptoms can give no assurance that other illogical fears will not emerge. What is desirable, then, is for the therapist to attack the core of the irrational thinking and to teach clients how to substitute rational beliefs and attitudes for the irrational ones.

The therapist who works within the RET framework functions differently from most other therapists. Because RET therapy is essentially a cognitive and active/directive behavioral process, it often minimizes the intense relationship between the therapist and the client. RET is educative, and the therapist's central task is to teach the client ways of self-understanding and changing. The therapist mainly employs a rapid-fire, highly directive, persuasive methodology that emphasizes cognitive aspects. Ellis (1979b, p. 206) gave a picture of what the rational-emotive practitioner does:

1. Pins clients down to a few basic irrational ideas that motivate much disturbed behavior.
2. Challenges clients to validate their ideas.
3. Demonstrates to clients the illogical nature of their thinking.
4. Uses a logical analysis to minimize clients' irrational beliefs.
5. Shows how these beliefs are inoperative and how they will lead to future emotional and behavioral disturbances.
6. Uses absurdity and humor to confront the irrationality of clients' thinking.
7. Explains how these ideas can be replaced with more rational ideas that are empirically grounded.
8. Teaches clients how to apply the scientific approach to thinking so that they can observe and minimize present or future irrational ideas and illogical deductions that foster self-destructive ways of feeling and behaving.

CLIENT'S EXPERIENCE IN THERAPY

To a large measure, the client's role in RET is that of a student, or learner. Psychotherapy is viewed as a reeducative process whereby the client learns how to apply logical thought to problem solving.

The therapeutic process focuses on the client's experience in the present. Like the person-centered and existentially oriented approaches to therapy, RET mainly emphasizes here-and-now experiences and clients' present ability to change the patterns of thinking and emoting that they acquired earlier. The therapist does not devote time to exploring clients' early history and making connections between their past and present behavior. Nor does the therapist explore in depth their relationships with their parents or siblings. Instead, the therapeutic process stresses that, regardless of clients' basic, irrational philosophies of life, they are presently disturbed because they still believe in their self-defeating views of themselves and their worlds. Questions of where, why, or how they acquired their irrational philosophies are of secondary importance. The central issue is how clients can become aware of their self-defeating messages and challenge them. Ellis (1974) asserted that clients will often improve even if they never understand the origin or development of their problems.

A central experience of the client in RET is gaining insight. Ellis (1967) defined emotional insight as "the patient's knowing or seeing the causes of his problems and *working,* in a determined and energetic manner, to apply this knowledge to the solution of these problems" (p. 87). Thus RET emphasizes interpretation as a therapeutic tool.

RET postulates three levels of insight. For an illustration of these levels, let us assume that a male client is working on his fear of women. He feels threatened by attractive women, and he is afraid of how he might react to a powerful woman and what she might do to him. Using this example we can distinguish the three levels of insight. In the first, the client becomes aware that there is some antecedent cause of his fear of women. This cause is not that his mother tried, for example, to dominate him. Rather, it is his irrational beliefs that she should not have tried to dominate him and that it was, and still is, awful that she did try.

On the second level of insight, the client recognizes that he is still threatened by women and feels uncomfortable in their presence because he still believes in, and keeps repeating endlessly to himself, the irrational beliefs that he once accepted. He sees that he keeps himself in a state of panic with women because he continues to tell himself "Women can castrate me!" or "They'll expect me to be a superman!" or some other irrational notion.

The third level of insight consists of the client's acceptance that he will not improve unless he works diligently and practices changing his irrational beliefs by actually doing things of a counterpropaganda nature. Thus, his "homework assignment" might be to approach an attractive woman and ask her for a date. While on this date, he needs to challenge his irrational notions and his catastrophic expectations and beliefs of what might happen. Merely talking about his fears will not do much to change his behavior. What is important is that he engage in activity that will torpedo the underpinnings of his irrational fears.

RET stresses particularly the second and third levels of insight—namely, the client's acknowledgment that it is he who is keeping the originally disturbing ideas and feelings alive, and that he had better rationally/emotively face them, think about them, and work to eliminate them.

RELATIONSHIP BETWEEN THERAPIST AND CLIENT

The issue of the personal relationship between the therapist and the client takes on a different meaning in RET than it has in most other forms of therapy. According to Ellis (1979b), a warm relationship between the client and the therapist is neither a necessary nor a sufficient condition for effective personality change. He contended that, although RET therapists accept their clients as fallible humans, they can do so without giving *personal* warmth (or even liking their clients). Therapists can use a variety of impersonal therapeutic procedures, including teaching methods, activity-oriented homework assignments, and a range of behavioral procedures.

Note that, although the personal relationship or warmth and affection between the therapist and the client is not viewed as primarily important in RET, this does not mean that transference is not viewed as significant. Ellis (1967, p. 87) maintained that RET emphasizes the importance of therapists as models for their clients. During the course of therapy, they model that they are not highly emotionally disturbed and that they are living rationally. They also model courage for their clients, in that they directly present the clients' irrational belief systems to them without being worried that they will lose the clients' love and approval.

RET thus stresses the help a client can get from a highly trained and rational therapist. Further, RET stresses the therapist's full tolerance and unconditional positive regard for the personhood of the client, in that the therapist avoids blaming the client. The therapist continues to accept the client as a worthwhile human being because the client exists, not because of the client's accomplishments.

Application: Therapeutic techniques and procedures

THE PRACTICE OF RATIONAL-EMOTIVE THERAPY

RET therapists invariably use a variety of cognitive, affective, and behavioral techniques. In this sense RET is an eclectic approach, employing diverse methods and tailoring them to individual clients. The approach is pragmatic, in that techniques that have proven useful are applied, and techniques that do not yield favorable results with a given client are abandoned. What follows is a brief summary of the major cognitive, affective, and behavioral techniques that were described in some detail by Ellis (1979a).

Cognitive methods. RET therapists usually incorporate into the therapeutic process a pronounced and forceful amount of cognitive methodology. From the cognitive perspective, RET demonstrates to clients in a quick and direct manner what it is that they continue to tell themselves to make and keep themselves emotionally disturbed. Then, RET teaches these clients how to deal with these self-statements so that they no longer believe them; it teaches them to acquire a reality-based philosophy. RET relies heavily on thinking, disputing, debating, challenging, interpreting, explaining, and teaching. A few of these cognitive techniques that are available to the RET therapist are:

1. *Disputing of Irrational Beliefs.* The most common cognitive method of RET consists of the therapist's actively/directively disputing the client's irrational beliefs. The therapist shows clients that they are disturbed not because of certain events or situations but because of their perceptions of these events and because of the nature of their self-statements. The therapist quickly challenges these irrational beliefs by asking questions such as: Where is the evidence for your beliefs? Why is it *terrible* and *horrible* if life is

not the way you want it to be? Where is it written that you *cannot stand* a situation? Why do you assume that you are a *rotten person* because of the way you are?

2. *Cognitive Homework.* RET clients are given homework assignments, which is a way of tracking down the absolutistic *shoulds* and *musts* that are a part of their internalized self-messages. For example, a person with a talent for acting, who is afraid to act in front of an audience because of fear of failure, may be asked to take a small part in a stage play. In this situation, the person would be instructed to replace her negative self-statements such as "I will fail, I will look foolish, no one will like me" with more positive messages such as "I can act, I will do the best I can. It is nice to be liked, but not everybody will like me, and that isn't the end of the world." The theory behind this and similar assignments is that people often create a negative, self-fulfilling prophesy and actually fail because they told themselves in advance that they would. Clients are expected to carry out specific assignments during the sessions and, especially, in everyday situations in between sessions. In this way they gradually learn to deal with anxiety and challenge basic irrational thinking.

3. *Client's Disputing of an Irrational Belief.* With this technique, clients take one major irrationality (especially one absolutistic *must*) and work on it in a systematic way each day for at least ten minutes. Clients go over this particular irrational belief until they no longer hold it, or at least until it is diminished in strength.

4. *Bibliotherapy.* An important RET cognitive technique consists of asking clients to read rational-emotive literature, which is designed to assist them in their process of cognitive restructuring. Two useful books are *Humanistic Psychotherapy: The Rational-Emotive Approach* (Ellis, 1973) and *A New Guide to Rational Living* (Ellis & Harper, 1975).

5. *Employing New Self-Statements.* After clients learn to dispute self-destructive beliefs, RET uses teaching methods that lead to rational self-statements and constructive assumptions. Once clients discover that their lives are determined by *shoulds* and *musts,* then they are in a position to replace these demands with nonabsolutistic preferences.

Emotive techniques. Emotively, RET therapists use a variety of procedures, including unconditional acceptance, rational-emotive role playing, modeling, self-statements, rational-emotive imagery, and shame-attacking exercises. Clients are taught the value of unconditional acceptance. Even though their behavior may be difficult to accept, *they as persons* do have intrinsic worth. They are taught how destructive it is to engage in "putting oneself down" for perceived deficiencies. One of the main techniques that RET therapists employ to teach their clients this self-acceptance is modeling. RET therapists are able to be themselves in the therapy sessions; they avoid seeking the approval of their clients, do not live by *shoulds* and *musts,* and are willing to risk themselves as they continue to challenge their clients.

Behavioral techniques. RET practitioners use most of the regular behavior-therapy procedures, especially operant conditioning, self-management principles, systematic desensitization, instrumental conditioning, biofeedback, relaxation techniques, and modeling. Behavioral homework assignments to be carried out in real-life situations are particularly important. These assignments are done in a systematic way and are recorded and analyzed on a form; then, the results are brought back to the sessions for further analysis. These homework assignments involve desensitization, skill training, and assertive training. Clients actually *do* new and difficult things, and in this way they put to use their insights in the form of concrete action.

APPLICATIONS OF RET TO CLIENT POPULATIONS

What are the areas of application of RET? Ellis and Grieger (1977) have written about the uses of RET as it applies to sex therapy, education, group work, assertion training, depression, and child therapy. Ellis (1979c) wrote that RET has inspired a large number of publications and studies on its application to the treatment of anxiety, depression, hostility, character disorder, and psychosis; to problems of sex, love, marriage; to child rearing and adolescence; and to assertion training and self-management. As a treatment approach, RET can be applied to individual therapy, group therapy, marathon encounter groups, marriage counseling, and family therapy.

Ellis does not assert that all clients can be helped through logical analysis and philosophical reconstruction. Some are not bright enough to follow a rigorous rational analysis. Some are too detached from reality. Some are too old and inflexible. Some are too philosophically prejudiced against logic to accept rational analysis. Some are chronic avoiders or shirkers who insist on looking for magical solutions. Some are simply unwilling to do the hard work that RET demands. And some seem to enjoy clinging to their misery and refuse to make any basic changes.

Application to individual therapy.   RET, as applied to one-to-one work, is generally designed for relatively brief therapy. Ellis (1979b, p. 217) contended that it is preferable that individuals with severe emotional disturbances continue both individual and group therapy for a period of six months to a year so that they have a chance to practice what they are learning. As for individuals with a specific problem or those who are going to stay in therapy only for a short time, RET can teach clients many of the basics of how to attack the underlying sources of their problems in from one to ten sessions. These sessions consist basically of explaining the A-B-C method of understanding any emotional disturbance, pointing out the irrational premises undergirding the problem, and teaching how to start working and practicing at converting irrational ideas into rational philosophies.

Ellis (1979b, p. 215) stated that most clients who are seen individually have one session weekly for anywhere between 5 and 50 sessions. The clients begin by discussing their most pressing problems and describing their most upsetting feelings. Then the therapist discovers the precipitating events that lead to the upsetting feelings. He or she also gets the clients to see the irrational beliefs that they associated with the events and gets them to dispute their irrational beliefs by assigning them homework activities that will help them directly work on undoing their irrational ideas and assist them in practicing more rational ways of being. Each week the therapist checks their progress, and the clients continually learn how to dispute their irrational system until they do more than merely lose their symptoms—that is, until they learn a more tolerant and rational way of living.

Application to group therapy.   RET is very suitable for group therapy, for all the members are taught to apply RET principles to one another in the group setting. They get an opportunity to practice new behaviors that involve taking risks, and they get abundant opportunities to do homework assignments. In the group setting members also have an opportunity to experience assertive training, role playing, and a variety of risk-taking activities. They can learn social skills and practice interacting with others in after-group sessions. Both other group members and the leader can observe their behavior and give feedback. In individual therapy a client usually gives after-the-fact reports, but in a group setting clients are able to engage in contacts designed to foster a radical philosophical change. Ellis recommends that most RET clients experience group as well as individual therapy at some point.

Ellis (1969) has developed a special form of group therapy, known as "A Weekend of Rational Encounter," that utilizes RET methods and principles. The weekend marathon is divided into two parts. The first part consists of 14 hours of continuous rational-encounter therapy, followed by 8 hours of rest; the second part includes about another 10 hours of therapy. During the initial stages of the weekend encounter members experience a series of directed activities, both verbal and nonverbal, designed to get them to know one another. Participants are asked to share their most shameful experiences and are encouraged to engage in risk taking.

In the beginning stages emotive-evocative procedures are used, and neither problem solving nor decision making is attempted. As the marathon progresses, the same logical principles of rational thinking that are used in one-to-one therapy are applied to the group. Thus, the marathon, which consists of a heavy dose of cognitive and action methods, is more than an experiential session during which feelings are explored and shared. At the later stages of the marathon, some of the deepest personal problems of the group members are explored with cognitive procedures. Ellis (1969) indicated that, during the closing hours "the group and the leader usually tend to smoke out anyone who has not as yet brought up a problem for detailed discussion. Such individuals are directly asked why they have not said too much about themselves previously and are induced to look for a major problem and to discuss it openly" (p. 121). Also toward the end of the session, specific homework assignments are given to the group members. A postsession is held six to eight weeks later to check the progress they have made with their assignments as well as to evaluate their current status.

Summary and evaluation

There are aspects of RET that I find to be very valuable as I work with clients, either individually or in groups. I believe that significant others in our past have contributed to the shaping of our current life-style and philosophy of life. Yet, in strong agreement with Ellis, I contend that we are the ones who are responsible for maintaining certain self-destructive ideas and attitudes that influence our daily transactions. We may have learned that we should be perfect, and that it is essential to be loved and approved of by everyone; the problem, however, is that we still apply these notions relentlessly to ourselves. I see value in confronting clients with questions such as What are your assumptions and basic beliefs? Have you really scrutinized some of the core ideas that you live by to determine if they are your own values or merely introjects?

In addition, I value thinking as well as feeling and experiencing in psychotherapy. I am critical of many group approaches, particularly encounter and sensitivity groups, where thinking, judging, and evaluating are looked on with scorn and where experiencing here-and-now feelings and "gut reactions" is seen as equivalent to psychological health. After a person has experienced a cathartic or highly intensive emotional experience related to earlier traumas, it seems, some attempt at conceptualization and giving meaning to the experience is essential if it is to have any lasting effect. RET does offer the cognitive dimension and does challenge clients to examine the rationality of many of their decisions and values.

Another contribution of RET is its emphasis on putting newly acquired insights into action. The homework-assignment method is well suited to enabling clients to practice new behaviors and assisting them in the process of their reconditioning. Reality therapy, behavior therapy, and Transactional Analysis share with RET this action orientation. Clients can gain a multitude of insights and can become very aware of the nature of their problems, but I question the value of self-understanding unless specific plans that lead to behavioral changes desired by the client are implemented. RET insists on this action phase as a crucial part of the therapy process.

RET has some definite limitations, many of which Ellis, as cited earlier in this chapter, has pointed out. Because the approach is highly didactic, I believe that it is essential for therapists to know themselves well and to take care not to merely impose their own philosophy of life on their clients. The issue of what constitutes rational behavior is central here. The fact that the rational therapist assumes such a confrontive and directive position creates certain dangers. The therapist's level of training, knowledge and skill, perceptiveness, and accuracy of judgment are particularly important in RET. Because the therapist has a large degree of power by virtue of persuasion and directiveness, psychological harm is more possible in RET than in the less directive person-centered approach. The RET therapist must be aware of when to "push" clients and when not to. There is the danger that an untrained therapist who uses RET might view therapy as "beating down" clients with persuasion, indoctrination, logic, and advice. Thus, a practitioner can misuse RET by reducing it to dispensing quick-cure methods—that is, by telling clients what is wrong with them and how they should change.

Questions for reflection and discussion

Below is a series of questions designed to stimulate your own critical evaluation of the advantages and disadvantages of RET.

1. Do you believe that it is desirable for one to "think" one's way through "irrational" aspects of life such as joy, ecstasy, craziness, sadness, despair, abandonment and loneliness, rage, fear, and hatred? Should one be "cured" of those feelings? What would life be like if one were almost exclusively rational?

2. RET views anxiety as the result of self-blame. Ellis maintains that blaming ourselves or others is pernicious. Do you agree? Is it desirable to remove all guilt? If one gets to a point where one never experiences guilt, does this mean that one is an accomplished psychopath? What kind of guilt is healthy? What kind is unhealthy?

3. Do you agree with the contention that one does not need love and acceptance from other significant people? Is it realistic to teach a client ways of enjoying life while feeling unloved? Is this a persuasive form of denial?

4. Can you apply to yourself the view that one tends to keep irrational ideas alive by repeating those ideas to oneself? What are some examples in your own life?

5. Review Ellis's list of common irrational ideas that many of us have learned in society. What is your evaluation of these ideas? What other irrational ideas could you add to the list? What ideas can you relate to personally? In what ways do you still cling to some irrational premises? Have you tried to eradicate them?

6. The rational-emotive therapist teaches a client a philosophy of life. Whose philosophy is taught? Is teaching a philosophy of life appropriate in counseling? Does this approach assume that the therapist is the one with the "correct" beliefs? Do you consider indoctrination as therapy?

7. Do you think that RET is too simplistic? Is it really teaching a client how to successfully suppress basic feelings? Take, for example, a client who says "I know I feel guilty over

```
  * ..        2095
  * ..         895
  * ..         150
 .993         3140    TX

 .993        3141 U CHK
A .993       000 CHG

         04/19/86
```

U.W.M.
BOOKSTORE

```
T *                  20.95
T *                   8.95
* *                   1.50        TL TX
A * 9 9 3            31.40


A * 9 9 3            31.40   CHK
                            TND
A * 9 9 3             0.00   CNG
```

. 0 0 0 1 0 6 / 1 9 / 8 4

an abortion, and I've been through the experience 98 times in my therapy. I know it's dumb, but I still feel guilty, though I wish I didn't. So, what can I do about it?" Ellis appears to believe that intellectual persuasion will eventually convince the client that she no longer need blame herself, nor will she need to cling to the "irrational belief" of her guilt. Could this form of therapeutic intervention aid her in suppressing her feelings? Would she have merely persuaded herself that she should not feel the way she actually does?

8. What criteria do you employ to determine whether or not a person's philosophy of life is rational?
9. Would a constant repetition of corrective sentences make one more of a robot than a spontaneous creator?
10. Do you believe that, with its emphasis on thinking, RET gives enough attention to the emotional aspects of therapy?

Recommended supplementary readings

If you are interested in suggesting rational-emotive self-help books to your clients or want to read this kind of material for yourself, there are two good references. *Humanistic Psychotherapy: The Rational-Emotive Approach* (Ellis, 1973) presents in a clear, straightforward manner most of the key concepts and basic issues of RET. *A New Guide to Rational Living* (Ellis & Harper, 1975) applies the principles of RET to problems of everyday living. Both books are easy to read and well-written.

For an excellent updated summary of the rational-emotive theory of personality and therapy and a survey of the research data relating to RET, I recommend *Theoretical and Empirical Foundations of Rational-Emotive Therapy* (Ellis & Whiteley, 1979). The *Handbook of Rational-Emotive Therapy* (Ellis & Grieger, 1977) is one of the most comprehensive up-to-date overviews of the theory and practice of RET. This book is especially good on application of the principles of RET to sex therapy, education, group work, assertion training, depression, and work with children.

References and suggested readings

Books highly recommended as supplementary reading are marked with an asterisk.

Corey, G. *Theory and practice of group counseling.* Monterey, Calif.: Brooks/Cole, 1981.
Corey, G. *Case approach to counseling and psychotherapy.* Monterey, Calif.: Brooks/Cole, 1982.
* Ellis, A. *Reason and emotion in psychotherapy.* New York: Lyle Stuart, 1962.
Ellis, A. Rational-emotive psychotherapy. In D. Arbuckle (Ed.), *Counseling and psychotherapy.* New York: McGraw-Hill, 1967.
Ellis, A. A weekend of rational encounter. In A. Burton (Ed.), *Encounter: The theory and practice of encounter groups.* San Francisco: Jossey-Bass, 1969.
* Ellis, A. *Growth through reason.* Hollywood: Wilshire Books, 1971.
Ellis, A. *Humanistic psychotherapy: The rational-emotive approach.* New York: Julian Press, 1973.
Ellis, A. Rational-emotive theory: Albert Ellis. In A. Burton (Ed.), *Operational theories of personality.* New York: Brunner/Mazel, 1974.
Ellis, A. The practice of rational-emotive therapy. In A. Ellis & J. Whiteley (Eds.), *Theoretical and empirical foundations of rational-emotive therapy.* Monterey, Calif.: Brooks/Cole, 1979. (a)
Ellis, A. Rational-emotive therapy. In R. Corsini (Ed.), *Current psychotherapies* (2nd ed.). Itasca, Ill.: F. E. Peacock, 1979. (b)

Ellis, A. Rational-emotive therapy. In A. Ellis & J. Whiteley (Eds.), *Theoretical and empirical foundations of rational-emotive therapy*. Monterey, Calif.: Brooks/Cole, 1979. (c)

Ellis, A. The theory of rational-emotive therapy. In A. Ellis & J. Whiteley (Eds.), *Theoretical and empirical foundations of rational-emotive therapy*. Monterey, Calif.: Brooks/Cole, 1979. (d)

Ellis, A. Toward a new theory of personality. In A. Ellis & J. Whiteley (Eds.), *Theoretical and empirical foundations of rational-emotive therapy*. Monterey, Calif.: Brooks/Cole, 1979. (e)

* Ellis, A., & Grieger, R. *Handbook of rational-emotive therapy*. New York: Springer, 1977.

* Ellis, A., & Harper, R. *A new guide to rational living* (Rev. ed.). Hollywood: Wilshire Books, 1975.

* Ellis, A., & Whiteley, J. (Eds.). *Theoretical and empirical foundations of rational-emotive therapy*. Monterey, Calif.: Brooks/Cole, 1979.

10

Reality Therapy

Introduction

I selected William Glasser's reality therapy for inclusion in this book for several reasons. First, this approach (as does Ellis's rational-emotive therapy) provides a good contrast to most of the other counseling approaches explored. Second, reality therapy has gained popularity among school counselors, teachers, and principals and rehabilitation workers. Third, it presents many of the basic issues in counseling that underlie such questions as What is reality? Should a therapist teach his or her patients? What should be taught? What model should the therapist provide? Whose philosophy should be taught? What is the role of values in counseling? As you read this chapter keep these questions in mind and compare reality therapy with the other therapeutic approaches you have studied.

Reality therapy focuses on present behavior. The therapist functions as a teacher and a model and confronts clients in ways that help them face reality and fulfill basic needs without harming themselves or others. The heart of reality therapy is acceptance of personal responsibility, which is equated with mental health. Glasser developed this therapy from his conviction that conventional psychiatry is based largely on mistaken assumptions.

Thus, practitioners of reality therapy focus on what clients are *able* and *willing to do* in the *present* situation to change their behavior and on the means for doing so. This includes making a commitment to change, developing a plan for action, and following through with the commitment.

Reality therapy rejects the concept *mental illness,* calling it an evasion of personal responsibility. Value judgments and morality are stressed, for individuals are challenged to evaluate the quality of their behavior to determine whether it is leading to autonomy and success.

Like behavior therapy, Transactional Analysis, and rational-emotive therapy, this model is basically active, directive, didactic, and cognitive, and it employs the contract method. The therapist's central task is to encourage clients to face reality and make value judgments regarding their current behavior. Thus, behavior is the focus, not attitudes, insight, one's past, or unconscious motivation.

Reality therapy is applicable to individual therapy and counseling, social work, teaching, group work, marriage counseling, family therapy, rehabilitation counseling, crisis intervention, institutional management, and community development. It is a popular therapeutic approach in state mental hospitals, correctional institutions, and other institutions designed for the rehabilitation and treatment of youthful and adult offenders. Reality therapy is a form of behavior modification, for, particularly in its institutional applications, it is essentially a type of nonrigorous operant conditioning. In my opinion, one reason for Glasser's popularity is that he has succeeded in transplanting some concepts of behavior modification into a relatively simple and straightforward model of practice. Another reason is reality therapy's emphasis on the strengths within clients and what they are able to do *now* to make constructive changes in the way they are living. Reality therapy is opposed to the medical model and all that it implies. Instead, it is based on the growth model, and it teaches people how to achieve success.

Key concepts

VIEW OF HUMAN NATURE

Reality therapy is based on the premise that there is a single psychological need present throughout life: the need for identity, which includes a need to feel a sense of uniqueness, separateness, and distinctiveness. The need for identity, which accounts for the dynamics of behavior, is seen as universal among all cultures.

According to reality therapy, it is most useful to consider identity in terms of a "success identity" versus a "failure identity." In the formation of identity, others play a significant role in helping us see ourselves as a success or as a failure. Having love and acceptance is directly related to a "success identity;" lacking love and acceptance is related to a "failure identity." According to Glasser (1965), the basis of reality therapy is to help clients fulfill the basic psychological needs, which include "the need to love and to be loved and the need to feel that we are worthwhile to ourselves and to others" (p. 9).

The view of human nature includes a contention that a "growth force" impels us to strive for a success identity. As Glasser and Zunin (1979) wrote: "We believe that each individual has a health or growth force. Basically people want to be content and enjoy a success identity, to show responsible behavior and to have meaningful interpersonal relationships" (p. 315). Personal suffering can be changed only with a change in identity. This viewpoint asserts that, because individuals can change how they live, feel, and behave, they can thus change their destinies. Identity change is contingent on behavioral change.

It is clear, then, that reality therapy does not rest on a deterministic philosophy of human nature but is built on the assumption that the person is ultimately self-determining. This principle implies each person's responsibility to accept the consequences for his or her behavior. Apparently, the person becomes what he or she decides to become.

CHARACTERISTICS OF REALITY THERAPY

There are at least eight characteristics that define reality therapy:

1. Reality therapy rejects the concept *mental illness* and does not deal with psychological diagnoses. It assumes that specific behavior disorders are the result of irresponsibility, and it equates mental health with responsible behavior.

2. Reality therapy focuses on behavior rather than on feelings and attitudes. Although it does not assert that feelings and attitudes are unimportant, it does stress becoming aware of present behavior. Also, the reality therapist does not depend on insight to change attitudes but maintains that attitude change follows behavior change.

3. Reality therapy focuses on the present, not on the past. Because a person's past is fixed, all that can be changed is the present and the future. If the past is discussed in therapy, it is always related to the client's current behavior. The therapist is open to exploring all aspects of clients' present life, including their hopes, fears, and values. Therapy stresses their strengths, potentials, successes, and positive qualities, not merely their misery and symptoms. Glasser (1965) urged that the client be seen as a "person with wide potential, not just as a patient with problems" (p. 31). He discouraged devoting therapy time to rehashing problems and failures and suggested that the therapist look for a client's strengths and emphasize them in the conversations. He did not advocate recounting history and exploring the past, for this is an unproductive venture. "Why become involved with the irresponsible person [the client] was? We want to become involved with the responsible person we know he can be" (p. 32).

4. Reality therapy emphasizes value judgments. It places central importance on clients' role in judging the quality of their own behavior in order to determine what is contributing to their failure in life. It holds that change is unlikely unless clients make some determination of the constructiveness or destructiveness of their behavior. If clients come to realize that they are not getting what they want and that their behavior is self-destructive, there is a real possibility for positive change to occur, simply because they decide that alternatives might be preferable to their present unrealistic style.

5. Reality therapy does not emphasize transference. It sees transference as a way for the therapist to remain hidden as a person. Reality therapy calls for therapists to be themselves, not play the role of the client's mother or father. Glasser (1965) contended that clients do not look for a repeat of unsuccessful involvements in their past but that they seek a satisfying human involvement with a person in their present existence. The therapist can help them fulfill their needs in the present by establishing a personal and genuine relationship.

6. Reality therapy stresses the conscious, not the unconscious, aspects of personality. Psychoanalytic theory, which assumes that insight and awareness of unconscious processes are a requisite for personality change, emphasizes ways of tapping unconscious conflicts through techniques such as analysis of transference, dream analysis, free associations, and analysis of resistance. By contrast, reality therapy emphasizes what clients are doing wrong, how their present behavior is not getting them what they want, and how they might plan for successful behavior based on responsible and realistic

actions. The reality therapist examines clients' present life in detail and assumes that they will discover the conscious behavior that does not lead to the fulfillment of their needs. Thus, reality therapy contends that to emphasize the unconscious is to sidetrack the central issue of clients' irresponsibility and give them an excuse for avoiding reality. Also, whereas insight might be interesting, reality therapy does not see it as essential to producing change.

7. Reality therapy eliminates punishment. Glasser maintains that punishment aimed at changing behavior is ineffective and that punishment for failing to implement plans results both in reinforcing the client's failure identity and in harming the therapeutic relationship. He cautions against the therapist's use of deprecating statements, for this is punishment. Instead of using punishment, Glasser advocates allowing the client to experience the natural consequences of his or her behavior.

8. Reality therapy emphasizes responsibility, which Glasser (1965) defined as "the ability to fulfill one's needs, and to do so *in a way that does not deprive others of the ability to fulfill their needs*" (p. 13). Learning responsibility is a lifelong process. Even though all of us possess the need to love and be loved and the need to feel a sense of worthiness, we are not naturally endowed with the ability to fulfill these needs. Responsibility consists of learning how to meet these needs in reality. Glasser contended that "we must learn to correct ourselves when we do wrong and credit ourselves when we do right" (p. 10). In order to improve our conduct when it is below our standards, we need to evaluate our own behavior or have it evaluated. Thus, an essential part of reality therapy involves morals, standards, value judgments, and right and wrong behavior, for they are all intimately related to the fulfillment of the need for self-worth. According to Glasser, responsible people do that which gives them a feeling of self-worth and a feeling that they are worthwhile to others.

Glasser (1965) contended that teaching responsibility is at the core of reality therapy. Whereas most animals are driven by instinct, humans have developed the capacity to learn and to teach responsibility. Reality therapy thus stresses the therapist's teaching function. The therapist teaches clients better ways to fulfill their needs by exploring the specifics of their daily lives and by making directive statements and suggestions of ways to solve problems more effectively. Therapy becomes a special kind of education wherein definite plans are made, and realistic and responsible means of meeting personal needs are examined.

The therapeutic process

THERAPEUTIC GOALS

As is true of most systems of psychotherapy, the overall goal of reality therapy is to help the individual achieve autonomy. Essentially, autonomy is the state of maturity that accounts for the person's ability to relinquish environmental support and substitute internal support. This maturity implies that people are able to take responsibility for who they are and what they want to become and to develop responsible and realistic plans to fulfill their goals. Reality therapy assists people in defining and clarifying their life goals. Further, it assists them in clarifying the ways they are frustrating their progress toward these goals. The therapist helps clients discover alternatives in reaching goals, but it is they who decide their own goals of therapy.

Glasser and Zunin (1979) agreed that the therapist should have some general goals in mind for clients in terms of individual responsibility but that clients must determine behavioral goals for themselves. They wrote that the criteria for successful psychother-apy depend largely on the client-determined goals. Although there are no rigid criteria for the termination of therapy, the general criteria of attaining responsible behavior and fulfilling the client's goals indicate that clients are able to follow through with plans independently, and that there is no longer a need for treatment.

THERAPIST'S FUNCTION AND ROLE

The basic job of the reality therapist is to become involved with clients and then get them to face reality. Glasser (1965) wrote that, when the therapist confronts clients, he or she forces them to decide whether or not they will take the "responsible path." The therapist does not make value judgments and decisions for clients, for to do so would take away the responsibility that belongs to them. The therapist's task is to serve as a guide to help them realistically appraise their own behavior.

Some of Glasser's readers have developed a distorted notion that the therapist should function as a moralist. Glasser (1972), asserting that his principle of evaluating behavior has been frequently misunderstood, disavowed the role of the moralist:

> Some people accept and others reject Reality Therapy because they misunderstand this prin-ciple. Both groups believe the Reality Therapist acts as a moralist, which he does not; he never tells anyone that what he is doing is wrong and that he must change. The therapist does not judge the behavior; he leads the patient to evaluate his own behavior through his involvement and by bringing the actual behavior out in the open [p. 119].

The reality therapist is expected to give praise when clients act in a responsible way and to show disapproval when they do not. Clients demand this type of judgment, according to Glasser (1965, p. 28). The therapist must also teach the client that the aim of therapy is not happiness. The reality therapist assumes that clients can create their own happiness, and that the key to finding happiness is through accepting responsibility. Therefore, the therapist does not accept any excuses or ignore reality, nor does he or she let clients blame anything or anybody else for their own present unhappiness.

In his more recent writings Glasser (for example, 1976a) emphasizes the value of an accepting attitude on the counselor's part. Although he does not endorse unconditional acceptance (acceptance is always conditional on clients' facing their problems and mak-ing plans to solve them), his recent thinking is that the therapeutic climate should be free of excessive criticism. While still maintaining that it is essential to "get down to brass tacks and make realistic plans," he makes it clear that clients need a reasonably noncritical therapeutic milieu if they are to acquire the strength to carry these plans out.

Another important function of the reality therapist is to set limits, including those in the therapeutic situation and those that life places on the individual. Glasser and Zunin (1979) pointed to the contractual arrangement as prescribing limits. Contracts, which are often a part of the therapy process, might include having clients report on their successes as well as failures in work outside the therapy situation. Frequently a contract determines a specific time limit for the duration of therapy. At the end of this time clients are allowed to fend for themselves. Some clients function more effectively when they are aware that the therapy sessions are limited to a certain number.

Apart from those functions and tasks, the therapist's ability to get involved with clients and to get them involved in the therapeutic process is considered to be paramount. This is often a difficult function, especially when clients are not seeking counseling or when they are coming for "help" solely as a provision of their probation. According to Glasser (1965), some of the personal attributes or qualities that lead to successful outcomes are the ability and willingness of therapists to be demanding yet sensitive; to fulfill their own needs in reality; to openly share their own struggles; to be personal and not maintain an aloof stance; to allow their own values to be challenged by the client; not to accept excuses for evasion of responsible action; to demonstrate courage by continually confronting the client, regardless of the opposition; to understand and empathize with the client; and to establish a genuine involvement with the client.

CLIENT'S EXPERIENCE IN THERAPY

Even though clients' behavior is inadequate, unrealistic, and irresponsible, it is still an attempt to fulfill their basic needs of being loved and loving and of feeling a sense of self-worth. Their behavior is an attempt to gain a sense of identity, even though it might well be a "failure identity." The therapeutic concern is with those who have not learned, or have lost their ability, to live responsible lives.

Clients are expected to focus on their behavior instead of their feelings and attitudes. The therapist challenges them to take a critical look at what they are doing with their lives and then make value judgments regarding the effectiveness of their behavior in attaining their life goals. If a man complains of feeling anxious, the therapist might ask "What are you doing to make yourself anxious?" The focus is not on the anxious feeling but on helping the client gain awareness of what he is now doing to make himself anxious. Constant examination and evaluation of what the client is doing continues throughout therapy.

Once clients make certain judgments about their behavior and decide how they want to change, they are expected to develop specific plans to change failure behavior into success behavior. Clients must make a commitment to carry out these plans; action becomes a must. They cannot escape their commitment by blaming, explaining, or giving excuses. They must be actively involved in implementing their therapeutic contract in a responsible way if any progress is to occur.

Glasser's recent thinking (for example, 1976a) involves giving attention to how individuals evaluate their behavior. He points out that it is important that they do so in a way that is not excessively self-critical. Although Glasser still maintains that self-evaluation and self-correction are the foundation of reality therapy, his updated writings include the caution that "how we criticize ourselves, however, is vitally important because we must learn to direct our criticism at those activities which it is possible to correct; otherwise we will be too hard on ourselves and may lock ourselves into failure" (1976a, p. 59).

In *Positive Addiction* Glasser (1976a) consistently referred to the importance of learning to be noncritical in our endeavors. He wrote about two forms of "positive addiction," running and meditation, and he related positive addiction (PA) to Maslow's "peak experiences." Glasser described people who have freed themselves of negative addictions such as to alcohol or drugs by developing some form of PA. In order to attain such a state, Glasser stressed, these activities must be approached in a noncritical way. As people try to improve, they must be careful not to criticize themselves harshly, which could bring the process of change to an abrupt halt.

RELATIONSHIP BETWEEN THERAPIST AND CLIENT

Before effective therapy can occur, an involvement between the client and the counselor must develop. Clients need to know that the helping person cares enough about them to both accept them and help them fulfill their needs in the real world. Specific principles that provide the framework for the client/therapist relationship are briefly reviewed below (Glasser, 1965; Glasser & Zunin, 1979):

1. Reality therapy is based on the personal relationship and involvement of the therapist with the client. The therapist, by warmth, understanding, acceptance, and belief in the capacity of a person to develop a success identity, must communicate that he or she cares. Through the personal involvement with the therapist clients learn that there is more to life than focusing on failures, misery, and irresponsible behavior. The therapist also demonstrates caring by refusing to accept blaming or excuses from clients. The therapist cares enough to view them in terms of what they can become if they decide to live by facing reality. While a warm relationship is being established, entanglements are avoided. It is the therapist's job to define the therapeutic situation so that the client understands the nature, purpose, and direction of the relationship.

2. Planning is essential in reality therapy. The therapeutic situation is not limited merely to discussions between the therapist and the client. They develop plans that, once established, must be carried out; action is another essential part of reality therapy. Much of the most significant work of the therapeutic process, then, consists in helping the client identify specific ways to change failure behavior into success behavior. Plans should be within the limits of the motivation and capacities of each client. They are not absolute but are mainly alternative ways to solve problems and expand successful life experiences. Plans for action must be specific, concrete, and measurable. They need not be rigid; an endless number of plans can be applied to problem solving. If one plan does not work, it should be reevaluated, and other alternatives can then be considered. Glasser and Zunin (1979, p. 321) wrote that it is valuable to put the plan in writing, in the form of a contract. Then the client can be accountable for his or her subsequent actions in carrying it out.

3. Commitment is the keystone of reality therapy. After individuals make value judgments about their behavior and decide on plans for action, the therapist assists them in making a commitment to implement their plans in their daily life. Resolutions and plans become meaningless unless there is a decision to carry them out. Glasser and Zunin (1979) pointed out that "a primary characteristic of individuals who have failure identities is that they have a strong unwillingness to commit themselves" (p. 322). Hence, it is in following through with plans that clients acquire a sense of self-worth.

4. Reality therapy accepts no excuses. It is clear that not all the client's commitments will be actualized. But when plans do fail, the therapist is not interested in listening to the client's explanations. Glasser stresses that the therapist should not blame or depreciate the client for failing or "play detective" and search for the reasons for the failure. Glasser thinks that people know why things went wrong; thus, instead of focusing on why, the therapist focuses on what the client intends to do to accomplish what he or she decided to do. Glasser (1965, p. 27) contended that it is essential that the therapist "insist that the patient face the reality of his behavior." The therapist's task is to care enough for the client that he or she makes the client "face a truth that he has spent his life trying to avoid; *he is responsible for his behavior.*" The therapist never condones or excuses any of the client's irresponsible behavior.

Application: Therapeutic techniques and procedures

MAJOR TECHNIQUES AND PROCEDURES

Reality therapy is verbally active. Its procedures focus on clients' strengths and potentials as related to their current behavior as they attempt to succeed in life. In assisting a client to create a success identity, the therapist might use a range of techniques such as the following:

1. Engage in role playing with the client.
2. Use humor.
3. Confront the client and not allow any excuses.
4. Help the client to formulate specific plans for action.
5. Serve as a role model and teacher.
6. Set definite limits and structure the therapy situation.
7. Use "verbal shock therapy" or appropriate sarcasm to confront the client with his or her unrealistic behavior.
8. Get involved with the patient in his or her search for more effective living.

Reality therapy does not include some commonly accepted therapeutic approaches. Psychiatrists who practice reality therapy apply drugs and medications conservatively, for medication tends to remove personal responsibility for behavior. Further, the practitioner of reality therapy does not devote time to searching for reasons but attempts to convey an attitude of working together with clients to help them achieve their stated goals. Diagnostic techniques are not a part of reality therapy, being seen as, at best, a waste of time and, at worst, damaging to a client by pinning on a label (such as *schizophrenic*) that tends to perpetuate irresponsible and unsuccessful behavior. Other techniques not used are interpretation, insight, nondirective interviews, prolonged silences, free association, analysis of transference and resistance, and dream analysis.

APPLICATIONS TO COUNSELING SITUATIONS

Glasser and Zunin (1979) wrote that the techniques of reality therapy are applicable to a wide range of behavior and emotional problems. They asserted that the procedures of reality therapy have been successful in treating such specific individual problems as anxiety, maladjustment, marital conflicts, perversions, and psychoses.

An area in which reality therapy has been used extensively and with great success is the treatment of youthful law offenders. Glasser's work at the Ventura School for Girls in southern California indicates that reality-therapy procedures significantly reduced recidivism rates (Glasser & Zunin, 1979).

Reality therapy is well suited to individual therapy, group therapy, and marriage counseling. In individual therapy, therapists usually see their clients once a week for a 45-minute session.

Group psychotherapy is an effective vehicle by which to apply the procedures of reality therapy. The group process can be a powerful agent in helping clients implement their plans and follow through with their commitments. The members are encouraged to write down a specific contract and read it to the group. Involvement with other group members in a meaningful way is an inducement to stick by the commitments made. The use of cotherapists is frequent and has been found to be a valuable adjunct in reality-therapy groups (Glasser & Zunin, 1979).

Marriage counseling or conjoint marital therapy is often practiced by the reality therapist, according to Glasser and Zunin. This type of counseling is usually limited to from 5 to 15 visits. At the end of this time an evaluation is made to determine what if any progress has been made and whether continued sessions are in order. It is important to establish at the outset whether the couples are (a) deciding to terminate the relationship; (b) exploring the pros and cons of continuing the relationship; or (c) quite sure they wish to remain married but seeking help in improving their relationship. The therapist is encouraged to be active and should raise questions leading to understanding the general marriage dynamics and style as the partners relate to each other. Some questions that are likely to be posed are "What are you doing that makes you feel good (or bad) about yourself?" "What is your spouse doing that makes you feel good (or bad) about yourself?" "What specific changes would each of you most like to make in your marriage?"

Summary and evaluation

Reality therapy seems well suited to brief interventions in crisis-counseling situations and to working with youths or adults who are in institutions for criminal behavior. Realistically, in those situations and with that type of population, long-term psychotherapy that explores unconscious dynamics and explores one's past may be extremely limited. Glasser developed his approach because of his contention that psychoanalytic procedures did not work for that population.

The advantages of the approach appear to be that it is relatively short-term therapy, and that it deals with conscious behavioral problems. The client is confronted with the necessity of evaluating his or her behavior and making a value judgment. Insight and awareness are not seen as enough; a plan of action and a commitment to following through are seen as the core of the therapeutic process. Clients might want to manufacture excuses, play blaming games, and make others responsible for their current problems. Because reality therapy accepts no excuses and insists on clients' accepting responsibility for the way they are, they must look inward and search for alternatives. Assume that a youth in a correctional facility is a product of a miserable environment in which his parents hated him and abused him physically and psychologically. Regardless of the reasons for his conflicts with the law, he now needs to decide whether his behavior is getting him what he wants. In this respect, reality therapy encourages clients to exercise freedom and responsibility.

I especially like the factor of accountability that this model stresses. If individuals say that they want to change certain behaviors, then they are confronted by the counselor with what is stopping them from doing so. I like the focus on strongly encouraging clients to evaluate their behavior and current life situation and decide if they really are willing to do what is necessary to make changes. If they determine that their behavior is not getting them what they want, then they are ripe for a plan of action.

Reality therapy provides a structure for both clients and therapists to evaluate the degree and nature of changes. I emphasize action-oriented procedures as a way for clients to actually make the changes they say they want to make. The contract approach is one such method that can lead to specificity and accountability. Although I like the idea of not accepting excuses for violating contracts, I also like the avoidance of punishment and blaming that is basic to reality therapy. If clients do not carry out their plans, it is important to frankly explore with them the implications of this situation.

In my estimation, a shortcoming of reality therapy is that it does not give enough emphasis to the place of unconscious psychodynamics and the person's past as a determinant of present behavior. Whereas Glasser apparently accepts the role of the past and the unconscious as causal factors of present behavior, he rejects the value of those factors in modifying present behavior. As he put it, "Certainly patients, like everyone else, have reasons of which they may be unaware for behaving the way they do. ... But we are doing therapy, and not research into the causes of human behavior, and we have found that knowledge of cause has nothing to do with therapy" (1965, p. 53). He discounted the contributions of the psychoanalytic approach and gave little credit to Freud's discoveries.

My major concern is that reality therapy can become a superficial type of intervention, because it utilizes an overly simplistic framework for therapeutic practice. As is rational-emotive therapy, reality therapy is vulnerable to the practitioner who could assume the role of expert in deciding for others questions such as how life should be lived, what is realistic or unrealistic, what is right or wrong behavior, and what constitutes responsible behavior. Thus, a therapist who is unaware of his or her own needs to "straighten people out" can stunt clients' growth and autonomy by becoming overly moralistic and by strongly influencing them to accept the therapist's view of reality instead of searching within for their own answers. Further, this approach reduces solutions of all problems to a few common denominators: acceptance of personal responsibility, commitment to realistic values, and conscious decision making. There are other dimensions stressed by the various therapies that are not seriously considered within the framework of reality therapy.

Another area of criticism that I have of reality therapy relates to Glasser's total rejection of the existence of mental illness. Glasser (1965, 1976a) has continued to see mental illness as a form of irresponsibility or as a basic weakness. According to him, it is a myth that there is such a disorder as schizophrenia. He prefers the term *crazy person* because he thinks that people *choose* their craziness as a way of avoiding reality. In my opinion, this extreme view of denouncing all mental illness as a myth is both naive and potentially harmful to mentally ill people. I see this view as increasing the difficulties therapists have in making real contact with such people. In general, it is not enough to merely appeal to people to decide now to give up irresponsibility and weakness. Further, some mental illness may *not* be merely chosen, but rather a reaction to a combination of causal factors, including excessive and prolonged stress, faulty psychological and social development, and biochemical or other physiological factors.

I want to add that I do not favor the medical model, for I agree that this approach frequently fosters passivity, dependency, and helplessness on the part of people who are rigidly categorized by some diagnostic label. I agree with Glasser that *some* people do choose craziness as a way of avoiding responsibility for their actions. I am also impatient with those mental-health professionals who are too ready to excuse some people who commit crimes and engage in antisocial behavior as "insane and therefore not held responsible for their acts." I am convinced that some "mentally ill patients" discover that it is convenient and expedient to be crazy, for this way they are not held accountable for their actions, regardless of whom they hurt.

Finally, Glasser (1976a) maintained that there has been no basic change in his approach since its development in the early 1960s. However, it seems clear from his more recent works that he now gives increased emphasis to a noncritical and accepting therapeutic milieu. This atmosphere is the opposite of what many beginners consider to be the essence of reality therapy—namely, a critical confrontation of the client's irresponsibility, with "no excuses" accepted for failing to make constructive changes. Glasser (1976a) mentioned that he would surely be misunderstood in this respect. He suggested that some would contend that he had deviated from the no-nonsense approach that stressed facing reality, making decisions, taking specific steps to change, and solving problems. Glasser added that he was continuing to teach the value of facing reality, yet that he had also learned that clients need to gain strength to accomplish their plans.

In closing I want to add that even though I am critical of reality therapy on the ground that it tends to oversimplify some complex issues, this does not mean that I do not see value in most of its principles and concepts. Many of them can be incorporated in a dynamic and personal way into the style of counselors, and there is a basis for integrating them with most of the other therapeutic approaches covered in this book.

Questions for reflection and discussion

The following questions are directly related to the theory and practice of reality therapy. I suggest that you review them as a basis for integrating certain aspects of reality therapy into your counseling philosophy.

1. How can a therapist judge acceptable, realistic behavior? Whose creeds and values should be used to judge the acceptability of behavior?
2. Wrestle with the problem of defining "reality." Is the therapist's view of reality more real than the client's? What about the problem that exists when the therapist and the client live in different experiential worlds? Can a White, middle-class therapist who has experienced little divergence in life-styles effectively guide a Black or Brown youngster who lives in the ghetto or in the barrio? Can the therapist enter the world of reality of the client? Can he or she understand values and behavior that are sharply divergent from his or her own?
3. Do you see a contradiction in the idea that a therapist must reject irresponsible behavior yet accept clients and maintain involvement with them? Is rejection of a person's behavior a subtle rejection of that person?
4. How realistic is it to assume that real involvement between a therapist and a client can occur when the client makes it frankly known that he or she wants no part of "head-shrinking"? Assume that your client is a "delinquent" in a youth authority camp and that she has to see you for therapy. She comes for several sessions, remains closed, and tells you each time that she does not want to be there and wants to quit. How would you handle this? What are your own values in regard to "mandatory counseling"? What if your views conflict with the agency that employs you?
5. Glasser's approach suggests that the therapist be a model for the client to emulate. Should the therapist be so? How can a therapist decide whether he or she is a model worth emulating? Should the therapist seek to have clients pattern themselves according to all the counselor's values? Which values should be emulated?
6. Glasser maintains that clients need to know that the therapist cares for them, and that one way of evidencing caring is to reject behavior that does not help them fulfill their needs in a responsible way. Do you agree? How can you determine whether a client feels that you care? What does caring imply to you? What if the truth of the matter is that you do not care for your client? What would you do if you had a strong aversion to the client?
7. Where do you stand on Glasser's idea that a therapist should give praise when clients act responsibly and show disapproval when they act irresponsibly? Do you think that these responses might encourage them to adopt your values so that they are liked and accepted by you? Is this type of value judgment conducive to developing inner direction? Is it appropriate to therapy? Can it really be avoided? Do all therapists make value judgments in some form or another?

8. What advantages do you see in the insistence on focusing exclusively on the present? How does it avoid digging for useless artifacts in a person's history? How does it eliminate the blaming game?
9. What limitations do you see in insisting that your client not explore past experience? Can one really understand or change one's present if one refuses to become aware of one's past? Are you not a victim now unless you understand your past?
10. Do you agree with Glasser's concept that mental illness is the result of irresponsibility? Can you think of any other causes of mental illness besides irresponsibility?

Recommended supplementary readings

A good place to begin your extended reading program in reality therapy is with *Reality Therapy: A New Approach to Psychiatry* (Glasser, 1965). It outlines the basic concepts and gives examples of how this approach works in private practice and in institutionalized settings with delinquent girls, with psychotics, and with students in the public schools.

For an updated work consult *Positive Addiction* (Glasser, 1976a). This is basically a self-help book, which describes how people can grow through some form of solitary activity such as jogging or meditation.

For those who are interested in applying the principles and procedures of reality therapy to school settings, good material can be found in *Schools without Failure* (Glasser, 1969).

References and suggested readings

Books highly recommended as supplementary reading are marked with an asterisk.

Bassin, A., Bratter, T. E., & Rachin, R. L. (Eds.). *The reality therapy reader.* New York: Harper & Row, 1976.

Corey, G. *Theory and practice of group counseling.* Monterey, Calif.: Brooks/Cole, 1981.

Corey, G. *Case approach to counseling and psychotherapy.* Monterey, Calif.: Brooks/Cole, 1982.

Glasser, W. *Mental health or mental illness?* New York: Harper & Row, 1961.

* Glasser, W. *Reality therapy: A new approach to psychiatry.* New York: Harper & Row, 1965.

Glasser, W. *Schools without failure.* New York: Harper & Row, 1969.

Glasser, W. *The identity society.* New York: Harper & Row, 1972.

* Glasser, W. *Positive addiction.* New York: Harper & Row, 1976. (a)

* Glasser, W. Reality therapy. In V. Binder, A. Binder, & B. Rimland (Eds.), *Modern therapies.* Englewood Cliffs, N. J.: Prentice-Hall, 1976. (b)

Glasser, W., & Zunin, L. M. Reality therapy. In R. Corsini (Ed.), *Current psychotherapies* (2nd ed.). Itasca, Ill.: F. E. Peacock, 1979.

Zunin, L., & Zunin, N. *Contact: The first four minutes.* New York: Ballantine Books, 1973.

11

Case Illustration:
Comparison of Approaches

Introduction

The case of Stan
STAN'S LIFE SKETCH

The various approaches
PSYCHOANALYTIC THERAPY
EXISTENTIAL THERAPY
PERSON-CENTERED THERAPY
GESTALT THERAPY
TRANSACTIONAL ANALYSIS
BEHAVIOR THERAPY
RATIONAL-EMOTIVE THERAPY
REALITY THERAPY

My eclectic approach
FROM THE PSYCHOANALYTIC PERSPECTIVE
FROM THE EXISTENTIAL PERSPECTIVE
FROM THE PERSON-CENTERED PERSPECTIVE
FROM THE GESTALT PERSPECTIVE
FROM THE TRANSACTIONAL-ANALYSIS PERSPECTIVE
FROM THE BEHAVIOR-THERAPY PERSPECTIVE
FROM THE RATIONAL-EMOTIVE PERSPECTIVE
FROM THE REALITY-THERAPY PERSPECTIVE

Working with Stan: Integration of therapies
A PLACE TO BEGIN
CLARIFYING THE NATURE OF OUR RELATIONSHIP
CLARIFYING GOALS OF THERAPY
IDENTIFICATION OF FEELINGS
EXPRESSING AND EXPLORING FEELINGS
THE THINKING DIMENSION IN THERAPY
THE ROLE OF THE PAST
DOING: ANOTHER ESSENTIAL COMPONENT IN THERAPY

Introduction

The purpose of this chapter is to illustrate how the various therapies might approach the understanding of the same client. One client, Stan, will be viewed in the light of how each therapeutic approach might answer questions such as What particular dimensions of Stan's life and behavior should be given focus? What are the psychodynamics or concepts that explain the existence of his problems? What are the general goals? What possible techniques and methods would implement these goals? What might be some characteristics of the relationship between Stan and the therapist? How might the therapist proceed, and what would be the therapist's function?

Presenting a single case is of particular value in pointing out the contrasts among the approaches and the parallels among therapies that emphasize similar or compatible concepts and practices. The case illustration of Stan exposes you to the approaches of eight different models in an attempt to provide some basis for integration among them and to help you gain more understanding of their practical applications. (For the sake of brevity, I am not including the heirs of psychoanalysis in this section.) I hope that you will be able to sharpen your focus on certain attributes of each approach that can be incorporated into a personalized style of counseling.

To make this chapter more personally meaningful, I suggest that you put yourself in the situation of seeking psychological counseling. Provide your own background information, and develop your own goals for what you hope to accomplish. Then, *as a client,* work through each of these therapies.

The case of Stan

The setting is a college counseling center, where both individual and group counseling by a qualified staff are available. Stan comes in for an intake counseling interview and gives the counselor these facts: "I'm a 25-year-old junior in college, a psychology major, and I've recently decided to eventually work toward a master's degree in counseling psychology. I took a course, 'Psychology of Personal Adjustment,' last semester that was group-oriented with a self-understanding and personal-growth slant. We were asked to write an autobiographical paper, and as a result of that I became aware that there are certain areas in my life that I want to change, or at least understand better. In this class we were told about the services offered in the counseling center, and I decided that, if I hope to work with people as a counselor someday, I'd better take a closer look at myself. I'd like to have weekly, individual counseling sessions and would like to join a counseling group, because I need experience in relating to others and could gain from their feedback. My hope is that I can continue counseling for at least a semester, and maybe for a year."

That is the essence of Stan's introduction. Before leaving this initial session, he gives the counselor his autobiography so that the counselor will have a better understanding of where he has been, where he is now, where he would like to go, and what he wants for himself.

STAN'S LIFE SKETCH

Stan's autobiography reads as follows:

Where am I *currently* in my life? At 25 years of age, I feel I've wasted most of my life. By now I should be finished with college and into a good job, but instead I'm only a junior. I realize that I can't do that much with a B.S. in psychology, so I hope to get a master's degree in counseling and eventually work as a counselor with kids who are in trouble. I feel I was helped by someone who cared about me, and I'd like to have a similar influence on young people. At this time I live alone, have very few friends, and feel very scared and inferior with people my own age or older. I feel good when I'm with kids, because they are so honest. I worry a lot whether I'm smart enough to get through all the studies I'll need to do before I can become a counselor. One of my problems is that I drink heavily and frequently get drunk. This happens mostly when I feel all alone and scared that I'll always feel as lonely and isolated as I do now. In the past I used drugs heavily, and once in a while I still get loaded. I'm scared of people in general but of strong and attractive women in particular. I feel all cold, sweaty, and terribly uptight when I'm with a woman. Maybe I think they are judging me and I know they'll find out that I'm not much of a man. I'm afraid I just can't measure up to what they expect of a man—you *always* have to be so strong, and tough, and perfect. And I'm not all this, so I often wonder if I'm adequate as a man.

I feel a terrible anxiety much of the time, particularly at night. Sometimes I feel so terrified that I feel like running, but I just can't move. It's awful because I often feel like I'm dying at times like this. And then I fantasize about committing suicide and wonder who would care. Sometimes I see my family coming to my funeral feeling very sorry that they didn't treat me better. Much of the time I feel guilty—like I haven't worked up to my potential, that I've been a failure, that I've wasted much of my time, and that I let people down a lot. I can really get down on myself and wallow in my guilt, and I feel very *depressed*. At times like this I tell myself how rotten I am, how I'll never be able to change, and how I'd be better off dead. Then I would not have to hurt anymore, and I wouldn't have to want either. It is very difficult for me to get close to anyone—and I can't say that I have ever loved a person and I surely know that I have never felt fully loved or wanted.

Everything isn't so bleak, because I did have enough guts to leave a lot of my shady past behind me and did struggle to get into college. And I like my determination—I *want* to change, and I have sought out counseling because I know I need someone to help me keep honest. I'm seeking a woman therapist because I feel more afraid of women than men. I like about myself that I feel scared a lot but that I also can feel my feelings and that I am willing to take risks even though I'm scared. That's why I chose to work with a woman.

What was my past like? Where have I been and what are some significant events and turning points in my life? A major turning point was the confidence my supervisor had in me at the summer youth camp where I worked during the past few summers. He encouraged me to go to college and said he saw a lot of potential in me for becoming a fine counselor with young people. That was hard for me to *really* believe, but his faith inspired me to begin to believe in myself. My marriage and divorce was another turning point. This "relationship" didn't last long before my wife left me. That was a severe blow to my manhood. She was a strong and dominant woman who took delight in telling me how worthless I was and how she couldn't stand to get near me. We had sex only a few times, and most of the time I was impotent. That was another blow to my ego. I'm so afraid to get close to a woman for fear that she will swallow me up. My parents never got a divorce, but I wish they had. They fought most of the time. I should say, she did most of the fighting. She was dominant and continually bitching at my father, whom I always saw as weak, passive, and mousy next to her. He'd *never* stand up to her. My folks always compared me unfavorably to my older sister and older brother—they were "perfect" children, successful, and honor students. My younger brother and I fought a lot, and he was the one who was spoiled rotten by them. I really don't know what happened to me and how I turned out to be the failure of all the four children.

In high school I took to the drug scene and got involved with the wrong crowd and got thrown into a youth rehabilitation facility for stealing. Later I was expelled from regular school for fighting, and I landed in a continuation high school, where I'd go to school in the mornings and have afternoons for on-the-job training. I got into auto mechanics and was fairly successful and even managed to keep myself employed for three years as a mechanic.

Back to my parents. I remember my father telling me: "You are really dumb. Why can't you be like your sister and brother? You'll never amount to a hill of beans! Why can't you ever do anything right?" And my mother treated me much like she treated my father. She would say: "Why do you do so many things to hurt me? Why can't you grow up and be a man? You were a mistake—I wish I didn't have you! Things are so much better around here when you're gone." I recall crying myself to sleep many nights—feeling so terribly alone and filled with anger and hate. And feeling so disgusted with myself. There was no talk of religion in my house, nor was there any talk about sex. In fact, I always find it hard to imagine my folks ever having sex.

Where would I like to be five years from now? What kind of person do I want to become, and what kinds of changes do I most want in my life? Most of all, I'd just like to start feeling better about myself. I really have an inferiority complex, and I really know how to put myself down. I want to like myself much more than I do now. I hope I can learn to love at least a few other people and, most of all, women. I want to lose my fear that women can destroy me. I'd like to feel equal with others and not always have to feel apologetic for my existence. I don't want to suffer from this anxiety and guilt. And I hope that I can begin to think of myself as an OK person. I really want to become a good counselor with kids, and to do this I know I'm going to have to change. I'm not certain how I'll change, or even what are all the changes I hope for. I do know that I want to get free of my self-destructive tendencies and learn to trust people more. Maybe when I begin to like myself more, then I'll be able to trust that others might find something about me that is worth liking.

The various approaches

PSYCHOANALYTIC THERAPY

The psychoanalytic approach would focus on the unconscious psychodynamics of Stan's behavior. Considerable attention might be given to material that he repressed such as his anxiety related to the threatened breakthrough of his sexual and aggressive impulses. In his past he had to rigidly control both these impulses, and when he did not he got into trouble. He also developed a strong superego by introjecting parental values and standards and making them his own. These aspirations were unrealistic, for they were perfectionistic goals. He could be loved only if he became perfect; yet no matter what he attempted, it never seemed adequate. He internalized his guilt, which became depression. At the extreme, Stan demonstrated a self-destructive tendency, which is a way of inflicting punishment on himself. His depression could be explained as the hostility he felt toward his parents and siblings, but instead of directing these feelings toward them he turned them inward toward himself. Stan's preoccupation with drinking could be hypothesized as evidence of an "oral fixation." Because during his early childhood he never received love and acceptance, he is still suffering from this deprivation and still desperately searching for approval and acceptance from others. Stan's sex-role identification was fraught with difficulties. He learned the basis of female/ male relationships through his early experiences with his parents. What he saw was fighting, bickering, and discounting. His father was the weak one who always lost, and his mother was the strong, domineering force who could and did hurt men. Stan identified with his weak and impotent father; he generalized his fear of his mother to all women. It could be further hypothesized that he married a woman who was similar to his mother and who stimulated his feelings of impotence in her presence.

Because Stan selected a woman therapist, the opportunity to develop a transference relationship and work through it would be the core of the therapy process. An assumption is that Stan would eventually relate to his therapist as he did to his mother, and that the process would be a valuable means of gaining insight into the origin of his difficulties with women. The analytic process would stress an intensive exploration of his past. The goal would be to make the unconscious conscious, so that he would no longer be determined by unconscious forces. Stan would devote much therapy time to reliving and exploring his early past. As he talked, he would gain increased understanding of the dynamics of his behavior. He would begin to see connections between his present problems and early past experiences in childhood. Thus, he would explore memories of relationships with his siblings and with his mother and father and also explore how he generalizes his view of women and men from his view of these family members. It could be expected that he would reexperience old feelings and would uncover buried feelings related to traumatic events. Some questions for Stan could include: What did you do when you felt unloved? What did you have to do as a child with your negative feelings? Could you express your rage, hostility, hurt, and fears? What effects did your relationship with your mother have on you? What did this teach you about all women?

The analytic process would focus on key influences in Stan's developmental years. As he came to understand how he had been shaped by these past experiences, he would become increasingly able to exert control over his present functioning. Many of his fears would become conscious, and then his energy would not have to remain fixed on defending himself from unconscious feelings. Instead, he could make new decisions about his current life. He could do this only if he worked through the transference relationship, however, for the depth of his therapy endeavors would largely determine the depth and extent of his personality changes.

EXISTENTIAL THERAPY

The counselor or therapist with an existential orientation would approach Stan with the view that he has the capacity to expand his consciousness and decide for himself the future direction of his life. The therapist would want Stan to realize more than anything else that he does not have to be the victim of his past conditioning but can be the architect in redesigning his future. He can free himself of his deterministic shackles and accept the responsibility that comes with the freedom of directing his own life. This approach would not stress techniques but would emphasize the importance of the therapist's understanding of Stan's world primarily by establishing an authentic relationship as a means to a fuller degree of self-understanding.

What are some possible dimensions that might be explored with Stan? He could be confronted with the ways he is attempting to escape from his freedom—through alcohol and drugs. His anxiety would not be seen as something that needs to be "cured"; rather, Stan would need to learn that realistic anxiety is a vital part of living with uncertainty and freedom. Because there are no guarantees and because the individual is ultimately alone, Stan could expect to experience some degree of healthy anxiety, aloneness, guilt, and even despair. These conditions are not neurotic in themselves, but the way Stan orients himself to these conditions and how he copes with his anxiety would be seen as critical.

Stan talks about feeling so low at times that he imagines suicide. The existential therapist might view this as symbolic. Could it be that Stan is feeling that he is dying as a person? Is he using his human potential? Is he choosing a dead way of merely existing instead of affirming life? The existentially oriented therapist would confront Stan with the issue of the meaning and purpose in his life. Is there any reason for Stan to want to continue living? What are some of Stan's projects that enrich his life? What can he do to find a sense of purpose that will make him feel more significant and more alive?

Guilt is a dominating force in Stan's life. However, much of his guilt is neurotic guilt, for it is based on his view of letting others down and not meeting their expectations. He must learn that guilt can serve a valuable function if it is based on his awareness of not utilizing his own potentials. Stan also needs to accept the reality that he may at times feel alone, for choosing for oneself and living from one's own center accentuates the experience of aloneness. He is not, however, condemned to a life of isolation, alienation from others, and loneliness. The existential therapist would see Stan's hope in his learning to discover his own centeredness and in living by the values he chooses and creates for himself. By doing so, Stan could become a more substantial person and could learn to appreciate himself more. When he does, the chances are lessened that he will have a clinging need to secure approval from others, particularly his parents and parental substitutes. Instead of forming a dependent relationship, he could relate to others out of his strength. Only then would there be the possibility of overcoming his feelings of separateness and isolation.

PERSON-CENTERED THERAPY

Stan's autobiography indicates that he has a fairly clear idea of what he wants for his life. He has stated goals that are meaningful for him. He is motivated to change and seems to have sufficient anxiety to work toward these desired changes. The person-centered counselor would thus have faith in Stan's ability to find his own way and would trust that he has within himself the necessary resources for personal growth. Thus, this orientation would not emphasize diagnosis or probe for information from his past. Instead, he would be encouraged to speak freely about his feelings of being a failure, being inadequate, or being unmanly; about his hopelessness at times; and about his fears and uncertainties. The therapist would allow Stan the freedom and security to explore threatening aspects of himself and would refrain from judging and criticizing him for his feelings. To do this the counselor would have to do much more than merely reflect the content of Stan's verbalizations. The person-centered practitioner would attempt to fully experience in the present moment what it must be like to live in Stan's world. As more than a mechanical technique, the therapist's authentic relationship with Stan would be based on a concern, a deep understanding and appreciation of his feelings, a nonpossessive warmth and acceptance, and a willingness to allow him to explore any and all of his feelings during the therapeutic hour. The therapist would convey to Stan the basic attitudes of understanding and accepting, and through her positive regard he might well be able to drop his pretenses and more fully and freely explore his personal concerns.

Basically, Stan would grow personally in the relationship with his therapist, who would be willing to be genuine. He could use the relationship to learn to be more accepting of himself, with both his strengths and limitations. He would have the opportunity to openly express his fears of women, of not being able to effectively work with people, and of feeling inadequate and stupid. He could explore how he feels judged by his parents and by authorities. He would have an opportunity to express his guilt—that is, the ways he feels he has not lived up to his parents' expectations and how he has let them and himself down. He could also relate his feelings of hurt over not having ever felt loved and wanted. He could express the loneliness and isolation that he so often feels, as well as the need to blunt these painful feelings with alcohol or drugs.

In relating his feelings Stan would no longer be totally alone, for he would take the risk of letting his therapist into his private world. In doing so, how would he be helped? Through the relationship with the therapist he would gradually get a sharper focus of his experiencing and would be able to clarify his own feelings and attitudes. He would be seen as having the capacity to muster his own strengths and make his own decisions. In short, the therapeutic relationship would tend to free Stan from his self-defeating ways. Because of the caring and faith he would experience from his therapist, he would be able to increase his own faith and confidence in his ability to resolve his difficulties and discover a new way of being.

GESTALT THERAPY

The Gestalt-oriented therapist would surely want to focus on the unfinished business that Stan has with his parents, siblings, and ex-wife. It would appear that this unfinished business is mainly feelings of resentment that he has toward them; yet he turns this resentment inward toward himself. His present life situation would be spotlighted, but he might also need to reexperience past feelings that could be interfering in his present attempts to develop intimacy with others. In Gestalt therapy Stan would not merely talk about past experiences; rather, he would be asked to imagine himself in earlier scenes with his wife, as though the painful situation were occurring in the here and now. He would relive and reexperience the situation, perhaps by talking directly to his wife. He could tell her of his resentments and hurts and eventually complete his unfinished business with her. It would be important also that he speak with his older brother and sister, toward whom he feels resentment because they were always seen as the "perfect" children in the family. He would need symbolically to talk with his mother and father, as though he were the child again. It is not necessarily a part of the Gestalt approach that in real life he actually speak with these significant people, but it is essential that he deal with them in his therapy sessions. He would be encouraged to say to them (in the sessions) what he had never told them before. The therapist might ask: "What are your resentments toward each of these people?" "What did you want from them that you never received?" "How would you have liked to have been treated by them?" "What do you need to tell them now so that you can keep from being destroyed by your resentments?"

Through awareness of what he is now doing and how he keeps himself locked into his past, Stan can increasingly assume personal responsibility for his own life. In working toward this end, he might engage in a "game of dialogue" in which his "top-dog" side talks with his underdog side. For Stan, these dimensions within himself are struggling for control. He would play both parts for himself, and the empty-chair technique could be used. Through this procedure, it is hoped, he could realize the self-torture game he continues to play with himself. Stan also maintains that he has difficulty in feeling like a man, especially in relationships with strong women. He might become the little boy in exaggerated fashion and talk to a powerful woman (in the empty chair), and then he could become the threatening woman and talk back to his little-boy side. The main point is that he would face his fears and engage in a dialogue with the polarities that exist within him. The aim is not to extract his feelings but to learn to live with his polarities. Why must he be either a "little boy" or a "powerful superman"? Cannot he learn to be a man who at times feels threatened and weak?

Most of the techniques and Gestalt exercises would serve one main function for Stan: to assist him in gaining a fuller sense of what he is doing in the present to keep significant figures alive and powerful within himself. As he gained more complete awareness of how dependent he allows himself to be on them, he would have the opportunity to find a center within himself and live for his own purposes rather than remaining controlled by them.

TRANSACTIONAL ANALYSIS

Because Transactional Analysis (TA) is a contractual form of therapy, Stan would begin by developing with the therapist a contract that specifies areas of his life he desires to change. A general area that Stan indicates that he would like to modify is learning how to feel "OK," for now he feels "not OK" much of the time. How might his therapy proceed with a TA orientation? Whereas the focus would be on present behavior and transactions with others as well as on his attitudes toward himself, exploration of the past, to the extent that early decisions could be identified, would also be important. Essentially, he would need to learn that his decision about the way he had to be in order to survive when he was a child may no longer be appropriate, and that he can modify his early decision. For Stan, the decision was "I am stupid, and it is best that I am not here, and I am a loser."

In addition to making this early decision, Stan accepted a list of injunctions and messages that he still lives by, including "don't be"; "be a man, which means be strong always"; "be perfect"; "don't trust women"; "you'll never become anything"; and "you can't do anything right." Perhaps the basic injunction, and the most dangerous one, is the message "don't be." In many ways Stan was programmed with the message "You were an accident, and the best way for you to be is to become invisible." He received many negative strokes, and he was discounted as a person of worth. Now he finds it difficult to maintain intimate relationships and to accept positive strokes. He has invested considerable energy in collecting "bad feelings"—including his feelings of anxiety, guilt, self-deprecation, and his suicidal thoughts—which would be explored as a part of the therapeutic process.

The TA therapist would probably confront Stan with the games that he is playing, such as "Poor Me," "Victim," "Martyr," and "Helpless One." Stan's "racket," the collection of feelings that he uses to justify his life script and his early decision, is at once both a "guilt racket" and a "depression racket." Stan appears to be saving up his feelings of guilt and depression, and the games he plays with others often have depression and guilt as a pay-off. In his case, when he finally gathers up enough self-condemnation and depression, he could feel justified in taking his life, which is the concluding action that his life script calls for. His accepting the message "don't be" is a particular problem that would be essential to explore in therapy.

Throughout the course of his therapy, Stan would be taught how to analyze his life scripts. He would be shown that he bases his lifetime plan on a series of decisions and adaptations. Through script analysis he would identify the life pattern he appears to be following, and, as he became more aware of his life script, he would be able actively to do something about changing his programming. It is through increased awareness that he could break free of his early scripting.

Stan's autobiography indicates that he has introjected a "Critical Parent" who punishes him and drives him to feel that whatever he does is not quite enough. If he hopes to learn how to love others more fully, it will be important for him to learn how to be kinder to and less demanding of himself. He must be able to nourish himself, accept his successes, and open himself to others.

BEHAVIOR THERAPY

The initial task of a therapist with a behavioral orientation would be to help Stan translate some of his general goals into concrete and measurable ones. Thus, if Stan said "I want to feel better about myself," the therapist might ask: "What do you mean?" "When do you feel good?" "What can you do to narrow down your broad goal?" If Stan said "I want to get rid of my inferiority complex," the therapist might counter with "What behaviors lead to your feelings of inferiority?" In Stan's case some concrete aims include his desire to function without drugs or alcohol. Aversion conditioning would probably not be used, but he might be asked to keep a record of when he drinks and what events lead up to his drinking.

Stan indicated that he does not want to feel apologetic for his existence. He might then be asked to engage in some assertive-training exercises with his therapist. If Stan has trouble in talking with his professors, the therapist could demonstrate to Stan ways in which he could approach his professors more directly and confidently. This procedure would include modeling, role playing, and behavior rehearsal. Stan could then try new behaviors with his therapist, who would play the role of his professors and then give feedback on how strong or apologetic Stan seemed.

Stan's anxiety in relation to women could also be explored by behavior-rehearsal methods. The therapist could play the role of a woman whom Stan wants to date. Stan could practice being the way he would like to be with his date and could say the things to his therapist that he might be afraid to say to his date. He could thus explore his fears, get feedback on the effects of his behavior, and experiment with more assertive behavior.

Systematic desensitization may be appropriate to working with Stan's fear of failing. First, he would learn relaxation procedures. Then he would list his specific fears relating to failure. At the top of his list might be sexual impotence with a woman. At the bottom of the list might be talking to a female student whom he does not feel threatened by. He would then imagine a pleasant scene and begin a desensitization process beginning with his lesser fears and working up to the anxiety associated with his greatest fear.

Therapy would focus on modifying the behavior that results in Stan's feelings of guilt and anxiety. This approach would not place importance on his past except to the extent necessary to modify his faulty learning. The therapist would not explore Stan's childhood experiences but would work directly with the present behaviors that are causing his difficulties. Insight would not be seen as important, nor would having him experience or reexperience his feelings. The assumption would be that, if he can learn more-appropriate coping behaviors, eliminate unrealistic anxiety and guilt, and acquire more-adaptive responses, then his presenting symptoms will decrease and he will report a greater degree of satisfaction.

RATIONAL-EMOTIVE THERAPY

The rational therapist would have as broad objectives minimizing Stan's self-defeating attitudes and helping him to acquire a more realistic outlook on life. To begin with, he would be taught that he is keeping alive some of his irrational ideas by reindoctrinating himself in an unthinking manner, and that he can learn to challenge the source of his difficulties. If he learned how to think more rationally, then he might begin to feel better. What are some of the steps that a rationally oriented therapist might employ to assist Stan in ridding himself of irrational beliefs and in internalizing a rational philosophy of life?

First, the therapist would challenge Stan to examine the many *shoulds, oughts,* and *musts* that he had blindly accepted. She would confront Stan on the issue of his continued repetition of specific, illogical sentences and irrational beliefs, which in his case are "I always have to be strong, tough, and perfect." "I'm not a man if I show any signs of weakness." "If everyone didn't love me and approve of me, then things would be cata-strophic." "If a woman rejected me, then I really would be diminished to a 'nothing.'" "If I fail, then I am a rotten person." "I feel apologetic for my existence because I don't feel equal to others."

Second, the therapist would ask Stan to evaluate the ways he now keeps reindoctri-nating himself with those self-defeating sentences. She would not only attack specific problems but would also attack the core of Stan's irrational thinking by confronting him with ideas such as the following: "You are not your father, and you do not need to continue telling yourself that you are just like him." "What your parents told you about yourself you have bought fully, but you no longer need to accept without question their value judgments about your worth." "You say that you are such a failure and that you feel inferior. Do your present activities support this? Why do you continue to be so hard on yourself?" "Does having been the scapegoat in your family mean that you need to continue making yourself the scapegoat?"

Third, once Stan has understood the nature of his irrational beliefs and become aware of how he maintains faulty notions about himself, the therapist would urge him to work diligently at attacking them by engaging in counterpropaganda. She would give Stan specific "homework assignments" to help him deal with his fears. For instance, at some point the therapist would probably ask Stan to explore his fears of attractive and powerful women and his reasons for continuing to tell himself "They can castrate me." "They expect me to be strong and perfect." "If I am not careful, they will dominate me." His homework could include approaching a woman for a date. If he succeeded in getting the date, he could challenge his catastrophic expectations of what might happen. What would be so terrible if she did not like him or if she refused the date? Why does he have to get all his confirmation from one woman?

In addition to using homework assignments, the therapist might use many other behavioral techniques such as role playing, humor, sarcasm, modeling, behavior rehearsal, and desensitization. Basically, she would work in an active/directive manner and would focus on cognitive and behavioral aspects. The therapist would give little attention to Stan's past but would highlight his present, illogical thinking by bringing it to his attention, by demonstrating the illogical links, and by teaching him to rethink and reverbalize in a more logical and constructive way. Thus, Stan could learn how to be different by telling himself a new set of statements that might include "I can be lovable." "I am able to succeed as well as fail at times." "I need not make all women into my mother." "I don't have to punish myself by making myself feel guilty over past failures, because it is not essential to always be perfect."

REALITY THERAPY

Reality therapy would not dwell on Stan's past experiences with failure but would focus on what he can do in the present to achieve a "success identity." Stan has already indicated what he considers success for himself, and he has indicated some specific changes that he desires. Therapy would emphasize Stan's desired behavioral changes, not his feelings and attitudes about himself. The assumption would be that, if Stan can begin to increase his self-esteem and come to recognize his strengths, his negative feelings about himself will change.

How might the therapist with a reality-therapy orientation proceed with Stan? Possible strategies and ways of approaching him would include, first, a specific contract that would set a time limit for the duration of the sessions and for the goals of therapy. The goals would have to be specific and concrete, and the therapist would help Stan determine how realistic his goals are by asking, for example: "Are your needs now being met?" "Are you satisfied with your current behavior?" Because Stan would respond negatively to both those questions, the therapist would challenge him to make a value judgment concerning his present life by asking: "How do you want to change?" "What can you do now to change?" "Are you willing to make a commitment to changing certain self-destructive behaviors? For instance, your drinking interferes with your studies and with forming close relationships, and it contributes to low self-esteem." The therapist could ask Stan to judge whether his drinking patterns are worth the price he pays for these immediate pleasures. If he agreed that drinking is not conducive to getting what he wants in terms of long-range satisfaction, he could make specific plans to eliminate his drinking. There would be no excavation into his past to explore the reasons for his drinking, nor would he be allowed to offer excuses or blame others. Regardless of how or why he began doing things that contributed to his "failure identity," the point is that Stan would be able to do something to change his behavior so that he can enjoy successes.

Specific suggestions that the therapist could make to Stan to help him change his behavior might include the following: "Next time you are lonely and want to get drunk, make a decision to call a friend and talk with him or her about your loneliness. Decide to do something with your feelings besides blunting them with alcohol." "You mention that you are uncomfortable when meeting people. Even though you may experience uneasiness, put yourself into situations where you can make new acquaintances. Write down your feelings, and observe and make a note of what you do when you are in these situations, and bring a report to your next therapy session." "Instead of exploring why you feel inferior, focus on what you do when you feel this way and on situations that accentuate your feelings of inferiority."

Reality therapy might give considerable emphasis to Stan's strong points. A few years ago he saw himself as a "loser," and today he has made significant progress toward utilizing his talents. He is doing well in college, he is involved in volunteer work, and he relates well with young people. Therapy could help him formulate plans to continue in the direction of his successes. In short, Stan would receive credit for the gains he has made and encouragement to face the fact that he is responsible for the kind of life he is currently leading. He would see that he can do more than he once believed to be possible.

My eclectic approach

To illustrate how each of the therapies might work with a single client, I have dealt with them as separate entities. However, a basic theme of this book has been learning how to select concepts and techniques from all of the approaches as a basis for building one's own unique and eclectic counseling style. To show how I might approach working with Stan, I will first describe the aspects that I would be most inclined to extract from each of the eight models.

FROM THE PSYCHOANALYTIC PERSPECTIVE

I value what I learn from the psychoanalytic model about the unconscious and early-childhood experiences and about their influence on Stan's present personality. Drawing on this approach, I would encourage Stan to recall and talk about his early memories of his parents. I would use his reactions to me as one basis of making interpretations about his early childhood, thinking that he is relating to me in some ways as he did to other significant people in his life. I would also work with Stan's difficulties in relating to women by making some connections with his mother. Although I do not see that Stan is determined by his past, I do assume that for him to eventually be free he needs to understand his past as it is evident in his present.

FROM THE EXISTENTIAL PERSPECTIVE

One of my basic assumptions is that people are more than mere victims of their past, and that they can assume responsibility for changing those aspects that they most want to change. Therefore, I might work with Stan by focusing on his fear of suicide. I take this fear to mean that he is tired of living a half-dead existence, that he wants to live in new ways, and that he no longer will settle for some of the deadening ways in which he has lived. I would probably ask him to look at what it would be like if he were to die now. One of the things I value from the existential model is the view that death is a stimulus to living; death jars us into taking a look at how we are living to determine if we are merely existing or are really alive. In keeping with this notion, I might ask Stan to relate all the ways in which he feels that he has been a victim, and how he has kept himself a prisoner of his past. This would be a starting point for working with the choices that are open to him.

I do make the assumption that his anxiety is a motivating force, and that his anxiety attacks are really significant existential messages indicating that it is time for him to take an inventory and realize his options. On this basis, I would also explore with him how he has been numbing himself with alcohol as an attempt to avoid dealing with the anxiety he feels over the freedom that comes with choosing for himself.

FROM THE PERSON-CENTERED PERSPECTIVE

The one central concept I value most from the person-centered perspective is the importance of the therapist's using himself and his relationship with his client as the major force for change. Thus, I would share with Stan my perceptions of him and the reactions I was having by being with him in these sessions. And I would let him know how I was affected by being in this relationship with him. In many ways I would let Stan point the direction he wants to travel; he relates a lot of rich material, and I believe that he does have the capacity to understand himself and move in a constructive direction.

From this model I would also draw on the factor of trust as a major attribute of a productive relationship. One way I would attempt to build this trust is to be honest with Stan in these sessions. I would also encourage him to talk openly about feelings that he has felt the need to tuck away and keep secret. Furthermore, I assume that the best way to create trust in the therapeutic relationship is by modeling the very behaviors and attitudes that I hope Stan will acquire. Thus, if I am genuine in the session and do not hide behind pretenses and roles, then I assume that Stan will drop his masks and be genuine with me. If I can *really* listen to him in a nonjudgmental way, then I have the basis to come to know him and thus to care for him. If I am able to hear, appreciate, respect, and care for Stan, the chances are increased that he will be able to do these things for himself.

FROM THE GESTALT PERSPECTIVE

I especially like the action-oriented techniques that I can use from Gestalt therapy. With them, I can challenge Stan to relive unfinished situations from his past that are cluttering up his ability to live fully in the present. For example, one area that is unfinished (and begs for closure) is his feelings toward women. Stan allows himself to feel weak, ineffectual, intimidated, and impotent when he even *thinks* about being in the presence of a strong woman. Because he has mentioned his feelings of resentment (and guilt) toward his former wife and his mother, I would be inclined to have him bring both of them to a session now—in a symbolic way—and speak to them.

I might say: "Stan, in this chair sits your mother, and next to her sits your ex-wife. You've talked about them and all the terrible things you imagine they've done to you, and in doing so you've rendered yourself helpless. Here is a chance to take for yourself some of that power you continue to give them. Are you willing to talk to each of these women, telling them now some of the things that you've been carrying around inside of you, yet keeping from them?" If Stan agreed, I would ask him to pick which woman he wanted to address first and to speak to her as though she were present. At some point I might also ask him to sit in "mother's chair" and "speak to Stan"; then he could sit in "ex-wife's chair" and "reply" as he imagines she would. The possibilities are many for lively exchanges and for following any leads of a verbal or nonverbal nature that Stan might provide. I would attempt to stay with him and focus him on whatever he was feeling at the moment, using this material as the basis of where to proceed with him.

FROM THE TRANSACTIONAL-ANALYSIS PERSPECTIVE

Early in our sessions I would work with Stan in formulating a clear contract that would provide the direction for his therapy. From Transactional Analysis, one of the aspects that I find exceptionally meaningful is the exploration of injunctions and the early decisions that were made in relationship to these parental messages. Surely, Stan heard messages such as "don't be," "don't be you," "don't succeed," "don't feel," "don't be important," "don't get close," and "don't trust." On the basis of these injunctions, Stan may have made a number of *early decisions*:

- "I won't let myself get close to women, because if I do they will dominate me and take away any power I have."
- "I don't have what it takes to be as successful as my brothers and sisters, so I will settle for being a failure."
- "I really don't deserve to feel important, so if I begin feeling important, then I'll do something to make sure that I mess things up."

Rather than merely talking with Stan about his early decisions in an intellectual manner, I would be inclined to ask him to recreate a situation as a child in which he remembers telling himself that he had better keep his distance from women. Using some of the experiential techniques of Gestalt therapy, I would ask him to relive this scene and create a dialogue for everyone in it. I would hope that the direction I was pursuing with him would give Stan a chance to make a new, more appropriate decision, but on an emotional level as well as a cognitive level. I would also explore what he has gotten from buying into these injunctions and the price he is paying for still striving to live by parental expectations.

FROM THE BEHAVIOR-THERAPY PERSPECTIVE

I value the action-oriented methods of behavior therapy, for with this model insight alone is not considered enough to cause behavior change. If Stan hopes to change, he will have to take specific action in the real world, and this approach provides plenty of techniques for helping him gain this needed practice. For example, he mentioned that he wants to resolve his inferiority feelings in dealing with professors and be able to approach them and talk with them about how he is doing in the course.

I might ask Stan to approach me as though I were his professor and role-play his typical approach. I would ask him to talk out loud about whatever he is telling himself, so that we could both hear his self-talk. Initially, I would want to show him how his cognitions affect his behavior—how the things he is telling himself cement his feelings of worthlessness and stupidity, which have a direct effect on his behavior around professors. It would be important to help Stan approach his professors with new self-talk and a new set of expectations, such as "I am worth asking for my professor's time, and if I ask I'll be able to work out some problems I've been having."

After we role-played more positive approaches in the session itself, I would encourage Stan to keep a record (in a spiral notebook that he could carry around in his pocket) of his negative self-statements when he is near professors. Also, he would be encouraged to seek out one of his professors and talk with him or her, actually implementing some of the ideas that we discussed in this session. Next week at the session, we would follow up and see how well he was changing behavior in his everyday world.

FROM THE RATIONAL-EMOTIVE PERSPECTIVE

One of the first things that I would draw on from the rational-emotive model is the value of teaching Stan that it is he who is keeping himself disturbed through the process of self-indoctrination of irrational ideas. Early in the session Stan would be challenged to see that only he can uproot his faulty thinking by difficult work, both in the session and out. A place where we might begin is a core irrational idea that he carries around: "If everyone doesn't approve of me and tell me that I am worth something, then I am doomed to feel rotten, and in fact I *am not* worth much." This irrational belief seems especially strong as it relates to women, for he gives them the power to devastate him.

Because Stan continually rates himself silently, I would ask him to engage in a self-rating process out loud. I would have him mention all of the things he does and then follow up by asking him to assign himself a grade for each of these functions. I would focus on the self-destructive things he tells himself when he is with a woman. For example, he wants to approach an attractive woman, yet he stops himself, because he is convinced that if she turned him down he simply could not stand this rejection. My work with him would be directed to having him learn that her rejection is not the cause of his feeling terrible but rather *his evaluation* of the situation and what he tells himself about rejection. Thus, I would get him to challenge his own fatalistic thinking and see that he has been living with untested assumptions. For homework, I would ask Stan to practice by approaching women, if that is something he wanted to do, and to work actively at learning to critically evaluate those beliefs that are self-defeating.

FROM THE REALITY-THERAPY PERSPECTIVE

The perspective of reality therapy teaches me the value of paying attention to what clients are saying by observing how they are actually behaving. Thus, if I am interested in really hearing and understanding Stan, one good way is to notice his behavior in the session and ask him to report what he has been doing the previous week about taking steps to change. It does not mean that I would avoid an exploration of feelings; nor would I avoid talking with Stan about attitudes that seem to be getting in his way. The focus, however, would be: "Stan, what do you want from these therapy sessions? What are some current behaviors that you *most* want to change? How can you go about doing so?"

From this perspective I also value the place of *planning* for change. Thus, I would work with Stan on specific steps that he can see are open to him to make the changes he has indicated he wants to make. In a kind and caring manner, yet with firmness, I would expect Stan to make some *commitments*—to state some specific things he *will* do, *how* he will go about doing them, and *when* he will do them. For example, Stan mentioned that he wanted to get involved in doing volunteer work in a mental-health agency. During the session we would go over the specifics of *how* he might proceed (with possibilities of role playing with feedback). I would seek a commitment on his part to actually *do something* before the next session to get a volunteer placement. He might agree to interview in one agency, or he might at least agree to write a resumé and bring it to his next session. Each week we could assess his progress in terms of what he is actually doing or not doing to bring about changes. As needed, we could revise his action plan for change.

Working with Stan: Integration of therapies

I draw on each of the eight therapeutic approaches to differing degrees in my work with a client. This section will show how I might integrate what I have chosen from the various theories into a therapy suited for Stan. Underlying my counseling of Stan will be a desire to work with him on the levels of *feeling, thinking,* and *doing.* Keeping these three aims in mind, here is how my sessions with him might evolve.

A PLACE TO BEGIN

I would want to start by giving Stan a chance to say how he feels about coming to the initial session. Questions that I might explore with him are:

- What brings you here? What has been going on in your life recently that gave you the impetus to seek professional help?
- What expectations do you have of therapy? Of me? What are your hopes, fears, and any reservations? What goals do you have for yourself through therapy?
- Could you give me a picture of some significant turning points in your life? Who have been the important people in your life? What are some significant decisions you've made? What are some of the struggles and conflicts you've dealt with, and what are some of these issues that are current for you?

CLARIFYING THE NATURE OF OUR RELATIONSHIP

I do not want to give the impression that I would bombard Stan with all of the preceding questions at once. However, early in our sessions those would be some of the questions that I would have in the back of my mind. At the outset I would work with Stan to develop a working contract, which would involve a discussion of our mutual responsibilities and a clear statement of what Stan wants from these sessions and what he is willing to do to obtain it. I believe that it is important to openly discuss any factors that might perpetuate a client's dependency on the therapist, so I would invite Stan's questions about this therapeutic relationship. One goal would be to demystify the therapy process; another would be to get some focus for the direction of our sessions. That is why I value a contract, one that puts the responsibility on the client for deciding what he or she wants from the process.

This emphasis is consistent with several of the therapeutic approaches: reality therapy, behavior therapy, and Transactional Analysis. Also, the existential approach and the person-centered approach both stress a real client/therapist relationship as the basis for productive work. Thus, I value being open about myself and about the process of therapy. I think it is a mistake to hide behind "professionalism" as a way of keeping distance from the client. Therefore, I would begin by being as honest as I could be with Stan as the basis for creating an effective relationship.

CLARIFYING GOALS OF THERAPY

It is not enough to simply ask clients what they hope they will leave with at the conclusion of therapy. Typically, I find that clients are vague, global, and unfocused about what they want. Especially from behavior therapy and from reality therapy I borrow the necessity of getting clients to be specific in defining their goals. Thus, Stan may say: "I want to stop playing all these games with myself and others. I'd hope to stop putting myself down. I want to get rid of the terrible feelings I have. I want to feel OK with myself and begin living." My reply is: "So Stan, let's see if we can narrow down some of these broad goals into specific enough terms that both you and I will know what you are talking about. What exactly are these games that you talk about? In what ways do you put yourself down? What are some of these terrible feelings that bother you? In what specific ways do you feel that you are not living now? What would it take for you to begin to feel alive?"

Again, I would not barrage Stan with all these questions at once. They are merely illustrations of ways that I would work with him toward greater precision and clarity. If we merely talked about lofty goals of self-actualization, I fear, we would have direction-less sessions. Thus, I value focusing on concrete language and specific goals that both of us can observe and understand. Once this is ascertained, Stan can begin to observe his own behavior, both in the sessions and in his daily life. This self-monitoring itself is a vital step in any effort to bring about change.

IDENTIFICATION OF FEELINGS

The person-centered approach stresses that one of the first stages in the therapy process involves identifying, clarifying, and learning how to express feelings. Because of my relationship with Stan, I would expect him to feel increasingly free to mention feelings that he has kept to himself. In some cases these feelings are out of his awareness. Thus, I would encourage him to talk about any feelings he has that are a source of difficulty. Again, drawing on the person-centered model, I would expect these feelings to be vague and difficult to identify at first.

Therefore, during the early stages of our sessions I would rely on empathic listening. If I can really hear Stan's verbal and nonverbal messages, some of which may not be fully clear to him, then I can respond to him in a way that lets him know that I have some appreciation for what it is like in his world. I need to do more than merely reflect what I hear him saying; I need to share with him my reactions to what is being generated within me as I listen to him. As I come to communicate to him that he is being deeply understood and accepted for the feelings he has, Stan has less need to deny or distort his feelings. His capacity for clearly identifying what he is feeling at any moment grad-ually increases.

EXPRESSING AND EXPLORING FEELINGS

My belief is that it is my authenticity as a person that encourages Stan to begin to identify and share with me a range of feelings. But I do not believe that an open and trusting relationship between Stan and myself is sufficient to change personality and behavior. I am convinced that I must also use my knowledge, skills, and experiences.

As a way of helping Stan express and explore his feelings, I would tend to draw very heavily on Gestalt techniques. Eventually I would ask Stan to avoid merely talking about situations and about feelings. Rather, I would encourage him to bring whatever reactions he is having into the present. For instance, if he reported his feeling of tension, then I would ask him *how* he experiences this tension and *where* it is located in his body. One of the best ways that I have found to encourage clients to make contact with their feelings is to ask them to "be that feeling." Thus, if Stan has a knot in his stomach, he may intensify his feeling of tension by "becoming the knot, giving it voice and personality." If I notice Stan's moist eyes, I may direct him to "be his tears now." By putting words to his tears, he avoids merely abstractly intellectualizing about all the reasons *why* he is sad or tense. Before Stan can change his feelings, he must allow himself to *fully expe-rience* these feelings. And the experiential therapies give me valuable tools for guiding him to the expression of feelings.

THE THINKING DIMENSION IN THERAPY

I part company with those Gestaltists who argue that "thinking is a form of bullshitting." Once Stan has gotten in touch with some intense feelings and perhaps experienced catharsis (release of pent-up feelings), some kind of cognitive work is essential. Stan needs to be able to experience his feelings fully, and he may need to express them in symbolic ways. This may include getting his anger toward women out by hitting a pillow and by saying angry things that he has never allowed himself to say. Yet eventually Stan needs to begin to make sense of the emotional range of material that is surfacing.

To bring in this cognitive dimension, I would draw heavily on Transactional Analysis to focus his attention on early parental messages that he has incorporated and the early decisions that he made as a child. I would get him to think about the reason that he made certain decisions as a child—namely, to ensure basic psychological survival. Yet I would challenge him to think about the degree to which he still needs to cling to some archaic and nonfunctional decisions. I would challenge him to look at his decisions about life, about himself, and about others and to make necessary revisions that can lead him to getting on with his living.

From rational-emotive therapy, I especially value the emphasis on learning to think rationally. I would look for the ways that Stan contributes to his negative feelings by the process of self-indoctrination with irrational beliefs. I would get him to really test the validity of the dire consequences that he predicts. I value the stress put on doing hard work in demolishing beliefs that have no validity and replacing them with sound and rational beliefs. Surely, I do not think that Stan can merely think his way through life, or that merely examining his faulty logic is enough by itself for personality change. But I do see this process as an essential component of therapy.

Behavior therapy offers a range of cognitive techniques that could help Stan recognize connections between his cognitions and his behaviors. He should also learn about his inner speaking and the impact it has on his day-to-day behavior. Eventually, our goal would be some cognitive restructuring work by which Stan could learn new ways to think, new things to tell himself, and new assumptions about life. This would provide a basis for change in his behavior.

THE ROLE OF THE PAST

From the psychoanalytic model I value the emphasis placed on becoming aware of how the past influences present personality development. Thus, I would not rule out an exploration of Stan's past in therapy. In fact, I would focus on it, although I would use Gestalt methods of working with toxic introjects. I would help Stan develop insight into his own dynamics, especially by pointing to connections between earlier experiences and current struggles. I find interpretations helpful if they are timed well, yet I would present them as hunches that I have about what certain of Stan's behaviors seem to mean. Then I would ask him to consider the degree to which my interpretations seem to fit for him. This would also encourage him to think for himself, especially about the role his past continues to play in his life today.

DOING: ANOTHER ESSENTIAL COMPONENT IN THERAPY

Stan can spend countless hours in gathering interesting insights about why he is the way he is. He can learn to express feelings that he kept inside for so many years. And he can think about the things he tells himself that lead to defeat. Yet in my view feeling and thinking are not enough for a complete therapy process. *Doing* is a way of bringing these feelings and thoughts together by applying them to real-life situations in various action programs. I am indebted to behavior therapy, reality therapy, rational-emotive therapy, and Transactional Analysis, all of which give central emphasis to the role of action as a prerequisite for change.

With this in mind, I would ask Stan to think of as many ways as possible of actually bringing into his daily living the new learning that he is acquiring in our sessions. Practice is essential. Homework assignments (preferably ones that he could give himself) are an excellent way for him to become an active agent in his therapy. He must do something himself for change to occur. I would hope that Stan sees that the degree to which he will change is directly proportional to his willingness to get out in life and experiment. I would want him to learn from his new behavior in life. Thus, each week we would discuss his progress toward meeting his goals and review how well he was completing his assignments. If he failed in some of them, we could use this as an opportunity to learn how he might adjust his behavior. His plans might need revision. Yet at the same time I would insist on a commitment from him that he have an action plan for change, and that he continually look at how well his plan was working.

12

Basic Issues in Counseling and Psychotherapy

Introduction

This chapter deals with certain basic issues that cut across all the theoretical approaches. It reviews key concepts related to human nature and their implications for counseling and psychotherapy. By comparing views about the therapeutic process, I attempt to show that some integration of the goals and procedures of the various approaches is possible. The issues of the therapist's role and function, the experience of the client, and the client/therapist relationship are highlighted.

A further aim of this chapter is to summarize the key ideas of the various therapies and to unify some concepts. Six tables are presented to help you see more clearly the areas of convergence and divergence among the eight therapy approaches with respect to these basic issues.

Key concepts and philosophy

In a survey of the current approaches to counseling and psychotherapy, it becomes evident that there is no common philosophy unifying them. Each of them has a different view of human nature, different goals of therapy rooted in that view, and different techniques. Differences are especially noticeable among the philosophical assumptions underlying three very different models: the psychoanalytic approach, the behavioral approach, and the existential approach. It is my conviction that our view of human nature and the basic assumptions that undergird our view of the therapeutic process have significant implications for the way we develop our therapeutic practice. I am also persuaded that many practitioners, because they do not pay sufficient attention to their philosophical assumptions, operate as though they had no set of assumptions regarding their clients. In my opinion, a central task is to make our assumptions explicit and conscious, so that we can establish some consistency between our beliefs about human nature and the way we implement our procedures in counseling or therapy. Our philosophical assumptions are important because they specify how much reality we are able to perceive, and they direct our attention to the variables that we are "set" to see. Thus, a Freudian analyst and a person-centered therapist work in ways that vary considerably from each other, and they have very different views of human nature. Let us now review some of the contrasting viewpoints.

PSYCHOANALYTIC APPROACH

The Freudian psychoanalytic approach views human nature through deterministic spectacles. It assumes that human beings are determined largely by the unconscious, by drives and irrational forces, by psychic energy, by seeking a homeostatic balance, and by early-childhood experiences. In practice this approach stresses an impersonal and anonymous role for the therapist. It puts the therapist in the expert role of diagnosing, formulating a conceptualization of the client's history, determining a treatment plan, and using interpretation techniques to gradually uncover unconscious material. It stresses insight and understanding of the past, which is achieved by skillful interpretation. It is definitely a long-term approach to psychotherapy and is aimed at major personality change. A basic assumption of the psychodynamic theories is that the therapy process has to be long and involved if it is to be effective. Because the analytically oriented approaches focus on factors such as unconscious conflicts, resistance, transference, regression to early-childhood experience, personality restructuring, and gaining insight, they assume that therapy will be a long-term process. At the same time, they view the briefer therapies as superficial approaches that deal with symptom removal or immediate problem solving. These approaches are not seen as dealing with underlying dynamics or the basic conflicts of clients. This raises the issue of whether therapy has to be lengthy to be effective.

TABLE 12-1 The basic philosophies

Psychoanalytic therapy	Human beings are basically determined by psychic energy and by early experiences. Unconscious motives and conflicts are central in present behavior. Irrational forces are strong; the person is driven by sexual and aggressive impulses. Early development is of critical importance, for later personality problems have roots in repressed childhood conflicts.
Existential therapy	The central focus is on the nature of the human condition, which includes capacity for self-awareness, freedom of choice to decide one's fate, responsibility and freedom, anxiety as a basic element, the search for a unique meaning in a meaningless world, being alone and being in relation with others, finiteness and death, and a self-actualization tendency.
Person-centered therapy	The view of humans is positive; humans have an inclination toward becoming fully functioning. In the context of the therapeutic relationship the client experiences feelings that were previously denied to awareness. The client actualizes potential and moves toward increased awareness, spontaneity, trust in self, and inner directedness.
Gestalt therapy	The person strives for wholeness and integration of thinking, feeling, and behaving. The view is antideterministic, in that the person is seen to have the capacity to recognize how earlier influences are related to present difficulties.
Transactional analysis (TA)	The person has potential for choice. What was once decided can be redecided. Although the person may be a victim of early decisions and past scripting, self-defeating aspects can be changed with awareness.
Behavior therapy	Humans are shaped and determined by sociocultural conditioning. The view is basically deterministic, in that behavior is seen as the product of learning and conditioning.
Rational-emotive therapy (RET)	Humans are born with potentials for rational thinking but also with tendencies toward crooked thinking. They tend to fall victim to irrational beliefs and to reindoctrinate themselves with these beliefs. Therapy is cognitive/behavior/action oriented and stresses thinking, judging, analyzing, doing, and redeciding. This model is didactic and directive. Therapy is a process of reeducation.
Reality therapy	The person has a need for identity and can develop either a "success identity" or a "failure identity." The approach is based on growth motivation and is antideterministic.

BEHAVIORAL APPROACH

Unlike the psychoanalytic practitioner, the behavior therapist is not concerned about matters such as unconscious conflicts, transference, or the basic characteristics of human nature. The focus in behavior therapy is on identifying specific problems and behaviors to be changed, formulating specific goals to be worked on in the sessions, developing a treatment plan including specific behavioral techniques, and continually assessing the results to determine how well therapy is meeting the stated goals. This approach emphasizes objective assessment of the treatment procedures. Although it does not spell out philosophical concerns, it does assume that human beings are to a large extent conditioned by external forces, and that one's behavior is shaped by reinforcement or the lack of it. Although extreme, or radical, behaviorism views humans as passive puppets that are controlled by environmental strings, the new perspective of behavior therapy provides room for client self-determination and for the critical role that cognition plays in human experience. The trend in behavior therapy has been toward an increased

TABLE 12-2 Key concepts

Psychoanalytic therapy	Normal personality development is based on successful resolution and integration of psychosexual stages of development. Faulty personality development is the result of inadequate resolution of some specific stage. Id, ego, and superego constitute the basis of personality structure. Anxiety is a result of repression of basic conflicts. Ego defenses are developed to control anxiety. Unconscious processes are centrally related to current behavior.
Existential therapy	Essentially an approach to counseling and therapy rather than a firm theoretical model, it stresses core human conditions. Normally personality development is based on the uniqueness of each individual. Sense of self develops from infancy. Self-determination and tendency toward growth are central ideas. Psychopathology is the result of failure to actualize human potential. Distinctions are made between "existential guilt" and "neurotic guilt" and between "existential anxiety" and "neurotic anxiety." Focus is on the present and on what one is becoming; that is, the approach has a future orientation. It stresses self-awareness before action. It is an experiential therapy.
Person-centered therapy	The client has the potential for becoming aware of problems and the means to resolve them. Faith is placed in the client's capacity for self-direction. Mental health is a congruence of ideal self and real self. Maladjustment is the result of a discrepancy between what one wants to be and what one is. Focus is on the present moment and on the experiencing and expressing of feelings.
Gestalt therapy	Focus is on the what and how of experiencing in the here and now to help clients accept their polarities. Key concepts include personal responsibility, unfinished business, avoiding, experiencing, and awareness of the now. Gestalt is an experiential therapy that stresses feelings and the influence of unfinished business on contemporary personality development.
Transactional analysis (TA)	Focus is on games played to avoid intimacy in transactions. The personality is made up of Parent, Adult, and Child. Clients are taught how to recognize which ego state they are functioning in with given transactions. Games, rackets, early decisions, scripting, and injunctions are key concepts.
Behavior therapy	Focus is on overt behavior, precision in specifying goals of treatment, development of specific treatment plans, and objective evaluation of therapy outcomes. Therapy is based on the principles of learning theory. Normal behavior is learned through reinforcement and imitation. Abnormal behavior is the result of faulty learning. This approach stresses present behavior and has little concern for past history and origins of disorders.
Rational-emotive therapy (RET)	Neurosis is irrational thinking and behaving. Emotional disturbances are rooted in childhood but are perpetuated through reindoctrination in the now. A person's belief system is the cause of emotional problems. Thus, clients are challenged to examine the validity of certain beliefs. The scientific method is applied to everyday living.
Reality therapy	This approach rejects the medical model and its concept of mental illness. Focus is on what can be done now, and rejection of the past is a crucial variable. Value judgments and moral responsibility are stressed. Mental health is equated with acceptance of responsibility.

acceptance of subjective factors—beliefs, thoughts, inner speech, and other cognitive activities. Out of this new emphasis on cognition, behavior therapists have developed a wide range of cognitive procedures.

As does psychoanalysis, the behavioral approach assumes that the client is able to change by learning new modes of thinking. What has been learned can be unlearned, and new patterns of effective behavior can replace ineffective behaviors. If clients are deficient in social skills, these skills can be taught. It is further assumed that certain cognitive structures (beliefs, expectations, self-fulfilling prophecies) that lead to problems in living can be identified. Through the use of systematic behavioral and cognitive procedures, these, too, can be changed.

Behavior therapy utilizes specific treatment methods toward the attainment of specific goals. As such, it places the therapist in the role of the expert. Although the client is expected to be active and, usually, to select the specific goals of therapy, it is up to the therapist to direct the course of therapy. Thus, behavioral approaches are action orient- ed and are characterized by a variety of therapeutic strategies that are available to the practitioner. In many respects the therapist is seen as a skilled technician, and it is assumed that his or her level of skill is of paramount importance. Further, although behavior therapists admit that the client/therapist relationship affects the outcome of therapy, they tend to minimize its importance. They maintain that their technical skill in the use of many behavioral procedures is of greater significance.

Finally, because of the basic philosophy undergirding behavior therapy, this model is typically a short-term approach, as opposed to the depth-probing psychoanalytic ap- proach. Because psychotherapy is viewed largely as a teaching/learning process, clients are taught specific skills, many of which they can use on their own. In this respect behavior therapy does tend to work toward self-direction on the part of clients. They learn specific skills, exercises, and techniques that they practice outside of the sessions. This indicates that clients do have the capacity to eventually become their own therapists, and that they can draw on newly acquired skills to effectively meet new problems that they will encounter after they terminate therapy.

EXISTENTIAL APPROACH

A third major force is the existential approach. The existential view assigns willing, choosing, and deciding a central place in therapy. It views humans as possessing the awareness and freedom to make fundamental choices that shape their life. The practice of existential therapy is based on an encounter between the client and the therapist in which the client is a partner in his or her search for self. Based also on understanding the subjective aspects of experiencing, it tends to stress the affective dimension. It is geared to helping clients reclaim their responsibility for choosing the quality of their life. It tends to be a future-oriented therapy. Both Frankl and May stress that people can best be understood by observing what they are becoming, not by delving into the past. The existential approach also stresses insight and awareness, which clients gain through direct experience rather than through the therapist's interpretations. They are expected to talk, and they decide what will be explored during the therapy hour.

Unlike the psychoanalytic practitioner, the existentially oriented therapist is not con- cerned with diagnosis or assessment or with fostering a transference relationship. Be- cause there are few designated techniques, the practitioner is free to use any technique that may seem appropriate. Unlike the behavioral approach, the existential approach does not call for a treatment plan; there is little planning, for existential counseling is seen as a spontaneous experience and encounter between two humans. Thus, there is no expert, for both the client and the therapist are said to grow from the therapeutic encounter. The therapist is not viewed as a skilled technician or as a transference object. Rather, the therapist's basic attitudes and personal characteristics are viewed as critically related to progress in therapy. Existential therapists assume that who they are as persons and how they relate to their clients in the here and now are what really count. It is through the realness of this therapeutic relationship that clients come to realize the power within themselves to change the direction of their life.

The fact that a therapist's view of human nature is vitally related to his or her view of the nature of the therapeutic process has definite implications for the application of therapeutic techniques. I want to emphasize that each of the counseling approaches provides a different dimension of understanding the person, and each can provide the framework for increasing understanding of behavior and for examining reality.

Although there are among the various models some points of divergence in philosophy, concepts, and practice, there are also some points of convergence. The models are not necessarily incompatible and mutually exclusive. Thus, one's existential orientation does not necessarily preclude one's use of techniques drawn from behavior therapy or from some of the more objective, rationally-oriented cognitive theories. That all these theories represent different vantage points for understanding human behavior doesn't mean that one theorist has "the truth" and the others are in error. Each point of view can offer the counselor a perspective for helping clients in their search for self. My plea is that we study all the theories, that we not allow ourselves to be converted to any single doctrine, and that in taking something from every viewpoint we integrate their perspectives into our own style. I call for an integration of these values and caution against rigidly adhering to any one mode as the one with all the truth.

What effect does our theoretical preference have on our behavior in our relationship with clients? My position is that our view of human nature dictates our goals and our manner of working with clients. We need to be careful of expectancy. If, for example, I am strictly Adlerian, I expect my client to struggle with power and superiority. Chances are that my vision will be distorted. I will look for certain behavior, expect certain behavior, and may even twist what I experience from my client to fit my preconceived model. My client, out of a desire to please, may unconsciously (or very deliberately, with awareness) fit into my expectations by accommodating me. A word of caution, then: beware of subscribing exclusively to any one central or universal view of humanity; remain open and selectively incorporate a framework for counseling or therapy that is consistent with your own personality.

Goals in counseling and psychotherapy

In surveying the goals of counseling and psychotherapy, one finds a diverse group, including personality restructuring, finding meaning in life, curing an emotional disturbance, adjusting to society, attaining happiness and satisfaction, attaining self-actualization, reducing anxiety, and unlearning maladaptive behavior and learning adaptive patterns. Is there a common denominator in this range of goals? Can there be any integration of the various theoretical viewpoints on the issue of goals?

The problem of the diversity of goals can be simplified by viewing the issue in terms of the degree of generality or specificity of goals. Goals can be seen as existing on a continuum from general, global, and long-term objectives to specific, concrete, and short-term objectives. The humanistic, or relationship-oriented, therapies tend to stress the former; behavior-oriented therapies stress the latter goals. The goals at opposite ends of the continuum are not necessarily contradictory; it is just a matter of how specifically the goals are defined. Several writers have noted that an integration of the goals of behavior therapy and those of the humanistic approaches is possible and desirable. Truax and Carkhuff (1967) contended that behavior therapy need not be antagonistic to humanistic approaches and may even be complementary. They cited evidence that suggests its applicability to psychotherapy in general and to person-centered therapy in particular. Wrenn (1966) considered it possible for the "two psychological worlds" to become integrated for the practicing counselor. He raised the question Must the practitioner accept one approach and reject the other? In his view the relationship-oriented therapies can contribute to determining meaningful goals in counseling, and the behavioral approach can contribute the methodologies for producing desired behavior and attitude changes. Thus, a convergence of the "two psychological worlds" is possible.

Let me examine in more detail the goals of counseling from both the humanistic and the behavioral orientations. As I mentioned earlier, the humanistic and relationship-oriented approaches tend to stress broad, or ultimate, long-term goals, which are frequently difficult to measure objectively. Those goals might include finding autonomy and freedom, becoming more fully functioning or becoming a self-actualizing person, discovering an internal locus of evaluation, becoming more self-integrated, and so on. Some other global objectives could include the following:

1. That clients become more self-aware and deny and distort less.
2. That clients accept their own feelings, avoid blaming their environment or others for their condition, and come to recognize that they are now responsible for what they are doing.
3. That clients avoid playing the helpless role and come to accept the power they possess for altering their life.
4. That clients clarify their own values, get a clearer perspective on their problems, and find within themselves the resolutions to their conflicts.
5. That clients become more integrated and face, recognize, accept, and work through fragmented and disowned aspects of self; and that they integrate into their total being all their feelings and experiences.
6. That clients learn to take risks that will open new doors for new ways of being and that they appreciate living with some uncertainty, which is necessary for breaking ground for growth.
7. That clients come to trust themselves more fully and be willing to extend themselves in doing what they have chosen to do.
8. That clients become more conscious of possible alternatives and be more willing to make choices for themselves and accept the consequences of choosing.

Behavioral approaches specify therapeutic objectives that are, in contrast to the broad goals just listed, concrete, short term, observable, and measurable. This does not mean that the behavioral counselor is opposed to global humanistic goals, but that the broad goals should be defined through subgoals that can be evaluated. Krumboltz (1966) admitted that he was not opposed to goals of self-actualization, better understanding of self, or promoting adaptive behavior, but he did say that

all of these ways of stating goals suffer from being so global and general that they provide no guidelines for what is to be accomplished. ... In order to make such generalities useful they must be translated into specific kinds of behavior appropriate to each client's problem so that everyone concerned with the counseling relationship knows exactly what is to be accomplished [pp. 9–10].

Some examples of specific therapeutic goals are to stop smoking, to reduce or eliminate a specific fear, to be more assertive with coworkers, to decide on a vocation, to get a

TABLE 12-3 Goals of therapy

Psychoanalytic therapy	To make the unconscious conscious. To reconstruct the basic personality. To assist clients in reliving earlier experiences and working through repressed conflicts. Intellectual awareness.
Existential therapy	To provide conditions for maximizing self-awareness and growth. Removal of blocks to fulfillment of personal potential. To help clients discover and use freedom of choice by expanding self-awareness. To enable them to be free and responsible for the direction of their own life.
Person-centered therapy	To provide a safe climate conducive to clients' self-exploration, so that they can recognize blocks to growth and can experience aspects of self that were formerly denied or distorted. To enable them to move toward openness to experience, greater trust in self, willingness to be a process, and increased spontaneity and aliveness.
Gestalt therapy	To assist clients in gaining awareness of moment-to-moment experiencing. To challenge them to accept responsibility for internal support as opposed to depending on external support.
Transactional analysis (TA)	To help clients become script-free, game-free, autonomous people capable of choosing how they want to be. To assist them in examining early decisions and making new decisions based on awareness.
Behavior therapy	To eliminate clients' maladaptive behavior patterns and help them learn constructive patterns. To change behavior. Specific goals are selected by the client. Broad goals are broken down into precise subgoals.
Rational-emotive therapy (RET)	To eliminate clients' self-defeating outlook on life and assist them in acquiring a more tolerant and rational view of life.
Reality therapy	To guide clients toward learning realistic and responsible behavior and developing a success identity. To help them make value judgments about behavior and decide on a plan of action for change.

successful divorce, to cure migraine headaches, to learn how to make friends, to cure impotence or frigidity, to cure stuttering, to lessen test anxiety, to develop better study habits, and to cure a specific behavior disorder.

A central question is Who should establish the goals of counseling? Almost all theories are in accord with the principle that it is the client's responsibility to decide the objectives of his or her own counseling, but they recognize that the therapist also has some basic, general goals. I believe that goal definition is a joint and evolutionary process—that is, something that is done by the client and the therapist as therapy proceeds. The therapist has general goals, and each client has his or her goals. I believe that therapy ought to begin with an exploration of the goals expected from the therapeutic relationship. Perhaps at the beginning clients have very vague and confused ideas of what they expect from therapy. They may simply want answers to their "problems," they may want to stop hurting, or they may ask for ways in which they can be different so that some significant persons in their lives will accept them more fully. In some cases, clients may have no goals; they are in the therapist's office simply because they were sent there by their parents, probation officer, or teacher, and all they want is to be left alone. So, where can a counselor begin? My belief is that the intake session can be used most productively by focusing on the issue of the client's goals or lack of them. The therapist might begin by asking such questions as "What do you expect from counseling?" "What do you want?"

"What do you hope to leave with?" "What about yourself or your life situation would you most like to change?"

A therapist will probably experience frustration when he or she hears the client utter "I'd just like to understand myself more, and I'd like to be happy." The therapist, however, can bring that global and diffuse wish into sharper focus by asking: "What is keeping you from feeling happy?" "What *do* you understand about yourself *now?*" "What would you like to understand about yourself that you don't now understand?" The main point is that setting goals seems unavoidable, and, if there is to be any productive direction, both the client and therapist need to explore what they hope to obtain from the counseling relationship. The two need to decide at the outset whether they can work with each other and whether their goals are compatible.

One other point needs to be highlighted. I observe in many counselor interns the tendency to embrace some goals only superficially. In my view, goals are vitally related to the values and personhood of the therapist, and the only way to know if one really accepts goals is to examine critically one's activity as a therapist and a person. What seems imperative is that therapists look at what they do in practice, not merely at what they say they believe.

It would also be good here to review some questionable or objectionable therapeutic goals. One common misconception is that therapy should "straighten out" clients by teaching them "right" and "appropriate" values. Many novice therapists have an urge to impose their own goals on clients and indoctrinate their own beliefs. In their need to make "proper" decisions for clients, they freely dispense advice. As Corlis and Rabe (1969) wrote: "There is no therapy as long as the patient only asks advice. There is no therapy when the therapist decides for the patient what he ought to do" (p. 16).

Another questionable goal is client contentment and happiness. I have heard many counselor interns say that this is their objective, and that they want to eliminate suffering, pain, and uncertainty from their clients' experiences. I feel strongly that, if we settle for contentment as an end in counseling or therapy, we are cheating the clients. If therapy is geared to growth, then some degree of discontent, confusion, anxiety, and pain seems inevitable. In regard to this issue, I think that the therapist's job is to encourage clients to take risks that might well lead to an increase of discontent for a time but that might also result in longer-term satisfaction.

Still another questionable therapeutic aim is social adjustment. Many counseling agencies and practitioners in schools and mental-health clinics do not focus their efforts on significant change in accordance with the client's needs but instead aim at fostering adjustment to the social environment. Whereas an exploration of the demands of society is surely in order in the therapeutic process, I do not think that adjusting a client so that he or she "fits" well should be the primary concern. In his collection of essays *The Radical Therapist,* Jerome Agel (1971) made the point that therapy as it is now practiced has failed. His view is that the only people helped are the therapists, whose lives are already fairly comfortable. Agel's essays are all based on one thesis: "Therapy is change, not adjustment. This *means* change—social, personal and political" (p. xi). The point is argued that therapy aimed at adjustment is more than useless; it is destructive. To remedy the situation, drastic changes need to be made in demystifying the therapeutic process. For significant personal change to occur, the alienating and oppressing social forces must be changed. Because Agel's thesis implies political and social change, one might raise the questions What good does it actually do merely to work with the individual alone? Is any long-lasting change effected, particularly when the client returns to an undesirable social environment? Should therapists get outside their offices and broaden their goals to include changing certain social situations that produce human misery?

Evaluating the effectiveness of counseling and psychotherapy

Related to the topic of therapeutic goals is the issue of how well the various psychotherapeutic techniques actually do meet the stated goals of each therapy. In this brief section I want to examine the effectiveness of counseling and psychotherapy in achieving the goals of constructive personality and behavioral change. Questions that can be asked are Does therapy make a significant difference? Are people substantially better with therapy than they are without it? Can therapy actually be more harmful than helpful? A thorough discussion of these questions is beyond the scope of this book, and in this section I will not review the literature relating to the outcomes of therapy. For those who are interested in such a review I suggest the following sources: Bergin (1971); Bergin and Lambert (1978); Bergin and Strupp (1972); Eysenck (1966); Garfield, Prager, and Bergin (1971); Luborsky, Singer, and Luborsky (1975); Meltzoff and Kornreich (1970); and Strupp, Hadley, and Gomes-Schwartz (1977). Instead of dealing with a survey of the literature here, I want to address what I consider basic issues related to evaluating the effectiveness of psychotherapy.

One of the first issues relates to the extent of research that has been done on the therapeutic approaches presented in this book. Most of the studies have been done by two divergent approaches: the behavior therapists, who have based their therapeutic practice on empirical studies, and the person-centered researchers, who have made significant contributions to the understanding of both process and outcome variables. To a lesser extent, rational-emotive therapy has also been subjected to research to support its main hypotheses, although the empirical rigor of these studies has been called into question by several other researchers with a behavioral orientation. Finally, an analytically oriented group of practitioners has also been concerned with the evaluation of psychotherapy. Aside from these four approaches, most of the other models that were covered in this book have not produced significant empirical research dealing with how well therapy works.

If we are looking to hard data to support the concepts and procedures of most of the therapeutic approaches discussed, we will be disappointed. A reason for this is that one approach's "cure" is another approach's "resistance." In other words, because each approach works toward different outcomes, it is almost impossible to compare them. Thus, factors other than scientific data must be considered if we are to determine the validity and usefulness of most of the therapy approaches.

Garfield (1980) argued that the question Is psychotherapy effective? is a poor one destined to receive poor answers. He made the point that psychotherapy is not a clearly defined and uniform process, and that there is thus no basis for any objective answer to the question.

A guideline for improving on this global question was provided by Paul (1967) with the following question: "*What* treatment, by *whom,* is the most effective for *this* individual with *that* specific problem, and under what set of circumstances"? Thus, the question of the effectiveness of psychotherapy needs to be narrowed down to a specific type of therapy, and usually narrowed further to a certain technique. However, it is not sufficient merely to conduct studies of certain therapeutic approaches. Practitioners who claim adherence to the same approach may function vastly differently, using techniques in various ways and relating to clients in diverse fashions. They may function differently depending on the type of client and the clinical setting.

I am in full agreement with Garfield (1980), who contended that, if we expect to improve research designs to meaningfully measure the effectiveness of therapeutic procedures, we must state questions more precisely: What therapeutic procedures will work best with what clients? What kind of therapist will work best with what procedures and with what clients? He contended that we need to individualize our therapeutic procedures and systematically investigate their effectiveness for specific problems.

The typical pattern in outcome evaluation has been to deal with group research, in which the results of a number of therapists with many clients are reported. This practice may be misleading in several ways. Some of the therapists may be functioning at a high level and succeeding, whereas others may be functioning at a low level and having negative outcomes. Thus, such group research may cancel itself out and yield no significant difference. On this point the essence of the Truax and Carkhuff (1967) study is relevant here. They stated that "the evidence now available suggests that, on the average, psychotherapy may be harmful as often as helpful, with an average effect comparable to receiving no help" (pp. 20–21). After an extensive evaluation of the research evidence, Truax and Carkhuff concluded that

1. the therapeutic endeavor is, on the average, ineffective;
2. therapy itself is a non-unitary phenomenon;
3. some counselors and therapists are significantly helpful while others are significantly harmful, with the resulting *average* helpfulness not demonstrably better than the effect of having no professional treatment; and
4. through research it is possible to identify the major ingredient of helpful and harmful therapy, and thus markedly increase the average effectiveness of counseling and psychotherapy [p. 2].*

On the surface those conclusions drawn from research evidence might seem discouraging, in that they seem to suggest that counseling and psychotherapy do not make a significant difference in helping people to achieve the goals of improved behavioral functioning. Yet there is some hope. Note that the fourth conclusion is that research has identified the specific variables that account for constructive changes. Truax and Carkhuff wrote that "research seems consistently to find empathy, warmth and genuineness characteristic of human encounters that change people—for the better" (p. 141). They found that, conversely, therapists who offer low levels of these "therapeutic conditions" produce either deterioration or no change in clients.

A significant implication here is that counselor-education programs can be designed to include teaching of interpersonal skills as well as theoretical content and techniques. In my estimation education should focus on the personal development of the counselor by including group therapy designed for personal growth and awareness. It can be integrated into supervision practices and practicum experiences in which the trainee gets actual experience in applying his or her knowledge and skills to real situations. In addition to paying attention to "problems" of clients, the program can also focus on the dynamics of the counselor intern's behavior. I believe further that a concern for the

---

*From *Toward Effective Counseling and Psychotherapy* by C. B. Truax and R. R. Carkhuff, Aldine Publishing Company, 1967. Copyright 1967 by C. B. Truax and R. R. Carkhuff. This and all other quotations from this source are reprinted by permission.

trainee's personhood should be the core of the program. The conclusions of Truax and Carkhuff appear to support my bias if the concern is to produce therapists who can affect clients for better instead of for worse. I will explore this important issue with more detail in the final chapter, on the personhood of the counselor.

Therapist's function and role

A basic issue that all therapists must face concerns the definition of their role. Is the therapist a friend? An expert? An advice-giver? A helper? A clarifier? An information-giver? A confronter? A provider of alternatives? A guru? Is the therapist all of these at various times, and, if so, what is his or her basic role in the helping process?

The fact that a range of proper roles exists often confuses beginning therapists. How do therapists determine their roles? What influences does the setting in which therapists practice have on their roles? What do counselors do when they are in conflict with the agency's view of what they should be doing? There is no simple and universal answer to the question of the therapist's proper role; such factors as the type of counseling, personal characteristics, level of training, the clientele to be served, and the therapeutic setting all need to be considered.

One problem that counselors might have to struggle with is what to do when their view of their role is in basic conflict with the requirements of their job position. For example, I have worked with school counselors who perceived their role as doing psychological counseling. Their interests were in "real counseling," both individually and in groups, and they resisted adopting what they saw as "inappropriate functions," or roles that were inconsistent with being an effective counselor. However, the school administrators perceived the counselors' roles differently, for they expected them to perform the following tasks: policing the bathrooms to detect smokers, supervising the halls during lunchtime, supervising football games, acting as disciplinarians by sus-pending and expelling students, administering group tests, and working with students primarily as schedule changers and academic programmers. If the counselors were to accept all those noncounseling functions, little time would be left for doing their main work of counseling. In real situations like that, I believe that it is part of the professional responsibility of counselors to define their roles and to educate their administrator Admittedly, that is not always feasible; thus, people who feel that they are being asked to perform functions that are inconsistent with their views of counseling or their levels of training must decide whether they can in good conscience remain with a particular agency if they cannot bring about certain essential changes.

At times mental-health workers will find themselves in jobs that demand that they function in multiple roles and perform functions that do not mix well. In a state hospital in which I serve as a consultant, the treatment staff is typically assigned a wide variety of therapeutic and nontherapeutic tasks. Psychiatric technicians, psychologists, and social workers are expected to function as therapists to a group of involuntarily committed patients, many of whom are mentally disordered sex offenders, psychotics, and socio-paths. In addition to providing one-to-one contacts, they are expected to regularly hold group-therapy sessions. Yet at the same time they are responsible for making a deter-mination of when the patients are ready to be released and returned to the community. This is a major burden for many of these workers, because they are aware of the possibility that some of their patients may commit new offenses (including rape, child molestation, or murder). Patients know that they make judgments concerning their detention or release. Hence, there is the possibility that these patients will learn the language expected and say all the "right things" to impress the treatment team, when in effect they may not have made any substantial changes. Thus, these mental-health workers carry out multiple functions: therapist, sponsor, nurse, friend, teacher, judge, guard, parent, and administrator.

Although having to perform the dual roles of therapist and evaluator may be far less than ideal, it is often impractical and unrealistic to think that such workers can involve themselves strictly in therapy functions. Like it or not, the reality of most institutions demands that they participate in treatment-team staffings and meetings in which they make evaluative judgments about their patients and decisions that may affect their ability to create a climate of trust in which they can function ideally. Therefore I think it is best for such workers to frankly tell their patients at the outset the reality of the situation and then not apologize for it. This type of directness with patients can go a long way in establishing trust.

I encourage each counselor to make a critical evaluation concerning appropriate counseling functions. Counselors could also benefit from deciding in advance certain functions they feel are inconsistent with real counseling. I believe that the central function of counseling is to help clients recognize their own strengths, discover what is preventing them from using their strengths, and clarify what kinds of person they want to be. I do not believe that problem solving is the primary function of counseling; rather, counseling is a process by which clients are invited to look honestly at their behavior and life-style and make certain decisions about the ways in which they want to modify the quality of their life. My view is that the counselor's job is multifold: he or she needs to provide support and warmth yet care enough to challenge and confront.

Thus, an essential function of the counselor is to give honest and direct reactions to the client. How does one perceive the client? What feelings does one have toward the client? How does one experience the client during the counseling sessions? Effective counseling entails a personal commitment and investment of self on the counselor's behalf. I strongly believe that counselors must do more than administer techniques, and that they must be willing to reveal themselves in the relationship with the client. Clients can then sift and sort the responses they receive from the counselors and make appropriate decisions.

An issue related to the therapist's function and role is the degree to which the therapist exercises control of client behavior both during and outside the session. What is the therapist's job in structuring the therapeutic process? All the various approaches are in basic agreement that the therapist does bring structure to the counseling experience, although they disagree over the nature and degree of this structuring. For example, rational-emotive therapists operate within a highly directive, didactic, persuasive, and confrontive structure. They frequently prescribe "homework assignments" that are designed to get clients to practice new behavior outside therapy sessions. By contrast, person-centered therapists operate in a much looser and undefined structure, but they do provide a general structure. Even an extremely nondirective practitioner works within some framework; the client defines the direction of the course of therapy by deciding what to talk about, and the therapist follows the lead of the client and stays within the client's frame of reference.

Therapists need to realize the importance of the influence of their behavior on their clients. The issue of influence is closely related to the issue of the therapist's authenticity as a person. In my opinion, it is a mistake for therapists to restrict themselves primarily to teaching responsibility, reflecting feelings, or the like. Instead, I advocate a wide range of behavior that becomes incorporated into the therapist's own style of being. Thus, I encourage potential counselors to study various counseling schools and to integrate useful methods from diverse approaches. At times reflection of feeling and simply listening to a client's verbal and nonverbal messages are what is called for, but to restrict oneself to these tactics is to unduly hamper one's effectiveness.

There will be times when it is appropriate to confront clients with their evasions of reality or their illogical thinking. Again, for therapists to focus primarily on this behavior is to restrict themselves unnecessarily. At times they will need to be interpretive, and at other times they will invite their clients to interpret for themselves the meaning of their behavior. Sometimes it may be appropriate to be very directive and structured, and at other times it may be appropriate to flow without a clear structure. So much depends on the purpose of therapy, the setting, the personality and style of the therapist, and the qualities of a particular client. To be prescriptive and to establish a formula are not helpful. This is where the art of therapy reveals itself. Although therapists can learn attitudes and skills and acquire certain knowledge about personality dynamics and the therapeutic process, so much of effective therapy is the product of this art. I often wonder whether this creativity, this capacity to be an artful and resourceful therapist, can be taught. My main point is that it is misleading to dupe student counselors into the idea that counseling is a science that is separate and distinct from the behavior and personality of the counselor.

Thus, a significant issue is the degree to which a counselor should be his or her real self during a session. What limitations are appropriate? I believe that as a therapist one ought constantly to ask oneself: What am I doing? Whose needs are being met—my client's or my own? What is the effect of my behavior on my client?

Another basic issue regarding structuring is that of division of responsibility. This issue must be clarified at the intake session. In my view, it is the therapist's responsibility early in the counseling context to discuss specific matters such as length and overall durations of the sessions, confidentiality, general goals, and methods used to achieve goals. I strongly believe that both the therapist and the client need to assume responsibility for the direction of therapy. If therapists primarily make decisions of what to discuss and are overdirective, they perpetuate clients' dependency. Clients should be encouraged to assume as much responsibility as possible in the early stages of therapy. Here is where I find contracts and assignments most useful. In both my individual practice and my group work, I typically suggest homework assignments that clients might try before the next session. I make the suggestion when I intuitively feel that clients might be resisting doing something for themselves out of fear or passivity. I also invite people I work with to choose something specific that they would like to experiment with outside the session. The assignments can be very small beginnings, or they can be rather demanding tasks.

Much of this methodology depends on the motivation of the client to change. For example, a client might reveal that he often feels "put down" by his wife and that, when he does, he typically feels hostility, which he swallows. My suggestion might be: "Next time you feel even slightly put down by your wife, why not take the risk of letting her know how you feel *at that moment?* Why not experiment for one week with expressing your anger instead of swallowing it, just to see what happens?" Another client might hurtfully disclose that she feels a real distance from her father and that she would like to have some closeness with him before it is too late. I might suggest that she write a long letter to her father, telling him exactly what she feels and what she would like with him—and then I might suggest that she *not* send the letter. It is strategy to invite her to come into closer touch with her hurt and with what she intends to do with the hurt. At the next session, she and I could explore the outcome of her assignment, and she could make her own decision about what she would like to do: to pursue the issue with her father, to write more on her own and keep it private, or simply to forget the issue.

I believe that it is centrally important for the therapist to be alert to clients' efforts to manipulate the therapist into assuming responsibility that they are capable of assuming. Many clients will push for the "magic answer" from the therapist as a way of escaping the anxiety of making their own resolutions. Client-initiated contracts and specific assignments are extremely helpful in keeping the focus of responsibility on the client. Contracts can be changed, and new contracts can be developed. Formulating contracts can be continued during the entire counseling relationship. As therapists we must ask ourselves Are my clients doing now what will move them toward greater autonomy and toward a place where they can increasingly find their answers within? If we allow clients to find their directions primarily from us, we foster their dependence and further reinforce their lack of potency. If we care enough, we will be demanding. We can still be tender and compassionate, but it seems to me that caring involves strongly inviting clients to become what they are capable of being, and when they consistently choose to remain less than they could be, we must care enough to demand more. In brief, perhaps the best measure of our general effectiveness as therapists is the degree to which clients are able to say to us "I appreciate what you've been to me, and, because of your faith in me, I feel I can now go it alone." Eventually, if we are good enough, we will be out of business!

Client's experience in therapy

What are clients like? Who should be a client? What are the expectations clients have as they approach therapy? What are their responsibilities in the process? Is therapy only for the "disturbed"? Can the relatively healthy person benefit from therapy? Are there any commonalities among the diverse types of client?

Generally, clients have in common some degree of suffering, pain, or at least discontent. There is a discrepancy between how they would like to be and how they see themselves presently functioning. Some initiate therapy because of their awareness of wanting to cure a specific symptom or set of symptoms: they want to get rid of migraine headaches, free themselves of chronic anxiety attacks, lose weight, or get relief from depression. Many seek some resolution to conflicts with a marital partner in the hope that they can enjoy their marriage. Increasingly, people are entering therapy with existential problems; their complaints are less defined but relate to the experiences of emptiness, meaninglessness in life, boredom, dead personal relationships, a lack of intense feelings, and a loss of the sense of self.

The initial expectations of many clients are expert help and a fast change. They often have great hope for major changes in their life. All too often they have the unrealistic notion that, if they merely reveal their "problem," the therapist will draw on his or her magic to "cure" them. As therapy progresses, they discover that they must be active in the process, for they must select their own goals, do much of the "work" in the therapy sessions, and be willing to extend the work beyond the sessions into their outside life. Hence, some clients discover the value of homework assignments, experiments with new behavior outside the session, and contracts—all of which are geared to getting clients to put their new learning into action. Other clients quit or find therapy too much work.

I believe that people are increasingly seeing the value of psychotherapeutic help for developmental purposes as well as for remedial goals. With the impetus created by humanistic psychology, people began to be educated to the idea that one need not be "sick" to benefit from some form of therapy.

Whether clients seek therapy to cure a disorder or to enhance the quality of their personal life, what are the characteristics of "successful" clients? Truax and Carkhuff (1967) described the client who is most likely to benefit from counseling and psychotherapy in the following way: The person has a high degree of inner disturbance but a low degree of behavioral disturbance. This definition is consistent with Rogers's idea that a basic requisite for therapy is that clients perceive that they have a problem, which supplies the motivation to change. Also, the successful client exhibits a high degree of readiness for change and has a positive expectancy for personal improvement. Finally, the successful client engages in deep and extensive exploration of self.

Most of this discussion has dealt with clients who seek out a therapeutic experience, either because they are in crisis and want relief, have long-standing problems that they want to solve, or hope to understand themselves more fully and move to a higher level of personal integration. But what about the involuntary clients who sit before you because the judge ordered them to do so, or the clients who must attend group-therapy sessions as a part of their treatment program in the hospital setting? Again, going back to my in-service training workshops for mental-health specialists, I have learned what it is like to be an involuntary client, as well as some of the difficulties in working with such a population. I have come to the conclusion that it is possible for clients to benefit from some type of therapy even if they do not initiate the process and in fact may be quite resistant.

As I mentioned earlier, I think it is essential that practitioners who work with involuntary clients begin by openly and directly discussing the nature of the relationship, that they promise nothing that they cannot or will not deliver, and that they make clear the limits of confidentiality as well as any other factors that might affect the course of therapy. Further, because I see psychotherapy as a learning experience, I believe it is essential to *prepare* clients. This is especially true for involuntary clients. What is the therapy about? What are the joint responsibilities of both parties? How can therapy help? What can the client do to increase the chances that the therapy experience will be a positive one? What are the potential risks and dangers involved? What might the client expect in terms of the general course of treatment? This kind of preparation can go a long way in dealing with resistance. Often, in fact, resistance is brought about by a therapist who fails to do any preparation of clients, and who merely assumes that all clients are open and ready to benefit from therapy.

To their credit, the behavior therapists do an especially good job of preparing clients for a treatment program. They systematically work with their clients to identify specific therapy goals, break down these goals into measurable ones, and discuss the procedures to be used. The clients are also involved in continually assessing the progress of the therapy. Although there are various ways to prepare clients for therapy, practitioners of other schools can learn something from the behaviorists in this regard.

Relationship between therapist and client

Most approaches share common ground in accepting the importance of the therapeutic relationship. The existential and person-centered views are based on the personal relationship as the crucial determinant of the outcomes of the therapeutic process. It is clear that some other approaches, such as rational-emotive therapy and behavior therapy,

TABLE 12-4 The therapeutic relationship

Psychoanalytic therapy	The therapist, or analyst, remains anonymous, and clients develop projections toward the analyst. Focus is on reducing the resistances that develop in working with transference and on establishing more rational control. Clients experience intensive, long-term analysis and engage in free association to uncover conflicts. They gain insight by talking. The analyst makes interpretations to teach them the meaning of current behavior as related to their past.
Existential therapy	The therapist's main tasks are to accurately grasp clients' being-in-the-world and to establish a personal and authentic encounter with them. They discover their own uniqueness in the relationship with the therapist. The human-to-human encounter, the presence of the client/therapist relationship, and the authenticity of the here-and-now encounter are stressed. Both the client and the therapist can be changed by the encounter.
Person-centered therapy	The relationship is of primary importance. The qualities of the therapist, including genuineness, warmth, accurate empathy, respect, and permissiveness, and the communication of these attitudes to clients are stressed. They use this real relationship with the therapist for translating self-learnings to other relationships.
Gestalt therapy	The therapist does not interpret for clients but assists them in developing the means to make their own interpretations. They are expected to identify and work on unfinished business from the past that interferes with current functioning. They do so by reexperiencing past traumatic situations as though they were occurring in the present.
Transactional analysis (TA)	An equal relationship exists, with deemphasis on the status of the therapist. The client contracts with the therapist for the specific changes desired; when the contract is completed, therapy is terminated. Transference and dependence on the therapist are deemphasized.
Behavior therapy	The therapist is active and directive and functions as a teacher or trainer in helping clients learn more effective behavior. Clients must be active in the process and experiment with new behaviors. Whereas a personal relationship between them and the therapist is not highlighted, a good working relationship is the groundwork for implementing behavioral procedures.
Rational-emotive therapy (RET)	The therapist functions as a teacher, and the client as a student. A personal relationship is not essential. Clients gain insight into their problems and then must practice actively in changing self-defeating behavior.
Reality therapy	The therapist's main task is to get involved with clients and encourage them to face reality and make a value judgment regarding present behavior. After clients decide on specific changes desired, plans are formulated, a commitment to follow through is established, and results are evaluated. Insight and attitude change are not deemed crucial.

do not ignore the relationship factor, even though they do not give it a place of central importance.

Therapists' degree of caring, their interest and ability in helping the client, and their genuineness are factors that influence the relationship. Clients also contribute to the relationship with variables such as their motivation, cooperation, interest, concern, attitudes, perceptions, expectations, behavior, and reactions to the therapist. Counseling or psychotherapy is a personal matter that involves a personal relationship, and evidence indicates that honesty, sincerity, acceptance, warmth, understanding, and spontaneity are basic ingredients of successful outcomes.

Patterson (1973) stressed the importance of the therapeutic relationship, maintaining that research indicates that the effective element in therapy is that relationship. He made the point that the therapist serves as a reinforcer, for the therapist's respect and concern for clients become powerful influences on their behavior. The therapist also provides a model of a good personal relationship that clients can use for their own growth. Patterson made it clear that therapy cannot be mechanical, and that the process cannot be reduced to technique alone, for the personhood of the therapist is crucial. He also stated that

> the evidence seems to point to the establishment of a particular kind of relationship as the crucial element in counseling or psychotherapy. It is a relationship characterized not so much by what techniques the therapist uses as by what he is, not so much by what he does as by the way he does it [1973, pp. 535–536].

Truax and Carkhuff (1967) supported Patterson's contention: "The central ingredients of empathy, warmth, and genuineness do not merely represent 'techniques' of psychotherapy or counseling, but are interpersonal skills that the counselor or therapist employs in *applying* his 'techniques' or 'expert knowledge'" (p. 31).

What are the basic characteristics of a therapist that lead to constructive personality and behavior change in the client? Truax and Carkhuff (1967, p. 25) found three sets of characteristics that appear to thread through almost every major therapeutic approach: accurate empathy, nonpossessive warmth, and genuineness. In summary, most therapeutic approaches emphasize the importance of the therapist's ability to be an integrated, mature, honest, sincere, authentic, and congruent person in therapeutic encounters; to provide a safe, nonthreatening, and trusting climate by demonstrating nonpossessive warmth for clients, which allows them to engage in deep and significant self-exploration; and to be able to grasp the internal frame of reference of clients' experience and deeply understand their meanings.

Issues related to techniques and procedures

DIAGNOSIS

Some practitioners view psychological diagnosis as an essential part of the therapeutic process, and others view it as a detriment to counseling. Psychological diagnosis generally means analyzing the client's problems, their causes, and the nature and development of patterns of maladjustment. Diagnosis also implies specifying certain therapeutic interventions and predicting the outcomes in terms of future client behavior. It frequently has a broader meaning than merely classifying and labeling, for diagnosis has come to be associated with a complete description of the client and his or her present functioning.

The purpose of diagnosis in counseling and psychotherapy is to gain sufficient knowledge of present behavior so that a differential treatment plan can be tailored to the client. Behavioral practitioners stress a diagnostic approach with their emphasis on a clear specification of treatment goals. Here an objective appraisal of specific functioning and definite symptoms is in order, for, after an evaluation has been made of what the disturbing behaviors are, then a treatment plan can be developed, and eventually some evaluation can be made of the effects of the treatment.

Many are critical of diagnosis in therapy. Rogers (1951) maintained that diagnosis is detrimental because it is an external way of understanding a client. It tends to pull the client away from his or her internal and subjective experience and foster an external, objective, intellectualized conception *about* the client. According to Rogers, the client is the one who knows the dynamics of his or her behavior, and for change to occur the client must experience a perceptual change, not simply receive data about himself or herself.

As a proponent of the existential view of therapy, Arbuckle (1975) saw diagnosis as inappropriate in counseling because "diagnosis misses entirely the reality of the inner person. It is the measure of me from the outside in, it is a measure of me by others, and it ignores my subjective being" (p. 255). Instead of an external diagnostic picture of the client, Arbuckle contended, counselors should attempt to grasp the internal world of the client.

Carkhuff and Berenson (1967) opposed traditional diagnostic categories and saw them as "not only intellectually repugnant but usually meaningless for purposes of differential treatment" (p. 234). But it seems clear that they were not against diagnosis that is a continuing part of the therapeutic relationship. According to them, "A meaningful diagnostic process flows out of an ongoing interactional process between therapist and client. There is no separate and distinct diagnostic process" (p. 235).

Is there a way to bridge the gap between the extreme view that diagnosis is the essential core of therapy and that it is a detrimental factor? In my opinion, a broad view of diagnosis is a basic part of the therapy process. I conceive of diagnosis as a continuing process that focuses on understanding the client. Both the therapist and the client are engaged in the search-and-discovery process from the first session to the last. Even though a practitioner might avoid the formal diagnostic procedures and terminology, it seems important that he or she raise certain questions, such as What is going on in the client's life now, and what does the client want from therapy? What are the client's strengths and limitations? How far should therapy go? What are some of the basic dynamics involved in the client's life at this time? In dealing with these questions, the therapist is formulating some conception about what clients want and how they might best attain their goals. Thus, diagnosis becomes a form of making tentative hypotheses, and these hunches can be formed with clients and shared with them throughout the process.

I do have serious reservations about pinning on clients shorthand labels such as *paranoid, schizophrenic,* or *psychopathic.* Frequently these labels categorize and stereotype a client, and an entire staff might react to the label and treat the "schizophrenic patient" the way it expects that type of "case" to behave. Instead of seeing the person's uniqueness and individuality, one can easily ignore his or her personhood. Also, the client may soon begin to live up to expectations—that is, to behave in a manner based on the way he or she is viewed and treated.

A point that needs to be stressed is that, just because some diagnostic procedures are

carried out in a technical/mechanical or objective/detached style that characterizes diagnosis as something done externally *by* an expert *to* a passive client, this does not
mean that all diagnosis needs to be done in such a manner. Diagnosis, if it is seen in a
broader context, can be a dimension of the therapeutic process as practiced by a behavior therapist or an existentially oriented therapist. I am in agreement with the view
of Brammer and Shostrom (1977): "We find it difficult to escape the fact that the therapeutic psychologist must make some decisions, do some therapeutic planning, be alert
for pathology to avoid serious mistakes, and be in the position to make some prognoses
or predictions" (p. 141).

TESTING

The place of testing in counseling and therapy is another controversial issue. Models
that emphasize the objective view of counseling are inclined to use testing procedures
to get information about clients or to provide them with information so that they can
make more realistic decisions.The person-centered and existential orientations view
testing much as they do diagnosis—as an external form of understanding that has little
to do with effective counseling. Arbuckle (1975) took a skeptical view of testing and
diagnosis:

> Thus if one sees the other person, in the traditional scientific pattern, as being what one is
> measured to be by outside and external criteria, then testing—and diagnosis—should be an
> integral part of the counseling process. If, on the other hand, one sees the basic reality of the
> human being from within, then testing and diagnosis will tend to remove the person even
> further from the reality of who he is [p. 261].

I do not share Arbuckle's view that testing and diagnosis "will tend to remove the
person even further from the reality of who he is." A wide variety of tests can be used
for counseling purposes, including measures of interest, aptitude, achievement, attitudes
and values, and personal characteristics and traits. In my view tests can be used as an
adjunct to counseling; valuable information, which can add to a client's capacity to make
decisions, can be gleaned from them. From my experiences in working in a university
counseling center, I have formulated some cautions and guidelines regarding the use
of tests:

1. Clients should be involved in the test-selection process. They should decide which general
   types of tests, if any, they wish to take.
2. A client needs to be aware that tests are only tools, and imperfect ones at that. As means to
   an end, tests do not provide "the answer" but at best provide additional information about
   the client that can be useful in exploring in counseling and in coming to certain decisions.
3. The counselor needs to clarify the purposes of the tests and point out their limitations. This
   implies that a counselor has a good grasp of what the test is about and that he or she has
   taken it.
4. Clients' reasons for wanting tests, as well as their past experience with tests, should be
   explored.
5. The test results, not simply scores, should be given to the client, and the meanings that the
   results have for the client should be explored. In interpreting the results, the counselor's
   attitude should be one of tentativeness and neutrality. It should be remembered that testing
   is only one avenue to gain information and that the information derived from tests needs to
   be validated by other measures. In presenting the results, the counselor needs to refrain
   from judgment as much as possible and allow the client to formulate his or her own meanings
   and conclusions.

6. Clients need to be involved in test interpretation as well as in test selection. The counselor needs to determine their readiness for receiving test information and for integrating it into their self-concept.

I have found that many students seek tests in the hope of finding "answers." Thus, I believe that it is important to explore why a person wants to take a battery of tests and to teach the person the values and limitations of tests. If that is done, I see less chance that tests will be undertaken in mechanical fashion and less chance that unwarranted importance will be attributed to the results. I have also found that a discussion with students about tests and testing can open the possibilities of counseling to them. Instead of seeking shortcut methods, they might be willing to invest in counseling as a way to clarify their thinking and to aid their decision making. In short, my view is that testing itself is not destructive; rather, the way that tests are used or perceived by some counselors is the source of the problem. Tests are simply tools that can be used properly or misused.

QUESTIONING AND PROBING FOR INFORMATION

The issue of questioning and its value in therapy needs to be discussed. Unfortunately, there are therapists whose main technique is to ask a barrage of questions. They interrogate the client. The therapy session is a question-and-answer period rather than an exploration session. The client frequently leaves feeling thoroughly interrogated but not understood. Used excessively, questioning can detract from the intensity of therapy and can provide the therapist with a safe but ineffectual mode.

In Gestalt therapy *why* questions are not asked, because searching for reasons for behavior typically takes one on an intellectualized and unproductive expedition. Instead, the Gestaltist asks a different set of questions such as "What are you doing?" "How are you behaving now?" "What is going on with you now?" These *what* and *how* questions are designed to get clients to focus on here-and-now experiencing, not to produce an explanation of the cause of their behavior. Nor does the reality therapist ask *why* questions. The reality therapist sees knowing the reasons for behavior as unessential.

Questioning is a main procedure in rational-emotive therapy. The hope is that, as a result of the therapist's challenging and questioning of clients' irrational beliefs and behavior, they will begin to look critically at their own thinking and beliefs that they have in the past accepted wholesale. The Transactional-Analytic therapist also uses questions to get clients to discover some early decisions and to make new decisions.

There is a place for questioning in counseling, but therapists need to be aware that excessive use of questions becomes distracting and leads to ineffective therapy. A cross-examination is not helpful. I have often recommended to counselor interns that they tape-record some of their sessions (with the client's permission) and that, in listening to the tape later, they pay attention to the function of their questioning.

One kind of question that I find useful is an open-ended, rhetorical question designed to generate some thought. I might ask: "What do you expect that you'll be like in five years if you continue as you are now?" "What is the worst thing that can happen to you if you take a risk and fail?" "How would you like to be different from the way you are now?" "What or who is preventing you from being a different person?" Questions that lead clients to search within themselves for honest answers are different from those that probe for information.

SUPPORT AND REASSURANCE

Reassurance and active support are part of every theory of counseling surveyed in this book. All practitioners agree that some kind of support is an essential ingredient of an effective therapeutic relationship. Person-centered therapy emphasizes the value of creating a supportive atmosphere in which clients will feel the freedom to explore threatening aspects of themselves. This therapeutic climate is created by a therapist's actively attending and listening to clients' subtle messages, accepting them as worthwhile, understanding their internal world and communicating this understanding, expressing a genuine faith and hope in their capacity to change, and granting permission to explore any and all feelings. All these are ways a counselor can provide the support that will allow clients to explore feelings and thoughts and that will encourage action. By the therapist's "being there" as fully as possible for clients as they struggle with uncertainty, they are moved to do and become what they might previously have considered impossible. The reassurance of the therapist gives them a sense of confidence to continue taking risks even though they might make mistakes and experience setbacks.

There are some dangers in and limitations to the use of reassurance methods. A major misuse is the "Band-Aid" approach, whereby the therapist rushes in to "aid" and "comfort" a client who is experiencing anxiety and pain. This approach, which short-circuits the client's struggle, is not at all therapeutic. I am convinced that for personal growth to occur a certain degree of pain and uncertainty is necessary. Instead of giving a Pollyanna response such as "I'm sure everything will be OK," the therapist can share in clients' moments of anxiety and be supportive as they go ahead and do what they fear. Another limitation of reassurance is that, if it is used excessively, it fosters a sense of dependence on the therapist for approval and sanction; clients might look mainly to the therapist for affirmation instead of ultimately attaining their own approval and confirmation.

CONFRONTATION

Support is related to confrontation, for a therapist who would limit his or her style to being predominantly reassuring and comforting would not encourage clients to become much more than they presently are. When a climate of trust is created by genuine support, the relationship can endure challenge. Egan (1973) put it well: "Confrontation without support is diastrous; support without confrontation is anemic" (p. 132).

Therapists often misunderstand the nature of confrontation. It is sometimes perceived—and implemented—as a ruthless attack, a dumping of hostile feelings, and a tearing down of the defenses of a vulnerable client. In my view, a brutal approach is not responsible confrontation. Authentic confrontation is basically an invitation to the client to consider some dimension of self that is preventing positive behavioral or attitudinal change. The therapist might do a number of things to challenge clients: call attention to possible forms of self-deception; confront discrepancies between what they say and what they do; point out their games and manipulations; point out resistances and evasions; note the way they are not recognizing their potentials or resources; and confront them with the way they engage in self-deprecation.

Confrontation is aimed at more than the client's untapped resources. It is essential that confrontation be an act of caring and that the therapist demonstrate caring by investing himself or herself in the act of confrontation. Instead of merely confronting clients with what they are doing or not doing, the therapist can share his or her personal reactions to their playing certain games, for example. The involvement, as well as the timing and appropriateness, of confrontation is crucial if it is to have a therapeutic effect. The purpose of a confrontational style is to encourage clients to nondefensively consider certain aspects of themselves that they are missing, in the hope that this process will lead to constructive action. Therefore, the manner in which the therapist confronts and the way a client receives the confrontation become critical.

Confrontation is very much a part of some of the theoretical approaches discussed in this book. The Gestalt approach is highly confrontational, in that clients are continually made aware of how they are at the moment and what they are doing. They are challenged on discrepancies between their verbalizations and their body language. The Gestaltist confronts clients on the ways they resist internal support and seek as a substitute external support. Rational-emotive therapy stresses confrontation of an irrational belief system. The therapist challenges clients to critically examine definite irrational beliefs that they have incorporated and that they continue to keep alive with self-indoctrination. Reality therapy is basically a confrontational approach, for it continually urges clients to determine whether their behavior is realistic and responsible and to see whether their needs are being fulfilled by irresponsible behavior. The Transactional-Analytic therapist confronts clients on the games that they use to avoid intimacy and challenges them to reevaluate early important decisions that still affect their lives. They are encouraged to decide for themselves how they want to change and what new decisions they want to make. The contractual approach keeps clients focusing on the therapeutic goals. The existential view confronts clients with their unused capabilities and challenges them to make use of their freedom in deciding whether to actualize their potentials. The existential therapist's encounter with clients is largely a confrontational process that encourages them to become aware of their being-in-the-world and to make choices of how they want to be. The person-centered approach deemphasizes confrontation and, in my judgment, overemphasizes support. Listening, hearing, and understanding are limited. In my opinion they are essential but insufficient qualities in a therapeutic relationship. Krumboltz (1966) contended that counselor understanding and empathy are necessary but not sufficient for therapy to progress. As he put it: "After the client's problem is clarified and the feelings about it are understood by both client and counselor, the client must still learn how to resolve his difficulty. Understanding alone is not enough. It provides only the beginning step upon which appropriate learning experiences can be arranged" (p. 8). In my view confrontation that is done in a caring and responsible way can be a major tool in helping the client acquire the new learning necessary for constructive behavior change.

INTERPRETATION AND REFLECTION

Recall the detailed discussion in the chapter on person-centered therapy of the technique of reflection and that in the psychoanalytic chapter of the technique of interpretation. I will not repeat those discussions here; rather, I will examine how the techniques of reflection and interpretation relate to the various models and explore the values and limitations of the techniques.

Reflection of feeling is a primary technique in person-centered therapy. The therapist focuses on the subjective elements of what clients say in order to help them clarify their feelings and experience them with more intensity or to think about some of the things that they are saying on a deeper level. It is important that more than the surface meaning of what clients are saying be reflected; if it is not, no movement toward increased awareness occurs. The therapist does not reflect content but the subtle messages underlying the content. On the other hand, the person-centered view assumes that interpretation fosters resistance because it is an external view of understanding. Therefore, the person-centered therapist does not interpret for clients, because to do so would take the therapeutic responsibility away from them.

On the other end of the continuum is the psychoanalytic approach, which gives a place of central importance to interpretive techniques. Transference, resistances, dreams, free associations—all are interpreted. The analyst assumes a teaching function and indicates to clients the meanings of their underlying psychodynamics.

In my view the therapist can interpret in a tentative way by presenting hypotheses or hunches. In this way clients can consider the meanings of certain behaviors and begin to examine the relationship between earlier behavior and present behavior. Instead of pontificating, the therapist can share hypotheses in words such as "I wonder if. . . ." "As a hunch. . . ." "Why not try . . . on for size to see how it fits?"

There is a danger in making interpretations, particularly for the inexperienced therapist. The obvious danger is that the therapist might be wrong. Even if the therapist is accurate, he or she might inappropriately make an interpretation by springing it on the client too soon—that is, before the client is able to recognize and integrate the interpretation—or by giving an interpretation that is too deep for the client's present readiness. Another problem with making excessive interpretations is that clients may depend on the therapist to sort out meanings instead of searching for their own meanings.

The Gestalt approach to interpretation is relevant here, for it suggests that learning is acquired through personal discovery and experiencing. In its focus on the what and how of clients' immediate experiencing, the Gestalt approach is geared to assisting them to make their own interpretations instead of engaging in abstract intellectualizing. As an example, the Gestalt approach to dream work demands that they reenact all the parts of their dream to discover for themselves the meanings of the dream. By contrast, the psychoanalytic approach relies heavily on the insightfulness of the therapist in interpreting the meaning of a dream to the client.

In summary, reflection and interpretation that are done appropriately and nonmechanically can add significantly to the client's self-exploration and self-understanding. The degree to which these techniques are used depends on the therapist's skill and training, the client's readiness, and the nature of the therapist's theoretical orientation.

A COMMENTARY ON THE USE OF TECHNIQUES

Regardless of what model you might be working with, you must decide *what* techniques, procedures, or intervention methods to use, *when* to use them, and with *what* kinds of client. A related question that counselors need to ask themselves frequently is *why* they use the techniques they use. Some counselors are eager to learn techniques, and they treat them as a bag of tricks to be pulled out and tried whenever they are stuck in a counseling session. There should be a rationale for the techniques used, and the techniques should in some way be tied into the goals of therapy. This does not mean that therapists should attempt to draw on accepted techniques and procedures within a single model; quite the contrary. However, professional counselors and therapists avoid using techniques in a hit-or-miss fashion; they typically avoid using techniques to fill time or to get things moving. Nor do they hide behind the mystery and aura of the techniques they use.

In many ways, I believe *you,* as a counselor or therapist, are your very best technique. There is no substitute for developing techniques that are an expression of your personality and ones that fit for you. I contend that the main purpose of techniques is to facilitate progress in a counseling session, and that it is really impossible to effectively separate the techniques you use from your personality and the relationship you have with your clients. There is the ever-present danger of becoming a mechanical technician and simply administering techniques to clients without regard for the relationship variables. I do not think that techniques should be used as gimmicks, or tricks, to get clients to open up or do certain things. Nor do I think that techniques should be used as a substitute for the hard work that it takes to develop a constructive client/therapist relationship.

I encourage students and those with whom I consult to experience a wide variety of techniques themselves *as clients.* Reading about a technique in a book is one thing; actually experiencing it from the vantage point of a client is quite another matter. For example, if you have actually practiced relaxation exercises, you will have a much better feel for how to administer relaxation procedures and will know more about what to look for as you work with clients. If you have carried out your own real-life homework assignments as a part of your own self-change program, you will have a lot more empathy for your clients and their potential problems. If you have experienced guided imagery, then you are likely to suggest fantasy exercises to your clients in a more sensitive and effective manner. It is important to realize that particular techniques may be better suited to some therapists' personality than to others'. Thus, the active/directive and highly confrontational techniques used in RET may or may not be suited to you personally or to your style of counseling.

In my view it is a mistake to equate counselor effectiveness simply with proficiency in a single technique or even a set of techniques. For example, some counselors might become specialists in confrontational techniques. They might develop a style of relating to clients geared to provoking them, goading them to "get their anger expressed," or merely focusing on techniques to deal with anger. These therapists might derive a sense of power from becoming "confrontation specialists." For a different set of motives, other counselors might limit themselves to techniques of reflection and clarification. Perhaps they are fearful of getting involved with clients on more than the empathic/supportive level; thus, they continue to reflect and reflect because there are few risks involved, and in this way they never have a real interaction with a client. By reviewing the models presented in this book and the techniques that flow from them, we can learn that effective counseling involves proficiency in a combination of *cognitive, affective,* and *behavioral* techniques. Such a combination is necessary to help clients *think* about their beliefs and assumptions, to *experience* on a *feeling* level their conflicts and struggles, and to actually carry out their insights into *action* programs by behaving in new ways in day-to-day living.

I contend that counselors would do well to honestly examine their motivations for using or avoiding certain techniques. This process is a continuing one, not done once and for all. It could be useful to think over the following questions to determine which techniques you see yourself being drawn to. You might also reflect on the meanings they have for you.

- Do you use a lot of questions in your counseling? If so, are they *open* questions, which encourage further client talk and exploration, or *closed* questions, which have a simple answer or do not lead to deeper self-exploration? Do you ask *what, how,* or *why* questions most frequently?
- Are your techniques mainly cognitive? Or affective? Or behavioral?
- Do the techniques you use fall within a particular school or therapeutic approach? Or are they representative of various approaches?
- Do your techniques intensify what a client is feeling, or do they have the effect of closing up certain feelings? How comfortable are you with pain? Anger? Jealousy? Conflict?
- Who does most of the talking during the session, you or the client? Do you tell, direct, and persuade?
- Do you use techniques to get clients moving, or do you wait until they express some conflict or feeling and then develop a technique geared to help them experience this feeling more fully?
- What techniques have you personally experienced from the vantage point of a client? What were some of your positive experiences? Did you have any negative experiences?
- How do you imagine it would be if you avoided using any techniques or counseling procedures other than simply being with your clients and relating to them in dialogues?

SYSTEMATIC DEVELOPMENT OF COUNSELING SKILLS

It is impossible to overemphasize that techniques cannot be effectively used if they are things that are grabbed onto. Techniques are not isolated procedures that can be learned in mechanical ways, nor can they be effectively learned by reading alone. Furthermore, in the acquiring and practicing of these skills we cannot overlook the importance of the quality of the person who is learning them. Skill development is associated with our development as a human being, and unless we are aware and vital people, we run the risk of becoming *skilled technicians* at best and *unskilled helpers* at worst.

In the selection and training of therapists, Palmer (1980) suggested, there is usually only a vague focus on basic personality characteristics. Therefore, he contended, it is better to stress "natural skills"—those abilities that are acquired through life experiences rather than through formal training. Palmer wrote that

> the nascent psychotherapist should at least have been under enough stress to drive her or him to be observant of others, sensitive to others' feelings, curious about others, and a bit skeptical, and at the same time to have a basic respect for the rights of others and for the differences of others [p. 297].

Egan (1975) advocated a systematic-skills approach as a basis for counselor education. His model, basically an eclectic one and a translation of many of the concepts of Carkhuff (1969), called for helpers to learn and practice a series of helping skills. These include attending and responding skills; supportive skills, which include empathy, genuineness, and respect; confrontational skills such as advanced accurate empathy and self-disclosure; and action-oriented skills. Ivey and his associates (1978, 1980) developed a similar approach to developing specific skills. Ivey maintained that counselors can become proficient in the use of techniques by breaking them down into components, by experiencing them in the role of helper and "helpee," by getting evaluations on their level of skill development, and by refining their skills and eventually integrating them.

Besides learning the necessary skills through a wide range of life experiences, the

TABLE 12-5 Therapy techniques

Psychoanalytic therapy	The key techniques are interpretation, dream analysis, free association, analysis of resistance, and analysis of transference. All are designed to help clients gain access to their unconscious conflicts, which leads to insight and eventual assimilation of new material by the ego. Diagnosis and testing are often used. Questions are used to develop a case history.
Existential therapy	Few techniques flow from this approach, because it stresses understanding first and technique second. The therapist can borrow techniques from other approaches and incorporate them into an existential framework. Diagnosis, testing, and external measurements are not deemed important. The approach can be very confrontive.
Person-centered therapy	This approach uses few techniques but stresses the attitudes of the therapist. Basic techniques include active listening and hearing, reflection of feelings, clarification, and "being there" for the client. Support and reassurance are often used when they are appropriate. This model does not include diagnostic testing, interpretation, taking a case history, and questioning or probing for information.
Gestalt therapy	A wide range of techniques is designed to intensify experiencing and to integrate conflicting feelings. Techniques include confrontation, dialogue with polarities, role playing, staying with feelings, reaching an impasse, and reliving and reexperiencing unfinished business in the forms of resentment and guilt. Gestalt dream work is very useful. Formal diagnosis and testing are not done. Interpretation is done by the client instead of by the therapist. Confrontation is often used to call attention to discrepancies. *How* and *what* questions are used.
Transactional analysis (TA)	A script-analysis checklist, or questionnaire, is useful in recognizing early injunctions. Many techniques of TA and Gestalt can be fruitfully combined. Some type of diagnosis may be useful to assess the nature of a problem. Clients participate actively in diagnosis and interpretations and are taught to make their own interpretations and value judgments. Confrontation is often used, and contracts are essential. Questioning is a basic part of TA.
Behavior therapy	The main techniques are systematic desensitization, implosive therapy, assertive training, aversion therapy, and operant conditioning. All are based on principles of learning, and all are geared toward behavior change. Diagnosis; data gathering; *what, how,* and *when,* (but not *why*) questions; and testing procedures are frequently used.
Rational-emotive therapy (RET)	The approach uses many diverse procedures such as teaching, reading, homework assignments, and applying the scientific method for problem solving. Techniques are designed to engage the client in a critical evaluation of a particular philosophy of life. A specific diagnosis is made. The therapist interprets, questions, probes, challenges, and confronts the client.
Reality therapy	This approach is an active, directive, didactic therapy. It often uses a contract; when the contract is fulfilled, therapy is terminated. It does not follow a medical model of diagnosis and evaluation. It aims at having the clients make their own interpretations and value judgments. This approach can be supportive and confrontational.

counselor can practice these skills in a practicum in the classroom. Eventually, these skills need to be integrated and tied to some type of theoretical framework.

To sum up, counselors need to have a basic knowledge of human behavior and counseling theory. They need to learn the skills to apply this knowledge in actual coun-

TABLE 12-6 Applications and contributions

Psychoanalytic therapy	This approach provides a conceptual basis for understanding unconscious dynamics, the importance of early development as related to present difficulties, anxiety and ego defenses as a way of coping, and the nature of transference and countertransference.
Existential therapy	This model provides an approach for individual and group counseling and therapy and for work with children and adolescents, and it can be usefully integrated into classroom practices. Its major contribution is the recognition of the need for a subjective approach based on a complete view of the human condition. It calls attention to the need for a philosophical statement on what it means to be a person.
Person-centered therapy	This approach has wide applicability to individual and group counseling and therapy for student-centered teaching. This approach's unique contribution is having the client take an active stance and assume responsibility to direct the course of his or her own therapy. This approach challenged the role of the traditional therapist, who commonly used techniques of diagnosis, probing, and interpretation, and challenged the view of the therapist as expert.
Gestalt therapy	These techniques are well suited for individual and group counseling and therapy. They are applicable to teaching/learning situations in classrooms. Gestalt's main contribution is the emphasis on doing and experiencing rather than on merely talking about feelings.
Transactional analysis (TA)	This approach can be applied to parent/child relations, to the classroom, to group and individual counseling and therapy, and to marriage counseling. A key contribution is its attention to transactions related to the functioning of ego states.
Behavior therapy	This approach has wide applicability to individual and group therapy, institutions, and the schools and other learning situations. It is a pragmatic approach based on experimental validation of results. Progress (or lack of it) can be continually assessed and new techniques developed.
Rational-emotive therapy (RET)	This approach calls attention to the importance of thinking as a basis for personal disturbances. Its main contribution is that it points out the necessity of practice and doing to actually change problem behavior.
Reality therapy	This approach was originally designed for working with youth in detention facilities. It is now widely used by educators in elementary and secondary schools. It is also applicable to individual therapy, groups, and marriage counseling.

seling situations. And they need to be healthy individuals who are able to employ these skills in such a way that the process becomes an extension of their uniqueness as a person.

Recommended supplementary readings

At this stage you may be interested in books that deal with an eclectic approach to psychotherapy, as resources to help you develop a basis for integrating the various theories and apply them to practice. Four excellent sources emphasize the counseling process and basic procedures and techniques:

A Primer of Eclectic Psychotherapy (Palmer, 1980) provides a very clear presentation of the stages in the therapy process, along with special techniques applied to adults, children, families, groups, and involuntary clients.

Psychotherapy: An Eclectic Approach (Garfield, 1980) provides a sound and readable treatment of both client and therapist variables in the therapeutic process. It also describes other specific variables and procedures associated with the various stages of therapy. There is a very good summary of research in psychotherapy and of evaluating the effectiveness of therapy.

Therapeutic Psychology: Fundamentals of Counseling and Psychotherapy (Brammer & Shostrom, 1977) provides a fine comprehensive review of the counseling process and counseling procedures from an eclectic framework. It has clear descriptions of commonly used counseling techniques.

Counseling and Psychotherapy: Skills, Theories, and Practice (Ivey & Simek-Downing, 1980) describes steps toward a general theory in counseling and psychotherapy, as well as addressing the question Which theory for which individual under what conditions? Its focus is on basic dimensions of the counseling process and specific skills.

For those who are interested in an advanced treatment of the various approaches to counseling and therapy, I recommend *Theories of Counseling and Psychotherapy* (Patterson, 1973 and 1980), which also contains an excellent chapter on the convergences and divergences among the major systems.

For those who want resources that deal with a skills approach to counseling I especially recommend *The Skilled Helper* (Egan, 1975) and *Microcounseling: Innovations in Interviewing, Counseling, Psychotherapy, and Psychoeducation* (Ivey & Authier, 1978).

References and suggested readings

Books highly recommended as supplementary reading are marked with an asterisk.

Agel, J. (Ed.). *The radical therapist.* New York: Ballantine, 1971.

Aguilera, D., & Messick, J. *Crisis intervention: Theory and methodology* (2nd ed.). St. Louis: C. V. Mosby, 1974.

Arbuckle, D. *Counseling and psychotherapy: An existential-humanistic view* (3rd ed.). Boston: Allyn & Bacon, 1975.

Bergin, A. E. The evaluation of therapeutic outcomes. In A. E. Bergin & S. L. Garfield (Eds.), *Handbook of psychotherapy and behavior change: An empirical analysis.* New York: Wiley, 1971.

Bergin, A. E., & Lambert, M. J. The evaluation of therapeutic outcomes. In S. L. Garfield & A. E. Bergin (Eds.), *Handbook of psychotherapy and behavior change* (2nd ed.). New York: Wiley, 1978.

Bergin, A. E., & Strupp, H. H. *Changing frontiers in the science of psychotherapy.* Chicago: Aldine, 1972.

Brammer, L. *The helping relationship: Process and skills.* Englewood Cliffs, N. J.: Prentice-Hall, 1973.

* Brammer, L., & Shostrom, E. *Therapeutic psychology: Fundamentals of counseling and psychotherapy* (3rd ed.). Englewood Cliffs, N. J.: Prentice-Hall, 1977.

Carkhuff, R. *Helping and human relations* (2 vols.). New York: Holt, Rinehart & Winston, 1969.

Carkhuff, R., & Berenson, B. *Beyond counseling and therapy.* New York: Holt, Rinehart & Winston, 1967.

* Corey, G. *Theory and practice of group counseling.* Monterey, Calif.: Brooks/Cole, 1981.

* Corey, G., Corey, M., & Callanan, P. *Professional and ethical issues in counseling and psychotherapy.* Monterey, Calif.: Brooks/Cole, 1979.

Corey, G., Corey, M., Callanan, P., & Russell, M. *Group techniques.* Monterey, Calif.: Brooks/Cole, 1982.

Corlis, R., & Rabe, P. *Psychotherapy from the center: A humanistic view of change and of growth.* Scranton, Pa.: International Textbook, 1969.

Dixon, S. *Working with people in crisis.* St. Louis: C. V. Mosby, 1979.

Dugger, J. *The new professional: Introduction for the human services/mental health worker* (2nd ed.). Monterey, Calif.: Brooks/Cole, 1980.

Egan, G. *Face to face.* Monterey, Calif.: Brooks/Cole, 1973.

* Egan, G. *The skilled helper.* Monterey, Calif.: Brooks/Cole, 1975.

Eisenberg, S., & Delaney, D. *The counseling process* (2nd ed.). Chicago: Rand McNally, 1977.

Eysenck, H. J. *The effects of psychotherapy.* New York: International Science Press, 1966.

* Garfield, S. L. *Psychotherapy: An eclectic approach.* New York: Wiley, 1980.

Garfield, S. L., Prager, R. A., & Bergin, A. E. Evaluation of outcome in psychotherapy. *Journal of Consulting and Clinical Psychology, 1971, 37,* 307–313.

Goldenberg, I., & Goldenberg, H. *Family therapy: An overview.* Monterey, Calif.: Brooks/Cole, 1980.

* Gottman, J., & Leiblum, S. *How to do psychotherapy and how to evaluate it.* New York: Holt, Rinehart & Winston, 1974.

Hackney, H., & Cormier, L. S. *Counseling strategies and objectives.* Englewood Cliffs, N.J.: Prentice-Hall, 1979.

Hatcher, C., Brooks, B., & Associates. *Innovations in counseling psychology: Developing new roles, settings, techniques.* San Francisco: Jossey-Bass, 1977.

* Ivey, A., & Authier, J. *Microcounseling: Innovations in interviewing, counseling, psychotherapy, and psychoeducation.* Springfield, Ill.: Charles C Thomas, 1978.

* Ivey, A., & Simek-Downing, L. *Counseling and psychotherapy: Skills, theories, and practice.* Englewood Cliffs, N.J.: Prentice-Hall, 1980.

Krumboltz, J. Promoting adaptive behavior: New answers to familiar questions. In J. Krumboltz (Ed.), *Revolution in counseling.* Boston: Houghton Mifflin, 1966.

Lewis, J. *To be a therapist: The teaching and learning.* New York: Brunner/Mazel, 1978.

Luborsky, L., Singer, B., & Luborsky, L. Comparative studies of psychotherapies. *Archives of General Psychiatry, 1975, 32,* 995–1008.

Lyon, W., with Duke, B. *Introduction to human services.* Reston, Virginia: Reston Publishing Co., 1981.

Meltzoff, J., & Kornreich, M. *Research in psychotherapy.* New York: Atherton Press, 1970.

Okun, B., & Rappaport, L. *Working with families: An introduction to family therapy.* North Scituate, Mass.: Duxbury Press, 1980.

* Palmer, J. O. *A primer of eclectic psychotherapy.* Monterey, Calif.: Brooks/Cole, 1980.

Patterson, C. H. *Theories of counseling and psychotherapy* (2nd ed.). New York: Harper & Row, 1973.

* Patterson, C. H. *Theories of counseling and psychotherapy* (3rd ed.). New York: Harper & Row, 1980.

Paul, G. L. Strategy of outcome research in psychotherapy. *Journal of Consulting Psychology, 1967, 31,* 109–118.

Rogers, C. *Client-centered therapy.* Boston: Houghton Mifflin, 1951.

Strupp, H. H., Hadley, S. W., & Gomes-Schwartz, B. *Psychotherapy for better or worse: The problem of negative effects.* New York: Aronson, 1977.

* Truax, C., & Carkhuff, R. *Toward effective counseling and psychotherapy.* Chicago: Aldine, 1967.

Wrenn, G. Two psychological worlds: An attempted rapprochement. In J. Krumboltz (Ed.), *Revolution in counseling.* Boston: Houghton Mifflin, 1966.

13

Ethical Issues in Counseling and Psychotherapy

Introduction

This chapter introduces you to some of the ethical principles and issues that will be a basic part of your professional practice. My main purpose is to stimulate you to do further thinking on these issues so that you can form a sound basis for decision making. I take the position that you will ultimately have to discover your own guidelines for responsible practice, and that as a professional you will not be able to rely on ready-made answers or prescriptions given from professional organizations.

I am not saying that students and practitioners are totally free to choose any set of ethics merely on the basis of personal whim or preference. Various professional organizations have established codes that provide broad guidelines. Some of these are the American Psychological Association (APA), the American Personnel and Guidance Association, the American Psychiatric Association, the American Academy of Psychotherapists, the American Association of Marriage and Family Therapists, the National Association of Social Workers, and the Association for Humanistic Psychology. Additionally, the many regional, state, and local professional organizations for social workers, psychologists, counselors, and other mental-health specialists have developed their own guidelines. As mental-health practitioners, you should know the ethical codes of your specialty and should be aware of the consequences of practicing in ways that are not sanctioned by your professional organizations.

The guidelines that are offered by most of these organizations are usually quite broad. Thus, they are not sufficiently explicit to deal with every situation, and it behooves you as a responsible practitioner to make specific decisions using informed and sound judgment. As you become involved in counseling, you may find that interpreting these guidelines and applying them to particular situations demand the utmost ethical sensitivity. Even among responsible practitioners there are differences of opinion over the application of established ethical principles to specific situations. Consequently, a vital dimension of becoming a professional counselor or therapist is facing questions to which there are no obvious answers. You will have to struggle with yourself to decide how to act in ways that will further the best interests of your clients.

Counselor-education programs ought to involve seminars in ethical principles and practices. Students should, as a beginning, thoroughly familiarize themselves with the ethical standards developed by the appropriate professional organizations. They should be sensitive to any ethical problems that arise in their practicum experiences and then discuss the problems in a seminar session or consult their supervisors. Part of a counselor's education is developing a sense of sound judgment, and basic ethical issues should receive top priority in a person's training.

In recent years there has been increased interest in developing ethical standards to guide practitioners and increased awareness of the role and responsibility of counselors and psychologists in alleviating human suffering. No longer can the practitioner be safely tucked away in the office; the trend is toward urging social action by professionals in cases of social injustice. Many professional associations emphasize the ethical responsibility of professionals to society by exerting their influence collectively against such wrongs as oppression of and discrimination against women and minority groups, the continuation of racism in society, the neglect of the aged, and certain inhumane practices against children. Seminars and workshops are conducted to awaken the dulled consciences of many professionals and to expand awareness of their personal responsibility. The trend is toward encouraging professionals to actively apply their knowledge and skills to the underlying causes of social injustice. It behooves the counselor or therapist to be acquainted with pressing social and political issues that have a direct bearing on human rights, and it is important to determine what definite steps to take in effecting necessary changes within the system. In short, psychological counselors are discovering that, to bring about significant individual change, they cannot remain blind and deaf to the major social ills that often create and foster individual sickness; they must become active agents of constructive social change.

Therapist's responsibilities

The therapist has a responsibility primarily to the client. But, because the client does not live in a vacuum and is affected by other relationships, the therapist has a responsibility also to the family members of the client, to the therapist's own agency, to a referring agency, to society, and to the profession.

There are times when a conflict of responsibilities arises or when there are clashes between the client's perception of his or her welfare and the therapist's perception.

The APA (1977) states that "the psychologist attempts to terminate a clinical or consulting relationship when it is reasonably clear to the psychologist that the client is not benefiting from it" (p. 23). But what does the therapist do when he or she believes that the client is "getting nowhere," but the client resists termination? Consider the following.

John generally shows up for his weekly session, but he typically reports that he has nothing really to discuss. He does not seem willing to do much for himself either during or outside the sessions. The therapist has confronted him a number of times on his unwillingness to invest much of himself in counseling and has shared with him that the sessions seem not to be of benefit. The client agrees, yet continues to return. Finally, the therapist becomes more forceful and judges that it is best to terminate this relationship. John raises objections and says that he does not want to end the counseling sessions. What should the therapist do? How long should the therapist continue to see John if he agrees to continue? What should the therapist do if John says he really does not want a therapist but just a friend to visit?

In a similar situation, what should a therapist do when he or she judges that a client should be referred, either because the therapist feels unqualified to continue working with the client or because the therapist believes that the type or duration of treatment at hand is too limited for what the client should receive? For example, Sue has been seeing her high school counselor, Mr. Smith, weekly for two months, and she feels that the sessions are extremely helpful to her. The counselor agrees that she is making progress but is also aware of some other realities: his time is limited, because he has 450 counselees; the school has a policy that long-term counseling should not be provided but that, when indicated, a referral should be made; and Sue's emotional problems are deep enough to indicate intensive psychotherapy. Because of these realities, he suggests a referral to Sue and gives her the reasons for the referral. Assume that Sue responds in one of these two ways: One, she might agree to accept the referral and see a private therapist. In this case, when does the counselor's responsibility to Sue end? The guideline is that the responsibility for the client's welfare would continue until she could begin seeing the other therapist. Even after that, some form of consultation with the other therapist might be in order. Two, Sue might refuse to be referred and say that she does not want to see anyone else. Should the counselor terminate the relationship? Should he continue but still encourage Sue to accept an eventual referral? What if the counselor feels that he is getting "in over his head" with Sue? The guideline from the APA (1967) is that "the psychologist carefully weighs the possible harm to the client, to himself, and to the profession that might ensue from continuing the relationship" (p. 67) when the client refuses a referral. The *Ethical Standards* of the American Personnel and Guidance Association (APGA, 1981) provides the following guideline on this issue: "If the member determines an inability to be of professional assistance to the client, the member must either avoid initiating the counseling relationship or immediately terminate that relationship. In either event, the member must suggest appropriate alternatives." As can be seen, there is frequently a fine line between operating in the client's best interests and dealing with the realities and limitations of a counselor's capacities in providing this help.

Another major ethical issue relating to client welfare is the use of drugs in mental-health and community clinics, rehabilitation agencies, psychiatric hospitals, and the schools. As a general guideline, the use of drugs is acceptable for therapeutic purposes in the client's best interests and not for making the client more tolerable to the staff. When drugs are used, a collaborating physician should provide appropriate safeguards for the client. Unfortunately, drugs are commonly used to sedate a client or repress problematic behavior for the benefit of others rather than to effect a change in the client. The counselor should be aware of the misuses of drugs and the need to take a position on the issue.

Therapist competence and issues in professional education and training

As a basic ethical principle, therapists are expected to recognize their own personal and professional limitations. Ethical therapists do not employ diagnostic or treatment procedures that are beyond the scope of their training, nor do they accept clients whose personal functioning is seriously impaired, unless they are qualified to work with those clients. A therapist who becomes aware of his or her lack of competence in a particular case has the responsibility to seek consultation with colleagues or a supervisor or to make a referral.

CRITERIA FOR DETERMINING COMPETENCE

What is the basis on which practitioners can decide whether they are qualified, or competent, to offer specific professional services? The APA's *Ethical Standards of Psychologists* (1977) provides the general standard: "Psychologists recognize the boundaries of their competence and the limitations of their techniques and only provide services, use techniques, or offer opinions as professionals that meet recognized standards" (p. 22). The APGA's *Ethical Standards* (1981) states: "With regard to the delivery of professional services, members should accept only those positions for which they are professionally qualified." Such a guideline still leaves unanswered the question "How can I recognize the boundaries of my competence, and how can I know when I have exceeded them?" This issue is not neatly solved by the mere possession of advanced degrees or of licenses and credentials. In my opinion there are many people who complete master's and doctoral programs in a mental-health specialty who still lack the skills needed to effectively function as practitioners. Further, licenses and certification are not necessarily any better criteria of competence than degrees. On the one hand, I have encountered some licensed practitioners who do not appear to possess the competencies specified by their licenses. On the other hand, I have worked with some unlicensed colleagues and even some undergraduate students who seemed far more competent than some licensed counselors, psychologists, and social workers.

Licenses mainly assure the public that the licensees have completed some type of formal academic program, have been exposed to a certain number of hours of supervision, and have completed a *minimum* number of hours of professional experience (some of which has been supervised by a licensed person). However, licenses do not assure the public that these practitioners can effectively and competently do what their licenses permit them to do. Further, licenses typically do not specify the types of client or problem the practitioner is competent to deal with or the specialized techniques he or she is skilled in. For example, a licensed psychologist may work very effectively with a certain population of adults yet not be qualified by virtue of training or experience to work with children or adolescents. The APA standard and most licensing regulations do specify that licensees are to engage only in those methods of intervention for which they have adequate training. Ultimately, this puts a lot of weight on practitioners to exercise honesty and good judgment in determining which services they are actually competent to provide.

Practitioners must continually assess their competence as related to particular clients to judge whether they should enter into relationships with them. There will be times when experienced counselors or therapists will need to consult colleagues or a specialist in a related field. It is possible that a therapist who has worked with one client over a long period of time might lose his or her perspective with that client. At times, it is wise for therapists to confer with colleagues to share their perceptions of what is occurring with their clients, within themselves, and between them and their clients. If a client continually complains of physical symptoms (such as headaches), it would seem essential that any organic problem be ruled out by a physician before the assumption is made that the client's problem is psychologically caused. What if the client had a brain tumor and the psychological counselor failed to refer him or her to a physician for a physical examination?

If experienced practitioners need occasional consultation, it goes without saying that beginning therapists need supervision and continuing consultation. In my work with counselors-in-training, I have found most of them eager for direction and supervision. They often ask for extra time and are quite willing to discuss openly their reactions, blockages, frustrations, and confusions in practicum meetings. Realizing that they need skills in working effectively with the problems that clients bring, they tend to want a chance to discuss their fieldwork. It thus becomes an ethical and practical concern that appropriate supervision be given to the intern, for the sake of the client's welfare and the intern's professional growth. A problem can arise when the counselor intern is placed in a community agency and the on-the-job supervisor is so steeped in the duties of the agency that he or she has little time left over for supervising interns. I have encouraged the counselor interns to actively and aggressively seek supervision and, at times, demand that they be given an hour a week to explore their case load. If the supervisor does not initiate close supervision, then trainees will have to learn to continue to ask for what they need.

TRAINING AND SUPERVISION

Related to the issue of competence are the questions What education, training, and supervision are necessary for ensuring competent practice? and What experiences are necessary for prospective counselors? There are two points of view about the preparation necessary for counseling. On the one hand is the position that clinical work of any form, even under supervision, should not be undertaken until late in a candidate's doctoral program or even until the postdoctoral period. This view regards as dangerous any untrained and unseasoned "amateurs" who have not acquired a Ph.D. and considers it unwise (perhaps unethical) to allow a person to practice counseling below a doctoral level. On the other hand are those who favor training in counseling and various practicum experiences at an early stage in the student's program. This viewpoint endorses the initation of supervised practical experience as early in the course of preparation as the maturity and responsibility of the individual student allow. I subscribe to the latter viewpoint. My view is that a counseling program ought to incorporate both academic and experiential phases and that counselors can be effectively trained at the sub-doctoral level.

CONTINUING EDUCATION

I would like to emphasize that professional competence is not something that we attain once and for all, even by the earning of advanced degrees and licenses. Continuing professional education is a must to keep up to date with new knowledge in your professional specialty, as well as to sharpen your skills. Most professional organizations support efforts to make continuing education a mandatory condition of relicensing. It is still possible in some cases to stop taking courses, workshops, and other forms of supervised experiences once an advanced degree, a license, or both have been earned. I question the ethics of practitioners who fail to keep current with new developments. I would like to see practitioners decide for themselves the kind of in-service and continuing education that would be most personally meaningful. This might include a combination of formal course work, attendance at professional workshops, participation in professional conferences where one can be challenged and stimulated, and some opportunities for having one's work observed and critiqued by other colleagues. This type of personalized continuing education and training seems more meaningful than merely complying with state regulations that stipulate completion of a minimum number of hours in a given area.

The client/therapist relationship

FACTORS AFFECTING THE CLIENT'S DESIRE TO ENTER THE RELATIONSHIP

The APGA (1981) provides the following general guideline on the issue of the client/counselor relationship: "The member must inform the client of the purposes, goals, techniques, rules of procedure and limitations that may affect the relationship at or before the time that the counseling relationship is entered." The APA (1967) specifies that "the psychologist informs his prospective client of the important aspects of the potential relationship that might affect the client's decision to enter the relationship" (p. 67). Several factors are likely to affect the client's decision. For example, the recording of an interview by videotape or by tape recorder might affect the client. Others besides the client and the therapist might listen to or view the tapes. Also, some agencies use observation through one-way glass, so that supervisors or trainees can monitor the sessions. Some school districts have a policy that, if clients reveal that they use drugs, the counselor is obliged to report their names to the principal. If a girl reveals to a counselor that she is pregnant or wants information about contraceptives or abortion, the counselor must report the girl to the school nurse, who must then inform the parents. Often people are required by others to seek counseling or psychiatric help; they do not voluntarily initiate a therapeutic relationship but are subjects of "mandatory counseling." It is clear that in each of these instances certain policies or conditions can affect the client's decision to enter a therapeutic relationship. Thus, it is ethical practice for the therapist to make known to the potential client the limitations of the relationship. Let us examine the issues underlying practices that may affect the therapeutic relationship.

First, there are the ethics of taping an interview or of using one-way glass for observational purposes. A clear guideline in using either of those procedures is to secure the client's permission in advance; it is considered unethical to make use of the procedures without the client's awareness and consent. Tape-recording for supervision purposes is a common procedure in counselor education. This can be important for the client as well as for the therapist. Clients may wish to listen to some earlier sessions as their therapy progresses. Their anxiety can be diminished by letting them know that observers wish to focus on the therapist's movement in the session. Whereas clients' anxiety may lessen, however, the therapist's anxiety may remain.

I typically find that therapists (beginning or experienced) are hesitant to tape-record their interviews. Many times a therapist will build a case for not recording the interview based, supposedly, on the client's mistrust or discomfort. I question where the mistrust and anxiety are—with the client or with the therapist. My hope is that supervisors can create a climate in which student counselors, even though they may be anxious, will be able voluntarily to bring in tapes for consultation. The supervisor's attitude is important. If supervisors adopt a harsh, critical, domineering style, then the intern is apt to conceal any element of uncertainty. Instead, if the counselor-in-training and the supervisor take the approach that one can learn by experience and that the trainee is not expected to be a polished therapist, then the chances of exposing oneself to opportunities for learning will be maximized.

A second issue, as mentioned earlier, that might affect the client's decision to enter a counseling relationship is that, unfortunately, some school districts have policies that are geared more to the legal protection of the district than to helping students in crisis. For example, some school counselors are prohibited from exploring a pregnant girl's alternatives unless the parents are notified and brought into the conference. This practice may have merit at times, but what becomes of the terrified girl who feels that she either cannot or, for her own reasons, does not want to tell her parents that she is pregnant? Must the counselor refuse even to see her or to have a session in which she can at least express her feelings of panic? In a related issue, I have been told by continuation-high-school counselors in some of my counselor-in-service training workshops that they must report the names of any students who admit using drugs. This puts a severe strain on a potential counseling relationship when we consider the reality that most their clients are dropouts from regular high school and drug users as well. If these counselors follow school policy, how much "real counseling" will occur? A point of ethics is that at the very least the counselor is obligated to inform potential clients of the limitations of confidentiality. Then they are able to decide how much they want to disclose or whether they even want to begin a counseling relationship.

A third issue to be explored here is whether therapy can occur under mandatory conditions. Is *mandatory counseling* a contradiction in terms? What can a counselor do when the population he or she serves consists of those who are required to come in for counseling but are generally unwilling to get involved? The issue is the ethics of forcing counseling on a person, even if he or she is clearly opposed to any form of therapeutic intervention. As a counselor, consider your position in the following four instances:

1. The client is sent to your private practice as a condition of probation. He is not much interested in counseling, but he is interested in being "out."
2. You work in a youth rehabilitation center, and you must see many resistant clients who are in your office only because they have been ordered to report to you.

3. The parents send their adolescent daughter to see you in the local counseling clinic, and she comes unwillingly.
4. A student with failing grades reports to your office for "counseling," because the school has a policy that any student who has an "F" must do so. He really does not want to be in your office.

In my opinion therapy can be effective only if the client is willing to cooperate with the therapist in working toward mutually acceptable goals. The clients mentioned above may not be willing to be cooperative. One avenue open to counselors is to present the resistant client with some of the possibilities that counseling might offer. For example, the counselor may agree to see the adolescent girl for three sessions simply to explore the possibilities of that relationship and then to terminate therapy if the girl still does not want to continue. The school counselor can see the student once and explain what he or she has to offer and then leave it to the student to decide whether he wants to seek counseling.

SOCIAL AND PERSONAL RELATIONSHIPS WITH CLIENTS

A special issue relating to the client/therapist relationship is how social and personal relationships mix with therapeutic ones. In general, although I think that friendships can be therapeutic (and good ones are), I find it difficult to be primarily concerned with a therapeutic relationship and at the same time maintain a personal and social relationship with a client beyond the sessions. Two questions that could be raised are Will I confront and challenge a client whom I am involved with socially as much as I do clients whom I have strictly professional relationships with? Will my own needs for keeping the friendship interfere with my therapeutic activities and thus defeat the purposes of therapy? One of the reasons that most counselors cannot counsel members of their own family is that they are too close to them, and their own needs interlock with the others' problems. The same dynamic, as I see it, operates in a social relationship. Another potential problem that occurs is that by the very nature of the therapeutic relationship counselors are in a more powerful and influential position than clients. Thus, there is the danger of subtle exploitation of clients when the relationship becomes other than a professional one. On this point the APA (1977) has the following principle on "dual relationships" with clients:

> Psychologists are continually cognizant of their own needs and of their inherently powerful position *vis à vis* clients, in order to avoid exploiting their trust and dependency. Psychologists make every effort to avoid dual relationships with clients and/or relationships which might impair their professional judgment or increase the risk of client exploitation [p. 23].

The APGA's (1981) guideline on this issue is "Dual relationships with clients that might impair the member's objectivity and professional judgment (e.g., as with close friends or relatives, sexual intimacies with any client) must be avoided and/or the counseling relationship terminated through referral to another competent professional." The issue of combining social with professional relationships does not have a simple answer. For example, some peer counselors contend that the friendships they have with people before or during counseling are a positive factor in building trust that leads to productive therapeutic results. What is essential is that counselors develop an awareness of their own motivations, as well as the motivations of their clients. They must honestly and accurately assess the impact that a social relationship might have on the client/therapist relationship. Further, counselors who as a matter of course tend to develop most of their friendships from their relationships with clients would do well to examine the degree to which they are using the power of their position to make social contacts.

SEXUAL INVOLVEMENTS WITH CLIENTS

Another pertinent issue that is currently controversial is that of erotic and sexual contact between clients and therapists. A number of professional organizations have established subcommittees to investigate and deal with ethical violations involving sexual activities of therapists with their clients. Licensing boards have suspended or revoked the licenses of some practitioners who became sexually involved with clients. Most professional codes of conduct now explicitly state that it is unethical to have sexual relations with one's clients or their spouse/partner. In my estimation most professional counselors and therapists take the position that sexual intimacy between therapists and clients is both unethical and professionally inappropriate.

There are several reasons for such a position. The general argument typically involves the abuse of the power that therapists have by virtue of their function and role. Clients are usually more vulnerable than the therapist. They are the ones who are revealing themselves in deeply personal ways. They are sharing their fears, past secrets, fantasies, hopes, sexual desires and conflicts, and it could be easy to take advantage of them. Another reason for the negative view of sexual involvement is that it is likely to foster dependence. Clients can very easily come to view therapists in an idealized way, especially when they see them in the limited context of the office. They may settle for this type of minimal contact, instead of working on the quality of their relationships with their spouse, or they may not look outside of the therapy relationship for longer-term meaningful relationships with others.

Most would say that, if therapists become sexually active with clients, then they lose their capacity for objectivity. These therapists will probably be far more concerned about the feelings their clients have for them than about challenging them to take an honest look at their life. Yet another reason for this position is that clients who have experienced sexual involvement with their therapists often tend to feel taken advantage of and used. They may discount the value of anything they learned in their therapy and may also be closed to any further kind of psychological assistance out of their bitterness and resentment. This is true even if some clients actually provoke and in some ways invite a sexual relationship. It becomes extremely important that therapists recognize their own areas of countertransference (extreme need to be needed or seen as sexually attractive), refuse to collaborate in sexually seductive game playing, and instead confront their clients with what is occurring.

When I have discussed the issue of sexual involvement between client and therapist with students, they have almost universally viewed it as unethical and unprofessional. In these discussions it has been brought out that the issue is more complex than merely whether to have sexual intercourse with a client. Although most of my students seem intellectually clear about the hope that they will not engage in intercourse with future clients, they do struggle with matters such as sexual attractions that they may have toward clients, with the attractions of their clients to them, with sexual fantasies and desires toward clients, and with touching. It is clear that romantic involvements and sexual behavior that do not lead to intercourse can have the similar effect of interfering with therapy. The primary focus of the sessions could be on sexual seduction and indirect methods of meeting the therapist's needs. Ideally, practitioners will be able to accept their sexual feelings and desires toward certain clients and at the same time see the distinction between *having* these feelings (and perhaps even expressing them to their clients if it is appropriate) and *acting* on them. This is an area in which beginning counselors can greatly benefit from consultation sessions with a supervisor. In this way they can explore how their own needs might negatively intrude into their work, and they can learn how to deal with their feelings in such a way that clients do not suffer.

TOUCHING AS A PART OF THE CLIENT/THERAPIST RELATIONSHIP

A topic that students inevitably raise is whether to engage in touching of their clients. They ask: "How can I tell when touching will be helpful or not?" "Do I have to hold myself back from expressing affection or compassion in a physical way?" "What if my touch is misinterpreted by the client?" "If I feel sexually drawn to certain clients, is it dangerous to express physical closeness?"

Although I agree with the position that erotic contact with clients is unethical, I think that nonerotic contact in the form of touching can be therapeutically valuable. What is important is that touching not be done as a technique, or something that a counselor does not genuinely feel. Touches that are not authentic and not spontaneous are detected as such; if clients cannot believe your touch, why should they believe your words or you? Another important dimension of this issue is the client's readiness and need to be touched. Sometimes counselors reach out too soon to comfort clients who are crying and expressing some pain. Clients do need at times to fully experience and express their pain, and touching them sometimes serves to cut off what they are feeling. Counselors may reach out physically not to meet the needs of their clients but to comfort themselves, because they are uncomfortable with the pain their clients are expressing. Although this is a complex issue, therapists need to be honest with themselves and their clients, and they need to be aware of whose needs are primarily being met when they have physical contact.

Confidentiality

Every therapist must come to grips with the thorny issue of the confidentiality of information. Surely no genuine therapy can occur unless clients trust the privacy of their revelations to their therapists. It is the therapist's responsibility to define the degree of confidentiality that can be promised. In making their determinations, therapists must consider the requirements of the institution in which they work and the clientele they serve. Although most therapists agree on the essential value of confidentiality, they realize that it cannot be considered an absolute. There are times when confidential information must be divulged, and there are many instances in which whether to keep or to break confidentiality becomes a cloudy issue.

Because these circumstances are not clearly defined by accepted ethical standards, counselors must exercise professional judgment. In general, confidentiality must be broken when it becomes clear that clients might do serious harm to either themselves or others. The following guideline is given by the APA (1977): "Information received in confidence is revealed only after most careful deliberation and when there is clear and imminent danger to an individual or to society, and then only to appropriate professional workers or public authorities" (p. 22). The APGA (1981) guideline is "When the client's condition indicates that there is clear and imminent danger to the client or others, the member must take reasonable personal action or inform responsible authorities. Consultation with other professionals must be used where possible." The crux of the issue often comes down to *when* do therapists know that their clients are likely to be a "clear and imminent danger" to themselves or others. Are all threats to be followed up with a report to authorities? What if the client does not make a verbal threat, yet the therapist has a strong hunch that the client could be suicidal or homicidal?

What is expected of counselors is that they use sound professional judgment, and that they seek consultation when they are in doubt about a given individual or situation. Further, those practitioners who work in mental-health clinics or agencies should inform their supervisors or directors and document in writing the nature of these consultations. If they determine that a client poses a serious danger of violence to others, they are obliged to use reasonable care to protect the potential victims. In addition to notifying the proper authorities, the intended victims should be notified; and in the case of a minor, the parents should also be notified. In this regard, counselors need to inform their clients of the possible actions they must take to protect a third party. Once again, because there are frequently no clear-cut answers, as these situations are often unique, it is a good policy for counselors to consult with professional colleagues for other opinions and suggestions concerning the gravity of a case, as well as for suggestions on how to proceed.

Because confidentiality is so vitally related to the therapeutic relationship, it is well for therapists to discuss its nature and purpose with their clients during the early sessions. When assuring their clients that what they reveal in sessions will in general be kept confidential, therapists should also tell clients the major circumstances in which this will not be so. Therapists should point out that they have obligations to others besides their clients. The APGA's *Ethical Standards* (1981) stresses the importance of confidentiality. "The counseling relationship and information resulting therefrom must be kept confidential, consistent with the obligations of the member as a professional person. In a group counseling setting, the counselor must set a norm of confidentiality regarding all group participants' disclosures."

With these general principles in mind, what would your position be if you were the counselor in the following four cases:

1. You have been seeing an adolescent girl in a community mental-health clinic for three months. Lately she has complained of severe depression and says that life seems hopeless. She is threatening suicide and even wants details from you concerning how she can successfully carry through with it. Are you obliged to disclose this information to her guardians because she is under legal age? What would you tell your client? What kind of consultation would you seek, if any?

2. Your client reveals to you that he has stolen some expensive laboratory equipment from the college where you are a counselor. A week later the dean calls you into her office to talk with you about this particular client. What do you tell the dean? And what do you not tell her?

3. In the course of a counseling session, a youth tells you that he is planning to do serious physical harm to a fellow student. What would you tell your client? Would you report this plan to anyone and, if so, to whom?

4. Your client is a 15-year-old girl sent to you by her parents. One day her parents request a session to discuss their daughter's progress and to see what they can do to help. What kind of information can you share with the parents, and what can you not disclose? What might

you discuss with the girl before you see her parents? What would you do if she made it clear that she did not want you to see her parents or tell them anything?

It is generally accepted that therapists will have no professional contact with the family or friends of a client without first securing the client's permission. It is accepted in addition that information obtained from therapeutic relationships should be discussed with others for professional purposes only and with persons who are clearly related to the case. In my opinion it is good practice to inform the client early in the relationship that you may be discussing certain details of the relationship with a supervisor or a colleague. This practice can also apply to the use of a tape recording. There are times when a therapist may want to share a recording of a particular session with a colleague simply to confirm his or her perspective by obtaining another viewpoint on the dynamics of the therapeutic relationship. The APGA's (1981) guideline on this issue is "The member may choose to consult with any other professionally competent person about a client."

The use of tape recordings and videotapings is also a part of the issue of safeguarding the confidentiality of client information. If these methods are part of the therapist's practice, he or she must secure the client's permission before making tapes. It is good practice to discuss with the client the purposes and possible uses for such tapes, and, of course, they should be shared only with professional persons who are related to the case or who are consulting with the therapist or supervising his or her work.

The issue of confidentiality takes on added dimensions for students who are involved in some type of practicum or internship as part of their program. In most cases, these counselor interns are required to keep notes on the proceedings with their individual clients or the members of their group. Also, group-supervision sessions at a clinic or university typically entail open discussions about the clients with whom these counselor interns are working. These discussions should always be conducted in a professional manner. If a particular individual client is being discussed, this person's identity can be protected. Also, I tend to focus on the intern's dynamics more than on a detailed presentation about a client. I have made it a practice to ask those interns whom I supervise to discuss this situation with their clients at the outset. If interns make clear that *they* will be the focus of any discussions, and that their clients will not be "an interesting case to dissect and analyze," then the chances are greatly increased that clients will be open in their sessions. With regard to safeguarding any information that is recorded about clients, there are many situations in which interns can actually show their clients what they are writing and discuss these notes with them. Again, last names might not have to be used. If clients receive this type of openness from their counselors, I have found, they respond with greater frankness, for they feel that information will be used *for* them, not *against* them.

Confidentiality is very important in therapy groups or in group-counseling settings. The therapist or group leader has the responsibility of pointing out the problem. Confidentiality should be introduced and discussed as a group is initially formed, but it should also be discussed as the process continues. Clearly, group members share in the responsibility of retaining the privacy of members' disclosures. If confidentiality is not secured, the group soon tends to disintegrate, for people are not willing to reveal private material that they suspect will become public knowledge. I have found that betrayed confidence in group work is generally not due to malicious gossip but more often to the carelessness of members. A person may reveal certain facts or events, and, as gossip is passed from person to person, distortions occur. Hence, it is crucial that the group leader make every effort to caution the members to keep the nature of the sessions private. On this issue, the *Ethical Guidelines for Group Leaders,* as approved by the Association for Specialists in Group Work (1980), makes the following comment: "Group leaders shall protect members by defining clearly what confidentiality means, why it is important, and the difficulties involved in enforcement."

Therapist's values and philosophy of life

Therapists are sometimes taught that they should remain "value neutral," that they should avoid passing value judgments on to their clients, and that they should keep their own value system and philosophy of life separate from the therapeutic relationship. I maintain that we cannot exclude our values and beliefs from the relationships we establish with clients, unless we do routine and mechanical "counseling." It is sensible to me that we make our values known to our clients and that we be willing to discuss openly the issue of values in counseling. To do so implies that we at times reveal our own biases, philosophy, and central values. I believe that, whereas we have an obligation to expose our values, we have an ethical obligation to refrain from imposing them on clients.

I do not view therapy as a form of indoctrination whereby the therapist lectures to or manipulates the client to act or feel in the "right way." Unfortunately, there are many well-intentioned therapists who are overzealous in "helping" to "straighten people out." The implication is that, by virtue of the therapist's greater wisdom, he or she will provide answers for the troubled client. But therapy is not synonymous with preaching or teaching. This is not to say that therapists should maintain an indifferent, neutral, or passive role by simply silently listening to and accepting everything the client reports. Instead, I propose that therapists challenge the values of their clients, and, if they care, when they sense that certain behavior is destructive, they will confront their clients and invite them to examine the pay-offs and the consequences of their actions.

A core issue in therapy is the degree to which the therapist's values should enter into a therapeutic relationship. A therapist cannot have goals for clients and yet be devoid of value judgments, for goals are based on our values. Let me pose a series of questions designed to help you search yourself for your own tentative answers with respect to the role of values in therapy:

1. Is it desirable that therapists not pass on to their clients value judgments about their clients' behavior and choices? Is it possible for therapists to make value judgments only about events that affect their own personal life and pass no judgments on to clients?
2. What kind of person is the therapist who insists that he or she does not make value judgments with respect to certain actions of clients? Do therapists have to deny much of themselves to remain "neutral"?
3. How can therapists retain their own sense of values and remain true to themselves, yet at the same time allow their clients the freedom to select values and behavior that differ sharply from theirs?
4. What is the essential difference between therapists who honestly expose their core values when appropriate and those who in subtle ways "guide" their clients to accept their own values or the values that they deem to be good for their clients?
5. In what way is the issue of values at the core of all therapy? Is it possible to separate the role of values from therapy?
6. What would you do if your client had a value system sharply contradictory to yours? What if you honestly felt that your client's values were destructive to him or her or to others?

The question of the influence of the therapist's values on the client has ethical impli-cations when we consider that the goals and therapeutic methods of the therapist are expressions of his or her philosophy of life. Even though therapists do not directly teach the client or impose specific values, they do implement a philosophy of therapy, which is, in effect, a philosophy of life. Ethically sensitive therapists become aware of their own values and encourage their clients to develop values. As counselors, they confront and challenge the values of clients and help them decide whether they are truly living by them or merely incorporating parental and societal values without evaluating them. Therapists need to be alert to the possibility of manipulating a client to accept values wholesale, for to do so would mean that they would simply become another parent substitute.

As an example of the influence that the therapist's philosophy of life can have on a client and of possible clashes over values between the client and the therapist, consider this case: The client is a married woman in her late thirties, with three children who are approaching their teen years. She has been in weekly individual therapy for six months. She is struggling to decide whether she wishes to remain married to her husband, whom she perceives as boring, uninvolved with her and the children, complacent, and overly involved in his work. Although she has urged him to join her in marriage coun-seling or some form of therapy for himself, he has consistently refused. He maintains that he is fine and that she is the one with the problems. She tells the therapist that she would divorce him immediately, "if it were not for the kids," and that, when the children finish high school, she will surely leave him. She is, however, presently ambivalent; she cannot decide whether she wants to accept the security that she now has (along with the deadness of her relationship with her husband) or whether she is willing to leave this security and risk making a better life for herself (as well as risk being stuck with even less than she has now). She has been contemplating having an affair so that someone other than her husband can meet her physical and emotional needs. She is also exploring the possibility of finding a job so that she will be less dependent on her husband. By getting a job she could have outside opportunities for personal satisfaction and still remain in her present marriage by deciding to accept what she has with him.

Several value orientations emerge here, and it seems imperative that the therapist examine his or her own values and the effects they might have on the client's decisions. In this light, consider the following questions and decide what value judgments can be made:

1. One of her reasons for staying married is for the "sake of the children." What if you, as her therapist, were to accept this value and believe that she should not challenge her marriage because children need both parents and a divorce is damaging? What if your judgment would be that she is better off by divorcing now? What do your beliefs about divorce, marriage, and children have to do with her possible decisions?
2. She is talking about an affair as a possibility. What are your values concerning monogamy and extramarital sex? Do you believe that having an affair would be helpful or destructive for your client? What influence might your views have on her?
3. There is the value question of security versus possible growth. If you are conservative and place primary value on security, what effects might your view have on your client? What are some of your own life experiences that might have some bearing on her decisions?

I think that we engage in self-deception when we attempt to convince ourselves that our own experiences and systems of values and beliefs do not enter into our therapeutic relationships, and that they do not have an influence on a client's decision making and behavior. It behooves us to clarify our positions on such controversial issues as the following:

1. *Religion.* If therapists call themselves "Christian counselors" and have definite beliefs about the "good life," salvation, sin, and the person's relationship with Christ, and if they see these beliefs as a central part of the therapeutic process, how does their view influence clients who are nonreligious? Or non-Christian? Or who are Christian but do not accept the therapist's religious beliefs? What potential impact does an atheistic therapist have on a client with a definite religious persuasion? Can the atheistic therapist allow the client to hold on to religious values, or will the therapist confront these values as forms of "immature defenses"?

2. *Abortion.* When a client who is unmarried and pregnant and wants to explore alternatives enters counseling, how might you work if you fully believed that she should have an abortion? If you were firmly and morally opposed to abortion on the ground that it is murder? How would your values affect the range of the client's exploring for herself possible alternatives?

3. *Sex.* In working with clients who are homosexual, with married people who are engaging in extramarital sex, and with unmarried people who are living together, what role do your values play? If you see homosexuality as immoral or as a form of psychopathology, would you be genuinely able to allow clients to retain their homosexual behavior and values? What does your viewpoint on marriage have to do with a client's freedom to explore alternatives ranging from a "traditional" marriage to an "open" marriage?

4. *Drugs.* Many of your clients may use various drugs. What are your values relating to drugs, and how might they influence your capacity to work with drug users? Assume that your client is a habitual drug user and, whereas your perception is that he is escaping through drugs, your client disagrees and sees no harm in "getting loaded" or going on "acid trips." What might you do when there is a clash of values and perceptions in a case like this?

On this issue of the role of values in the therapeutic process, my colleagues and I (Corey, Corey, & Callanan, 1979) took the position that it is neither possible nor desirable for counselors to be scrupulously neutral with respect to values in the counseling relationship. Although we do not see it as the counselor's function to persuade clients to accept a certain value system, we do think that it is crucial for counselors to be clear about their own values and how they influence their work and the directions taken by clients. Because we believe that counselors' values do inevitably affect the therapeutic process, we contend that counselors should be willing to express their values openly when they are relevant to the questions that come up in their sessions with clients.

My colleagues and I cautioned counselors of the tendency to assume either of two extreme positions. On one extreme, there are those counselors who hold definite and absolute beliefs, and who see it as their job to exert influence on clients to adopt their values. These counselors tend to direct their clients toward the attitudes and values *they* judge as being "right." At the other extreme are those counselors who maintain that they should keep their values out of their counseling, and that the ideal is to strive for "value-free counseling." Because these counselors are so intent on remaining "objective," and because they are so anxious not to influence their clients, they run the risk of immobilizing themselves.

My associates and I took the position that clients often want and need to know where their therapists stand in order to test their own thinking. Thus, clients deserve an honest involvement on the part of their therapists. We also believe that it seems arrogant to make the assumption that counselors know what is best for others. Therefore, counselors should avoid equating counseling with pushing people to conform to certain "acceptable" standards to live by. Counseling should be a process whereby clients are challenged to honestly evaluate their values and then decide for themselves in what ways they will modify these values and their behavior.

Influence of therapist's personality and needs

Just as therapists cannot exclude their values from the therapeutic relationship, neither can they hope to keep their needs and personality separate, for these attributes have a bearing on the client. I strongly believe that ethically sensitive counselors recognize the supreme importance of becoming aware of their own needs, areas of unfinished business, potential personal conflicts, and defenses and vulnerability. They realize how these realities might prevent their clients from freely and fully exploring certain dimensions of themselves. I am convinced that, unless practitioners develop this self-awareness, they will obstruct clients' change or in various ways will use them for satisfying their own needs. Therapy then shifts from a matter of client satisfaction to one of therapist satisfaction. The crux of the matter here is to avoid exploiting clients for the purpose of meeting the counselor's needs. The APGA (1981) ethical guideline on this issue is "In the counseling relationship, the counselor is aware of the intimacy of the relationship and maintains respect for the client and avoids engaging in activities that seek to meet the counselor's personal needs at the expense of that client."

What kind of awareness is crucial? We all have certain "blind spots" and distortions of reality. I see it as therapists' responsibility to themselves and to their clients to work actively toward expanding their own self-awareness and to learn to recognize their own areas of distortion, biases and prejudices, and vulnerability. Therapists need at least to become increasingly aware of the nature of their unfinished business that may come to the fore in their relationships with clients. They must develop a sensitivity to their unmet needs so that they do not use the therapeutic relationship as a main avenue of satisfying those needs. If they recognize and work through their own personality problems, there is less chance that they will project them onto clients. If certain areas of struggle surface and old conflicts become reactivated, then therapists have, in my opinion, the ethical obligation to seek their own therapy, so that they will be able to help clients explore these same struggles.

The APA offers guidelines on this issue of therapist self-awareness. Therapists recognize that their effectiveness depends on their ability to maintain sound personal relationships and that their own personal problems may interfere with creating these relationships. It would surely seem that the mental health and level of self-integration and self-awareness of practitioners are vitally related to their ability to establish and maintain a therapeutic relationship, as opposed to a toxic one. The APA (1977) guideline is that therapists "refrain from undertaking any activity in which their personal problems are likely to result in inadequate professional services or harm to the client; or if engaged in such activity when they become aware of their personal problems, they seek competent professional assistance to determine whether they should suspend, terminate, or limit the scope of their professional and/or scientific activities" (p. 22). As counselors, we have other aspects of our personality that we must examine if we hope to be instrumental in using ourselves to create therapeutic relationships. These other aspects include the need for control and power; the need to be nurturing and helpful; the need to change others in the direction of our own values; the need to teach and preach and to persuade and suggest as well; the need for feeling adequate, particularly when it becomes overly important that the client confirm our competence; and the need to be respected and appreciated. I am not asserting that these needs are neurotic or necessarily destructive; on the contrary, I believe that it is essential that our needs be met if we are to be involved with helping others to find satisfaction in their life. Nor do I think that there is anything amiss in our deriving deep personal satisfaction from our work.

And surely many of our needs for feeling worthwhile, important, respected, and adequate may be a function of the quality of our work with others.

The questions are Do we, as therapists, depend primarily on our clients to give us this confirmation? Do we use the therapeutic relationship to enhance our own glory and promote our own cause of self-interest? Are we able to place the client's welfare in a primary position? This is no simple matter; self-deception is a very real danger. It is the main reason that I urge that all people who offer counseling and psychotherapy for others have the courage and ethical sensibility to have experienced their own therapy. If they have, they will be better able to differentiate between fulfilling oneself in direct and healthy ways and attempting to compensate for one's own frustrations by vicariously living through another's experience. One of my strong biases is that it is an ethical responsibility to obtain counseling or therapy before attempting to intervene in the lives of others. As therapists, how can we help a client to face and work through fears of death if we are escaping from our own fears of death? If we are unaware of our own sexual needs or have not examined our sexual motivations and dynamics, can we possibly help a client develop sexual maturity? If we flee from intimacy and are afraid of experiencing the depths of our own feelings of depression, anxiety, guilt, uncertainty, hopelessness, or helplessness, then can we honestly expect to be able to "be there" with others as they come close to experiencing those same feelings within themselves? Will we actively disrupt clients in their own processes of struggle out of our feelings of uneasiness? If we refuse to look at these dimensions in our own life, I cannot see how we can encourage our clients to plunge into unknown territory that may be anxiety-arousing for us as well as for them. I make the broad assumption that ethical practitioners will recognize the value of taking for themselves what they offer as valuable to their clients and that, through some form of personal-growth experience, they will be better able to avoid inflicting harm on their clients.

I agree with Palmer's (1980) views on the values of psychotherapy for the student trainee. He maintains that individual or group psychotherapy gives student therapists the experience of perceiving things from the client's position. By experiencing the process of personal psychotherapy, trainees learn what it is like to deal with anxieties that are aroused by self-disclosure and self-exploration. They experience transference and thus know first hand what it is like to view their therapists as parent figures.

According to Palmer (1980), the main reason for having students receive some form of psychotherapy is to help them learn to deal with countertransference (the process of seeing themselves in their clients; or the tendency to overidentify with their clients; or the tendency to meet their needs through their clients). I am in agreement with Palmer when he says that, unless therapists are aware of their own conflicts, needs, assets, and liabilities, they are in danger of being carried away on the client's emotional tidal wave. Student therapists who have not healed their own psychological wounds and to some extent resolved their own conflicts will be in continuous conflict with their clients.

Now let us examine briefly some of the specific areas of the therapist's personality that may have a bearing on clients. First is the issue of the power of therapists and their use of control. In my estimation power is a quality that every effective helping person possesses. It is a vital component of good therapy, and I believe that many clients improve as a result of their sharing in the power of their therapists. It has been suggested that therapists be models, and one aspect of modeling is for therapists to be potent persons—that is, to have in their life what they want or to be in a position to know how to obtain the kind of life they desire. People who genuinely feel powerful do not dominate the lives of others and do not encourage others to remain in a dwarfed state so that they can feel superior. They do not enjoy power over others in a dictatorial and controlling fashion but are able to appreciate other people's potency and their own at the same time. The client's accomplishments, strengths, and newly discovered potencies are a source of joy to the potent therapist, not a source of threat as they are to the impotent therapist, who uses clients in his or her own attempt to achieve potency.

Clearly, the fact that power can be used against the client is an ethical concern. For example, consider the therapist's use of control as a way of reducing personal threat and anxiety. If therapists fear losing control because of their need to maintain control of the client and the relationship, then they may resort to all sorts of strategies (both consciously and unconsciously). Thus, if a female client is behaving seductively, and the male counselor is unsure of his own sexuality, he may deal with her by distancing her with abstract, intellectual interpretations or by assuming an aloof, "professional" stance. If she desires to become a sexually mature woman and he feels uncomfortable in the presence of powerful women (particularly sexually attractive and mature women), he may subvert her attempts to become a woman and encourage her to remain in a dependent, little-girl condition, because then he is not so threatened and can control the relationship.

Another issue is the counselor's need to nurture. It is my observation that many are attracted to the "helping professions" because of their need to "help others," to "teach people how to live the good life," to "straighten people out," and to "solve others' problems." There is also the motivation of people who at one point recognized that they were miserable or at least that they wanted to make basic changes in their life and who then did make a decision, with positive outcome, to embark on a self-exploration journey. Now these people may deeply desire to help others find their own way and, in so doing, provide for themselves a sense of meaningfulness and personal significance. One aspect of therapists' need to nurture frequently is their own need for succorance—that is, the need for others to nurture them through their respect, admiration, approval, appreciation, affection, and caring. The helping person quickly learns that the rewards are abundant for being nurturing to others.

Again, I see nothing amiss in therapists' need for being nurtured, nor even in the rewards that they receive from their acts of giving to clients. The ethical questions are What are the dangers to the client's well-being when the therapist has an exaggerated need for being nurtured by the client? Can therapists distinguish between therapy for the client's benefit and that for their own gains? Are therapists sufficiently aware of their needs for approval and appreciation? Do they base their perceptions of their adequacies strictly on reactions from clients? What are the dangers that exist when therapists depend too heavily on client confirmation of their adequacy, worth, and values as both a therapist and a person?

In summary, I believe that many are motivated to become "helpers" because of their needs for power, for feeling useful and significant, and for bolstering their feelings of adequacy. I see it as crucial that the therapist enter the therapeutic relationship as a person who is relatively integrated and fulfilled. If helpers must have others continually feed their ego and reinforce their personal adequacy, then it is apparent that they must keep others in a dependent position. Thus, such helpers must be in control of the relationships with their clients. Because of their own emotional hunger and their own need to be psychologically fed and nurtured, they are unable to genuinely focus attention on the client's deprivations and concerns. At the extreme, the relationship becomes one in which the helper is in greater need of the "helpee" than the other way around. For these reasons, ethical practice demands that helping persons recognize the central importance of continuously exploring themselves to determine in which direction—for betterment or for stagnation—their personality might influence clients.

Some guidelines for ethical practice: A summary review

Without setting out the following guidelines as absolute decrees, I would like to summarize this chapter by putting into focus some principles that I believe are important for counselors to review throughout their professional practice. My hope is that you will think about these as guidelines, apply them to yourself, and attempt to formulate your own views and positions on some of the topics raised in this chapter. I want to emphasize that developing a sense of professional and ethical responsibility is a task that is never really finished. Because there are no final or universal answers to many of these issues, I see it as essential to avoid falling into the trap of assuming that you will not have to reexamine your basic values and how they affect your practices. As I implied earlier, these ethical issues demand periodic reflection and an openness to change. I hope you will be willing to rethink your positions as you gain more experience.

1. Counselors need to be aware of what their own needs are, what they are getting from their work, and how their needs and behavior influence their clients.

2. Counselors should have the training and experience necessary for the assessments they make and the interventions they attempt.

3. Although professional practitioners know the ethical standards of their professional organizations, they are aware that they must exercise their own judgment in applying these principles to particular cases. They realize that many problems are without clear-cut answers, and they accept the responsibility of searching for appropriate answers.

4. It is important for counselors to have some theoretical framework of behavior change to guide them in their practice.

5. Because the therapist's primary responsibility is for the welfare of the client, it is essential that the therapist's own needs not be met at the client's expense.

6. Counselors need to recognize the importance of finding ways to update their knowledge and skills through various forms of continuing education.

7. Counselors should avoid any relationships with clients that are clearly a threat to the therapeutic/professional relationship.

8. It is the counselor's responsibility to inform clients of any circumstances that are likely to affect the confidentiality of their relationship and of any other matters that are likely to negatively influence the client/therapist relationship.

9. It is imperative that counselors be aware of their own values and attitudes, recognize the role that their belief system plays in the relationships with their clients, and avoid imposing these beliefs on their clients, either in a subtle or a direct manner.

10. It is important for counselors to inform their clients about matters such as the goals of counseling, techniques and procedures that will be employed, possible risks associated with entering the relationship, and any other factors that are likely to affect the client's decision to enter therapy.

11. Counselors need to become aware of the boundaries of their competence, and

they should seek qualified supervision or refer clients to other professionals when they recognize that they have reached their limit with a given client.

12. It is good for counselors to realize that they teach their clients through a modeling process. Thus, counselors should attempt to practice in their own life what they encourage in their clients.

Recommended supplementary readings

Professional and Ethical Issues in Counseling and Psychotherapy (Corey, Corey, & Callanan, 1979) is devoted entirely to the kinds of issue that were introduced briefly in this chapter. Some relevant chapters deal with the role of values in the client/counselor relationship, therapist responsibilities, therapist competence, factors influencing the client/therapist relationship, dealing with transference and countertransference, and ethical issues special to group work. The book is designed to involve readers in a personal and active way, and many open-ended cases are presented to help them formulate their thoughts on various issues.

Another useful resource is *Ethical and Legal Issues in Counseling and Psychotherapy* (Van Hoose & Kottler, 1977) which deals with professional issues such as incompetent and unethical behavior, legal regulations on professional psychology, problems of diagnosis and assessment, and value problems in therapy.

For those of you who have an interest in ethical and professional issues related to group work, separate chapters are devoted to these topics in *Groups: Process and Practice* (Corey & Corey, 1977); *Professional and Ethical Issues in Counseling and Psychotherapy* (Corey, Corey, & Callanan, 1979); *Theory and Practice of Group Counseling* (Corey, 1981); and *Group Techniques* (Corey, Corey, Callanan, & Russell, 1982).

For those who want to review ethical standards, I suggest the booklet *Ethical Standards* (American Personnel and Guidance Association, 1981), which lists ethical principles relating to counseling, testing, research and publication, private practice, and professional preparation. Another useful reference is *Ethical Standards of Psychologists* (American Psychological Association, 1967), which is both a casebook dealing with applications of ethical principles to specific situations and also a set of ethical guidelines for psychologists. Specific principles deal with the following areas: (1) responsibility, (2) competence, (3) moral and legal standards, (4) misrepresentation, (5) public statements, (6) confidentiality, (7) client welfare, (8) the client/therapist relationship, (9) impersonal services, (10) announcement of services, (11) interprofessional relations, (12) remuneration, (13) test security, (14) test interpretation, (15) test publication, (16) research precautions, (17) publication credit, (18) responsibility toward organization, and (19) promotional activities.

References and suggested readings

Books highly recommended as supplementary reading are marked with an asterisk.

American Personnel and Guidance Association. *Ethical standards.* Washington, D.C.: Author, 1961.
American Personnel and Guidance Association. *Ethical standards.* Falls Church, Virginia: Author, 1981.

American Psychological Association. *Ethical standards of psychologists.* Washington, D.C.: Author, 1967.

American Psychological Association. *Ethical principles in the conduct of research with human participants.* Washington, D.C.: Author, 1973.

*American Psychological Association. Ethical standards of psychologists. *APA Monitor,* March 1977, pp. 22–23.

Association for Specialists in Group Work. *Ethical guidelines for group leaders.* Falls Church, Virginia: Author, 1980.

Burgum, T., & Anderson, S. *The counselor and the law.* Falls Church, Virginia: American Personnel and Guidance Association, 1975.

Callis, R. (Ed.). *Ethical standards casebook.* Falls Church, Virginia: American Personnel and Guidance Association, 1976.

Corey, G. *Theory and practice of group counseling.* Monterey, Calif.: Brooks/Cole, 1981.

Corey, G., & Corey, M. *Groups: Process and practice.* Monterey, Calif.: Brooks/Cole, 1977.

*Corey, G., Corey, M., & Callanan, P. *Professional and ethical issues in counseling and psychotherapy.* Monterey, Calif.: Brooks/Cole, 1979.

Corey, G., Corey, M., & Callanan, P. *Casebook on ethical standards for group counseling and psychotherapy.* Falls Church, Virginia: Association for Specialists in Group Work, in press.

Corey, G., Corey, M., Callanan, P., & Russell, M. *Group techniques.* Monterey, Calif.: Brooks/Cole, 1982.

Fretz, B., & Mills, D. *Licensing and certification of psychologists and counselors.* San Francisco: Jossey-Bass, 1980.

*Goldberg, C. *Therapeutic partnership. Ethical concerns in psychotherapy.* New York: Springer, 1977.

London, P. *The modes and morals of psychotherapy.* New York: Holt, Rinehart & Winston, 1964.

Monahan, J. (Ed.). *Who is the client? The ethics of psychological intervention in the criminal justice system.* Washington, D.C.: American Psychological Association, 1980.

Palmer, J. *A primer of eclectic psychotherapy.* Monterey, Calif.: Brooks/Cole, 1980.

Stolz, S., & Associates. *Ethical issues in behavior modification.* San Francisco: Jossey-Bass, 1978.

*Van Hoose, W., & Kottler, J. *Ethical and legal issues in counseling and psychotherapy.* San Francisco: Jossey-Bass, 1977.

Wrenn, G. *The world of the contemporary counselor.* Boston: Houghton Mifflin, 1973.

14

The Counselor as a Person and as a Professional

Introduction

In this chapter you are asked to examine the assumption that one of the most important instruments you have to work with as a counselor is *yourself as a person*. As part of your preparation you can acquire a knowledge of the theories of personality and psychotherapy, you can learn diagnostic and intervention techniques, and you can learn about the dynamics of human behavior. Although this knowledge and these skills are essential, I do not think that they are, by themselves, sufficient for establishing and maintaining effective therapeutic relationships. I am convinced that to every therapy session we bring our human qualities and the experiences that have influenced us. In my judgment this human dimension is one of the most powerful determinants of the therapeutic encounter we create with clients. As counselors, if we hope to promote growth and change in our clients, we must be willing to promote growth in our own life. Our most powerful source of influencing clients in a positive direction is through our living example of who we are and of our willingness to continually struggle to become the person we are able to become.

Both in the Preface and the introductory chapter I recommended that you read this chapter before studying the counseling theories. I suggested this so that you could think about the personal implications of each of the therapeutic approaches. On a second reading, after you have studied these theories and been introduced to some ethical and professional issues in the practice of counseling, I ask you to reevaluate ways that you can work on your development as a person. You should look especially at the needs and personality traits that might interfere with your effectiveness as a counselor. By remaining open to self-evaluation you not only expand your awareness of self personally but also build the foundation for developing your abilities as a professional. The theme of this chapter is that the *person* and *professional* are intertwined entities that cannot be separated in reality.

Personal characteristics of effective therapists

THE AUTHENTICITY OF THE THERAPIST

Therapy, because it is a deeply intimate kind of learning, demands a practitioner who is willing to risk shedding stereotyped roles and being a real person in a relationship. In my view it is precisely within the context of the person-to-person relationship that the client experiences growth. If as therapists we hide behind the safety of our professional role, I believe, our clients will keep themselves hidden from us. If we become merely technical experts and leave our own reactions, values, and self out of our work, then I see the product as being sterile counseling. My view is that it is through our own realness and our aliveness that we are able to significantly touch our clients. If we make life-oriented choices, radiate a zest for life, are real in our relationships with our clients, and let ourselves be known to them, we can inspire and teach them in the best sense of the words. This does not mean that we are self-actualized persons who have "arrived" or that we are without our problems. Rather, it implies that we have not given up our willingness to look at our life and do what is necessary to make the changes we want to make. Because we have a sense of hope that we can change, and that changing is worth the risks and the efforts, then we can hold out hope to our clients that they have the capacity to become their own person and to like the person they are becoming.

In short, I think that as therapists we serve as models for our clients. If we model incongruent behavior, low-risk activity, and deceit by remaining hidden and vague, then we can expect our clients to imitate this behavior and to be untrusting. If we model realness by engaging in appropriate self-disclosure, then we can anticipate that our clients will integrate more of this characteristic in themselves. To be sure, psychotherapy is a process that can be for better or for worse. Clients can become more actualized, or they can become less healthy. In my judgment the degree of aliveness and self-actualization of the therapist is the crucial variable that determines the outcome.

THE THERAPIST AS A THERAPEUTIC PERSON

Tied to the issue of the therapist's personhood and behavior are two central questions: How can counselors *be* therapeutic persons? How can they be instruments, catalysts, and agents of the awareness and growth of their clients? I have examined, sometimes painfully, the issue of therapeutic personhood to determine for myself how I can be either a therapeutic or a toxic therapist. When I think of counselors who are therapeutic persons, I come up with a lengthy list of personal qualities and characteristics. Let me emphasize before I offer this list that I do not expect any therapist to be fully all these things, and I do not propose a perfection model. Rather, I suggest that these dimensions of a therapist's being are those that he or she is struggling to attain. For me the willingness not to become a finished product but to remain open to the struggle to become a more therapeutic person is precisely the quality that is most crucial for counseling experience. My list is incomplete and still evolving; I propose it, not as a dogmatic itemizing of the "right" ways to be a therapist, but as a stimulus for you to examine your own idea of what it means to be a therapeutic counselor. My view of therapeutic persons includes the following characteristics:

1. They have found their own way. They are in the process of developing a style that is uniquely theirs, and their counseling style is an expression of their philosophy of life and their own personal style of living. Although they might freely borrow ideas and techniques from many other therapists, they do not mechanically imitate another's style.

2. They possess self-respect and self-appreciation. They can give out of their own sense of self-worth and strength rather than out of a need to receive false feelings of strength. They are also able to ask, to be needed, and to receive from others, and they do not isolate themselves from others as a demonstration of pseudostrength.

3. They are able to be powerful, and they recognize and accept their own power. They are able to feel okay with others and allow others to feel powerful with them. They do not diminish others, nor do they encourage others to maintain a powerless stance so that they might feel a relative sense of power. They use their power and model for clients its healthy uses, but they attempt to avoid abusing it.

4. They are open to change, generally in touch with themselves, and willing to take risks. Rather than settling for less, they extend themselves to become more. They exhibit willingness and courage to leave the security of the known and to plunge into the unknown, where they might tap many of their untapped potentials.

5. They are expanding their awareness of self and others. They realize that with limited awareness comes only limited freedom, and that awareness increases the possibilities for choosing a richer life as it permeates several levels: feelings, values, beliefs, personal motivations, basic life attitudes, bodily reactions, sensory capacities, and so on. Instead of investing energy in defensive behavior designed to block out experiences,

they direct energy toward allowing for a maximum of experiences and an expansion of awareness.

6. They are willing and able to tolerate ambiguity. Most of us have low thresholds for coping with a lack of clarity. Because growth depends on leaving the familiar and entering unknown territory, therapeutic persons seek out a degree of ambiguity in life. Instead of perceiving it as a threat to their existence, they are attracted to it. As they build their ego strength, they develop more self-trust—more trust in their intuitive processes, more willingness to experiment with novel behavior, and more trust in both their feelings and their judgments. They eventually come to realize that they are trustworthy. Although their behavior may not be predictable at all times, they are usually reliable.

7. They have an identity. They know who they are, what they are capable of becoming, what they want out of life, and what is essential. They question life, and they are willing to reexamine their values. They are not mere reflections of what others expect or want them to be but strive to get in touch with their inner core and live from their own center. Essentially, their standards are internalized, and they have the courage to act in a way in which they believe, even though they might not be rewarded by others for their beliefs or actions.

8. They are capable of nonpossessive empathy. They can experience and know the world of the other. They are aware of their own struggles and pain, and they have a frame of reference for identifying with others while at the same time not losing their own identity by overidentification with others.

9. They are alive! Their choices are life-oriented. They feel intensely, can participate in life, and like to live. They are committed to living life rather than settling for mere existence.

10. They are authentic, real, congruent, sincere, and honest. They do not live by pretenses but attempt to be what they think and feel. They are willing to appropriately disclose themselves to selected others, and in this way they come to know themselves more fully. They do not hide behind masks, defenses, sterile roles, and facades; instead, they prefer to be genuine.

11. They are able to give and to receive love. They are able to give out of their fullness and from their souls, not out of their deprivations and inner emptiness. They are vulnerable to those they love, and they have capacities to care for others.

12. They live in the present. They do not badger themselves with what they should have done or could have done in the past, nor do they fixate on the future. They are able to experience the now, live in the now, and be present with others in the now.

13. They make mistakes and are willing to admit them. Although they are not over-burdened with guilt over how they could or should have been, they learn from their mistakes. They do not dismiss their errors lightly, yet they do not choose to dwell on misery.

14. They are able to become deeply involved in their work and their creative projects; they derive rich meanings in life through their projects. They can accept the rewards flowing from their work, and they can honestly admit the ego needs that are gratified in their work. Yet they are not slaves to their work, and they do not depend exclusively on their work to live full lives. They have other dimensions in life that provide them with a sense of purpose and fulfillment.

15. They are able to reinvent themselves and to revitalize and recreate significant relationships in their life. They make decisions about how they would like to change,

and they work toward becoming the person they would like to become. They are not bound by their past ways of being; they are capable of changing.

16. They have the ability to be emotionally present for others. They can be with others in their pain or their joy, for they are open to their own emotional experience.

17. They are in the process of making choices that shape their life. They are aware of early decisions they made about themselves, others, and the world. They are not the victims of these early decisions, for they are willing to make new and revised decisions if necessary.

18. They challenge unreasonable assumptions or any self-destructive beliefs or attitudes, rather than submitting to them. Because they are willing to engage in continuing self-evaluation, they do not hold themselves back needlessly by limiting self-talk.

19. They have a sincere interest in the welfare of others, based on respect, care, trust, and a real valuing of them. This caring implies that they are willing to challenge significant people in their life to also remain open to growth.

This picture of the characteristics of the therapeutic person might appear monumental and unrealistic. Who could ever be all those things? Again, I emphasize that, although none of us is fully actualized, the point is striving to become more of our potential self. I have presented the picture with the hope that you will examine it and develop your own concept of what personality traits you deem essential to work toward if you are to be able to facilitate personal growth. Researchers have identified many other traits of the effective therapist, including a deep interest in people, sensitivity to the attitudes and reactions of others, emotional stability and objectivity, a capacity for being trusted by others, a sense of humor, broadmindedness toward and tolerance of divergent beliefs and life-styles, intelligence and perceptivity, respect for people, knowledge of human behavior, and the interest in continuing to learn, just to mention a few. Today the trend is toward stressing the psychological aspects of the therapist as a human being. Much of the literature on counselor education emphasizes therapists' ability to look at, understand, and accept their own self as well as the self of the other person.

PERSONAL COUNSELING/PSYCHOTHERAPY FOR THERAPISTS

Discussion of the therapist as a person raises another debated issue in counselor education: whether therapists should experience counseling or therapy before they become practitioners. As I mentioned earlier, my view is that therapists should have the experience of being a client at some time. It might be prior to their training or during it, but I strongly endorse some form of personal-growth experience, either individual or group, or both, as a prerequisite to counseling others.

I do not assume that potential therapists are "sick" and need to be "cured," but I do believe that we all have our blind spots, that we all have forms of our own unfinished business that may interfere with our effectiveness as therapists, and that we can all become more. I do feel that therapy should be viewed not as an end in itself but as a means to help a potential therapist become more of a therapeutic person who will have a greater chance of having a significant and positive influence on clients.

I want to emphasize the value of continuing individual or group counseling as we begin to counsel. I found that, when I began counseling others, old wounds were opened and feelings that I had not explored in depth came to the surface. I found myself unable to encounter a client's depression, because I had failed to come to terms with the way I escaped my own depression. Being a therapist forces us to confront our unexplored blocks related to loneliness, power, death, sexuality, our parents, and so on. Also, as we begin our work as counselors, we often feel a sense of professional impotence, and we frequently feel like quitting. I encourage student counselors to feel their helplessness and despair but to decide not to quit too soon, at least not without giving themselves a chance to test their potential. Here is where I find personal counseling a natural adjunct for beginning therapists' work.

Through the process of being a client ourselves, we know what it is like to look at ourselves as we really are. It gives us a basis for compassion for our clients, for we can draw on our own memories of reaching impasses in our therapy, of both wanting to go further ahead and at the same time wanting to stay where we were. Personal or group therapy can help us become clearer about our unresolved personal conflicts. This does not mean that we need to be free of conflicts before we can counsel others, but it does mean that we should be aware of what these conflicts are and how they are likely to affect us as counselors. For example, if we have great difficulty in dealing with anger and guilt in our personal life, the chances are that we will do something to dilute these emotions when they occur in our clients. How can we be present for our clients and encourage them to express feelings openly that we are so intent on denying in ourselves? The key point is that, to the degree that unfinished business clutters up our life, we are not able to be a therapeutic agent for our clients. If we are enslaved by situations from our past that we are unwilling to look at, and if we feel burdened with current problems, how can we encourage our clients to free themselves? I firmly believe that as therapists we can take our clients no further than we have been willing to go in our own life. If we are not committed personally to the value inherent in the process of struggling, we will not convince clients that they should pay the price of struggling.

Ideally, I would like to see some individual counseling combined with group-oriented growth experiences. My preference is for personal-growth groups, for here counselor candidates can benefit from the reactions of many. The focus of the group experience should be on helping the person become more aware of why he or she wants to become a counselor. Some questions for exploration are Why do I want to pursue a career in the helping professions? What are my own needs and motivations? What rewards do I receive from being a counselor? How can I differentiate between satisfaction of client needs and satisfaction of my own needs? Some other questions that might profitably be asked in a personal-growth experience include What are some of my problems, and what am I doing to resolve them? How might my own problems get in the way of effectively working as a counselor? What are my values, where did they originate, and how will they affect my counseling style? How in touch am I with my own feelings? How courageous and willing to take risks am I? Am I willing to do what I would like my clients to do? What are some ways that I avoid using my own strengths? And how can I more fully utilize my potential power? What keeps me from being as open, honest, and real as I might be? Who are the people I am particularly attracted to, and who are those whom I take a dislike to? How do others experience me? What impact do I have on others? How sensitive am I to the reactions of others and to how they respond to me and I to them?

Those questions reflect but a few of the possible areas of focus in a personal-growth experience. The aim of the experience is to provide a situation in which counselors can come to greater self-understanding. I never cease to be surprised by the amount of resistance I encounter from the ranks of professionals on this issue. I hear this argument:

"Requiring the therapist to be a client in personal counseling is based on a medical model of sickness. It's like saying that a surgeon cannot perform an operation that he or she has not also undergone." I simply cannot accept the analogy. I am left with the strong conviction that therapists cannot hope to open doors for clients that they have not opened for themselves. If I am fearful of acknowledging my own demons and fears, how can I help others accept their demons and fears? If I have limited vision, how can I help my clients expand their visions of what they might become? However, although I deem a therapeutic experience necessary for prospective counselors, I do not believe it to be a sufficient and complete experience in itself. I believe that it is but one way in which therapists can actively do something about becoming more therapeutic in their relationships with people.

Issues faced by beginning therapists

This section is based on my observation and work with counselors-in-training and on my own struggles when I began practicing. My attempt is to identify some of the major issues that most of us typically face, particularly during the beginning stages of learning how to be therapists. I have become aware of a recurring pattern of questions, conflicts, and issues that provide the substance of seminars and practicum experiences in counseling. I believe that these issues are vitally related to the counselor as a person. When counselor interns complete their formal course work and begin facing clients, they are put to the test of being able to integrate and apply what they have learned. They soon realize that all they really have to work with is themselves—their own life experiences, values, and humanity. At that point arise some real concerns regarding their adequacies as a counselor and as a person and about what they can bring of themselves to the counseling relationship. In what follows I attempt to formulate some useful guidelines for beginning counselors.

OUR ANXIETY IS NOT NECESSARILY NEUROTIC

Most beginning therapists, regardless of their academic and experiential backgrounds, anticipate with ambivalent feelings meeting their initial clients. As beginners, if we have enough sense, we are probably anxiety ridden and ask ourselves such questions as What will I say? How will I say it? Will I be able to help? What if I make mistakes? Will my client return, and, if he does, what will I do next? In my view a certain level of anxiety demonstrates that we are aware of the uncertainties of the future with our client and of our abilities to really be there and stay with our client. Because therapy is serious business and can have an impact on the clients, we can accept our anxieties as normal. Whereas too much anxiety can torpedo any confidence we might have and cause us to be frozen, we have every right to experience some anxiety. We may also fear that our peers know far more than we do, that they are much more skilled and perceptive, and that they will see us as incompetent.

The willingness to recognize and deal with these anxieties, as opposed to denying them by pretenses, is a mark of courage. That we have self-doubts and anxiety seems perfectly normal; it is how we deal with them that counts. One way is to openly discuss them with a supervisor and peers. The possibilities are rich for meaningful exchanges and for gaining support from fellow interns, who probably have many of the same concerns, fears, and self-doubts.

BEING AND DISCLOSING OURSELVES

Because we are typically self-conscious and anxious when we begin counseling, we tend to be overconcerned with what the books say and with the mechanics of how we should proceed. In my work as a supervisor I have noted that inexperienced therapists too often fail to appreciate the values inherent in simply being themselves. I have suggested to many of my students that they attempt to put their theories and academic learning into the background and follow their intuitions, even though they do not fully trust their hunches. One hopes that course work, readings, fieldwork, and other training experiences have been integrated and that they can call on their acquired knowledge and skill as it is appropriate. I frequently encourage counselors-in-training to follow through with some of their hunches and later to confirm their intuitive directions with a fellow student, the client, a supervisor, or their own internal reactions.

A common tendency is for therapists to become passive. They listen. They reflect. They have insights and hunches but mull over them so long that, even if they decide to act on a hunch, the appropriate time for action has already passed. So they sit back, passively wondering whether internal reactions are correct. Thus, I tend to encourage an active stance for the student counselor, because I believe that it is generally better to risk being inappropriate (which is a risk with an active counselor) rather than almost to ensure bland results by adopting passive, nondirective stances.

Let me push further with the issue of being oneself. I do not believe that we should be either of two extremes: at one end are therapists who lose themselves in their fixed role and who hide behind a professional facade; at the other end are therapists who strive too hard to prove that they, too, are human. If we are at either of these poles, we are not being ourselves.

Take the first extreme. Here the role functions hide therapists' humanity; they are so bound up in maintaining stereotyped role expectations that little of them as a person shows through. Although we do have role functions, it is still possible for us to responsibly perform them without blurring our identity and becoming lost in our role. I believe that the more insecure, frightened, and uncertain we are in our professional work, the more we will cling to the defense afforded by a role. Also, I believe that the unrealistic expectation that to be therapists we must be superhuman leads to becoming ossified in fixed roles. Consider some unrealistic expectations that a beginning counselor often becomes ensnared with: I should always care; I need always to demonstrate warmth (whether I feel it or not); I should like and enjoy all my clients; I must be all-understanding and fully empathetic; I should know what is going on at all times; I can't be acceptable as a counselor unless I'm fully put together myself, and any indication of personal problems rules against my effectiveness; I am expected to have answers for clients, answers that they say they cannot find within themselves; and so on. If we accept these unrealistic notions, then we can fall victim to presenting a role to clients instead of presenting ourselves. By accepting these lofty standards, we deceive ourselves into being that which we are really not, because we indoctrinate ourselves with the idea that we should be a certain way. The role we play is not always congruent with the way we deeply feel. Thus, finding ourselves bored, we deny our boredom and force attention; or, discovering negative feelings toward clients, we deny our feelings by stressing the positive qualities we see in clients; or, becoming aware that we are uncaring in a particular moment, we trick ourselves into caring instead of letting the feeling stand.

At this extreme of too little self-disclosure, therapists are unwilling to discuss the reactions they are having toward clients or what has been going on with them during the session. They focus too much on the clients, often by questioning or probing, which is a subtle demand for them to be open and revealing. At the same time they are modeling closed behavior. They expect their clients to do what they are not doing themselves in the therapy relationship. Their clients are left guessing about what the therapist is experiencing during the session; thus, a valuable basis for an honest dialogue is lost.

At the other extreme, therapists actively work at demonstrating their humanness. Instead of getting lost in a professionally aloof and nondisclosing role, such therapists overreact and blur any distinction between helper and one who is helped. They would rather be seen as a buddy with similar hang-ups than as a therapist. Their approach is one of sharing their own problems, past and present, and of using the relationship to work on their own needs. A pseudorealness develops out of their need to be seen as human, and, in a desperate attempt to be themselves, they fail. At this extreme we tell clients too much about ourselves, and thus we take the focus off of them and put it on ourselves as therapists. We might make the mistake of inappropriately burdening them with fleeting reactions or impressions we are having toward them; our disclosures in these cases have the effect of closing them up. The key point is that disclosure should have the effect of encouraging clients to deepen their level of self-exploration or to enhance the therapeutic relationship. Excessive therapist disclosure often originates from the therapist's own needs, and in these cases the client's needs are secondary.

This kind of therapist has not learned appropriate self-disclosure, for facilitative disclosure generally entails revealing reactions that stem from the relationship with the client, not disclosing some unrelated experience out of the therapist's past. To be sure, facilitative disclosure enhances the therapeutic process, for it admits the client into the therapist's private world when to do so is relevant and timely within the context of the therapeutic relationship. Appropriate disclosure of self is not contrived, and it is one way of being oneself and revealing oneself to the other without working to prove one's humanity to the point of phoniness.

In working with professional mental-health workers at workshops and with trainees, I have found that it is difficult to learn the differences between appropriate and inappropriate self-disclosure. I attempt to teach that appropriate self-disclosure can focus on the reactions of the therapist to the client in the here-and-now encounter between them. Counselors do not necessarily need to share that much of their outside life, either past or current. With a few words, and often in nonverbal ways, therapists can let clients know that they are identifying with them and that they are really hearing them. I tend to stress the value of disclosures that are directly related to what is going on between the counselor and the client in the immediate moment, especially if doing so will enhance this relationship.

I have found the following guidelines useful in determining when self-disclosure is facilitative. First, disclosing my persistent feelings that are directly related to the present transaction can be useful. If I am consistently bored or irritated in a session, then it becomes essential to reveal my feeling. On the other hand, I think it is unwise to share every fleeting fantasy or feeling that I experience. Timing is important. I recall sharing my feelings of being "grouped out" at an initial session of a personal-growth group. This admission burdened the group with doubt about their willingness to place additional stress on me. If I had continued to feel distant and uninvolved, it would have been appropriate to reveal how I felt, but to do so with my opening statement had the effect of creating defenses within the group. Second, I find it helpful to distinguish between disclosure that is history telling and disclosure that is an unrehearsed expression of my present experiencing. For me to mechanically report events of my past might be pseudodisclosure. If it is easy to relate or if it sounds rehearsed and mechanical to me, I have a clue that I am trying too hard to be authentic. However, if my disclosure is an outgrowth of something I am feeling in the moment and if, as I share this feeling, it has some freshness of expression, I can be more sure that my self-disclosure is facilitative. Third, I often ask myself why I am revealing myself and to what degree it is appropriate. To use my group to explore my own feelings, I believe, is to burden the group. Perhaps one may need outside therapy, but I do not see it as appropriate that one should consistently use the group of which one is a leader for working through one's own problems.

WE NEED NOT BE PERFECT

One thing I attempt to teach counselor interns is that they do not need to burden themselves with thinking that they must be perfect. To be sure, we will make mistakes, whether we are beginning or seasoned therapists. I do not believe that our clients are fragile and that they will be destroyed for life because of our mistakes. If our energies are aimed at presenting the image of perfection, then where will we get the energy to pay attention to our clients—or to our reactions to them?

I find that many counselors-in-training are afraid of revealing their mistakes to their supervisors. Although I do not discount this fear, I urge students to have the courage to share their mistakes or what they perceive as errors. Only if we are willing to reveal our uncertainties with fellow students and supervisors can we hope to profit from our errors. Also, we might need consultation with others because we are too close to a situation to acquire a perspective. If we can discuss with others our feelings of frustration or of not handling a case as we would like, then consultation can help us through an impasse.

On this point I would like to share a personal experience. A while back I reached an impasse with a person whom I had been counseling for two years. The client began seriously examining the possibility of committing suicide, saying that death was preferable to living. This situation caused me to examine seriously what I had been doing in our relationship. At that time I felt both hopeless and helpless and not at all sure how to proceed. I decided to bring the case up for consideration in a colleague's seminar. At the seminar were ten students (many of them my own) and two fellow faculty members. After I gave some descriptive background on the case and spoke of my feelings of fear and uncertainty in proceeding with my client, we did some role playing. I received suggestions from most of those present. What I became aware of was how mechanical I had become with my client and how I really felt hopeless. Of course, the client sensed my hopelessness, and part of the motivation for suicide was a test to see if I cared about the client at all. I became aware not only of my own inauthenticity but also of my need to become more demanding. As a result of this experience I found myself demanding more of both myself and of the clients I was then seeing. To this day, I do not have any fear that my students lost confidence or respect in me because of my disclosure of my mistakes with my client.

BEING HONEST WITH CLIENTS

One fear that most of us have is in facing our limitations as therapists. We fear losing the client's respect if we say "I really feel that I can't help you on this point" or "I just don't have the kind of information or skill to help you with this problem." From client responses the evidence is overwhelming in favor of direct honesty as opposed to an attempt to fake competence. Not only will we perhaps not lose our clients' respect, but may gain their respect by frankly admitting our limitations. An illustration comes to mind. A counselor-in-training had intake duty in a college counseling center. Her first client came in wanting to discuss the possibilities of an abortion for his girlfriend. Many questions raced through her mind: "Should I admit to him my lack of awareness and skill in dealing with this problem, or should I somehow bluff my way through to avoid looking like a neophyte? Should I know how to help him? Will he get a negative impression of the counseling center if I tell him I don't have the skill for this case? What about the girl in this situation? Is it really enough to work only with him? Is all that he really needs at this point simply information? Will information resolve the issue?" Fortunately, the counselor-in-training let the client know directly that the matter was too complicated for her to tackle, and she got another counselor on duty to help him. A point of this illustration is that we sometimes burden ourselves with the expectation that we should be all-knowing and skillful even without experience. The counselor-in-training's willingness to be realistic helped her avoid the pitfalls of trying to look good for the client and of presenting a false image.

SILENCE: A THREATENING EXPERIENCE

Those silent moments during a therapeutic session may seem like silent hours to a beginning therapist. It is not uncommon to be threatened by silences to the point that we frequently do something counterproductive to break the silence and thus relieve our anxiety. I recall when I was a counselor intern and was tape-recording an individual session with a highly verbal high school girl. Toward the end of the session she became silent for a moment, and my anxiety level rose to the degree that I felt compelled to rush in and give several interpretations to what she had been saying earlier. When my supervisor heard the tape he exclaimed, "Hell, your talk really got in her way. You didn't hear what she was saying! I'll bet she doesn't come back for her session next week." Well, she came back, but by that time I was determined not to intervene and talk my anxiety away. So, rather than take the initiative of beginning the session, I waited for her to begin. We waited for about half an hour. We played a game of "you first." Each of us sat and stared at the other. Finally, we began exploring what this silence felt like for each of us.

Silence can have many meanings, and I believe that it is essential to learn how to effectively understand the meanings of silence. Some of the possible meanings of silence, either during an individual session or a group session, are the following: the client might be quietly thinking about some things that were discussed earlier or evaluating some insight just acquired; the client might be waiting for the therapist to take the lead and decide what to say next, or the therapist might be waiting for the client to do this; either the client or the therapist might be bored, distracted, preoccupied, or just not have anything to say for the moment; the client might be feeling hostile toward the therapist and thus playing the game of "I'll just sit here like a stone and see if he (she) can get to me"; the client and the therapist might be communicating without words, the silence might be refreshing, or the silence might say much more than words; and perhaps the interaction has been on a surface level, and both persons have some fear or hesitancy about getting to a deeper level.

I suggest that you explore alternative meanings of silences and that, when silences occur, you explore with your client what a particular silence means. You could first acknowledge the silence and your feelings about it and then, rather than pretending it does not exist and making noisy talk simply to make each other comfortable, pursue the meaning of the silence.

DEALING WITH DEMANDING CLIENTS

A major issue that puzzles many beginning therapists is how to deal with the over-demanding client. Typically, because therapists feel that they should extend themselves in being helpful, they often burden themselves with the unrealistic standard that they should give unselfishly regardless of how great the demands on them are. The demands might manifest themselves in a variety of ways. Clients might call you frequently at your home and expect you to talk at length over the telephone; demand that they see you more often or for a longer period of time than you can provide; want to see you socially; want you to adopt or in some other way take care of them and assume their responsibilities; expect you to manipulate another person (spouse, child, parent) to see and accept their point of view; demand that you not leave them and that you continually demonstrate how much you care; or demand that you tell them what to do and how to solve a problem.

It might be useful for you to review some of your encounters with clients to assess the ways you feel that you have been the victim of excessive demands. What are some demands that were placed on you? How did you handle those situations? Can you say no to clients when you want to? Are you able to value yourself enough that you can make demands for yourself? Do you confront demanding clients, or do you allow them to manipulate you in the same way that they have manipulated others? If you let them manipulate you, are you doing them a favor?

I suspect that one problem inexperienced therapists must work through is their need to be needed. The demanding client can feed the ego of a hungry therapist, just as there are pay-offs in the relationship between a spoiled child and an overprotective parent: at least the parent feels needed! We can delude ourselves into an exaggerated sense of importance by thinking that we must always be available or by believing that we are essential to the very lives of our clients. What would they do without us? I think that there are two imperatives in dealing with demanding clients: first, we need to be aware of the nature of the demands and our reactions to them; second, we must have the courage to confront them with our perceptions of their behavior and of our own demands.

DEALING WITH UNCOMMITTED CLIENTS

Related to the problem of demanding clients is that of clients who really have very little investment in their own counseling. Their lack of motivation might be evidenced by their frequent "forgetting" or canceling of appointments, stated indifference, or unwillingness to assume any of their own responsibility in the counseling process.

It is easy for beginning counselors to get drawn into unproductive games with these clients, to the extent that far more investment is being shown by the counselor than by the client. It is possible for counselors to try too hard to be understanding and accepting and therefore not to make any demands on their clients. I see it as a mistake to fail to confront clients who seem to lack personal investment. This is true even of the involuntary client.

I have seen too many instances in which the issue of the uncommitted patient was used as a reason to justify any possible movement in therapy. It is especially difficult for beginning counselors to confront a client who is not committed to working, for they fear that, if they do so, the client will surely not return. Perhaps this direct confrontation is the very factor that can lead to a level of commitment from clients. If they persistently seem to forget appointments or fail to do any work during or outside of the therapy session, they can be asked if they want to continue coming for counseling. At least a clear decision not to continue if they are not willing to get involved is some step. In the case of clients who are sent to counseling by the court, the therapist can still work with them by stating that, although they are required to attend sessions, it is up to them to decide how they will use this time. They can eventually be shown that, even though they are involuntary clients, they can use this time well.

In working with mental-health workers at a state hospital, I have initially found many of them uncommitted to the workshop. They typically say that they have come to the training workshop because a supervisor sent them to it. I have found with these people that it often helps to allow them to express their negative feelings about being sent to the workshop; in this way they sometimes open the door for some level of personal involvement.

INSTANT RESULTS ARE IMPOSSIBLE

Do not expect instant results. You will not "cure" clients in a few sessions. So many beginning therapists experience the anxiety of not seeing the fruits of their labor. They ask themselves: "Am I really doing my client any good?" "Is the client perhaps getting worse?" "Is anything really occurring as a result of our sessions, or am I just deceiving myself into believing we're making progress?" I hope that you will learn to tolerate the ambiguity of not knowing for sure whether your client is improving, at least during the initial sessions. Understand that clients might apparently "get worse" before they show therapeutic gains. After clients have decided to work toward self-honesty and drop their defenses and facades, they can be expected to experience an increase of personal pain and disorganization, which might result in a depression or a panic reaction. Many a client has uttered: "My God, I was better off before I started therapy. Now I feel more vulnerable than before. Maybe I was better off when I was ignorant." Also, realize that the fruitful effects of the joint efforts of the therapist and the client might not be manifest for months (or even years) after the conclusion of therapy.

The year that I began doing full-time individual and group counseling in a college counseling center was, professionally, the most trying year for me. Up until that time, I was teaching a variety of psychology courses, and I could sense relatively quick results or the lack of them. I found teaching gratifying, reinforcing, and many times exciting; by contrast, counseling seemed like a laborious and thankless task. The students who came to the counseling center did not evidence any miraculous cures, and some would come each week with the same complaints. They saw little progress, sought answers, wanted some formula for feeling better, or wanted a shot of motivation. I was plagued with self-doubts and skepticism. My needs for reinforcement were so great that I was antitherapeutic for some. I needed them to need me, to tell me that I was effective, to assure me that they were noticing positive changes, and so on. I became aware that I attempted to refer the depressed male students to other counselors, whereas I put effort into encouraging a bright, attractive, young female to continue in counseling. Learning the dynamics of my motivation did not come easily, and I appreciated the confrontation that several of my colleagues provided in helping me become more honest about whose needs were really being met. Eventually I discovered that growth and change did occur in a number of my clients as a result of our joint efforts. They were willing to assume their responsibilities for taking risks, and I became more willing to stay with them, even though I was not at all sure of the results.

My beginning experiences taught me that I needed to be able to tolerate not knowing whether a client is progressing or whether I am instrumental in that person's growth or change. I learned that the only way to acquire self-trust as a therapist was to allow myself to feel my helplessness, self-doubts, feelings of impotence, uncertainty about my effectiveness, and ambivalence over whether I wanted to continue as a counseling psychologist. As I became less anxious over my performance, I was able to pay increasing attention both to the other and to myself in the therapeutic relationship. Gradually, I found that clients did make changes in a direction that they liked, and that they influenced others in their life to become involved in personal counseling. Over the past 14 years that I have been in therapeutic practice, I have grown to trust myself more fully in my therapeutic skills; reports from former clients have confirmed my self-trust. But when we begin, we do not have the benefit of such success, and we may expect to flounder for a time as we wonder whether we will see any results.

WE WILL NOT SUCCEED WITH EVERYONE

We cannot realistically expect to succeed with every client. Even experienced therapists at times become glum and begin to doubt their value when they are forced to admit that there are clients whom they are not able to touch, much less reach in a significant way. Be honest enough with yourself and with your client to admit that you cannot work successfully with everyone. You may need to refer to other therapists, and you may often have to tell clients that you cannot work with them. I believe that we do prospective clients a disservice if we accept them when we deeply feel that we do not want to work with them. The image of an altruistic, selfless, and nondiscriminating therapist is one that needs to be smashed. Eventually, unwanted clients will sense that we really do not want to (or cannot) counsel them, and they may develop generalized resentments toward all therapy and therapists based on their encounters with our dishonesty in not being straight with them. I am not, however, suggesting that we send away all clients that we might have negative or mixed feelings toward, for we can in some cases profit from facing some of our internal dynamics that lead us to believe that we cannot work with a particular client.

There is a delicate balance between learning our realistic limits and challenging what we sometimes think of as being "limits." For example, we may tell ourselves that we could never work with the elderly because we cannot identify with them, because they would not trust us, because we might find it depressing, and so forth. However, in this case it might be good to test what we see as limits and open ourselves to this population. If we do, we may find that there are more grounds for identification than we thought. The same holds true for other populations (the handicapped, young children, mentally ill people, alcoholics, adolescents). Before deciding that we do not have the life experiences or the personal qualities to successfully work with a given population, we might do well to attempt working in a setting with a population we do not intend to specialize in. This can be done through diversified field placements or visits to agencies.

SELF-DECEPTION IN THERAPY

No discussion of guidelines for beginning therapists could be complete without mentioning the phenomenon of self-deception as it occurs in the counseling process—both by the therapist and the client. Self-deception is not necessarily conscious lying, for it can be subtle and unconscious. For both the client and the therapist, the motivation for deception may be based on the need to make the relationship worthwhile and productive; both have invested in seeing positive results. Our need to witness personal changes may blur reality and cause us to be less skeptical than we should be. Let us examine client self-deception first.

Clients want to be cured, and they want to be persuaded that their pains and struggles have been worth the effort. I have developed a healthy suspicion of some of the occurrences, for example, in group settings. There have been times when my coleaders and I suspected that participants did not want to be considered nonconforming, unproductive group members. During the course of a week-long session they might conduct a desperate search to uncover some traumatic event that would lend itself to dramatic catharsis and receive group approval. If most participants in the group have an intensive confrontation psychologically with their parents, some members will in a subtle way deceive themselves into pseudofeelings of anger, hurt, or the like. In such cases, I believe, the underlying dynamic is their need for group approval and approval of self, so that they can say: "I really got a lot from the group. I am working, and changing, and doing a lot for myself." Another manifestation of self-deception consists of clients' eagerness to blindly accept an interpretation, diagnosis, or appraisal from a therapist, a group leader, or another group member. Instead of critically evaluating the interpretation, they might contribute to their shaky judgment of self by incorporating everything another says.

Therapist self-deception needs to be explored as well. Just as clients have an investment in seeing a pay-off for their pain, so has a therapist an investment in seeing clients get well. What would happen if most clients complained that they did not get better, or if most groups were a flop? I have asked myself this question often. Our need to feel that we are instrumental in assisting another to enjoy life more fully and our need to feel a sense that we do make significant differences do at times lead to self-deception. We look for evidence of progress, and we rationalize away elements of failure. Or we give ourselves credit for our clients' growth when it may be due largely to another variable, perhaps to something unrelated to the therapeutic relationship. My point is that being aware of a tendency toward self-deception in a counseling relationship can lead to an exploration of the phenomenon and thus lessen the chances of its occurring.

THE DANGER OF LOSING OURSELVES IN OUR CLIENTS

A common mistake for beginners is to worry too much about clients. There is a danger of incorporating clients' neuroses into our own personality. We lose sleep wondering what decisions they are making. We sometimes identify so closely with clients that we lose our own sense of identity and assume their identity. Empathy becomes distorted and militates against a therapeutic intervention. We need to learn how to "let clients go" and not carry around their problems until we see them again. The most therapeutic thing is to be as fully present as we are able to be (feeling with our clients and experiencing their struggles with them) but to let them assume the responsibility of their living and choosing outside of the session. If we become lost in clients' struggles and confusion, we cease being an effective agent in helping them find their way out of the darkness. If we take on ourselves the responsibility our clients need to learn to direct their lives, then we are blocking rather than fostering their growth.

This discussion relates to an issue that we all need to recognize and face in our work as counselors—namely, *countertransference,* which occurs when a counselor's own needs or unresolved personal conflicts become entangled in the therapeutic relationship. Because countertransference that is not recognized and not successfully dealt with has the effect of blurring therapist objectivity (and actually intruding in the counseling process), it is essential that counselor trainees focus on *themselves* in supervision sessions. By dealing with the reactions that are stirred up in them in their relationship with a particular client, they can learn a lot about how their needs and unfinished business in their own life can bog down the progress of a client. Here are a few illustrations of common forms of countertransference:

- The need to be liked, appreciated, and approved of by clients.
- The therapist's fear of challenging clients lest they leave and think poorly of the therapist.
- Sexual feelings *and* sexually seductive behavior on the therapist's part toward clients (to the extent that the therapist becomes preoccupied with sexual fantasies or deliberately focuses clients' attention on sexual feelings toward the therapist).
- Extreme reactions to certain clients who evoke old feelings in the therapist—for example, clients who are perceived by the therapist as judgmental, domineering, paternalistic, maternalistic, controlling, and the like.
- The therapist's need to take away clients' pain or struggles because their experience is opening up old wounds or unrecognized conflicts in the therapist.
- Compulsive giving of advice. The therapist assumes a superior position of wanting to dictate how clients should live and the choices they should make.

This brief discussion is not a complete treatment of the issue of learning how to work through our feelings toward clients. Because it may not be appropriate for us to use clients' time to work through our reactions to them, it makes it all the more important that we be willing to work on ourselves in our own sessions with another therapist, supervisor, or colleague. Although recognizing *how* our needs can intrude in our work as counselors is one beginning step, we need to be willing to continually explore what we are seeing in ourselves. If we do not, we increase the danger of losing ourselves in our clients and using them to meet our unfilled needs. In the process, our clients end up being the losers.

DEVELOPING A SENSE OF HUMOR

Although therapy is a responsible matter, it need not be deadly serious. Both clients and therapists can enrich a relationship by laughing. I have found that humor and tragedy are closely linked and that, after allowing ourselves to feel some experiences that are painfully tragic, we can also genuinely laugh at how seriously we have taken our situation. We secretly delude ourselves into believing that we are unique in that we are alone in our pain, and we alone have experienced the tragic. What a welcome relief when we can admit that pain is not our exclusive domain. The important point is that therapists recognize that laughter or humor does not mean that work is not being accomplished. There are times, of course, when laughter is used to cover up anxiety or to escape from the experience of facing threatening material. The therapist needs to distinguish between humor that distracts and humor that enhances the situation.

ESTABLISHING REALISTIC GOALS

Realistic goals are essential for a potential relationship with a client. Assume that your client is truly in need of a major overhaul. He presents himself as a man who is intensely dissatisfied with life, rarely accomplishes what he begins, and feels inadequate and helpless. Now for the reality of the situation. He comes into a community crisis-counseling clinic where you work. Your agency has a policy of limiting a person to a series of six counseling sessions. There are long lines, waiting lists, and many people in need of crisis counseling. The man comes to you because of his personal inability to function; his wife has just abandoned him. Even though both of you might agree that he needs more than a minor tune-up, the limitations of the services at hand prevent exploring his problems in depth. Both counselor and client need to decide on realistic goals. This does not mean that the two need to settle on patch-up work. One possibility is to explore the underlying dynamics of the presenting problem, with attention to what alternatives are open beyond the six sessions. If our aims are realistic, we may be sad that we could not accomplish more, but at least we will not be steeped in frustration for not accomplishing miracles.

ON GIVING ADVICE

A mistaken notion of those who are unsophisticated about the nature of therapy is to equate giving advice with the therapy process. Quite often clients who are suffering come to a therapy session seeking and even demanding advice. They want more than direction; they want a wise counselor to make a decision or resolve a problem for them. Therapy should not be confused with the dispensing of information or advice. As I view it, a therapist's tasks are to help clients discover their own solutions and recognize their own freedom of action, not to deprive them of the opportunity to risk exercising their freedom. It seems to me that a common escape by many clients is not trusting themselves to find solutions, use their freedom, or discover their own direction. Even if we, as counselors or therapists, were able to effectively resolve their struggles for them, we would be fostering their dependence on us. They would continually need to seek our counsel for every new twist in their difficulties. Our job is to help them independently make choices and have the courage to accept the consequences of their choices. Giving advice (as a style) does not work toward this end.

I am not ruling out occasional use of the technique of giving advice. There are appropriate times for direct advice, particularly when clients are clearly in danger of harming themselves or others, or when for the time being they are unable to make choices. Also, information can be used legitimately in therapy as a basis for helping clients make their own choices. Essential to decision making is having pertinent information.

My caution is to avoid overusing the technique of giving information and advice and considering doing so as therapy. Far too many inexperienced therapists fall into the trap of believing that they are not doing their job unless they are being prescriptive and meeting the apparent demands for advice from clients. I recommend that, instead of merely being advice givers, we ask our clients questions such as "What alternatives are open to you?" "What possibilities do you see?" "If I were able to solve this particular problem, how would this help you with future problems?" "Are you asking me to assume your responsibility for you?" "How have you avoided accepting the responsibility for directing your own life in the past?" "Can part of your present problem stem from listening to the advice of others earlier?"

SUGGESTION AND PERSUASION IN THERAPY

Closely related to the issue of giving advice is the role of suggestion and persuasion in therapy. Let me begin by admitting that most of us do suggest and persuade as we counsel. I do not see how we can avoid doing so unless we assume an extremely passive stance of keeping ourselves out of the relationship with clients, a stance from which we operate chiefly as a mirror reflecting to others our observations. Whereas suggestion is related to giving advice, I do not link the two inseparably, for we can make suggestions and stimulate clients to see other avenues. Let me give some examples of instances when I use suggestion and persuasion.

A person hesitates to apply for college because he feels that he will never succeed. I might urge him to take some beginning steps to test out his suspicion of failure, perhaps only by enrolling in an evening class. (But I would explore his feelings of being doomed to failure, the realism of his view, and his perpetuating of a fatalistic view.)

A person experiences ambivalence over whether she should attend a weekend marathon group. She states her fears that she will be overwhelmed, that she is too fragile, that she is not yet ready for such a "heavy" experience, and on and on. If I feel that she is ready for such an experience, I may strongly urge her to attend the group. Many members have told me that my enthusiastic salesmanship of the benefits of a group was the determining factor that tilted the scale in favor of their risking attending. (But first I would explore my client's presenting fear, not merely relying on my convincing manner to persuade her to do something against her will.)

Suggestion can be a supportive device if used appropriately and if not overdone. In essence, we are saying: "I have confidence in you even though you may not yet feel that confidence in yourself. Trust my confidence in you, and perhaps you'll discover this confidence in yourself." I recall a letter from a client who was certain that not even a junior college would accept him. He allowed his poor record during high school to determine his decision whether to enter college. As a result of my persuasion, he enrolled in a junior college and took on a light load. In a letter a year later he related that he was carrying a full load and was on the dean's list.

Although suggestion and persuasion might produce results, I want to caution against the abuses of these techniques in therapy. Clients may strive to follow our suggestions out of their need to receive our approval. If they sense that we have certain expectations for them, they may incorporate them into their own expectations for themselves. Instead of working for self-approval, they perpetuate their need to be liked, thought well of, and respected by the therapist. Pleasing the counselor is counterproductive to therapeutic growth when it becomes more important a goal than pleasing oneself.

SOME REALISTIC CAUTIONS

I have developed the policy of encouraging beginning therapists to proceed with caution when taking risks. I feel that being a bit more conservative during the beginning stages is safer for both the client and the therapist. A cautious approach is specifically applicable to lessening the tendency of the beginning therapist to provoke the expression of anger in a client. Sometimes an unsuspecting counselor or group leader will tease a client, even to the point of becoming physically aggressive, to get the client's hostility out into the open. Although an explosive person needs to have a safe outlet to explore this repressed rage, there are times when the therapist will attempt prematurely to lift the lid off this dynamo and then be very unprepared for what follows. It is relatively easy for a therapist to encourage a client to stomp and pound and have a grand catharsis, but my question is usually "So the catharsis is over, now what?" I do not wish to encourage the development of impotent therapists who are afraid of taking risks and who become hesitant to the point that they fail to be active, but I want to underscore the value of developing a healthy respect for possible hazards.

DEVELOPING OUR OWN COUNSELING STYLE

Counselors-in-training need to be cautioned about the tendency to mimic the styles of their supervisor, therapist, or some other model. It is important that we accept that there is no "right" way of therapy, and that wide variations in approach can be effective. I believe that we inhibit our potential effectiveness in reaching others when we attempt to imitate another therapist's style or when we fit most of our behavior during the session into the Procrustean bed of some expert's theory. Although I am fully aware that one's style as a therapist will be influenced by teachers, therapists, and supervisors, I caution against blurring one's own potential uniqueness by trying to imitate them. At best one becomes a carbon copy, a poor imitation of the other. I do not have any formula for the way to develop a unique therapeutic style, but I do think that the awareness of our tendency to copy our teachers is critical in freeing ourselves and finding a direction that is compatible with our personality. I advocate borrowing from others but, at the same time, finding a way that is distinctive to oneself.

Staying alive as a person and as a professional

If the thesis that I have presented in this chapter is valid—that ultimately the single most important instrument we have to work with as a counselor is the person that we are, and that our most powerful technique is our ability to model aliveness and realness—then taking care of ourselves so that we remain fully alive is essential. We need to consciously work at dealing with those factors that threaten to drain life from us and render us helpless.

A topic that is receiving a great deal of attention is professional burn-out. I hesitate to write *professional burn-out,* because it has almost become a catch phrase to justify a general sense of ineffectiveness, both personally and professionally. I have heard counselors complain that they are just going through the motions on their jobs, that they feel that whatever they are doing makes no difference at all, that they have nothing left to give, and that they feel deprived of any confirmation that the work they are doing has any worth. Thus, some of these practitioners have convinced themselves that burn-out is one of the inevitable hazards of the profession, and that there is not much that they can do to revitalize themselves. This assumption is lethal, for it cements the feeling of impotence and leads to a giving up of hope.

There are many ways in which burn-out can manifest itself. Those who experience this syndrome typically find that they are tired, drained, and without enthusiasm. They talk of feeling pulled by their many projects, most of which seem to have lost their meaning. They feel that what they do have to offer is either not wanted or not received;

they feel unappreciated, unrecognized, and unimportant, and they go about their jobs in a mechanical and routine way. They tend not to see any concrete results or fruits from their efforts. Often they feel oppressed by the "system" and by institutional demands, which, they contend, stifle any sense of personal initiative. A real danger is that the burn-out syndrome can feed off itself, so that practitioners feel more and more isolated. They may fail to reach out to one another and to develop a support system.

Because burn-out can rob us of the vitality we need to be effective as persons and as professionals, it is important to look at some of its causes, possible remedies, and ways of preventing it. Surely, staying alive as a person and as a professional is a top priority, for if we are personally devitalized, then our knowledge, skills, and experience cannot be put to use for the service of clients.

CAUSES OF BURN-OUT

Recognizing the causes of burn-out can be itself a step in dealing with it. A few of them are the following:

1. Doing the same type of work with little variation, especially if this work seems meaningless.

2. Giving a great deal personally and not getting back much in the way of appreciation or other positive responses.

3. Being under constant and strong pressure to produce, perform, and to meet dead-lines—many of which may be unrealistic.

4. Working with a difficult population—those who are highly resistant, involuntary clients, or those who show very little progress or change.

5. Conflict and tension among staff; an absence of support from colleagues and an abundance of criticism.

6. Lack of trust between supervisors and mental-health workers—a condition in which they are working against each other instead of toward commonly valued goals.

7. Not having opportunities for personal expression or for taking initiative in trying new approaches—a situation in which experimentation, change, and innovations not only are not rewarded but are actively discouraged.

8. Having jobs that are both personally and professionally taxing without much opportunity for supervision, continuing education, or other forms of in-service training.

9. Unresolved personal conflicts beyond the job situation—problems that drain away energy needed for working. These may include marital tensions, chronic health problems, family problems, and so on.

REMEDIES FOR BURN-OUT

Learning ways to take care of ourselves is a necessary step beyond this initial recognition of the problem of burn-out. I see acceptance of *personal responsibility* as one of the most critical factors. In my experience in conducting professional training workshops, it has almost become standard to hear mental-health workers blame the system and other external factors for their condition; the more they look outside of themselves for the reasons why they feel dead, the greater becomes their sense of impotence and hopelessness. At these workshops I often hear statements such as:

- "I'm failing as a counselor because my clients are highly resistive and they really don't want to change—besides, they're not capable of much change!"

- "The system here keeps us down. We're merely small cogs in the machinery that need to keep functioning if this big machine is to continue working."
- "I have far too many clients, and I also have too many demands on my time. All these demands make me feel useless, because I know I'll never be able to meet them."

Notice that in these sample statements the responsibility is placed *outside* of the person, and that someone else or some other impersonal factor is *making* the person ineffective. This is the passive stance that so often contributes to the general feelings of hopelessness and powerlessness. To the degree that professionals continue to place blame on external factors, they also surrender their own personal power and assume the position of victim. This very passive state lends itself to the development of cynicism that makes it very difficult to harness energy and apply it toward meeting tasks. What I see as critical is that counselors recognize and accept that, even though there are external realities that exert a toll on personal energy, they see their own role in allowing themselves to remain passive. For example, although there are bureaucratic obstacles that do make it difficult to implement sound ideas or to function effectively, it is possible to learn ways to survive with dignity within an institution and to engage in meaningful work. This means that counselors will have to become active and stop blaming the system for all that they *cannot do.* Instead, as a place to begin, they can focus on what they *can do* to bring about *some* changes and to create a climate in which they can do work which has meaning to them.

PREVENTING BURN-OUT

Learning to look within ourselves to determine what choices we are making and not making to keep ourselves alive can go a long way in preventing what some people consider as an inevitable condition associated with the helping professions. There are other ways that we can prevent professional burn-out, most of which include assuming the responsibility to actively nourish ourselves:

1. Finding other interests besides work.
2. Thinking of ways to bring variety into work.
3. Taking the initiative to start new projects that have personal meaning and not waiting for the system to sanction this initiative.
4. Attending to one's health through adequate sleep, an exercise program, proper diet, and some meditation.
5. Developing a few friendships that are characterized by a mutuality of giving *and* receiving.
6. Learning how to ask for what one wants, though not expecting to always get it, and learning how to deal with not getting what is asked for.
7. Learning how to work for self-confirmation and for self-rewards, as opposed to looking externally for validation and rewards.
8. Playing, traveling, or seeking new experiences.
9. Taking the time to evaluate the meaningfulness of one's projects to determine where personal investment and time will continue to be spent.
10. Avoiding assuming the burden of responsibility that is properly the responsibility of others—for example, worrying more about clients than they are seeming to worry about themselves.
11. Reading, both professional literature and books for fun.

12. Taking new classes or workshops or attending conferences and conventions to get new perspectives on old issues.

13. Exchanging jobs with a colleague for a short period or asking a colleague to join forces in a common work project.

14. Taking the initiative to form a support group with colleagues to openly share feelings of frustration and to find better ways of approaching the reality of certain job situations.

15. Cultivating some hobbies that bring pleasure.

Although this is not an exhaustive list, it does provide some direction for thinking about ways to keep ourselves alive. If we feel a personal zest for living, I think, we will find ways to keep growing professionally. However, I do not believe that our attempts to keep ourselves professionally updated will mean much if we feel dead to ourselves. This is why we must make periodic assessments of the direction of our own life to determine if we are living the way we want. If we are not, we must decide what we are willing to actually do to *make* changes occur, rather than simply waiting for new life to enter us. By being in tune with ourselves, by having the experience of centeredness and solidness, and by feeling a sense of personal power, we have the basis for integrating our life experiences with our professional experiences. Such a synthesis can provide the basis for being an effective professional.

Concluding comments

I have found a big difference in the students with whom I work from the beginning to the end of the introductory course in theories and techniques of counseling. Typically, at the outset their reaction is "How will I ever be able to learn all these theories, and how can I make sense out of what appears to be a mass of knowledge?" By the end of the course students are often surprised by how much work they have done *and* by how much they have learned. Although an introductory survey course will not make students into accomplished counselors, they generally have the basis for selecting from the many models to which they are exposed.

At this point in your reading, you may be able to begin putting the theories together in some meaningful way for yourself. This book will have served its central purpose if it has encouraged you to read further and to expand your knowledge of the theories that most caught your interest. I hope that you have made friends with some theories that were unknown to you before, and that you have seen something of value that you can use from each of the approaches described. Further, I hope that this book has introduced you to some of the major professional and ethical issues that you will eventually encounter, that it has stimulated you to think about your position on them, and that you have been convinced that there is no single theory that contains the total truth. Finally, the book will have been put to good use if it has stimulated and challenged you to think about the ways in which your philosophy of life, your values, your life experiences, and the person you are becoming is vitally related to the quality of counselor you can become and to the impact you can have on those who establish a relationship with you personally and professionally.

Now that you have finished this book, I would be very interested in hearing about your experience with it and with your course. I will welcome and value any suggestions for making this book more useful in future revisions. You can write to me in care of

Brooks/Cole Publishing Company, Monterey, California 93940, and you can complete the reaction sheet at the end of the book.

Recommended supplementary readings

I Never Knew I Had a Choice (Gerald Corey, Brooks/Cole, 1978) is a good resource with which to continue a reading program on the counselor as a person. Topics include our struggle to achieve autonomy; the roles that work, love, sexuality, intimacy, and solitude play in our lives; the meaning of loneliness, death, and loss; and the ways in which we choose our values and philosophy of life. Readers are continually encouraged to actively apply what they read to their personal life and to examine the choices they have made and how these choices affect their present level of satisfaction. The central theme of the book can be summed up in these words: "As we recognize that we are not merely passive victims of our circumstances, we can consciously become the architects of our lives. Even though others may have drawn the blueprints, we can recognize the plan, take a stand, and change the design."

Professional and Ethical Issues in Counseling and Psychotherapy (Gerald Corey, Marianne Schneider Corey, & Patrick Callanan, Brooks/Cole, 1979) is also relevant to the issues in this chapter. Especially appropriate are the chapters on the counselor as a person, the counselor as a professional, the counselor's values, the counselor and community involvement, and learning to work within the system.

Group Techniques (Gerald Corey, Marianne Schneider Corey, Patrick Callanan, & J. Michael Russell, Brooks/Cole, 1982) deals with a rationale for creating and using techniques for each stage of group work. The theme of the book is that techniques are most effective when they are an expression and an extension of the personality of the group leader. Examples of group techniques, all of which reflect the authors' personal styles, are given throughout the book.

Name Index

Subject Index

To the owner of this book:

We hope that you have enjoyed *Theory and Practice of Counseling and Psychotherapy* (Second Edition). We would like to know as much about your experiences with this book as possible. Only through your comments and those of others can we learn how to enhance it for future readers.

School: _____ Instructor's Name: _____

1. What I like *most* about this book is _____

_____

_____

2. What I like *least* about this book is _____

_____

_____

3. My specific suggestions for improving the book are _____

_____

_____

4. Did your instructor require or recommend that you use the *Manual* that accompanies this textbook or *A Case Approach to Counseling and Psychotherapy?* _____

_____

5. My general reaction to this book is _____

_____

6. In what course did you use this book? _____

_____

7. In the space below or in a separate letter, please let us know what other comments about the book you would like to make. We welcome your suggestions!

Optional:

Your name: _____ Date: _____

May Brooks/Cole quote you, either in promotion for *Theory and Practice of Counseling and Psychotherapy* or in future publishing ventures?

Yes _____ No _____

Sincerely,

 Jerry Corey

FOLD HERE

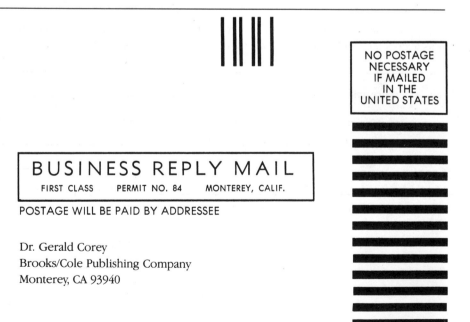

**NO POSTAGE
NECESSARY
IF MAILED
IN THE
UNITED STATES**

BUSINESS REPLY MAIL
FIRST CLASS   PERMIT NO. 84   MONTEREY, CALIF.

POSTAGE WILL BE PAID BY ADDRESSEE

Dr. Gerald Corey
Brooks/Cole Publishing Company
Monterey, CA 93940